Regulatory Competition in the Internal Market

PRIVATE REGULATION

Series Editor: Fabrizio Cafaggi, *European University Institute, Italy*

Under the general editorship of Fabrizio Cafaggi, and the guidance of a small, international advisory board including leading figures David Levi Faur, Katharina Pistor and Colin Scott, this *Private Regulation* series is a forum for monographs and collaborative, interdisciplinary volumes on private regulation through the lenses of law, economics, political science, sociology and philosophy. The role of transnational regulation and global governance is reshaping the distribution of power and opportunities across the world, calling for a radical conceptual transformation. Each of the books in the series will appeal not only to an academic audience but will also engage policy makers and practitioners involved in designing, implementing and enforcing regulatory policies.

Books in the series include:

Enforcement of Transnational Regulation
Edited by Fabrizio Cafaggi

Regulatory Competition in the Internal Market
Comparing Models for Corporate Law, Securities Law and Competition Law
Barbara Gabor

Regulatory Competition in the Internal Market

Comparing Models for Corporate Law, Securities Law and Competition Law

Barbara Gabor

Public Official, European Commission, Belgium and member of Tilburg University's Law and Economics group 'TILEC'

PRIVATE REGULATION

Edward Elgar

Cheltenham, UK • Northampton, MA, USA

Published by
Edward Elgar Publishing Limited
The Lypiatts
15 Lansdown Road
Cheltenham
Glos GL50 2JA
UK

Edward Elgar Publishing, Inc.
William Pratt House
9 Dewey Court
Northampton
Massachusetts 01060
USA

A catalogue record for this book
is available from the British Library

Library of Congress Control Number: 2012948847

This book is available electronically in the ElgarOnline.com Law Subject Collection, E-ISBN 978 1 78100 338 1

FSC
www.fsc.org
MIX
Paper from
responsible sources
FSC® C018575

ISBN 978 1 78100 337 4

Typeset by Columns Design XML Ltd, Reading
Printed and bound by MPG Books Group, UK

To Mirko

Contents

Foreword

Barbara Gabor's book provides an excellent example of interdisciplinary work on a hotly debated subject: regulatory competition (RC). The book develops her EUI PhD thesis, which was awarded the Cappelletti Prize in 2010.

Barbara primarily, but not exclusively, uses sophisticated law and economics tools to show when RC arises, which preconditions have to be met for being welfare enhancing, and how it differs across fields. She builds on different approaches from the economics of federalism to public choice, and uses insights from game theory, in a language accessible to academics in all fields as well as policy makers.

She examines regulatory competition in its broad sense, including also trade competition and yardstick competition in her analysis, focusing on what institutional and economic factors drive regulatory competition, and which factors may make it welfare enhancing or welfare reducing.

Barbara looks at the topic from a regulatory perspective, comparing company, securities, and competition law in order to evaluate the relevance of sector specificity in devising the institutional design that best promotes RC. The current literature often derives, from observations drawn from a single sector, general implications about the desirability of RC and its institutional features. She takes a different approach and compares different sectors. Her analysis integrates a comparative methodology with the tools of comparative institutional analysis, building on the social science toolkit. The comparative institutional analysis carried out by Barbara suggests that it is hard to reach homogenous conclusions because sectors matter. In particular they matter for the nature of external effects that choices of rules might generate. But they matter also in terms of regulatees' as well as regulators' incentives, as rules in various sectors have a different magnitude of impact on costs of compliance and on international trade advantages. Finally, sectors matter also for the differences within legal contexts in which their institutions are embedded.

After introducing the theoretical framework of regulatory competition, the central part of the book is dedicated to a deep analysis of the three sectors: company law; securities law; and competition law. For each one she analyses:

- the economic rationale of regulatory intervention;
- the competence allocation among legal actors at EU and MS level;
- the governance mechanisms shaping the competitive or cooperative interaction of legal actors with competence;
- the scope for legal divergence within the European legal framework, which at the same time sets the limits to legal arbitrage for regulatees;
- the channels of economic openness that may give rise to competitive interactions, and, when there is free choice of law or mobility involved, who gets to decide over such choice of legal regime;
- the occurring patterns of arbitrage, and/or competitive interactions across various legal actors, both within and across jurisdictions, and the welfare implications of these, if applicable.

The comparative chapter of the book contains conclusions on both regulatory competition theory and recent policy developments within the Internal Market. As regards normative, theoretical findings, interesting conclusions emerge, for example, concerning the responsiveness of different legal actors to different channels of competition, and the relevance of institutional design in promoting cooperation instead of competition. In terms of positive, descriptive conclusions, the book gives an account of recent trends across policy fields, such as the spread of economic theory as a regulatory paradigm and axis of competition, the spreading use of what could be called network-governance, and the narrowing of private regulators' competences.

The goals of the analysis are both positive and normative. She describes, through the lenses of RC, the evolution of the three fields, examining the concurrent roles of different institutions in shaping and steering the process. The differences in her three chosen fields concern regulatory objectives and instruments. RC is based primarily on choices among rules and to some extent among institutions. Parties are given a menu of regulatory options and correlated institutional set-ups within which they can choose. The choice-space is dictated by several factors, among which the mandatory or default nature of the rules plays a significant role. The three sectors are characterised by different degrees of contractual or organisational freedom ranging from a high level in company, to a medium that is constantly decreasing in securities, and a relatively low level in competition law.

Clearly one of the main methodological puzzles is whether the nature of rules should be the dependent or independent variable for the institutional design. The author examines both possibilities. In the positive analysis, she assumes the nature of rule as an independent variable. Given the mandatory or default nature of the rule, different types of, or even no, RC arises. In the normative account, she changes the approach and considers both choice of rules and institutions as variables, dependent upon the selection of the desirable regulatory strategy.

The comparative analysis thence includes not only rules but also institutions. She not only considers how various European institutions have contributed in different ways to the introduction or rejection of RC, but also their interaction. She points out that regulatory competition may be triggered by institutional competition between legislatures and regulators or between regulators and courts. She emphasises how institutional incentives may contribute to stimulate – or temper – regulatory competition. At the same time, she analyses the hypothesis, frequently raised, of conflicting institutional incentives, as is the case when, for example, regulators favour regulatory cooperation while courts may promote regulatory competition.

I am extremely pleased to host her book in the Private Regulation series. It will provide both scholars and policy makers with new insights on the desirability and the limits of regulatory competition. Barbara's analysis can hopefully trigger more research and debate on the role of private regulatory competition at national, European and transnational level.

Fabrizio Cafaggi
Fiesole June 2012

Preface

Regulatory competition is an 'old' subject that has taken on new 'functions' in a fast changing world, thereby reviving the interest of policy makers as well as academic research. Competitive interaction among different legal actors changes along with the legal framework that sets competences, choice of law and substantive legal rules in any market. The results, the allocative and overall welfare implications of such competition, are also susceptible to change each time the legal framework changes.

Regulatory competition is thus a sort of moving target; but should policy makers eradicate competition or embrace it? Ignoring competition is definitely not an attractive option, although current policy making rarely accounts for regulatory competition, and almost never employs competition as a means to achieve the desired outcome – at least not deliberately. This is probably due to old (mis-)conceptions about regulatory competition and the lack of an easily applicable toolkit to design optimal competitive interactions.

This book looks at competition from a regulatory perspective, having the above issues in mind. It explores the concept and different channels of regulatory competition, and analyses the drivers of competitive interactions through the description of its actual functioning in the EU's Internal Market. Its contribution to existing literature consists in deeper general theoretical insights, as well as policy-specific conclusions in three EU policy fields: company law; securities law; and competition law.

As for the theory, Chapter 1 reviews the definition of regulatory competition and the conditions for its success or failure, with a more in-depth analysis of presumptions and underlying concepts that often remain under-explored in the literature. A closer look is offered at the broad and the narrow definition of regulatory competition, the concept of a 'race to the bottom'; co-opetition; the measurement of the outcome of competitive interactions; and legal actors' incentives. A number of issues are identified as possible 'drivers', determinants, of the functioning of regulatory competition. These include

- The channel of competitive interactions
- Which legal actor has competence
- The incentives of legal actors
- The governance mechanisms in place
- The allocation of choice of law or capacity for mobility across jurisdictions
- The potential externalities, both cross-border and across stakeholder groups
- The types of market failures that legal norms are aiming to correct
- The underlying theory of what efficient markets should look like and what outcomes they should achieve.

The descriptive part of the book (Chapters 2 to 4) then also serves the purpose of testing the general, theory-related questions. In order to better understand what the impact of these potential drivers are on competitive interactions, the current forms of regulatory competition are described in three legal areas: company law (Chapter 2); securities law (Chapter 3); and competition law (Chapter 4). The analysis looks at the issues identified above, and each chapter is structured in a similar manner, addressing:

- market failures and the various theories of efficiency;
- the channels of competitive interactions;
- existing legal norms, allocation of competences, allocation of choice of law (where applicable);
- the legal actors involved and governance mechanisms in place;
- the potential functioning of regulatory competition in a different legal environment.

The inquiry for each field thus starts with the analysis of that market, continuing with a positive description of regulatory competition, and closing with a hypothetical inquiry into how (a more intensive form of) regulatory competition would work in that policy field.

The scope of analysis necessarily had to be limited to some selected regulatory aspects within each policy field. Topics covered include: minimum capital requirements and employee participation within company law; transparency and market abuse rules in securities regulation; the functioning of the Modernisation Regulation and damages actions in competition law.

Chapter 5 offers some conclusions that emerge from the comparison of the three policy fields under analysis. General theoretical conclusions are drawn for the various drivers of competitive interactions, with an emphasis on legal actors, the institutional environment and the governance mechanisms for different actors' interaction. Cross-cutting trends across the policy fields under examination are identified with regard to regulatory competition within the EU Internal Market. A research agenda is also set out, enumerating issues that require further analysis.

Readers interested only in regulatory competition in a certain policy field can go directly to the chapter dealing with the field of their interest. Those wishing to read the general theoretical conclusions can go from Chapter 1 to Chapter 5. My hope is that the book will provide useful insights and interesting new angles for both policy makers and academics.

Barbara Gabor
Brussels, May 2012

Acknowledgements

This work builds on my doctorate thesis completed at the European University Institute in Florence, Italy. I owe thanks to many people who helped me with this book. I would like to name a few of them in particular.

I am grateful to Professor Fabrizio Cafaggi for his guidance on this research. I am also thankful for the most useful comments from Professor Hanns Ullrich, Professor Pierre Larouche and Professor Wolfgang Kerber. It is an honour to have received an endorsement for this book from Professors Daniel Rubinfeld and Jonathan Faull. I also benefited from the stimulating discussions at Tilburg University's TILEC group. I owe thanks to Professor Joseph McCahery for his help at the early stages of my research. I would like to thank also for the support of my colleagues at the European Commission, particularly Werner Stengg, Kamil Kiljanski, Emiliano Tornese, Larisa Dragomir and Tim Shakesby, both in terms of insights on the subject matter and in terms of encouragement. All remaining errors are mine.

The general disclaimer applies that the views expressed in this book are those of the author and cannot be attributed to the European Commission.

1. Regulatory competition: what it is and what remains to be explored

1. INTRODUCTION

In order to present a structured analysis, this chapter defines the scope of this book and establishes an analytical framework for it. It starts with a definition of regulatory competition, continuing with a review of the main drivers of competitive interactions. The aim of this review is not only to integrate the latest theoretical developments into the analysis that follows, but also to go beyond the existing literature in examining some of the most important drivers of regulatory competition.

Within this chapter, Section 2 gives a brief summary of what is most often understood by regulatory competition in the literature, or the narrow meaning of this concept. Section 3 continues with a description of different forms of competition. It examines the broader meaning of regulatory competition, distinguishing different channels of competitive interaction among legal actors, and introduces the concept of vertical, horizontal and intra-jurisdictional competition, of which the latter is often neglected in existing literature. This review of different forms of competition closes with an analysis of 'co-opetition', a concept offered – but not fully explored – by previous studies. Section 4 explains the challenges of measuring the outcome of regulatory competition, and of determining when competition occurs. It also makes some basic distinctions between concepts that are sometimes misunderstood, such as 'race to the bottom' and 'regulatory laxity'. Section 5 identifies the actors of institutional competition, including independent regulatory agencies and private regulators, and reviews legal and economic literature with regard to their incentives. Section 6 concludes with the research questions that emerge from the preceding overview, identifying the subject matter for further analysis (the 'what') and the methodology to be followed (the 'how').

2. REGULATORY COMPETITION FROM TIEBOUT TO CORPORATE CHARTERS AND BEYOND

2.1 Tiebout's Model of Fiscal Federalism

The first economic model of the benefits of decentralisation is attributed to Charles Tiebout.[1] He claimed that giving people the freedom to choose between the offerings of different governments, thus having these governments compete in pleasing their voters, is a good thing. The original model for local public finance demonstrated that, subject to certain conditions, competition among local jurisdictions will result in an optimal allocation of local public goods. Tiebout examined the provision of public goods to local 'consumers' (that is taxpayer voters) in exchange for taxes paid to local government. The model looked at the effect of perfect competition between jurisdictions on selection by citizens, in a setting where there are several jurisdictions competing to attract taxpayer voters, and where taxpayers have divergent preferences as to the optimal range and mixture of public goods to be provided to them. Tiebout's prediction was that each taxpayer voter would move to the local jurisdiction providing the package of public goods closest to his or her own personal preference. The assumptions of this model were the following:

- taxpayer voters are fully mobile;
- they have perfect information/knowledge about what is offered to them;
- they can choose from amongst a large number of diverse communities;
- employment opportunities do not influence their choice;
- there are no external economies or diseconomies; and
- there is an optimal community size with communities below this size trying to attract more residents in order to lower their average cost of providing public goods.

Already at the early stage of research, Tiebout pointed out that these assumptions are *sine qua non* conditions for optimal selection. In other words, taking away any of the above conditions would modify the results. This meant that the model had only a limited application in practice.

---

[1] Tiebout, C. (1956), 'A Pure Theory of Local Expenditures', *Journal of Political Economics*, vol. 64. no. 5, p. 416.

Indeed, when considering practical examples, it is rare to find situations perfectly corresponding to the above set of assumptions. But the more realistic the model becomes, the more its outcome will depart from the predicted optimal results. One example of this is the relation between mobility and the predicted outcome: the lower the mobility of citizens, the further from optimal is the outcome of competition.

2.2 Adaptation of the Tiebout Model to Regulatory Federalism

Despite the slim prospects of the original model being applied in reality, Tiebout's model had a lively afterlife. Several subsequent studies elaborated on the Tiebout model, relaxing its assumptions,[2] while others proved its viability in practice through empirical research. The real upswing in its popularity came with the idea to apply this framework to the provision of law, rather than conventional public goods such as defence or infrastructure. The model has thus been further developed to be applicable also to regulation as a public good.[3]

The model of regulatory competition applies the Tiebout model to the provision of regulation by legislators as a public good in exchange for taxes or other fees paid by regulatees. In this narrower sense,[4] regulatory competition refers to a competition between governments for regulatees: that is, the process of legislators selecting and de-selecting rules through the process of competition.[5] The prerequisites for the emergence of regulatory competition through mobility of regulatees are the following:

- Co-existence of two or more regulators (multiple jurisdictions) providing diverse rules that create regulatory arbitrage;
- Mobility of regulatees, either through moving to another jurisdiction (free movement), or by mere choice of law (free choice) that

---

[2] For a review of how the Tiebout model works when relaxing some of its assumptions, see e.g., Inman, R.P. and Rubinfeld, D.L. (1997), 'The Political Economy of Federalism', in Muller, D.C. (ed.) *Perspectives on Public Choice: A Handbook* (Cambridge: Cambridge University Press).

[3] One of the most relevant studies in this regard is: Oates, W.E. and Schwab, R.M. (1988), 'Economic Competition Among Jurisdictions: Efficiency Enhancing or Distortion Inducing?', *Journal of Public Economics*, vol. 35, p. 333.

[4] Later sections will introduce further forms of competitive interaction, which are sometimes also labelled regulatory competition (in a broader sense).

[5] Bernard, K. and Deakin, S. (2001), 'Market Access and Regulatory Competition', *Jean Monnet Working Paper* 9/01, p. 4.

provides them with the possibility of taking advantage of regulatory arbitrage arising from the differences amongst legal norms;[6]

- Incentives for governments to attract more regulatees, which can actually alter the normative outcome (supply side of regulatory competition);
- Further factors, such as perfect information and rationality, which contribute towards the optimal outcome (positive welfare effects) of regulatory competition.

As in the case of the original public finance model, here also the assumptions form an essential element of the model: relaxing the assumptions will affect the welfare outcome. And here, also, these pose a problem. In most cases, perfect information and costless mobility cannot be observed, and it is often argued that externalities render regulatory competition inefficient in reality. But the literature recognises that the welfare effects of regulatory competition have to be analysed on a case-by-case basis, since each legal field has its own specific features.[7]

In parenthesis, the conditions of mobility and threat of exit require some further clarification here. The phenomenon of regulatory competition does not presuppose the actual migration or opt-out of regulatees. Competitive law-making can also emerge from the mere threat of exit, provided there are sufficient incentives for states to retain regulatees within their jurisdiction by means of providing competitive norms matching their preferences.[8] Regulatory arbitrage refers to the additional benefits regulatees could derive from being subjected to the norm or set of norms of a foreign jurisdiction. If such arbitrage poses a threat of movement from one jurisdiction to another, it might trigger preventive action by the law-maker.

Besides, regulatees often do not have to move physically in order to change jurisdictions. They may be permitted to choose the applicable law, or arrange for a transaction outside the jurisdiction, to take advantage of another regulatory regime. The difference between free choice

---

[6] This is often called the 'demand side' of regulatory competition through mobility.

[7] See Esty, D.C. and Geradin, D. (2001), *Regulatory Competition and Market Integration* (Oxford: Oxford University Press).

[8] The other possible motive behind making such law-making responsive to the preferences of regulates, even without mobility, is trade competition, where states favour their home industries in order to provide them with comparative advantage over foreign industries. The difference between these two types of competition will be explained in this chapter.

and the mobility of regulatees also needs to be further clarified. If we take a pragmatic approach, free choice of law should refer to cases where there is not only a *de iure* possibility of choosing the governing legal regime, but also a *de facto* feasibility of doing so without prohibitive costs, time delays, or other severe consequences. The same is true for mobility: is there a mere theoretical possibility provided for in a legal provision, or is mobility a feasible option for regulatees? Often the answer is in the balancing of gains from switching legal systems and its costs. But what is important is to note that free choice and physical mobility are to a large extent the same, just perhaps positioned differently on a scale of the costs of switching.[9]

2.3 The Main Benefits from Regulatory Competition

Simplifying the vast literature on this subject, we can group the main advantages of competitive decentralisation into three categories.

2.3.1 Satisfaction of diverse preferences

The first positive implication of having several jurisdictions compete over regulatees is that this set-up, when conditions are met, has the potential to satisfy diverse preferences. As the original Tiebout model already assumed diversity of regulatees, it is self-evident that many different rules are more desirable than one single rule for all.

The conditions of optimal regulatory outcome should not be forgotten here, however. Regulatees need to be able to migrate or opt into the regime of their preference, not only to pose competitive threats, but potentially also to achieve so-called perfect sorting.

2.3.2 A process of discovery of the best rules

Several authors describe regulatory federalism as a process of discovery.[10] This feature of decentralisation, also referred to as 'laboratory

---

[9] It may be that physical mobility becomes determinative of the welfare impacts of competition, for example when polluting activities are relocated, or when physical presence itself will trigger the applicability of other, unrelated legal norms (such as taxation for example). Therefore, again, each legal field should be examined case by case.

[10] See e.g. Deakin, S. (2006), 'Legal Diversity and Regulatory Competition: Which Model for Europe?', *European Law Journal*, vol. 12, no. 4, pp. 440–454; Tietje, Ch. and Lehmann, M. (2010), 'The Role and Prospects of International Law in Financial Regulation and Supervision', *Journal of International Economic Law*, vol. 13, no. 3, pp. 663–682; or Zumbansen, P. (2006), 'Spaces and

federalism', is a strong argument in favour of allocating competences to several legal actors.

If information is not perfect, centralised decision-makers will not be able to arrive at the best possible solution without trial and error. The process of creative destruction is described by Schumpeter[11] and has since been further developed to apply the concept to product market competition as well as regulatory competition. In the latter context, competition as a trial and error process is also a well-known approach, referred to, among others, by Van den Bergh.[12]

2.3.3 Restraint of the Leviathan state

Hobbes describes the state as a Leviathan that overstretches its powers, and over-regulates when left unconstrained.[13] Regulatory competition can have the positive effect of restraining the Leviathan state.[14] The idea is that governments would over-tax and over-spend if they were to act as monopolist regulators. In a competitive setting there are constraints on their taxation and spending patterns, rendering the states less interventionist than they otherwise would be. The economic models in fiscal and regulatory federalism show the optimality of competition among jurisdictions in this respect.

2.4 Limitations of the Model

Certain market failures may prevent regulatory competition from functioning correctly, leading to decreased welfare. In principle, the necessary assumptions of the model, when not present, are likely to lead to such results.[15] The main limitations of regulatory competition over regulatees

Places: A Systems Theory Approach to Regulatory Competition in European Company Law', *European Law Journal*, vol. 12, no. 4, pp. 534–556.

[11] Schumpeter, J. (1975), *Capitalism, Socialism and Democracy* (New York: Harper), at pp. 82–85.

[12] Van Den Bergh, R. (2000), 'Towards an Institutional Legal Framework for Regulatory Competition in Europe', *Kyklos* vol. 53, no. 4, pp. 435–466.

[13] Hobbes, Th. (1651), reprinted in Shapiro, I. (2010), *Leviathan: Or the Matter, Forme, and Power of a Common-Wealth Ecclesiastical and Civil* (New Haven: Yale University Press).

[14] Sinn, S. (1992), 'The Taming of Leviathan: Competition Among Governments', *Constitutional Political Economy*, vol. 3, no. 2, pp. 177–196.

[15] However, as will be argued later in this chapter, some of the preconditions, especially the mobility criterion, when abandoned, lead to other workable forms of competition.

(where the latter have mobility or choice between legal norms) are briefly summarised here.

2.4.1 Externalities

The possibility of imposing external effects on third parties is one of the most common sources of failure that may inhibit the proper functioning of regulatory competition. Externalities can arise both across borders, and among stakeholder groups. Once jurisdictions do not take account of either the positive or negative external effects of their domestic regulation, the provision of rules will not be set at the optimal level from an overall welfare perspective. In such situations allocative inefficiency will arise. The jurisdiction that can externalise costs (negative externality) will produce a given product (or undertake a given activity) up to a point where *domestic* costs equal benefits. Since other jurisdictions bear some of the costs, this production choice will, overall, be ruinous.

Externalities across stakeholder groups arise if, in the context of choice of law or mobility, the regulatee with choice does not fully account for the benefits or the costs of his choice as they are imposed on other parties.[16]

2.4.2 Imperfect information

A further market failure may arise due to information problems. If either regulatees' or regulators' information is imperfect (concerning the performance of the jurisdiction in comparison with other jurisdictions), neither side will be able to make fully-informed decisions – ultimately impacting on the welfare outcome.

In the European case, scholars point to information problems related to different languages and the difference of legal traditions.[17] But information deficiencies of a more general nature include, for example, the complexity of a certain regulation that renders accurate assessment impossible (or prohibitively costly) for regulatees. Similar arguments are put forward also on the supply side, the side of the regulator. Knowledge problems are the simplest argument in this field but there are other strong claims that equally predict market failures in regulatory competition.

---

[16] Later sections analysing other forms of competitive interactions will show that externalities can also arise in other contexts, where no choice or mobility is provided to regulatees.

[17] See, e.g. Geradin, D. and McCahery, J.A. (2004), 'Regulatory Competition and Coopetition', in Jordana, J. and Levi-Faur, D. (eds) *The Politics of Regulation: Institutions and Regulatory Reforms for the Age of Governance* (Cheltenham, UK: Edward Elgar).

Majone argues for example that optimal matching of preferences with regulation cannot take place if the individual jurisdictions lack information about each others' choices.[18]

2.4.3 Economies of scale and transaction cost savings

Another situation in which decentralised competitive rule setting may turn out to be undesirable is where economies of scale render regulation at the centralised level more efficient. Such natural monopolies in regulation may arise in cases where standards have significant positive networks. Whether centralisation is better than decentralisation depends, in this context, also on the size of the jurisdictions in question (as also, for example, with optimal currency areas and free trade areas). And it is of course also closely linked to the Tiebout conditions of diverse preferences, mobility and a sufficient number of competing jurisdictions. Furthermore, optimal regulatory areas also depend on the patterns of information asymmetries and externalities.

But it should be kept in mind that, just because there is a decentralised competitive setting as the starting point, it does not mean that competition will not lead to convergence on one single (superior) solution. If one single legal rule within an optimal regulatory area is desirable over several scattered standards, legal competition may be able to deliver such a result.[19]

2.4.4 Public choice and political problems

Some authors argue that regulatory capture is a further example of potential market failure.[20] If a regulatory body favours a particular lobby group instead of serving the welfare of the public, such behaviour may be aggravated by regulatory competition. While it is true that one of the main benefits of regulatory competition is that it can prevent regulatory capture in specific circumstances, it is often the case that the strongest domestic lobby interest is the regulated party with choice or mobility across jurisdictions, imposing externalities on other stakeholders.

---

[18] Majone, G. (2003), 'The Politics of Regulation and European Regulatory Institutions', in Hayward, J. and Majone, G. (1996), *Regulating Europe* (London: Routledge).

[19] See, for example, the emergence of Delaware as the lead provider of rules on company law within the US. (Chapter 2 gives a detailed description of regulatory competition in US company law.)

[20] Geradin and McCahery (2004).

2.4.5 Incentives to compete

The lack of incentives to compete may be another factor that impedes the emergence of regulatory competition. If the suppliers of norms do not have sufficient incentives to compete with others, no competition will take place. The analysis of the following chapters puts a great deal of emphasis on this aspect, arguing that incentives can be of different kinds, ranging from monetary reasons to peer pressure. The characteristics of the legal actor's institutional design, interaction with regulatees and other legal actors are important, but even geographical circumstances can determine incentives. For example, smaller jurisdictions may regard budget revenues created by successful competitive law-making as sufficient incentive to enter the competitive arena.[21]

2.4.6 Network externalities

Scholars argue that a further impediment to competitive law-making may be the presence of network externalities.[22] The investment in producing better norms has to pay off, and network effects may prevent such pay-offs from being realised. However, in some cases competition may lead to convergence around a set of norms that are identified as the 'best'.[23] It is argued that if a new legal product can be imitated by other jurisdictions, and its benefits reaped by them, this will take away any incentive from the jurisdiction to invent it in the first place – similarly to incentives to inventors and innovators in product markets. Expropriation of the innovator's reward after the innovation will eliminate *ex ante* incentives to invest in innovation in the first place.[24]

2.4.7 Bundling and pricing

The literature lists a further potential cause of regulatory competition failure: bundling of legal products.[25] The argument goes that bundling makes the assessment by the individual of the value of the products more uncertain. This uncertainty then contributes to information problems. But, even more importantly, due to the bundling, the regulatees cannot punish the regulator as easily as in the case of individually sold products, making competitive pressure less significant than it would ideally be under well-functioning regulatory competition.

---

[21] There is evidence for this in Delaware, and similarly evidence exists in tax competition.

[22] Geradin and McCahery (2004).

[23] Again Delaware is an example at hand. See Chapter 2 for further details.

[24] See for example the law and economics of intellectual property rights.

[25] Geradin and McCahery (2004).

2.4.8 Lack of mobility of regulatees

Finally, lack of mobility is identified as a main source of market failure in regulatory competition. It is argued that once market participants (firms or citizens) cannot move freely among jurisdictions, the disciplining effect of competition will be entirely eliminated.

However, other theories on institutional competition explain competitive interactions without free choice or mobility of regulatees. These are discussed below in Section 3.

2.5 Where Regulatory Competition Research Stands Today

The model of regulatory competition through mobility or choice of regulatees originated in, and has been most predominantly applied to, corporate law in the US. However, other legal fields have also been assessed under this model, such as environmental regulation,[26] labour law,[27] securities regulation,[28] immigration law,[29] family law,[30] antitrust,[31] and intellectual property rights,[32] just to mention a few examples.

With regard to the comparison of regulatory competition in different legal fields, studies point out that competition among jurisdictions

---

[26] Revesz, R.L. (1992), 'Rehabilitating Interstate Competition: Rethinking the "Race to the Bottom" Rationale for Federal Environmental Regulation', *New York University Law Review*, vol. 67, p. 1210.

[27] Langille, B.A. (1996), 'Competing Conceptions of Regulatory Competition in Debates on Trade Liberalisation and Labour Standards', in Bratton et al. (eds) *International Regulatory Competition and Coordination* (Oxford: Clarendon Press).

[28] Romano, R. (2001), 'The Need for Competition in International Securities Regulation', *Theoretical Inquiries in Law*, vol. 2, p. 387.

[29] Barbou des Places, S. (2003), 'Evolution of Asylum Legislation in the EU: Insights for Regulatory Competition Theory', IUE, *Robert Schumann Center Working Paper*, RSC No. 2003/16.

[30] Brown, J.G. (1996), 'Competitive Federalism and Legislative Incentives to Recognize Same-Sex Marriage'. in Bratton et al. (eds) *International Regulatory Competition and Coordination* (Oxford: Clarendon Press).

[31] Fox, E.M. (2001), 'Antitrust Law on a Global Scale: Races Up, Down, and Sideways', in Esty, D.C. and Geradin, D. (eds) *Regulatory Competition and Economic Integration* (Oxford: Oxford University Press).

[32] Govaere, I. and Demaret, P. (2001), 'The TRIPS Agreement: A Response to Global Regulatory Competition or an Exercise of Global Regulatory Coersion?', in Esty, D.C. and Geradin, D. (eds) *Regulatory Competition and Economic Integration* (Oxford: Oxford University Press).

demonstrates highly field-specific features. Therefore competitive law-making cannot be described through one single model that could predict the welfare implications within any legal field.[33]

Recent scholarly work on regulatory competition is focusing on identifying relevant determinants of competitive interaction. The emerging conclusions show the pieces of a puzzle,[34] revealing determinative elements of competitive interaction.

For example, the literature explores the concept of co-opetition, claiming that legal actors' interaction goes beyond mere competition.[35] Cooperation and competition can go hand-in-hand, and are likely to be mutually indispensable in a well-functioning system of competitive interactions. Currently there is no explanation of what makes actors compete or cooperate.

Further, scholars draw attention to the fact that legal actors' incentives to compete should not be presumed, but should instead be established on a case-by-case basis.[36] However the circumstances that would influence their incentives are not listed in the literature.

Other streams of literature, often referring to systems competition or institutional competition,[37] address regulatory competition in a broader context, examining also the interaction of legal actors through different channels of competition.[38]

These developments and propositions for further research are explored below in this chapter, in order to analyse and further extend them throughout the book.

---

[33] See Esty and Geradin (2001).

[34] The metaphor is used in Radaelli, C. (2004), 'The Puzzle of Regulatory Competition', *Journal of Public Policy*, vol. 24, no. 2, pp. 1–23.

[35] See, e.g. Geradin, D. and McCahery, J.A. (2004), 'Regulatory Competition and Coopetition', in Jordana, J. and Levi-Faur, D. (eds) *The Politics of Regulation: Institutions and Regulatory Reforms for the Age of Governance* (Cheltenham, UK: Edward Elgar).

[36] See, e.g. Radaelli (2004).

[37] For a recent collection of essays, see Bergh, A. and Hoijer, R. (2008), *Institutional Competition* (Cheltenham, UK: Edward Elgar).

[38] Kerber, W. and Budzinski, O. (2004), 'Competition of Competition Laws: Mission Impossible?', in Greve, M.S. and Epstein, R.A. (eds) *Competition Laws in Conflict: Antitrust Jurisdiction in the Global Economy* (Washington, DC: AEI Press).

3. DIFFERENT FORMS OF COMPETITION

3.1 The Four Channels of Competitive Interaction and their Potential Benefits

Although the denomination of different forms of legal competition is not always used in a consistent manner in the existing literature, regulatory competition most often refers to competitive interaction among jurisdictions' legal actors for mobile regulatees. Institutional competition, also referred to as 'systems competition' or 'competitive federalism',[39] is a broader concept that includes several other forms of competitive interaction.[40] Institutional competition can take place through four main different channels that correspond to different degrees of economic openness within an economy:[41]

- Yardstick competition;
- Trade competition;
- Production factor competition;
- Regulatory competition (in the narrow sense for mobile regulatees).

3.1.1 Yardstick competition

Yardstick competition is competition that takes place merely through the free flow of information about jurisdictions' policy performance. This is a form of competition where the mobility of production factors and goods are equally restricted and (political) competition occurs only through citizens' observations of, and comparisons with, other jurisdictions' performance.

---

[39] Tiebout, C. (1956), 'A Pure Theory of Local Expenditures', *Journal of Political Economics*, vol. 64, no. 5, p. 416; Oates, W.E. and Schwab, R.M. (1988), 'Economic Competition Among Jurisdiction: Efficiency Enhancing, or Distortion Inducing?', *Journal of Public Economics*, vol. 35, pp. 333–354; Kerber, W. and Vanberg, V. (1994), 'Institutional Competition Among Jurisdictions: An Evolutionary Approach', *Constitutional Political Economy*, vol. 5, pp. 93–219; Sinn, H.W. (1997), 'The Selection Principle and Market Failure in Systems Competition', *Journal of Public Economics*, vol. 88, pp. 247–274.

[40] For recent additions to this stream of literature, see Meessen, K. (2009), *Economic Law as an Economic Good: Its Rule Function and Its Tool Function in the Competition of Systems* (Munich: Sellier).

[41] See Kerber, W. and Budzinski, O. (2004), 'Competition of Competition Laws: Mission Impossible?', in Greve, M.S. and Epstein, R.A. (eds) *Competition Laws in Conflict: Antitrust Jurisdiction in the Global Economy* (Washington, DC: AEI Press).

The term 'yardstick competition' probably originates from the late 1920s.[42] The concept is rooted in economic theory that shows that even when there is no direct product market competition among firms, a weaker yardstick competition occurs by comparing the achievements of one firm against another's. In competition policy, it is argued that it is better to have several electricity providers with exclusive sales areas that are not in direct competition with each other, than to have one monopolist firm across the entire country because yardstick competition can emerge among them, improving their performances.[43] The same argument holds true for legal actors.

Yardstick competition in the law-making process can take place without any direct interaction of the economies of different countries, apart from a flow of information about each others' performance. It is merely this flow of information that opens a channel of competitive interaction among legal actors.

The competitive learning process improves the *domestic* efficiency of a country, which might be an aim for political actors in response to their electorate. But since the countries do not interact, such efficiency does not translate into competitive advantage in international trade, or into changes in endowment of production factors. In most real world cases, however, yardstick competition will be present in parallel with other forms of competition, since the economies of most countries are open and they do interact. How the model of yardstick competition performs in such a setting has not been fully explored yet in the literature, although existing studies look at cases of yardstick competition which exists in parallel to economic openness, that is not 'pure' forms of yardstick competition amongst completely closed economies.

In the case of 'pure' yardstick competition, there are no potential externalities involved, as there is no transmission mechanism between the countries. It is possible, however, that jurisdictions learn the 'wrong'

---

[42] Handy, W. (1929), *The Yardstick of Public Utility Operations and Construction Costs* (Baltimore: Williams and Wilkins), cited as the first use of this term by Harrison, J.L. (1979), 'Yardstick Competition: A Prematurely Discarded Form of Regulatory Relief', *Tulane Law Review*, pp. 465–491. Later appearances of the concept include Henderson, L. (1936), 'The Consumer and Competition', *Annuals of the American Academy of Political and Social Science*, vol. 183, Government Finance in the Modern Economy (Jan., 1936), pp. 263–271; and Stead, W.H. (1942), 'Democracy and Social Controls in Industry', *American Sociological Review*, vol. 7, no. 2, pp. 176–184.

[43] Nordhaus, R. R. (1998), 'Yardstick Competition in a Deregulated Electricity Industry', *Natural Resources and Environment*, vol. 12, pp. 256–260.

policies from each other, either because of information failures, or because of a failure of the democratic system and voters' control.

The yardstick competition model builds on the power of political competition within jurisdictions, something that advocates of regulatory competition through mobility of regulatees are sceptical of.[44] There are, however, strong arguments that point to the effectiveness of this type of competitive interaction.[45] This form of competition features in some of the early federalism models and fits into a continuum of models based on the different degrees of openness of national economies, therefore it will be further explored in the following chapters.[46]

To conclude, yardstick competition basically renders decentralised monopolistic competences (under certain conditions referred to in the previous section) superior to centralisation. The question is how to make yardstick competition achieve its potential advantages even in open economies where trade and factors of production circulate freely, such as within the EU.

3.1.2 Competition through international trade

Competition through international trade can emerge under trade openness, as the performance of one jurisdiction in the trading system will put pressure on the others to perform better. For this to happen the factors of production (capital and labour) or regulatees do not have to be mobile across jurisdictions; it is sufficient that there is trade between them.

With regard to trade, international economics tells us that, under the Ricardian model of the economy, countries will benefit from international trade based on comparative advantages while, in a specific factors model, the overall benefits from international trade can be attributed to the difference between countries' relative supply curves.[47] Similarly, in the Heckscher-Ohlin model, where factors of production are not internationally mobile but are mobile domestically across industries, the

---

44 Brennan, G. and Buchanan, J.M. (1980), *The Power to Tax. Analytical Foundations of a Fiscal Constitution* (Cambridge: Cambridge University Press).

45 Schleifer, A. (1985), 'A Theory of Yardstick Competition', *Rand Journal of Economics*, vol. 6, no. 3, p. 319.

46 Salmon, P. (1987), 'Decentralisation as an Incentive Scheme', *Oxford Review of Economic Policy*, vol. 3, no. 2, pp. 24–43; Besley, T. and Case, A. (1995), 'Incumbent Behavior: Vote-Seeking, Tax-Setting, and Yardstick Competition', *American Economic Review*, vol. 85, no. 1, pp. 25–45; Kerber and Budzinski (2004).

47 This model already points to problems of income distribution between domestically mobile and immobile industries.

capital or labour endowment of countries will lead to benefits from international trade in, respectively, capital intensive or labour intensive goods.[48] But, notwithstanding the voluminous economic literature describing the mutual and overall advantages of free trade, and condemning national restrictions and interventions, when looking at the competition of regulators, it can be observed that states still try to affect the competitiveness of their home industries through regulation (typically through trade subsidies, duties and quotas, state aids). Economic literature has criticised such interventions arguing that their overall effects will be detrimental also for the country implementing them.

However there is also another way in which domestic regulation can achieve international trade advantages: through more efficient internal regulation that increases domestic productivity, which does not qualify as an 'unfair advantage' created by the state for a specific firm or industry and does not have detrimental effects on overall welfare. In this respect, the domestic legal environment translates into one of the local features of the country or region affecting the competitiveness of firms.

3.1.3 Competition through production factor mobility

A further channel of competition, that can be distinguished from yardstick and international trade competition, is the mobility of factors of production, namely capital and labour.[49] Even when regulatees (citizens, companies) cannot move across borders, competition can still take place across jurisdictions through the channel of capital mobility. Here the main subject of competition is, in part, still international trade advantages, since changing a country's factor endowments will impact on trade performance as well as on domestic productivity.[50] As for the welfare impacts of this mobility itself, mainstream international economic theory predicts increased world output.[51]

The welfare effects of regulation are not always clear. States can engage in tax competition in order to attract foreign direct investment (capital) into their economies. Indeed, this type of competition among

---

[48] Krugman, P.R. and Obstfeld, M. (2009), *International Economics: Theory and Policy*, 8th edition (Boston: Pearson Education).

[49] Where, obviously, capital is more mobile than labour.

[50] The cross-border flow of technologies and know-how would be an interesting extension of this theory of competition as these can have a significant impact on economic performance (i.e. on productivity and as a result of trade performance).

[51] Krugman, P.R. and Obstfeld, M. (2009), *International Economics: Theory and Policy* (Boston: Pearson Addison Wesley).

countries usually involves taxation: factors of production are what states compete for (most often capital investment) and in exchange they offer reduced taxes, or more attractive public goods and regulation (or an optimal mix of the two).

However, a distinction should be made between competition for capital and competition for budget revenue in the form of taxes. While the first form of competition is tax competition for foreign direct investment (offering lower tax rates),[52] or institutional competition through production factor mobility (offering a more attractive legal environment), the second form is a competition between states in order to attract tax revenue (offering other locational advantages and public goods, such as infrastructure, regulatory environment, and so on).[53] This latter form of competition, if it attracts budget revenue from regulatees through offering a better regulatory environment, is already bordering on the most open form of competition: institutional competition through the mobility of regulatees.[54]

3.1.4 Regulatory competition with free choice by regulatees

The fourth category of institutional competition is regulatory competition with free choice of law or mobility of regulatees across legal systems.[55] Regulatory competition in the narrow sense, as it is most often referred to in the literature, refers to such competitive settings, with mobility or free

---

[52] In exchange for the creation of employment in production sites. With capital mobility, it is FDI competition that occurs; without capital mobility, it is the enhancement of national firms' international competitiveness, which in turn raises national tax revenues.

[53] In certain cases, a lower tax burden on individual firms will raise the overall tax revenue of the state.

[54] It is recognised here, however, that distinguishing regulatees and capital as the aim of competition is not easy. Firms are the channels of capital investment and they are subject to as many legal norms as regulatees. For example, relocating the corporate seat might be thought of as the movement of investment, but production facilities might not be moved together with the seat of administration.

[55] The expression 'regulatory competition' is most often used to describe interjurisdictional competition with free choice of law or mobility of regulatees, but there are exceptions to this. Regulatory competition is sometimes referred to in the broader sense of institutional competition, see, e.g. Paul, J.R. (1995), 'Free Trade, Regulatory Competition and the Autonomous Market Fallacy', *Columbia Journal of European Law*, vol. 29, no. 1. The lack of clear distinction between these concepts is due also to the fact that the borderlines are not clear. Capital is often regulated, therefore capital mobility is close to mobility of regulatees, etc.

choice of law on the side of regulatees. This form of competition has already been explained above in Section 2.

3.2 Vertical, Horizontal, Inter- and Intra-Jurisdictional Competition

3.2.1 Vertical and horizontal dimensions of competition

The ultimate question of normative regulatory competition studies concerns the optimal allocation of competences among legal actors. Competence allocation has several dimensions. In a horizontal context, decentralisation is described as a system with competences allocated at the state level,[56] where competitive law-making (regulatory competition) may emerge among national legislators or other legal actors.

However, regulatory competition can also be described in a vertical dimension. Competition may arise between the federal (in this case European) and state (that is Member State) legal actors. Vertical competition may arise between these two levels if European action does not pre-empt national action. This is the case, for example, when the European legislator introduces a new legal form that exists parallel with national legal forms, a so-called '21st regime', such as the Societas Europea.

The co-existence of legislation at both federal and state level is not necessary, however, in order to speak about vertical regulatory competition. Romano observes that the threat of pre-empting state level competences may provide sufficient incentive to the state legislator to provide 'good' laws.[57] This can be described as vertical regulatory competition, or at least vertical competitive pressure.

3.2.2 Inter- and intra-jurisdictional dimensions of competition

The interaction of legislators has been the main focus of regulatory competition literature. This form of competition can by definition only take place between different jurisdictions. However, as we broaden the scope of legal actors, their competitive interaction can be observed also within a single jurisdiction.

Courts' interpretative activity and the gap-filling and policy developing role of regulatory agencies may diverge from the legislator's original intents. Similarly, private regulators can shape the regulatory field in a

---

[56] In an EU context, this means Member States and the EU. But below the national level further vertical competence allocation may occur, as in federal states, local governments, etc.

[57] See Romano, R. (2005), 'Is Regulatory Competition a Problem or Irrelevant for Corporate Governance?', *ECGI Working Paper* no. 26/2005.

way that causes legislators, or regulators to experience competitive pressure from them and respond in a competitive way.

In the domestic setting, the competitive behaviour of, for example, the regulator (*vis-à-vis* the courts for example) does not necessarily result in systems competition on the international scene. It may well be that the courts aim to foster systems competition with other countries, and the regulator blocks this attempt. This means that intra-jurisdictional competition (competition for the field) may be a prerequisite for the emergence of international systems competition in the classical sense, but it is not a sufficient condition.

Further sections will examine different legal actors and their potential intra-jurisdictional interaction.

3.3 Competition and Cooperation Among Jurisdictions: Co-opetition

3.3.1 The possible interpretations of co-opetition

Regulatory competition literature has developed the dichotomy of competition and cooperation. Under such so-called 'co-opetition' legal actors not only compete but also cooperate.[58]

The concept of co-opetition can be interpreted in different ways as, in fact, the authors addressing this issue have not drawn clear contours for this concept. One reading of it is that legal actors compete in certain fields and cooperate in others (alternative model of 'competition-cooperation').[59] Another possibility is that actors cooperate at one stage and compete at another, in a cyclical sequence ('sequential co-opetition').[60] Finally, authors also refer to harmonisation and institutional competition as complements rather than mutually exclusive concepts, pointing out that harmonisation of international law rules are needed for example in national company laws in order to achieve a legal framework in which companies can move freely across the EU Member States.[61] Similarly, scholars often refer to setting the rules of the game, or

---

[58] Geradin and McCahery (2004).

[59] This interpretation is implied by the examples provided by Geradin and McCahery (2004).

[60] The concept of competition and cooperation in sequence was put forward by Radaelli (2004) at p. 20.

[61] Kerber, W. and Van den Bergh, R. (2008), 'Mutual Recognition Revisited: Misunderstandings, Inconsistencies, and a Suggested Reinterpretation', *Kyklos*, vol. 61 no. 3, pp. 447–465.

the framework international law rules, in terms of a cooperative agreement among jurisdictions' legal actors, which sets the scope and limits for competitive interactions.[62]

It is argued that such co-opetition (in all of its above interpretations) may in certain circumstances result in a better outcome than pure competition. Cooperation in this framework means, for example, cooperation as to the outcome of regulations resolving the conflict of different rules, such as harmonised standards or mutual recognition. But cooperation may also take the form of information or data exchanges, or exchange of policy experience.[63] The latter is an example of institutional arrangements that facilitate yardstick competition.

Co-opetition is documented by authors in a bilateral as well as a multilateral context. Among the examples are the enhanced cooperation between the EU and the US in the field of antitrust, and multilateral cooperation in intellectual property rights protection.[64] But, similarly, the European subsidiarity principle, as well as state-level enforcement of federal antitrust laws in the 1980s in the US, are described as 'co-opetition'.

3.3.2 The European Union as centralisation or cooperation of actors

In the specific European context, cooperation is of special significance, given that competences are shared in most legal fields between the Member States and the EU, with the latter operating under the requirements of subsidiarity. The subsidiarity principle, as enshrined in the Treaty, requires that, when cooperation at national level can provide a solution that is as efficient as the response of the European legislator would be, the former should have priority.

However the European legislator consists of national heads of state or government (Council), and directly elected members of the European Parliament.[65] Besides, when exercising powers of implementation and preparing legislative proposals, the European Commission often consults

[62] Holzinger and Knill interpret cooperation and competition as creating a framework for competition by a cooperative agreement: Holzinger, K. and Knill, Ch. (2005), 'Causes and Conditions of Cross-National Policy Convergence', *Journal of European Public Policy*, vol. 12, no. 5, pp. 775–796.

[63] Geradin and McCahery (2004).

[64] Geradin and McCahery (2004).

[65] See Art. 251 of the EC Treaty (Art. 294 TFEU), governing the most commonly used legislative procedure, the co-decision procedure.

or is under the obligation to consult specialised committees.[66] In this sense describing European harmonising measures as centralised decisions is an over-simplification.

On the other hand, cooperative arrangements among Member States may also take the form of consultation and cooperation procedures, where decisions are taken by representatives. Thus there is no sharp dividing line between centralised decisions and cooperative solutions.

Instead, the involvement of various actors (legislators, regulators, courts, private regulators) at different levels (EU or national) will presumably have an influence on the final outcome. Also, different models of European or national governance may alter the dynamics of institutional competition within a certain field.

3.3.3 Conclusions on the co-opetition concept and its possible application

It appears that competition, cooperation and centralisation will lead to different outcomes in terms of legal output and welfare effects. There is however, no indication in the literature so far as to when cooperation is likely to arise.

The comparative part of this book will examine how European governance models may alter the behaviour of legal actors in their interaction and thus influence the emergence of institutional competition, what the scope and limits of such competition may be, and ultimately, what outcome it leads to. It will examine whether the model of governance influences the propensity of legal actors to engage in cooperation rather than competition.

4. MEASURING THE ‘OUTCOME’ OF REGULATORY COMPETITION

4.1 Welfare and Efficiency as Measures of the Outcome of Regulatory Competition

Although we can all tell the difference between what is good and what is bad for us, describing this is not as easy as it first seems. Economic theory works with units we can count; values are also often expressed in

---

[66] Regulation 182/2011 of the European Parliament and the Council of 16 February 2011 laying down the rules and general principles concerning mechanisms for control by Member States of the Commission’s exercise of implementing powers.

monetary terms. Economics often also assumes that people have clear preferences and clear orders of preference and that, when it comes to choosing between two things (for example products, meals, holiday destinations), they choose in line with their stated preferences. Economists acknowledge, however, that in reality, subjective value and relative preferences are not so straightforward, and that often we don't know what our exact preferences are.

Against this background, this section reviews some interpretations of optimal delegated decision-making.

4.1.1 How do centralised decision-makers measure what is best for their constituency?

Decision theory extends the decision made by one individual to the decision of a group of individuals taken on their behalf by a centralised decision-maker. This is the situation when a political or legal actor decides on legal rules. Theory offers some alternative explanations as to how the decision maker is supposed to achieve the 'best' decision. The main ones are: 'multi-attribute utility' (MAU), and 'social choice'. 'Cost benefit analysis' describes individuals' utilities in monetary terms, and aggregates them in order to calculate the overall cost and benefit of each potential choice of the decision-maker. The central actor should then choose the option that has the highest value. This does not take into account the non-linear utility of money, or low income levels that affect people's ability to pay, thus distorting the signal about preferences.

The 'multi-attribute utility' avoids using monetary terms. It works instead with the cardinal utilities of individuals. This model is difficult to use in practice, as data on people's utilities is hard to collect and work with. However, cardinal utilities account better for individuals' preferences.[67] There are two further sub-theories within multi-attribute utility: the prospect theory and bounded rationality, both of which account for observed deviations of individuals from the predicted choices under rational actor models.

Finally the 'social choice' model describes the central decision-makers' objective as being to choose the option that is preferred by the most individuals within the group, without regard to how much each person gains or loses. This model is the closest description of political decision-making through the system of voting. However, as described by

---

[67] Lejano, R. (2006), *Frameworks for Policy Analysis: Merging Text and Context* (London: Routledge).

Arrow,[68] social choice rules can lead to counterintuitive decisions on the part of the centralised decision-maker.

4.1.2 How does academic literature define welfare and optimal policies?

'Pareto optimality' is a state of affairs in which nobody can be made better off without making someone else worse off.[69] While this concept eliminates the tricky question of interpersonal exchange, and therefore comparisons of welfare, its application is limited in practice exactly because there are few policy changes that would not create losers. In the 1930s an idea gained terrain that the interpersonal comparison of welfare is not scientific (economic) but rather ethical in nature, since utility cannot be measured.

The Kaldor-Hicks criteria are an attempt to respond to the questions raised about Pareto optimality. This efficiency concept acknowledges the limitations of Pareto optimality (that is the impossibility of interpersonal comparisons of welfare), but it claims their irrelevance. The Kaldor-Hicks efficiency concept requires an increase in aggregate welfare, which makes it possible, at least in theory, to compensate losers from the gains of a given policy change. Whether such compensation should take place 'is a political question on which the economist, qua economist, could hardly pronounce an opinion'.[70] In other words, the Kaldor test is passed if in the new state, after a policy change, redistributions are possible that would create a state superior to the original state. The Hicks test is passed if there are no redistributions possible in the original state (before the policy change) that would produce a situation Pareto superior to the new state (after the change).[71] Later scholars, among them Posner, still use the Kaldor-Hicks efficiency criteria when analysing efficiency.[72]

In 1957, Little pointed out that the separation of efficiency and distribution is not possible; any criteria, whether Kaldor-Hicks efficient

---

[68] Arrow, K. (1951), *Social Choice and Individual Values* (New York: Wiley).

[69] Pareto, V. (1896), *Cours d'Economie Politique* (Lausanne: F. Rouge).

[70] Kaldor, N. (1939), 'Welfare Positions of Economics and Interpersonal Comparisons of Utility', *The Economic Journal*, vol. 49, no. 195.

[71] Zerbe, R.O. (2001), *Economic Efficiency in Law and Economics* (Cheltenham, UK: Edward Elgar).

[72] Posner, R.A. (1985), *Antitrust Law* (Chicago: University of Chicago Press).

or not, rests on value judgement. Further technical[73] and moral[74] criticisms followed the elaboration of this efficiency concept. There are currently a number of studies that try to pave the way for more just, or better-founded, efficiency concepts. Reviewing these in any depth would exceed the scope of the present study. It should be mentioned however that one of the most discussed recent contributions to this debate is Kaplow and Shavell's 'Fairness vs. Welfare'.[75]

The authors there argue that social policies should be assessed 'entirely on the basis of their effects on individuals' well-being', and 'no independent weight should be accorded to notions of fairness (other than many purely distributive notions). They claim that notions of fairness perversely reduce welfare … by revealing numerous other deficiencies in the notions, including their lack of sound rationales.'[76]

The position they present is strongly criticised, however, by other scholars, claiming that, 'Fairness and welfare do not lie on the same plane. While welfare can provide a descriptive framework for classifying different states of the world, only fairness is able to provide a normative framework for assessing legal policies, that is, for choosing among possible states of the world, featured by different distributions of welfare. In this sense, fairness and welfare are not competing values.'[77] And that, '[t]he basic intuition we can extract from these reasonings is that the maximisation of welfare is an attractive aim, though only when it is pursued in a fair context …'.[78]

4.1.3 The approach followed in this book

Given that a fully-fledged review of the measure of economic efficiency is not feasible within this book, the approach followed here will be the Kaldor-Hicks efficiency concept. In what follows there will not be mathematical calculations of benefits and costs that would require precise quantification. Nonetheless, the efficiency concept does influence the

---

[73] For an overview of technical criticisms of the Kaldor-Hicks efficiency concept see Zerbe (2001).

[74] Dworkin, R. (1980), 'Is Wealth a Value?', *Journal of Legal Studies*, vol. 9, p. 191; Sen, A. and Williams, B. (eds) (1982), *Utilitarianism and Beyond* (Cambridge: Cambridge University Press).

[75] Kaplow, L. and Shavell, S. (2003), 'Fairness versus Welfare: Notes on the Pareto Principle, Preferences, and Distributive Justice', *NBER Working Paper No. 9622*.

[76] Kaplow and Shavell (2003).

[77] Denozza, F. (2007), 'Fairness and Welfare', in Cafaggi, F. et al. (eds) *Law, Economics and Institutional Complexity* (New York: Routledge).

[78] Ibid.

conclusions: hence the necessity of describing the concept of efficiency used here.

This book thus follows the more common approach of interpreting optimal policies as those that increase overall welfare (allowing for redistribution, at least in theory). Following through this theoretical approach to the end would mean that even in cases where redistribution is not a real option, the mere fact that more wealth is gained than lost (together with the difficulties of comparing utilities across groups of people) would justify a legal change.

This, in reality, is highly questionable from a moral and ethical viewpoint and, therefore, it is not argued here that any policy that leads to a perceived higher overall welfare should be followed through without regard to its distributional impact.

At the same time, this book also aims to explore whether competing jurisdictions have different efficiency concepts. This will be done not in terms of tracing competing economic theories on welfare economics and efficiency concepts, like the Kaldor-Hicks efficiency concept and its alternatives – which is done surprisingly rarely in academic discussion – but rather with regard to the distributive impact of jurisdictions' preferred legal solutions. It is beyond the reach of this book to examine the distributive effects of the entire system of legal rules, which could theoretically lead to very different distributive outcomes than the one single observed legal solution (for example on corporate governance).

4.2 When is Co-opetition Welfare Enhancing?

Federalism and regulatory competition literature has long examined the dichotomy of whether decentralisation is better than centralisation. But, the concept of co-opetition introduced above raises the question of optimality in a triangular setting: it calls for determining the value added of cooperation *vis-à-vis* both competition and centralisation. The existing literature on co-opetition up to now has not done this.

Therefore, we revisit the main points of each of the above competence settings here in order to clarify what the optimal place of cooperation is between competitive and centralised arrangements.

4.2.1 When is cooperation superior to centralisation?

Game theory shows that the agreement reached by the individuals participating in cooperation will be different from that of the 'collective decision' of one centralised decision maker.

However, as shown above, there are several ways to describe centralised decision-making, and there are differences between assuming perfectly benevolent decision-makers or ones that can be influenced by other incentives than pursuing the common good. If the central decision-maker is assumed to be benevolent and capable of aggregating the utilities, than the outcome will be optimal from this aggregated utility perspective. Moreover, if we want to take a different measure of optimality, and integrate equity into the efficiency concept (or fully replace economic criteria with it), it can be argued that the centralised decision-maker can be the best placed to take account of any social consideration – better placed than players of a cooperative game. As Parisi puts it: 'In some sense, whether regulatory fragmentation represents an increase or a decrease in total welfare is a valuation problem that depends upon the assessment of the value of the underlying regulatory mission. Clearly, if regulators are assumed to act benevolently and with full information, unified regulatory powers (or the coordination among multiple regulators) represent the value maximizing regulatory structure.'[79]

But does that mean that there is nothing that cooperative games can do for us that centralisation cannot?

4.2.2 Potential benefits of competition over centralisation

The first possible gain from decentralisation comes from polities that consist of people with diverse preferences. As decision theory shows, one of the main challenges for any centralised decision-maker, even if benevolent and with full information, is to arrive at one common solution in a polity with diverse preferences. Decentralised solutions may offer each local community its most preferred solution.

But if we remove the assumption that central decision-makers will always be able to act both benevolently and with full information, we arrive at the conclusion that competition may have further benefits over centralisation.

The second such potential benefit is the discovery process of what the best solution is. If the central decision-maker does not have full information, this may easily indicate good potential for decentralisation.

The third advantage of competitive decentralisation is present when the centralised decision-maker over regulates. Competition in such cases can restrain the Leviathan state.

---

[79] Parisi, F. et al. (2006), 'Two Dimensions of Regulatory Competition', *International Review of Law and Economics*, vol. 26, pp. 55–66.

Inefficient central solutions may thus emerge when the central decision-maker is captured,[80] when the regulated field is subject to local diversity, or quick changes that the central decision-maker is not well placed to keep pace with (for example securities regulation) or, simply, when the local decision-maker has better access to information (for example competition law).

So at an abstract level we can say that there may be cases where competition is better than centralisation.

4.2.3 Potential benefits of cooperation over competition

The co-opetition model basically means that institutional competition can turn from a non-cooperative game into a cooperative one. Several authors argue that once cooperative games emerge, these are welfare enhancing.[81] However, at present, descriptions of co-opetition do not tell us *when* cooperation is good or bad.

Examples for cooperation achieving better results than competition are ample, since cooperative strategies overcome 'prisoner's dilemma' problems. But, in several other cases, cooperation can lead to outcomes inferior to competition. The best-known example of this is the collusion of competitor firms.

It appears, thus, that when regulatory competition would lead to an optimal outcome, cooperation among the legal actors may be ruinous. On the other hand, when regulatory competition fails to achieve optimal outcome due to a 'prisoner's dilemma', cooperation may achieve better results. But when does regulatory competition fail?

At a very general level, we can observe that in a 'market for legal rules', just like in any other market, there can be market failures that lead to inefficient outcomes. In cases of market inefficiencies, like external effects, coordination among the actors who would otherwise be competing may lead to better overall welfare. Prisoner's dilemma situations can also be avoided with the introduction of cooperation. Therefore we can conclude that in some cases cooperation is better than competition, even if the latter delivered better outcomes than centralisation.

At a theoretical level this is because centralisation is modelled as a single decision-maker, whereas cooperation involves all of the concerned jurisdictions' decision-makers. But, in the particular case of the EU, cooperation and centralisation have to be understood differently. In this

---

[80] The empirical question of whether and how often this happens at the European level is assessed by political science studies with varying conclusions.

[81] Esty and Geradin (2001); Holzinger and Knill (2005); Geradin and McCahery (2004); Radaelli (2004).

case, centralisation refers to the decision-making process at EU level, which is very similar to a form of cooperation (for example negotiations in Council or the European Parliament). But what do we mean by cooperation then, in contrast to such cooperation-like centralisation? One important difference is that cooperation in a decentralised system is likely to take place among national or regional legal actors different from those that make up the Council or the Parliament. With their own incentive structure, problem solving and mission statement, these national legal actors are bound to arrive at different outcomes in cooperative situations from Council members. Besides, the interaction between these actors is set up differently from Council negotiations, and the rules governing such interactions may be important determinants of whether cooperation will emerge and what results it will bring.

It should also be added that such cooperation depends on the credibility of the actors who commit to a given strategy in the game. Again, in practice, this means that the institutional design of legal actors' interaction (such as repeated games, the observability of actions and the ability to punish deviations from agreed conduct) play a very important role in determining the likelihood and strength of cooperative interaction. Further chapters will analyse the governance mechanisms of legal actors' interaction to see to what extent those are conducive towards cooperative, rather than competitive, outcomes in a decentralised setting.

4.3 Races to Top and Bottom: A Clarification

As referred to above, the model developed by Tiebout claims that competition is welfare enhancing.[82] This claim opened a scholarly debate in which authors argued that competition among legal actors would not lead to optimal outcomes. On the contrary, it would be welfare decreasing, due to the relaxation of certain, otherwise welfare maximising, standards. The literature on regulatory competition (through choice or mobility) referred to welfare decreasing competition as a 'race to the bottom'.[83]

To counter the arguments of the race to the bottom literature, Vogel presented competitive interactions in environmental standard setting

---

[82] Tiebout (1956).

[83] Cary, W.L. (1974), 'Federalism and Corporate Law: Reflections Upon Delaware', *Yale Law Journal*, vol. 83, at p. 664, quoting Mr Justice Brandeis in an early case from 1933: *Ligett Co. v. Lee* 288 U.S. 517, 562–563 (1933).

where the outcome was a raising of standards and an overall welfare increase.[84] He called this effect the 'race to the top'.

In the above example, the relaxation of standards has been associated with an overall detriment to welfare, while stricter standards have been claimed as welfare increasing. This coincidence results in some confusion in the current literature about whether the moniker 'race to the bottom' refers to a relaxation of standards or to a decrease in (overall) welfare. It can be argued that non-competing states over-regulate, and competition corrects this with laxer norms which, nonetheless, increase overall welfare. In this study, 'race to the bottom' is used to refer to an overall welfare decrease, and 'race to the top' is used to describe welfare gains. The phrases 'race in stringency' and 'race in laxity' distinguish between the two directions of regulatory movements.

4.4 Convergence or Divergence – and the Potential Reasons Behind it

The outcome of regulatory competition can be measured not only in terms of welfare implications, but also in terms of direction of legal change. Earlier reference was made to the race in laxity or stringency. But, when comparing the legal outputs of different jurisdictions, we can also observe convergence or divergence among them. Comparative law acknowledges that convergence can occur among norms in their formulation as well as in their function. Political science literature makes a general distinction between the similarity of *policy outputs* (the policies adopted by a government) and *policy outcomes* (the actual effects of a policy in terms of goal achievement).

In the literature of regulatory competition, convergence or divergence of policies is not only a positive, but also a normative debate. If competition among legal actors leads to fully convergent solutions, experimentation and further innovation is limited and the regulatory competition circle is closed. It can be that, after convergence, there is a new problem to which the actors respond with new solutions, but they eventually converge on the leading innovator.[85] It is indeed plausible that strong economies of scale and network effects will always lead to convergence around a single set of rules, as the efficient solution (such as well-established case law that goes along with a growing number of

---

[84] Vogel, D. (1995), *Trading Up: Consumer and Environmental Regulation in a Global Economy* (Cambridge, MA: Harvard University Press).

[85] This is generally the case, for example, in US corporate law where Delaware is regarded as the leading provider of corporate charters across states. See, e.g. Bebchuck and Hamdani (2002).

regulatees opting into a given jurisdiction). In these cases, the only danger of full convergence is the lock-in (path dependence) with a sub-optimal legal solution, when other better solutions exist but cannot spread due to the strong network effects.

It is, in reality, often a degree of convergence that regulatory competition leads to. This is often for reasons of embedded differences between legal systems. Partial convergence can mean convergence of function, not only legal form; or it can mean convergence only on certain aspects. Well-established research shows that the mere transplantation of foreign legal rules into any domestic legal system is unlikely to deliver the same results as in the jurisdiction of origin.[86] Therefore, partial or functional convergence may be a superior outcome to full convergence.

Although there are reviews that categorise regulatory competition as consistently leading to policy convergence,[87] this will not be presumed here: divergence can also be the outcome of regulatory competition. Even in these cases of policy convergence, the jurisdiction that is copied by others starts the competition with a divergence move, a legal innovation of some kind. In other cases, a jurisdiction may find itself a niche in offering legal products that other jurisdictions do not have, and it may well be that other jurisdictions cannot (or do not find it worthwhile to) imitate these legal rules.

A framework from the political science literature for policy convergence and its causes is summarised below, in order to see how the categorisation followed here fits with this stream of research.[88]

According to Holzinger and Knill,[89] regulatory competition leads to mutual adjustments through competitive pressures. They distinguish other mechanisms of policy convergence, such as imposition that leads to submission, harmonisation that leads to compliance, and transnational communication, which is broken down to further cases, among them:

- lesson-drawing (perhaps closest to yardstick competition described here) which, according to their framework, leads to the transfer of a foreign model through problem pressure; and
- emulation, which they argue is the copying of a widely used model for reasons of a desire for conformity.

---

[86] See, e.g. Berkowitz, D., Pistor, K. and Richard, J.F. (2003), 'The Transplant Effect', *The American Journal of Comparative Law*, vol. 51, no. 1, pp. 163–203.

[87] See, e.g. Holzinger and Knill (2005).

[88] Ibid.

[89] Ibid.

The multitude of policy convergence mechanisms identified by Holzinger and Knill shows that mere convergence in legal output does not in itself prove that competitive interaction took place.

There are however similarities among several different channels of convergence. For example 'desire for conformity' presupposes that there is no other identifiable motive behind emulating other jurisdictions' policies. The challenge that remains in convergence research is the correct identification of causes. For example, distinguishing between 'problem pressure' and 'desire for conformity' is not always straightforward. How yardstick competition fits into the above categorisation remains to be seen. Also, in the framework of Holzinger and Knill, harmonisation automatically implies compliance. Here this will not be assumed. To sum up, while this framework of division of convergence causes and mechanisms is insightful for several purposes, the current analysis will not follow these exact categories and will not presume causal links between certain triggers and certain legal outcomes.

5. THE ACTORS OF COMPETITION AND THEIR INCENTIVES

This section provides an overview of legal actors involved in competitive interaction among jurisdictions. Several different categories of legal actors can be distinguished for such an analysis, and the existing literature already refers to most of these actors. It is therefore not a new initiative to look at different legal actors in the competitive interaction among jurisdictions. However, these actors and their incentives have not yet been extensively examined in the European context, and there is, so far, no systematic description of competition among them.

The incentives of the players are instrumental to the outcome of institutional competition. The behaviour of the different legal actors as public decision-makers is assessed here in order to find out whether the strategy of these actors is the same across the various groups or differs, and to analyse what role the institutional set-up can play in the features of each type of legal actor.

5.1 Legal Actors Selected for Analysis

The original Tiebout model of perfect sorting under fiscal decentralisation focused on horizontal competition between local governments in the provision of local public goods. This model has subsequently been adapted to providing law as a product from governments. The classical example of US corporate law has already extended the scope of legal actors to courts and lawyers, analysing systems competition through the active involvement of the judiciary. The advocates of regulatory competition in securities regulation also regard the US Securities and Exchange Commission (SEC), a federal regulatory agency, as a potential actor in competitive rule-setting.[90] Recent literature on regulatory competition has extended the number of actors to include not only governments but also international organisations and non-governmental organisations (NGOs).[91] The different divisions of government were also regarded as a platform of competition.[92] The idea of self-regulatory competition, that is competition among self-regulatory bodies, is also explored in recent literature.[93]

This study distinguishes among the following categories of legal actors:

- legislators and governments;
- independent regulatory agencies;
- courts;
- private regulators.

Governments, as regulators, are clearly distinguished from independent regulatory agencies (IRAs). Therefore governments and IRAs are analysed as two completely different legal actors, and the term 'regulator' refers here only to independent regulatory agencies. Governments are examined under the same heading as the 'legislator' in the tripartite distinction of legislator, regulator, and courts. In a deeper analysis, these three should be distinguished as legislator, regulator and independent regulatory agency. The reason for simplifying the list this way was that governments as regulators are closer in their behaviour and incentive structure to national parliaments than to independent regulatory agencies.

---

[90] Romano, R. (2001), 'The Need for Competition in International Securities Regulation', *Theoretical Inquiries in Law*, vol. 2, p. 387.

[91] Geradin and McCahery (2004).

[92] Ibid.

[93] Cafaggi, F. (2005) 'Self-Regulatory Competition' presentation prepared for the first SIDE Conference, Siena, 25 November; and Van den Bergh, R.J. (2004), 'Towards Efficient Self-regulation in Markets for Professional Services', in Ehlerman, C.D. and Atanasiu, I. (eds) *European Competition Law Annual 2004: The Relationship Between Competition Law and Liberal Professions* (Oxford: Hart Publishing).

Since the supervisory authorities are most often assigned some regulatory powers as well, here they will be assumed to have similar incentives and behaviour to regulatory agencies, unless otherwise specified in the text. Thus the legal actors whose incentives will be examined are: legislators; regulators; judges; and private regulators.[94]

5.2 The Legislator and the Government

Within the first category of legislators (national parliaments) and governments, the incentives of actors to attract firms into their jurisdictions have been extensively discussed in regulatory competition literature. Such incentives are very much field dependent.[95] They may focus on achieving increased tax revenues (attracting incorporations and start-ups), achieving international trade benefits (as in the model of mobility of goods) or attracting foreign investment (capital mobility).

The political accountability of governments makes these legal actors responsive to the preferences of their electorate and, potentially, also vulnerable to the capture of powerful lobby groups. This is a major determinant of the incentives of government, distinguishing it from the other actors analysed here. In political science terms 'the governments are the agents reacting to problem pressure, experience gained elsewhere, pressure of powerful external actors, economic pressure, and legal obligation'.[96] Governments are potentially influenced by a number of motivations: to satisfy their constituency; to answer to lobby groups' demands; to satisfy the personal preferences of actors within the government, and so on.

But, more broadly, the government has to be seen as a legislating bureaucracy. It is not only the political leaders of government whose incentives will influence the final output, but also the incentives of their bureaucrats. The internal functioning of a government, and the interaction between political leadership and technocratic staff, is a key element that

---

[94] Although the other legal actors' role is not less significant in general terms, the scope of the current study and the legal fields examined do not imply directly the involvement of NGOs and international organisations. As to the role of lawyers, they are undeniably involved in the shaping of legal solutions, however their role and influence is somewhat indirect, since ultimately it is the judiciary that will accept or reject a given legal solution. To limit the scope of this analysis, the lawyers' role in shaping legal norms will not be assessed here.

[95] Esty and Geradin (2001).

[96] Holzinger, K. and Knill, Ch. (2005), 'Causes and Conditions of Cross-National Policy Convergence', *Journal of European Public Policy*, vol. 12, no. 5, pp. 775–796.

determines the output of governments. To better understand the functioning of this institution that ultimately builds on bureaucrats, this section examines theories of political science literature on the functioning of bureaucracies.

5.2.1 Inside a bureaucracy: principal-agent theories of bureaucracies

National as well as federal governments are bureaucracies. Principal-agent theory has been adapted to describe them. It is argued that there are three types of agency relationships: between the electorate or citizens (principals) and the elected governments (agents); between the politicians (principals) and civil servants (agents); and a third one between the users of bureaucracy-provided goods and services (principals) and the bureaucracies (agents).[97]

The second agency type is further complicated by the fact that the bureaucracies are divided both vertically and horizontally into sub-units, also called *bureaux*, which exhibit their own agency characteristics *vis-à-vis* each other.

The basic features of all these agency types are that the actors pursue different goals, and that information is distributed asymmetrically between the agents and the principals – the latter have less information.

With regard to different goals, the agents are assumed to have incentives to shirk, and not to perform tasks as best they can. As to information asymmetries, it is argued that principals cannot see whether the outcome is the result of the agent's action or some other external event. This problem of information asymmetry is also called 'hidden action'. This leads to a moral hazard problem since agents will have an incentive to shirk. 'Hidden information', on the other hand, leads to adverse selection, when principals cannot verify whether the agents used the information available to them to the advantage of the principal.

Agency theory, as it describes bureaucracies, views these organisations as a nexus of contracts, with the main inquiry being directed at incentive contracts aiming to reduce agency costs.

Under an alternative model to the principal-agent theory, agents have some discretionary power, which they use in a way that alters the

---

[97] Based on the seminal work of Tirole, J. (1986), 'Hierarchies and Bureaucracies: On the Role of Collusion in Organizations', *Journal of Law, Economics and Organization*, vol. 2, p. 81; Laffont J.J. and Tirol, J. (1990), 'Politics of Government Decision Making: Regulatory Institutions', *Journal of Law, Economics and Organization*, vol. 6, no. 1, p. 1.

outcome of the decisions of the bureaucracy as a whole.[98] The agents aim to maximise their budgets, including amenities of office (salary, reputation, status, power). The main tenet of this model is that even if the political actor (political leadership, hierarchy) has clearly identifiable motivations, the bureaucracy may not act in full alignment with the intentions of the political actor, but may instead have its own incentives and objectives.

5.3 Independent Regulatory Agencies in a Systems Competition Setting

Independent regulatory agencies display different characteristics with regard to decision-making behaviour but their organisation is also bureaucratic, and all the principal-agent problems are applicable to IRAs. This section also builds on the observation that regulatory agencies have a certain scope for exercising discretionary decision-making powers.

5.3.1 Delegation of powers to regulatory agencies with discretion

Whilst the output of legislators is mainly dependent on the functioning of the political system,[99] the actions of regulatory bodies and judges have to be examined from a different perspective. The starting point for this analysis is the use of the discretion which these legal actors have.

Delegating regulatory power to agencies necessarily involves some discretion on the part of the regulator, and its use is often described as a principal-agent conflict between the legislator and the regulator. Legal, economic and political literature addresses the question of why the power of implementation is delegated to agencies.

Majone[100] argues that delegation is a way for governments to make credible commitments, as independent regulatory agencies enjoy autonomy and independence. Delegation may also occur due to the fact that in a given field special expertise is needed, and that governments have limited resources to deal with the details of all policies themselves.

The competing theories of economic self-interest versus ideas and values both feature in the more advanced political science literature on

---

[98] This model was described by Niskanen 1971, although its basis is Baumol's maximisation of sales theory for business firms, published in 1959.

[99] A substantial political science literature deals with the description of democratic elections and its restraining effects on legislative bodies.

[100] Majone, G. (1997), 'The Agency Model: The Growth of Regulation and Regulatory Institutions in the European Union', *European Institute of Public Administration Working Paper*.

agency behaviour. These studies take the perspective on discretion that agencies will use it to deviate from what has been originally envisaged by the legislator. It is important to remember, however, that agencies may be granted discretion on purpose, and may be acting in line with the legislators' interests.

In this sense regulatory competition may emerge between regulatory agencies of different jurisdictions even when the agency is acting in conformity with the legislator's preferences, as well as in the contrary situation. Regulatory competition between the regulator and the legislator within the same jurisdiction may however only emerge when the regulator is acting contrary to the legislator's original intent.

5.3.2 The use of discretion

Discretion allows these actors to arrive at legal solutions which are 'not necessarily predictable from the scrutiny of legal rules'.[101] By exercising discretion, these legal actors may influence the content of the law, further develop policies and arrive at solutions that were not envisaged by, and may even be contrary to, the intention of the legislator.[102]

In analysing the role of independent regulatory agencies (as well as supervisors and courts), this study takes a positivist approach, focusing on the central role of legal rules that determine the competences of these legal actors. It is therefore not argued here that courts or regulators (IRAs) necessarily exceed the limits of their discretion as they become actors of competitive law-making. Instead, this study analyses how such discretion can be exercised in practice in ways that lead to significant changes in the law as it is applied, as opposed to the law in books. Such a use of discretion is a relevant determinant of the dynamics of competition among legal actors.

---

101 Hawkins, K. (1992), *The Uses of Discretion* (Oxford: Clarendon Press).

102 This aspect is especially interesting in the case of regulatory agencies in a temporal context, where the legislator that created the agency was different (in composition, ideology, values and aims) from the one dealing with the agency and its output today.

5.3.2.1 Economic and sociological literature on legal actors' incentives Two different streams of literature emerged examining the incentives of regulators and judges:[103] One from the economic, the other from the sociological perspective. From the economic perspective, regulators are viewed as self-interested maximisers.

According to the sociological literature, the regulatory outcome has a driving force other than economic self-interest, namely ideas, values and culture.[104] This stream of literature points to some of the weaknesses of the materialistic approach, which fails to exactly predict the outcome of legal decisions, and explain the deviations from its predictions. This approach may be closer to reality but might have the disadvantage of not reflecting clear trends at the macro level (for example, judicial decisions' impact on the development of the law within a country over time).

Finally an alternative to the economic and sociological literature's predictions is the description of regulatory agents who have their own policy preferences.[105] Identifying which model better describes incentives and behaviour would be useful, but is beyond the ambit of the book. In general, the literature associates the independence of courts and regulatory agencies from political bodies with positive regulatory outcomes.[106] When comparing these models, which describe the interaction between the regulatory agency and the legislator, we arrive at the conclusion that for the legislator it is easier to control budget maximisation than the fixed policy preferences of an agency.[107] The positive or negative welfare implications of regulatory competition may be explained by economic self-interest as well as certain prevailing values and ideas.

5.3.2.2 Institutional set-ups that may impact the independence and activity of regulatory agencies Above, we examined *individuals*' economic or value-driven incentives within regulatory agencies. Here the *institutional* structure and independence of IRAs are analysed from the point of view

[103] See Black, J. (2003), 'Enrolling Actors in Regulatory Systems: Examples from UK Financial Services Regulation', *Public Law*, pp. 63–91.

[104] See, e.g. Meidinger, E. (1985), 'Regulatory Culture: A Theoretical Outline', *Law and Policy*, vol. 9, no. 4, pp. 355–386.

[105] Bendor, J., Taylor, S. and Van Gaalen, R. (1987), 'Politicians, Bureaucrats and Asymmetric Information', *American Journal of Political Science*, vol. 31, pp. 796–828.

[106] Thatcher, M. (2002), 'Delegation to Independent Regulatory Agencies: Pressure, Functions and Contextual Mediation', *West European Politics*, vol. 25, pp. 125–147.

[107] This might be relevant in the case of *intra*-jurisdictional regulatory competition.

of potential influence on the behaviour of regulatory agencies *vis-à-vis* other legal actors. The independence of the regulatory agency defines how far it can go in deviating from the original intention of the legislator (deriving its discretion from a delegation of powers). The broader the independence of the agency, the more scope it has to compete with other domestic legal actors, and thus to drive inter-jurisdictional competition.

Studies in political science and economic literature look at the independence of regulatory agencies and the impact of institutional setting on their activities.[108] The elements of independence are most often listed as relating to financing, the term, renewal and dismissal of the head of the agency and its key members, and the scope of competences it has. Alternative institutional aspects that may influence the independence of regulatory agencies include: the source and control of the agency's budget; regulatory competencies; relationship with government and parliament; which body, other than a court, can overturn the decisions of the agency, where the latter has exclusive competence; term of office; appointment and dismissal of head and management board; formal requirement of independence, and so on.

These criteria can serve as a useful starting point for further analysis.

5.3.2.3 Under which conditions is it likely that legal actors will engage in international regulatory competition? The incentives for any legal actor to enter into regulatory competition with other Member States' legal actors are assessed here from various angles. This is important because the first and most important condition for regulatory competition is that the agency and its individual members have an incentive to engage in it.

Overall actors' incentives may be threefold:

---

[108] See, e.g. Gilardi, F. (2008), *Delegation in the Regulatory State: Independent Regulatory Agencies in Western Europe* (Cheltenham, UK: Edward Elgar); and Gilardi, F. (2005), 'The Formal Independence of Regulators: A Comparison of 17 Countries and 7 Sectors', *Swiss Political Science Review*, vol. 11, no. 4, pp. 139–167; Voigt, S. (2006), 'The Economic Effects of Competition Policy: Cross-Country Evidence Using Four New Indicators' available at SSRN: http://ssrn.com/abstract=925794; Mateus, A.M. (2007), 'Why Should National Competition Authorities be Independent and how Should they be Accountable?' Paper presented at the 10th anniversary of the Romanian Competition Council. Available at: http://www.unctad.org/sections/wcmu/docs/c2clp_ige8p20aPortugal_pca_en.pdf.

1. Agencies may aim to attract regulatees for financial benefits (self-financing of the agency)[109] for example through mobility of regulatees or through competition in enforcement of norms.
2. Agencies may aim to achieve efficiency (the theory of policy ideas instead of budget maximisation).
3. They may be motivated by the goal of emanating the best rule: what Geradin and McCahery[110] describe as competition in the intellectual marketplace; and what Mulligan and Shleifer[111] describe as a preference for cases not to be overturned (in this case for example by courts on judicial review).[112]

Incentives to engage in regulatory competition depend on the legal framework, of course, but it may be compatible with budget maximising behaviour (in the context of the mobility of regulatees), or it can be a result of values and ideas (in the context of international trade), or it may stem from a wish to emulate the best rule (yardstick competition). When a given incentive is present, and strong enough, there is a further dimension that has to be taken into account: the independence of the agency from government and parliament.

The theoretical literature reviewed above implies that regulatory competition between the regulatory agency and the legislator is more likely to emerge – due to better institutional conditions – when the regulator has its own policy agenda (as compared to cases where it is acting as a budget maximiser). It is also predicted that as conflicts arise between the regulator and the legislator, the legislator is likely to reduce the scope of discretion of the regulatory agency, if it can.

The incentives for governments to attract firms into their jurisdictions mainly focus on achieving increased tax revenues (attracting the tax base with real seat relocations and start-ups), achieving international trade benefits (as in the model of mobility of goods), attracting foreign investment (capital mobility) or obtaining re-election (political and yardstick competition). As for IRAs and courts, these government

---

109 Although Delaware finances itself from the charter fees of companies, similar trends are not observed in Europe.

110 Geradin and McCahery (2004).

111 Mulligan, C. and Shleifer, A. (2005), 'The Extent of the Market and the Supply of Regulation', *Quarterly Journal of Economics*, vol. 120, no. 4, pp. 1445–1473.

112 This latter case is closest to rational decision theory, and theories of legal interpretation that assume there is a single interpretative outcome.

incentives, especially re-election in cases where nomination and dismissal are not linked to performance, are not so directly relevant, and in some cases they are insignificant.[113] However, values and ideas may include considerations such as enhancing the development of the national economy.

Thus, there are different assumptions about the incentives of regulatory agencies. Under the different assumptions, we arrive at different conclusions on whether competitive law-making can occur among these actors (vertically, horizontally, or within the same state), and the outcome of regulatory competition can also be different under the different incentives of actors.

5.4 Courts

The role of the judiciary in regulatory competition has been acknowledged in the US for some time. The courts of Delaware are considered to be the driving force behind competition for corporate charters.[114] Nevertheless, the later adaptations of regulatory competition to other fields largely neglected the role of courts, despite the fact that courts can become important actors in the regulatory competition setting whose role should not be underestimated. This study looks at the role courts play in advancing legal rules and standards in the course of applying them, without engaging in the constitutional debate on the role of courts and judicial activism. The active or passive role played by courts in shaping the law is only assessed here from the perspective of its potential impact on regulatory competition. To start exploring the judiciary as an actor in regulatory competition, this section looks at the incentives of courts in their decision-making.

5.4.1 Three models of judicial decision-making

Although substantial differences exist between common law and civil law jurisdictions, the role of the courts is significant for both shaping the final form and effectiveness of laws.[115] Judges and the regulatory agencies examined above have in common a scope of discretion to shape the applicable norms. Regulatory agencies possess regulatory power assigned to them by the legislator by delegation of powers, while courts

---

[113] Assuming relatively independent regulatory agencies and independent judiciary.

[114] Romano, R. (1993), *The Genius of American Corporate Law* (Washington: AEI Press).

[115] Berkowitz et al. (2003).

derive their powers to apply the law from the constitution. Another difference between the two legal actors is that courts are more focused on the *ex-post* assessment of individual cases, while regulators are setting up *ex ante* rules.[116]

In the literature describing judicial decision-making, different theories describe the behaviour of judges. The three main theories work with different assumptions about the incentives or character of a judge.

The first, so-called *legal model* of judicial decision-making, assumes that judges are impassive public officials aiming to perform their duties by applying the law as it stands, without any further considerations.[117] The second, the *cooperative model*, describes judges as acting cooperatively among themselves (within the court system) as they share common goals and face common challenges (coordination, division of labour). Finally according to the *bureaucratic model*, 'judges compete against each other in the promotion of their institutional power and they face problems of agency and strategy'.[118]

In a study combining some elements of the legal and the bureaucratic approach, Gennaioli and Schleifer[119] examined two factors that might influence the way in which judges may exercise their discretion. One is the given set of policy preferences of the judge, the other is his or her aversion to reversal on appeal when the law is unsettled. Both are found to play a role in judicial decisions.

With regard to judges' incentives to engage in regulatory competition, the bureaucratic model implies that courts will take a competitive rather than cooperative approach to other courts and other legal actors. Within the vertical setting of regulatory competition courts will aim to reach judicial decisions that will not be overturned by the ECJ. Such an

---

[116] Regulatory and supervisory powers are merged for example in the field of financial services.

[117] The rule of *stare decisis*, for example, requires the judge to follow a previous decision, even if he does not agree with it or considers it wrong.

[118] Ramos, F. (2002), 'Judicial Cooperation in the European Courts: Testing Three Models of Judicial Behavior', *Global Jurist Frontiers*, vol. 2, no. 4. See also Alter, K.J. (2001), *Establishing the Supremacy of European Law. The Making of an International Rule of Law in Europe* (Oxford: Oxford University Press) at p. 45, stating that '[j]udges are primarily interested in promoting their independence from political bodies, they want to exert influence to promote their ability to make decisions that can influence the policy process and the judicial process, and finally they want to preserve their authority, meaning that they protect their legal turf (their jurisdiction) and the finality of their decisions'.

[119] Gennaioli, N. and Schleifer, A. (2006), 'Judicial Fact Discretion', National Bureau of Economic Research, *NBER Working Papers*, no. w12679.

approach leads to cooperative outcomes. However, national judges, according to Alter's bureaucracy model,[120] also have an incentive to preserve their independence from political agents, meaning mainly the legislator.[121] This claim predicts a competitive approach towards government. Finally, courts are thought to aim to promote their ability to influence the policy process. This view coincides with models of regulatory agencies with their own policy ideas. This final assumption of the bureaucratic model of courts' incentives implies that courts will take a competitive approach not only towards the government, but also towards regulatory agencies.

The legal model does not leave much scope for courts to engage in regulatory competition, as it assumes that legal rules will determine the most important issues, and indeterminacy of law is either non-existent, or is filled in by other legal decision-makers to whom the courts will refer the case, or will be determined by the courts in complete alignment with the legislator's intent.

The cooperative model advocates a shared concept of what is the best decision. This shared concept may be national or Europe-wide. If the judiciary shares a Europe-wide concept of optimal decisions, this means that the courts will be cooperative around an idea coming from the EU level. This form of cooperation is therefore very different from the legal model, under which each court abides by the letter of the national (and, where appropriate, EC) law, because this cooperation model does not leave scope for national divergences. The courts under this model may be cooperative towards other courts, and in the vertical context, but non-cooperative towards the national legislator and regulatory agencies.

Thus, to conclude, the bureaucratic model predicts a competitive strategy towards the government and regulator, and a cooperative behaviour towards the higher courts. The legal model predicts cooperation with all other legal actors, to the extent that the discretionary power of courts is virtually non-existent in the framework of regulatory competition, while the cooperative model predicts cooperation vertically with courts higher in the hierarchy and horizontally with other courts. It predicts competition horizontally towards the national legislator or regulator as long as they do not share the Europe-wide concept of 'best policy decision'.

---

120 Alter (2001).

121 However, in cases of highly independent judiciary systems, preserving independence may be targeted against the European Court.

5.4.2 Institutional set-up and judicial behaviour

Posner[122] tests how changing some of the institutional setting (more precisely, imposing limits on terms or raising salaries) for federal judges influences their behaviour. He describes different types of judge,[123] and argues that the institutional setting may influence judges' behaviour.

Posner describes the continental European judiciary, as so-called career judges,[124] where appointment and promotion are by merit: '... there is so little difference between a career judiciary and other professional civil servants that the analysis of judicial behaviour in career judiciary should be like that of public bureaucratic behaviour in general, which should in turn resemble, though not be identical to, the behaviour of employees in a large business firm'.[125]

With regard to the self-interest of judges, and the possible institutional features that may influence the actions of the judiciary, Posner lists the carrots and sticks for performance, such as the possibility of removal from office, pay incentives, promotion possibilities, judges' power *vis-à-vis* each other (whether it is performance or seniority based), and whether they are allowed to have a personal involvement in cases that they decide.[126] Besides he notes that: 'We can also expect the criteria of judicial performance to vary with the constraints on judicial behaviour. In some judicial systems a judge's reversal rate might be a critical performance criterion, while in another more weight might be placed on how

---

[122] Posner, R.A. (2008), *How Judges Think* (Cambridge, MA: Harvard University Press), pp. 129–130.

[123] These include the difference between arbitrators (private judges) who are chosen by the litigants, career judges, elected judges (US), federal trial judges, federal intermediate appellate judges and US Supreme Court Justices.

[124] Career judges are lawyers who make their career out of being a judge.

[125] Posner (2008).

[126] He notes that '(US) Federal judges cannot be removed from office, short of gross misconduct, and cannot be docked pay, exiled to undesirable judicial venues or paid bonuses. Their powers vis-à-vis each other (for example, to preside, to make opinion assignments, to be promoted chief justice) are determined by seniority, rather than appointment. And their opportunities for promotion to a higher court ... are too limited to make concern with being promoted play a major role in the thinking of most of them ... Furthermore judges are forbidden to sit in cases in which they might have a personal stake, such as a case in which a relative is a party or a lawyer for a party, or in which one of the parties is a corporation in which the judge owns stock. So it is as if the designers of federal judiciary set out to remove every possible stick and carrot to which judges might respond ... .' Posner (2008).

often a judge's opinions are cited by other courts, or even on the political acumen exhibited by the judge in his opinion.'[127]

5.4.3 Allocation of jurisdiction in a federal court system

Beside the incentives of courts within the judicial hierarchy with respect to other legal actors *within* a state, the literature also extends to the allocation of jurisdiction among courts in a *federal system*.[128] Posner[129] describes an economic theory of jurisdiction allocation[130] between the state and federal level, where three issues are decisive for such allocation decisions. The first is the need to restrain regulatory capture, the second is the desirability of laboratory federalism, and the third is the consideration of costs.

With regard to the first consideration – the need to restrain regulatory capture – it should be noted as a starting point that mobility of production factors implies that labour and capital are mobile across jurisdictions. If we are trying to examine whether competition has a positive or a negative influence on overall welfare with regard to this phenomenon of mobility, we should remember that the mobility of different groups is not equal. Posner observes that in situations of regulatory capture, '[an interest group's] power to exploit will be limited by the threat that those whom it is trying to exploit will move to another state … '.[131] This implies that, if a group is immobile, it can be exploited more than a mobile factor. Posner argues that capture by interest groups can be much more harmful at federal level, thus it is preferable at the state level, which is an argument in favour of decentralisation.

Secondly, Posner considers laboratory federalism and yardstick competition to be the advantages of a decentralised jurisdiction allocation. As several distinct jurisdictions experiment with the legal solution to a given problem, it is more likely that a superior solution will be found in a decentralised system than if a single jurisdiction imposed a solution on the entire polity. By way of observing the achievements of others, each jurisdiction can identify the optimal solution and adopt it or aim to

---

[127] Posner (2008), p. 126.

[128] See, e.g. Dorf, M.C. (2006), 'Whose Ox is Being Gored? When Attitudinalism Meets Federalism', *Columbia Public Law Research Paper* No. 06-102.

[129] Posner, R.A. (1983), 'Toward an Economic Theory of Federal Jurisdiction', *Harvard Journal of Law and Public Policy*, vol. 6, pp. 41–50.

[130] Reference below to either the allocation of legislative power or court jurisdiction means both, in order to avoid lengthy repetitions.

[131] Posner, R.A. (1983), 'Toward an Economic Theory of Federal Jurisdiction', *Harvard Journal of Law and Public Policy*, vol. 6, pp. 41–50.

achieve an even better one through a mechanism of yardstick competition. With this analysis, Posner implicitly agrees that courts' enforcement does matter in shaping even uniform laws, and their role in regulatory competition, at least in one form of it – yardstick competition – is relevant.

Finally, the third decisive consideration in Posner's model of federalism is that of cost efficiency. He argues that on this aspect as well it is better to have decentralised jurisdictions to avoid inefficiencies in government.

Besides, Posner's model shows that when the courts have a certain discretion in enforcing the law, it is necessary to design an allocation of competence that takes account of the potential externalities that state courts may impose on other jurisdictions (or on the federal level) when enforcing the law.

5.5 Private Regulators

Private regulation is becoming increasingly widespread in the regulatory sphere,[132] even though there are also recent signs of the opposite trend, notably in financial services. In undertaking regulatory activity, self-regulatory bodies have incentive structures that are different from those of public legal actors (the legislator, the regulator, and the courts).[133] This suggests that the question whether these actors become involved in regulatory competition or cooperation should be examined separately.[134]

5.5.1 What is private regulation?

Although the definition of private regulation is a much broader question and would require deeper analysis than the scope of this book can offer, a basic working definition can be established, acknowledging that the concept of private regulation itself is debatable.

The forms of public vs. private regulation recognised by the literature are: public regulation; co-regulation; delegated private regulation; *ex post*

---

132 Black, J. (2003), 'Enrolling Actors in Regulatory Systems: Examples from UK Financial Services Regulation', *Public Law*, pp. 63–91.

133 Black, J. (1997), *Rules and Regulators* (Oxford: Oxford University Press).

134 Cafaggi, F. (2005), 'Self-regulatory Competition', paper presented at the first SIDE Conference, Siena, 25 November.

recognised private regulation; and pure private regulation.[135] These categories imply different rules for institutional set-up, that is the composition of the regulatory body and its interaction with public legal actors. Different private regulators can have identifiable, relatively homogeneous incentives if they form a homogenous group, similarly to the judiciary or regulatory agencies. However, when the regulatory body consists of several stakeholder groups, their incentives can be more diverse, and their legal output will largely depend on the rules governing their internal decision-making.

Finally, private legal actors can take on more than just regulatory functions in the strict sense of the word: they can also complement legislative and monitoring functions.[136]

5.5.2 Private regulators' incentives and institutional set-up

Private regulatory bodies are most often described as acting in their own self-interest as individual rational economic actors. Their actions are best analysed through the lens of self-interest and market dynamics. It was argued above that public regulatory agencies can also be described as self-interested maximisers. It is also important to note that private regulation can occur in exchange for monetary remuneration. However, the main difference between public and private regulators is that while the former acts through a democratic election mechanism (at least in the European case) or is embedded in an institutional design which determines its incentive structure and vulnerability to capture, private regulators' self-interests are determined directly by their market position or the transaction they aim to regulate. In other words, their individual incentives are naturally market driven, and their institutional environment is best described by the composition of the private regulatory body, and the rules governing its interaction with public legal actors – if any.

As Cafaggi points out:

> [t]here are at least two possible phenomena concerning rule-making:
>
> (a) private regulators regulate actions in a way that maximizes their own benefits without taking into account the public interest, but without specifically harming third parties;
> (b) private regulators, while regulating (by the setting or implementation of

---

[135] Cafaggi, F. (2006b), 'Rethinking Private Regulation in the European Regulatory Space', in Cafaggi, F. (ed.) *Re-framing Self-regulation in European Private Law* (The Hague: KLI).

[136] Cafaggi, F. (2006a), 'Self-regulation in European Contract Law', *EUI Working Paper Law 2006/43.*

> standards) externalize the costs of their regulating towards third parties (for example consumers, environment, workers or other industries that are not represented in the regulatory authority).[137]

The possibility of externalising costs to other industry participants or third parties towards whom the private regulation produces legal effects, but who may not be involved in the regulatory activity, is a recognised issue in the current literature, along with the specific agency problems arising in this context.[138]

Inter-stakeholder externalities will greatly depend on the composition of the private regulatory body. Table 1.1 displays a categorisation of different organisational forms. Single-stakeholder private regulatory bodies guarantee less resolution of conflicts of interest and internalisation of externalities than bilateral (dual-stakeholder) or multilateral (multi-stakeholder) bodies.

Table 1.1 Contractual and organisational arrangements of self-regulation

	Unilateral (single stakeholder)	Bilateral (dual stakeholder)	Multilateral (multi-stakeholder)
Contractual	Only among firms	Between trade and consumer (or other trade) associations	Among trade and consumer associations and public actors
Organisational		Composed of trade and consumer or other trade associations	Among trade and consumer associations and public actors

Source: Cafaggi (2006a).

Overall, it is thought that the main disadvantages of private regulation may be the lack of democratic legitimacy and the potential for the creation of the externalities described above, along with concerns for 'incumbent' private regulators restricting competition within a given

[137] Cafaggi, F. (2006b), 'Rethinking Private Regulation in the European Regulatory Space', in Cafaggi, F. (ed.) *Re-framing Self-regulation in European Private Law* (The Hague: KLI), pp. 55–57.

[138] Lindseth, P.L. (2006), 'Agents Without Principals? Delegation in an Age of Diffuse and Fragmented Governance', in Cafaggi, F. (ed.) *Re-framing Self-regulation in European Private Law* (The Hague: KLI).

market through their regulatory activity.[139] The potential benefits of private regulation include the information advantages of the private regulator (often business actors, industry), flexibility and responsiveness to market developments and potential internalisation of costs.

The incentives for private regulators to engage in regulatory competition or adopt a cooperative behaviour towards other legal actors is largely unexplored in the literature.[140] It would seem, however, that private regulators have more propensity to engage in competition, as soon as the business interests of their community requires it, since the motivations of the legal actors are much better aligned with the community they regulate. This being said, there is also a higher propensity to impose externalities on other constituencies, since there is no strong political accountability or rigorous objectives as for governments, regulatory agencies or courts.

When co-regulatory frameworks are used to counter the externalities of pure private regulation, the potential for regulatory competition *vis-à-vis* the co-regulator is lost by definition (even in cases of *ex post* recognised private regulation). But competition *vis-à-vis* other domestic or foreign legal actors is not excluded. On the contrary, a co-regulatory scheme in one Member State may be very competitive compared to other Member States' public regulatory schemes.

The following chapters aim to look at the role of private regulation in a competitive or cooperative setting, comparing the role private legal actors play in a potential setting of regulatory co-opetition.

5.6 Regulatees as Actors of Regulatory Competition

Legal norms do not exist without their subjects and thus should always be examined together. Regulatees are important actors also in regulatory competition, as their reactions to legal norms will determine the direction of competitive interactions as well as their welfare implications.

---

[139] Van den Bergh, R.J. (2004), 'Towards Efficient Self-regulation in Markets for Professional Services', in Ehlerman, C.D. and Atanasiu, I. (eds) *European Competition Law Annual 2004: The Relationship between Competition Law and Liberal Professions* (Oxford: Hart Publishing).

[140] For a thorough analysis of self-regulatory competition, see Cafaggi (2005).

In a study on regulatory competition from a comparative law angle, Ogus[141] distinguishes between so-called facilitative and interventionist legal rules. The difference between the two is that, while facilitative law provides rules that will benefit all parties to a given transaction or legal relationship, interventionist law is aimed at regulating certain conflicts of interests among the parties, and therefore results in a re-allocation of parties' original bargaining power.

The dividing line between facilitative and interventionist law is defined by Ogus as: 'Large areas of law are [...] interventionist in the sense that they protect defined interests and/or supersede voluntary transactions. This covers tort and regulatory law, but also those aspects of contract, property and corporate law which confer protection on parties assumed to be disadvantaged by processes of free bargaining, for example consumers, employees, tenants and (in some context) shareholders.'[142]

Interventionist law therefore creates a redistribution of costs and benefits. Rules of this nature will have beneficiaries and obligees. Although a clear distinction cannot always be made between facilitative and interventionist law, and the aim is not to elaborate further on this theory, we will in some cases distinguish between obligees (or regulatees) and beneficiaries (or protected parties). The former are direct subjects who have to comply with norms, while the latter are often indirectly targeted by those norms. In other words, those obliged to comply with the rules without necessarily benefiting from them directly – compared to free bargaining – will be called the 'regulatees', and those who directly enjoy its benefits as compared to free bargaining will be called the 'beneficiaries'.

In those situations where actors have a choice among several different legal regimes, the analysis will aim to identify the party who can effectively choose the applicable rules. In some cases, this is a very straightforward exercise (when for example a single natural person is entitled to choose the legal regime), in other cases the question requires some more analysis or caveats (for example in those cases where firms are entitled to such a choice but, due to conflicting interests among constituencies within the firm, it becomes relevant to identify which constituency has the final word, or more influence, over the final decision on choice of law).

---

[141] Ogus, A. (1999), 'Competition between National Legal Systems: a Contribution of Economic Analysis to Comparative Law', *The International Comparative Law Quarterly*, vol. 48, no. 2, pp. 405–418.

[142] Ogus (1999), p. 413.

The person of the 'chooser' can coincide with the regulatee or with the beneficiary, depending on the case, and this in turn is expected to impact on the (distributive and potentially the overall) welfare impacts of competition.

In the case of certain channels of inter-jurisdictional competition, choice of law or mobility is not permitted and therefore, in that context, the issue of who has the choice is not applicable.

As has been said, regulatees may not be a homogeneous group. They may have diverse preferences, which decentralised diverse legal solutions can satisfy better than one single rule. Regulatees should therefore be examined from this perspective as well.

5.7 Conclusions and Open Questions Concerning Legal Actors' Incentives

The above analysis reveals that the various legal actors can have slightly or significantly different incentives, which in turn may imply a different approach to regulatory competition.

The institutional design (rules determining the incentives and independence of the agents) will arguably influence the output. This means that the rules governing agents' appointment, removal, financing, accountability, and so on can possibly change their attitude, first towards other domestic legal actors, and secondly (directly or indirectly) towards regulatory competition.

This analysis makes a clear distinction between the (competitive/cooperative) interaction between legal actors domestically, and competition or the lack of it among the final legal outputs of jurisdictions. This implies also that the incentives of legal actors can be examined in both aspects: when will they have an incentive to challenge the legal output of other domestic actors; and when will they have an incentive to engage in competition or cooperative behaviour with other jurisdictions?

A further interesting question is whether different legal actors have different responsiveness to the various channels of competition. Do their incentives lead them to respond to different competitive pressures, such as international trade competition, yardstick competition, or competition for mobile regulatees?

Further chapters will analyse the effect of multi-level governance mechanisms on the incentives of legal actors to compete or cooperate although they will not adopt a rigorous methodology that would allow a direct causal relationship to be established.

6. CONCLUSIONS AND THE SUBJECT OF FURTHER INQUIRY

6.1 The 'What?'

This chapter has looked at the definition of regulatory competition, explaining the interpretation of this concept in a broad and in a narrow sense. In the broad sense, regulatory competition refers to competitive interaction among jurisdictions' legal norms, through various possible channels of competition as transmission mechanisms. These channels are: international mobility (or choice) of regulatees; cross-border mobility of factors of production (capital, labour, technologies); cross-border mobility of products (international trade); and information flows across borders (yardstick competition). This broad interpretation is often referred to in the literature as 'systems competition' or 'institutional competition'.

In the narrower sense, regulatory competition refers to the competitive interaction of jurisdictions through the transmission mechanism of regulatees' mobility or free choice of law.

This study will look at the broad interpretation of competitive interactions among jurisdictions.

Regulatory competition literature establishes that competitive design with mobility of regulatees can have one or more of the following three advantages: satisfaction of diverse preferences; parallel experimentation leading to superior legal outcomes; and constraint on the Leviathan state or legal actors.

The constraints of such competition with choice or mobility are: the presence of externalities; information asymmetries; public choice failures; network externalities; bundling of legal rules; economies of scale at federal level; a lack of incentives to compete on the side of legal actors; and similarly a lack of incentives to engage in legal arbitrage on the side of regulatees.

More recent scholarly work has focused on identifying the relevant determinants of competitive interactions. The emerging conclusions are worth examining further. In this study the following questions will be explored through the examples of company, securities and competition law.

- **On the side of regulatees:**
  - o *Do regulatees have diverse preferences?*
  - o *Do they have free choice or mobility?*
  - o *Is there bundling or tying of legal rules?*

  - *Are there information problems?*
  - *Do regulatees have incentives to engage in regulatory arbitrage?*
  - *Are regulatees an homogeneous group?*[143]
- **On the side of legal actors:**
  - *What are the market failures and what is the optimal regulatory intervention?*
  - *Who are the legal actors with competence?*
  - *Do they have incentives to compete or cooperate?*
  - *What is their organisational set-up?*
  - *How do different legal actors interact within one jurisdiction (intra-jurisdictional competition)?*
- **Finally, with respect to the legal norms or governance mechanisms in place:**
  - *Which channels of competitive interaction are open?*
  - *What are the legal or governance tools in place?*
  - *Do they incentivise convergence or divergence?*
  - *How do they impact the incentives of legal actors to compete or cooperate?*
  - *What legal paradigms and theories of efficiency are in place?*

The analysis undertaken here will also extend to legal actors and their incentives in competing or cooperating. A distinction is drawn here between competition and cooperation among national legal actors domestically and the international competition or the lack of it (decentralised powers without competition, spontaneous convergence for reasons other than competition, coordination, harmonisation, and so on) among jurisdictions. In other words, the interaction of legal actors will shape the final legal output of a given jurisdiction, which then may or may not be in competition with another jurisdiction's legal output.

The legal actors to be examined here are the legislator, the independent regulatory agency (mainly supervisory agencies and competition authorities), the court, and the private regulator – both at the national and at the European level. A brief summary of existing literature pointed out that the incentives of these legal actors may be different, and their behaviour

---

[143] Throughout the analysis in this study, reference is made to regulatees and beneficiaries of regulation. It is acknowledged that often the two can coincide, where the law plays a facilitative role in legal relationships between actors. In other cases, however, the rules impose an obligation on one party and grant a right, a benefit, on the other. These norms are intervening, changing the original bargaining powers of parties.

can be influenced by certain organisational settings affecting their independence and incentives.

This book will also analyse how European governance models may alter the behaviour of legal actors in their interaction and thus influence whether regulatory competition emerges or not, what its scope and limits may be and, ultimately, what outcome it leads to. It examines whether the model of governance influences the propensity of legal actors to engage in cooperation rather than competition, whether it alters actors' payoff structure or their incentives in such a way that it leads to a different outcome than under other forms of governance.

As noted above, there are three possible interpretations of the co-opetition model: an alternative of competition or cooperation, depending on the legal field or the issue at hand; a sequential model of cooperating and competing, as advocated by Radaelli;[144] and a framework model that argues that cooperation sets the field for competition.[145]

This study argues that the co-opetition model may be useful in exploring new possibilities in regulatory competition and federalism studies. The potential of individual jurisdictions and legal actors to not only compete but also cooperate may provide a long sought-for solution to the race to the bottom outcomes of competition. Instead of centralisation as an answer to the race to the bottom concern, the question should be which form of governance would provide the appropriate incentives and framework for co-opetition, where the rules of competition are set in a coordinated framework. The following chapters on substantive legal fields will examine whether co-opetition can be observed in the European legal arena and, if so, when and in what form?

6.2 The 'How?'

The above issues will be explored through the study of regulatory competition in three legal areas: company law; securities law; and competition law. The comparison of these should allow conclusions as to whether some answers to the above questions are field specific, or are of general applicability. The fields to be examined are selected according to several criteria, but some determinative features are that the regulated unit is the firm, but the regulated relationships, and thus the market failures they aim to correct, are different.

---

[144] Radaelli (2004).
[145] Holzinger and Knill (2005).

The scope and functioning of competition in the above three fields of law are examined in three separate chapters. Chapter 5 concludes by returning to the research questions identified here, drawing on a comparison of the three descriptive chapters.

The task of comparing regulatory competition models in three different legal areas – company law, securities regulation, and competition law – calls for a uniform, or at least comparable framework of analysis. Based on the previous observations concerning the relevant legal actors, the models and dimensions of regulatory competition, and the dichotomy of competition and cooperation, this study will focus on a number of relevant issues.

The structure of each chapter is similar. Within each legal field, different theories of the efficiency of markets and regulation are described and observed, in order to see how our assessment of welfare impacts may be altered by different theories of efficiency or political choice.

The available channels of competitive interaction are then reviewed briefly, and the allocation of law-making powers is assessed in each legal area, both in terms of the vertical allocation of powers (between the European and national levels) and in terms of the horizontal allocation of competences, among the legislator, the regulator, the private regulator and the judiciary.

Within this theme, the governance framework of each policy area is described and an analysis of who the regulatees are, and whether they have homogeneous preferences, forms part of the inquiry. Recent legal changes are also reviewed with a view to detect competitive or cooperative interactions. Legal developments are analysed in the light of (multilevel) governance mechanisms in place, to trace the impact of such governance models on the working of regulatory competition.

Finally, each chapter offers a look at hypothetical frameworks with free choice of law, examining what the overall and distributive welfare outcome of such competition would be in the three different legal fields.

Methodologically, this analytical framework would require a comparative analysis of existing legislation at a given point in time (static stage), and the analysis of legal change over a longer period of time (dynamic stage), optimally ending with a comparison of the laws at the end of that period, again in the form of a static comparative analysis. This exercise is not performed here: the present study is limited to examples that can provide relevant insights for the indicated inquiry.

The following three chapters will use the above framework to assess models of regulatory competition in the field of company law, securities law and competition law. The main goal of these chapters is not only to describe the existing frameworks of regulatory competition in these three fields, but also to create a basis for comparison in the final, concluding chapter.

2. Regulatory competition in European company law

1. INTRODUCTION

This chapter examines regulatory competition in company law within Europe. Section 2 starts with an overview of the economic rationale of regulation in company law. Given the significant impact that American literature has had on European thinking about competitive law-making, this chapter contains a brief summary of the US literature on the subject.

Section 3 continues with a review of the European legal framework focusing on the channels of competition. Existing forms of competitive law-making are presented in Section 4, including legal developments for private companies, public listed firms, employee participation and take-overs. The section closes with an overview of the legal actors that shape the norms of company law.

After the description of where regulatory competition stands today, a theoretical inquiry is presented in Section 5. This section analyses how competition with full mobility can impact on welfare, both overall welfare and the pay-offs of each stakeholder group in a hypothetical example of two jurisdictions. Section 6 concludes.

2. ECONOMIC THEORIES ON REGULATION AND REGULATORY COMPETITION IN COMPANY LAW

2.1 The Subjects of Regulation: European Firms and their Stakeholders

Regulatory competition in Europe was often depicted in the early regulatory competition literature as a mirror image of that in the US, the only difference being the lack of a widespread incorporation doctrine.[1]

[1] Jurisdictions following the incorporation doctrine require of the firms governed by their laws nothing else but to be incorporated within the jurisdiction.

While it is certainly true that the 'real seat' doctrine plays an important role in distinguishing US and EU decentralisation models, further differences between the two systems should be carefully considered before drawing either positive or normative conclusions about regulatory competition in company law in Europe.

The aim of this sub-section is to point out the main differences between the US and Europe not only in terms of the legal structure, but also in terms of the subject matter of regulation: the firms. Understanding the differences and similarities between the two markets is a prerequisite to distinguish the models of regulatory competition in the two jurisdictions.

2.1.1 Shareholders: ownership and control structure of firms

One significant difference lies in the *ownership and control structure* of European and US companies.[2] Shareholding (ownership) and voting rights (control) often go hand-in-hand under a 'one share one vote' regime. The two can diverge however for various reasons, such as multiple voting rights (dual or multiple class shares), golden shares, voting caps, or pyramid structures (firms having substantial cross-ownership). Continental European corporate ownership patterns display three distinguishing features: there is a significantly higher concentration of ownership in the hand of one shareholder than in the US or the UK;[3]

Conversely, the 'real seat' doctrine means that firms not only have to be incorporated within the jurisdiction, they have to have their main administrative office in its territory as well. For a more detailed interpretation of the latter, see Section 3.4.

[2] The ownership of firms refers to the pattern of shareholdings within a company, measuring what percentage of the firm's shares accumulate in a single owner's hands (be it a natural person or another company). Control structures in turn measure not just the accumulation of shares but the concentration of voting rights.

[3] Data collected on the control rights within companies shows how widely held firms without 5 per cent accumulated control rights dominate the US (40 per cent and 50 per cent, respectively, of companies on the NYSE and NASDAQ) and the UK (up to 25 per cent of companies). Conversely, companies without a 5 per cent concentration of control rights are rare in continental European countries (between close to 0 and 1 per cent in France, Belgium, Germany, Italy, Spain, Sweden, Austria and the Netherlands). See Barca, F. and Becht, M. (2002), *The Control of Corporate Europe* (Oxford: Oxford University Press). For comparative data see pp. 21–25.

pyramidal structures are more frequent;[4] and family ownership is more significant than in the two Anglo-Saxon jurisdictions.[5]

The difference between US-UK and continental Europe is valid for all listed companies, not only the largest ones. Enriques and Volpin find that ownership is highly concentrated in Germany and Italy, and diffused in the UK and the US, with France in an intermediate position. In half of all German and Italian listed companies, one blockholder owns at least 57 per cent, or 55 per cent of the votes.[6]

This difference in control structure is relevant to the present discussion given that the internal governance structure of companies matters in determining the overall direction of regulatory competition and its welfare implications. While some empirical studies find that family-controlled firms may be even more efficiently managed than widely held firms,[7] this ownership structure poses a different agency problem within the firm. In the US, dispersed ownership and control implies that the shareholder/manager conflict is acute. In Europe, on the other hand, the concentrated control of rights points in the direction of strong majority shareholders, implying less friction between controlling owners and managers, but at the same time inflating the shareholder conflict between majority and minority.[8]

The US debate about regulatory competition in company law very much concentrates on the question of whether managers choose incorporation freely and can go on to exploit that at the expense of shareholders.

---

4 Barca and Becht (2002).

5 When measured by the share of a country's total stock market capitalisation held by the 10 richest families, company ownership in continental Europe shows high concentrations in the hands of a small number of wealthy individuals. See Enriques, L. and Volpin, P. (2007), 'Corporate Governance Reforms in Continental Europe', *Journal of Economic Perspectives*, vol. 21, pp. 117–140.

6 Enriques and Volpin (2007).

7 See, e.g. Anderson, R.C. and Reeb, D.M. (2003), 'Founding Family Ownership and Firm Performance: Evidence from the S&P 500', *Journal of Finance*, vol. 58, no. 3, p. 1301, for the US, and Barontini and Caprio (2005), 'The Effect of Family Control on Firm Value and Performance. Evidence from Continental Europe', *ECGI Finance Working Paper* No. 80/2005 for Europe. In a sample of large US and European companies, studies found a significantly higher Tobin's Q for family-controlled firms than for widely held companies. Tobin's Q is the ratio of the market value of a firm to the replacement value of its assets (typically the book value of the firm's assets). A higher (industry-adjusted) Tobin's Q suggests that the assets are used efficiently – that is, they are worth more within the firm than in alternative uses. Enriques, L. and Volpin, P. (2007), 'Corporate Governance Reforms in Continental Europe', *Journal of Economic Perspectives*, vol. 21, pp. 117–140.

8 Randall, M. et al. (2005), 'Corporate Governance, Economic Entrenchment and Growth', *Journal of Economic Literature*, vol. 43, no. 3, pp. 655–720.

The main welfare questions culminate in the measurement of shareholder detriment from managerial behaviour. In Europe, it is perhaps appropriate to ask this question with a different focus. Given the specificities of the European control structure of companies, managers are presumably under closer scrutiny in taking decisions than under the US regime. The party that may be unprotected in this respect is the minority shareholder.

2.1.2 Employees and creditors

It is beyond the scope of this study to provide an overview and assessment of labour law differences between the US and the EU. Although such a complete analysis would show us the links between legal fields and would provide a fuller picture of overall impacts on employees as a stakeholder group,[9] here the assessment will focus on employees as actors of the firm's corporate governance.

With regard to *creditors* as another significant stakeholder group, it should be noted that firms in Europe have different financing models and therefore different creditors than in the US. The continental European system, often referenced by the German system of finance, is bank-based, while the US and UK have a market-based model of financing.[10] This means that, in terms of firm-creditor relations, companies in certain European Member States may face different agency problems from the US.[11]

2.2 Why Regulate? Agency Problems and the Optimal Regulatory Response

The theories of corporate governance for publicly held firms describe the relationships among the firm's constituencies and their agency problems. The main aim for corporate governance, according to the law and economic literature, is to reduce the agency costs and thus make the governance of the firm more efficient. The main agency problem examined in American literature for widely dispersed ownership is that between the owners of the company (shareholders) and its controllers

[9] It is acknowledged that corporate governance is very closely linked with securities regulations, labour laws and creditor protection and bankruptcy rules. The delineation among these legal fields is somewhat artificial as one will necessarily have an impact on the effectiveness of the other.

[10] The chapter dealing with financial regulation will give an overview of competing theories of financial structure.

[11] See Chapter 3, Section 2.4.1 for a comparison of advantages and disadvantages under these two models of finance.

(managers), however there is also some attention directed to creditors' and employees' agency problems. There are different variants of corporate governance theories, depending on what they envisage as the most efficient way to govern the firm.

2.2.1 The shareholder empowerment argument

One theory of achieving efficient governance is by empowering shareholders to exercise more power over management ('shareholder empowerment').[12] According to this proposition, the managers of the company should be put on a leash by more shareholder empowerment, as shareholders currently are not able to exercise sufficient (effective) control over the firm's affairs.[13] Under this theory, increasing shareholder power through the increase of their ability to make a direct intervention would reduce the agency costs between managers and shareholders.

The impact of increased shareholder power on other constituencies is also an important aspect. The issue of conflicts of interest between different constituencies of the firm, and how an increased power of intervention for shareholders would affect other stakeholders is part of the overall efficiency question.

Referring back to Oliver Hart, Bebchuk[14] argues that managers cannot be expected to maximise the overall welfare of all corporate constituencies, as courts would not be able to enforce such an obligation and thus management would be left without effective control.

Interests between employees and management are even less aligned than interests between management and shareholders. However, the comparison should be made between the alignment of interests between shareholders and employees and between management and employees in order to be able to assess which one (management or shareholders) is better placed to uphold employees' interests. In this regard, the so-called game-ending decisions, that end the company's life, also constitute a case for an overlap of interests between managers, employees and creditors.

Cases of a misalignment of interests are: opposing a takeover where management would be replaced while the situation for employees would be improved; or the opposite scenario of accepting an offer that benefits management and hurts stakeholders; or bargaining acquisition offers to the benefit of management rather than to the benefit of stakeholders.

---

[12] To demonstrate the main claims of this theory, I refer to Bebchuk's leading article on the topic: Bebchuk, L.A. (2005), 'The Case for Increasing Shareholder Power', *Harvard Law Review*, vol. 118, no. 3, p. 833.

[13] See Bebchuk (2005).

[14] Ibid.

Bebchuk argues that management would not serve the interests of stakeholders better than shareholders would; instead, the policy choice is between giving more power to self-interested managers or to self-interested shareholders. He also points out that if stakeholder interests require curbing shareholder intervention power,[15] this should hold across the board, to public as well as private companies. This argument presumes that shareholders with a controlling stake in a closely held firm will have the same incentives and behaviour as dispersed owners in a public company.[16]

2.2.2 Manager control as the efficient governance form

Proponents of the managerial theory point out that increasing shareholder empowerment will necessarily reduce the benefit of separating ownership from control: that of specialisation and centralisation of decision-making. Berle and Means describe not only the challenges but also the advantages of separating ownership from control.[17] According to this theory, the delegation of powers to managers is necessary in order to minimise the transaction costs of bringing decisions.

It should thus be remembered that such agency relationships involving delegation of powers have a clear advantage, as well as a necessary cost – the agency costs. To optimise the situation, the agency costs should be reduced to the greatest extent possible, measured against the necessary trade-off of compromising the benefits flowing from the delegation of powers to managers. Decreases in these latter benefits should be lower than the gains from reduced agency costs. It is ultimately a question of finding the right balance between the two sides, as there will always be a trade-off. Where exactly the right balance is, is the subject of the debate.

---

[15] Stakeholder protection concerns often lead to the conclusion that management needs to have more power in order to balance the, sometimes conflicting, interests of the different constituencies.

[16] This assumption may be disputed. While dispersed shareholders can be expected to make short-term profits from selling and buying shares, controlling owners are likely to have a more long-term interest in the firm for various reasons. One such reason is that selling a substantial stake in the firm will often influence share prices. Another reason may be that family-owned firms are not only looking to short-term profit making, but also to establishing and continuing a family business. A more detailed analysis of controlling owners in European firms is carried out below.

[17] Berle, A.A. and Means, G.C. (1967), *The Modern Corporation and Private Property* 2nd edition (New York: Harcourt, Brace and World).

2.2.3 Stakeholder theory of corporate governance

There is however another reason why management control could lead to superior outcomes. The stakeholder theory of corporate governance points out that it is not only the conflict between shareholders and managers that should be resolved, but the position of creditors, employees and society at large also deserve attention from an efficiency point of view.[18] Stout acknowledges that board governance increases agency costs but she argues that it yields benefits in the form of efficient and informed decision-making, less opportunism among shareholders, and more investment in corporate team production.[19]

As for the team production benefits, this theory recognises that shareholders are not the only group to make illiquid, 'firm specific' investments in corporations. Executives, customers, creditors, suppliers, employees, and other corporate 'stakeholders' also put time, money, and expertise into relationships with companies.

> Economists have long recognized that formal contracts cannot fully protect specific investments in team production. As a result, all 'specific investors' – whether they are stockholders, executives, customers, or rank-and-file employees – are vulnerable to the risk that someone given control over the corporation might use that control to threaten the value of their investment or exclude them from the corporate team. If shareholders controlled public corporations, at least some might be tempted to use shareholder control in an opportunistic fashion to 'hold up' other team members. This is because shareholders can profit from threatening other stakeholders' interests. For example, they can raise earnings by demanding that long-term employees accept reduced health benefits or risk being fired, or by requiring customers to purchase additional software in order to get continued customer support. When specific investments are large enough, the immediate financial returns from making such opportunistic threats can easily outweigh any longer term reputational costs. Anticipating this, many important corporate stakeholders would be justifiably reluctant to make specific investments in public companies run by widely dispersed but powerful shareholders, some of whom might be tempted to pump up the share price by making opportunistic threats.[20]

---

[18] It is important that there is a distinction between fairness and efficiency arguments. The stakeholder theory is not based on fairness claims but puts forward a theory of increased efficiency of production within the boundaries of the firm. For the purpose of presenting its main claims, I will make reference to Stout: Stout, L.A. (2007), 'The Mythical Benefits of Shareholder Control', *Vanderbilt Law Review*, vol. 93, p. 789.

[19] Stout (2007).

[20] Ibid.

With regard to the inter-shareholder conflicts, Stout points out that there is a different type of inter-shareholder opportunism, arising in the context of closed corporations, than in public companies. This is relevant in the case of European companies and their optimal governance structure, since the controlling shareholders we observe in Europe are not controllers of private companies, but big blockholders in publicly held firms.

Although these two theories of corporate governance seem to be in fundamental contradiction, and most jurisdictions clearly sign up to one system or another, it is true that there is some common understanding with regard to the role of stakeholders in corporate success. As a study comparing European corporate governance codes put it:

> Corporate governance is viewed increasingly as a means of ensuring that the exercise of economic power by the corporate sector is grounded in accountability. Different EU Member States tend to articulate the purpose of corporate governance in different ways; some emphasise broad stakeholder interests and others emphasise ownership rights of shareholders. Although the comparative corporate governance literature and popular discussion tend to emphasise 'fundamental' differences between stakeholder and shareholder interests, the extent to which these interests are different can be debated. The majority of corporate governance codes expressly recognise that corporate success, shareholder profit, employee security and well being, and the interests of other stakeholders are intertwined and co-dependent. This co-dependency is emphasised even in codes issued by the investor community.[21]

2.2.4 Agency problems in public firms with blockholder owners

Unlike big publicly held corporations, closely held companies have managers as the main residual claimants.[22] This does not hold true for European public companies with controlling shareholders, where the residual claimants are still the shareholders as in any public company.

Besides, there are a number of specific features of closely held firms that are not necessarily present in typical European publicly held companies. In private companies, the absence of a secondary market makes it difficult to value stock. The lack of liquidity for the shares means that shareholders have to rely on dividend policy, rather than

---

[21] Weil, Gotshal and Manges LLP (2002), *Comparative Study of Corporate Governance Codes Relevant to the European Union and its Member States*, Study on behalf of the European Commission, DG Internal Market. Available at: http://ec.europa.eu/internal_market/company/docs/corpgov/corp-gov-codes-rpt-part1_en.pdf (last accessed: 3 October 2012).

[22] See Easterbrook, F.H. and Fischel, D.R. (1991), *The Economic Structure of Corporate Law* (Cambridge, MA: Harvard University Press), pp. 229–235.

selling their investment, if they want a return. There is no monitoring due to the lack of an active market in the private company's shares. The lack of active markets also implies that uninformed investors will not have the advantage of being able to rely on market prices as an information revealing mechanism. None of the above features of private firms' information or agency problems will hold true in the same way or to the same extent for the typical European firm.

In public firms with controlling owner(s), shareholders may still have to rely on dividend policy, rather than selling their investment, for a return. However, there may well be an active and liquid market for the shares, which in turn means that minority shareholders in these firms do not rely exclusively on dividend policies: they will have a monitoring mechanism in place, and markets will also be able to process information about the firm to integrate it into the price.

At the same time, the situation of minority shareholders in these firms is very different from those in firms of a widely dispersed ownership pattern. In widely held firms, the shareholders will decide by majority or qualified majority, each having a more or less equal say in the outcome but, in blockholder structures, the shareholder with more votes will be able to represent his or her interests to a disproportionate degree. This is not a fairness argument, as it is acknowledged that those who pay for a controlling stake should have its benefits, but a description of how a majority is formed in a controlled, as opposed to a widely held, firm. It might be a minority of persons having a certain economic interest who will achieve the majority of votes. What this means for a minority shareholder is that his economic interests should be perfectly aligned with that of the blockholder, otherwise his interest may easily be expropriated. The logic of widely dispersed ownership in publicly held firms is that the shareholders are in the majority of cases a homogeneous group with aligned interests. Therefore, majority decisions are likely to be to the benefit of the majority and most often to all shareholders. An ownership structure that is distorted by a significantly more powerful shareholder will imply that, if his interests diverge from the interests of the rest of the shareholders, he will be able to exercise power over the others. This feature of conflict of interest between controlling and minority shareholders is similar in closely held and European-type public firms. The difference is that minority shareholders in European type public firms are more likely to be able to exit the investment through an active secondary market, thereby imposing a higher threat and thus more effective control on the blockholder owner than in the case of private firms.

At the same time a controlling owner will be able to exert much more effective control over management than shareholders in dispersed ownership structures. It is not necessarily true that a blockholder in a public listed company will have powers of management; this will depend in each case on the stake held by the block owner. In some cases this ownership stake may in fact result in *de facto* management, while in other cases it is perhaps more accurate to say that the controller will be able to exercise effective monitoring over management, without necessarily being able to directly take over management entirely.

The question of negative externalities from choice of applicable legal regime in a regulatory competition setting should be thus examined in the context of the specific agency problems of European firms as between managers, shareholders, creditors, and employees.

2.3 The US Model of Regulatory Competition in Corporate Law

The literature on regulatory competition originates from the US and current European literature is to a great extent inspired by it. So the main features of the academic debate are briefly summarised here.

2.3.1 The supply side of regulatory competition: the legal framework of competences

In the US, corporate law is decentralised, that is, it is the states, rather than the federal legislator, that has the competence to lay down rules governing corporations. Within the decentralised system of competences, since the articulation of the 'internal affairs doctrine',[23] it has been clear that the corporate laws of the states in the US follow the so-called 'incorporation doctrine'. In other words, if the company is incorporated in one state but carries on business in another, it is the state of incorporation, rather than the state of real business activity, that governs the company.[24] Under such a legal setting it is then relatively easy to

---

[23] Decisions such as *Smith* v *Mutual Life Insur. Co.*, 96 Mass. 336 (1867) and *Howell* v *Chicago & Nw. Rwy. Co.*, 51 Barb. 378 (Sup. Ct. NY 1868). See Tung, F. (2006) 'Before Competition: Origins of the Internal Affairs Doctrine', available at ssrn.com (last accessed: 28 May 2008).

[24] In certain states 'pseudo-foreign corporations rules' limit the scope of the incorporation doctrine. These rules apply to companies that are incorporated in one state but have significant economic links, e.g. a majority of shareholders, in another state. For a discussion of this rule see Buxbaum, R.M. (1987), 'The Threatened Constitutionalization of the Internal Affairs Doctrine in Corporation Law', *California Law Review*, vol. 75, p. 29.

choose a company's governing law, by choice of state of incorporation either at start-up stage, or later through reincorporation.

Scholars observe that 'incorporation or reincorporation in a jurisdiction different from where the firm physically operates is quite simple and inexpensive'.[25] This inexpensive choice of law opened up the way to the dynamics of regulatory competition for mobile regulatees.

In its analysis, US regulatory competition literature takes stock of the incentives and competitive interactions of legal actors (the so-called supply side). Not only the state level legislator, but also the judiciary and the bar are recognised as playing a significant role in shaping company law rules under competitive dynamics. The main incentives of legislator and judiciary have been identified as the creation and maintenance of a reputation as the leading corporate law jurisdiction within the US, as well as the creation of revenues to finance the judiciary system from incorporation taxes and franchise fees.[26]

2.3.2 The dynamics of competition in the US and the emergence of Delaware

How competition takes place, and where it leads to, will be labelled here the 'dynamics' of regulatory competition.

The first observation of US states' competition to attract incorporations probably dates back to the early twentieth century. It is interesting to note that the original regulatory competition phenomenon relates not to the

---

[25] Ventoruzzo, M. (2006), 'Experiments in Comparative Corporate Law: The Recent Italian Reform and the Dubious Virtues of a Market for Rules in the Absence of Effective Regulatory Competition', Bocconi University Research Paper no. 06–02. See also Ventoruzzo, M. (2006), 'Cost-based and Rule-based Regulatory Competition: Markets for Corporate Charters in the U.S. and the EU', Bocconi Legal Studies Research Papers no. 14, available at: http://papers.ssrn.com/sol3/papers.cfm?abstract_id=946730## (last accessed: 3 October 2012): 'the company need only file the articles of incorporation with the secretary of state of the jurisdiction, pay an incorporation fee and a franchise tax, and complete some additional minor paper work, all of which is usually accomplished through local legal and commercial support services that specialize providing such assistance.'

[26] For example, a company with authorised capital stock having an aggregate par value of $10 million would pay an initial incorporation fee of $1,200. See for more detailed information: Garon, P.S. et al. (2006), 'Challenging Delaware's Desirability as a Haven for Incorporation', *Wm. Mitchell Law Review*, vol. 32, p. 769.

state of Delaware, the infamous 'winner' of the regulatory race, but rather to New Jersey.[27]

The account by Cary of the birth and early stages of regulatory competition tells us that shortly after New Jersey adopted the 'first of the modern liberal corporation statutes' in 1896, Delaware followed suit, copying much of the content of the New Jersey law. The lead of New Jersey was lost when it tightened its corporate laws, while Delaware stayed with the liberal statute it had copied. With this development, Delaware became the most attractive jurisdiction for incorporations.

This historical perspective offers interesting lessons on the dynamics of regulatory competition – how it can emerge, which jurisdiction wins the race, and how the winner's position can be contested. By imitating New Jersey, the first-mover, Delaware could not obtain a significant position as a corporate charter provider. Being second was not enough to attract companies from other states. However, the position of Delaware changed immediately when the 'market leader', New Jersey, pulled back, abandoning its original 'winner strategy'.

Bebchuk and Hamdani[28] make an attempt to describe the competition interaction of states in the terms of the economic literature of industrial organisation. They point out that once a jurisdiction establishes an advantage as the first mover, there will be significant network externalities stemming from the use and interpretation of law by the judiciary, leading to higher legal certainty and better recognition by lawyers. In other words, the more firms incorporate in a given jurisdiction, the more attractive it will be for others to incorporate there.

2.3.3 Impact of regulatory competition on welfare

US regulatory competition literature explores also the effects of competitive law-making and legal arbitrage on the various constituencies of the firm and on overall welfare. As can be predicted from the focus on large public companies in a country with dispersed ownership structure, the debate on impacts concentrates on the agency problem between shareholders and management.

The early debate divided commentators into two camps. The arguments of those against regulatory competition can be outlined as follows.

---

27 See Cary, W.L. (1974), 'Federalism and Corporate Law: Reflections Upon Delaware', *Yale Law Journal*, vol. 83, p. 664, quoting Mr Justice Brandeis in an early case from 1933; *Ligett Co.* v *Lee* 288 U.S. 517, 562–563 (1933).

28 Bebchuk, L.A. and Hamdani, A. (2002), 'Vigorous Race or Leisurely Walk: Reconsidering the Competition over Corporate Charters', *Yale Law Journal*, vol. 112, pp. 553–615.

Since the majority of US firms are widely held, it is ultimately managers who decide where to incorporate or reincorporate. In order to attract incorporations, Delaware corporate law thus became overly management friendly. Shareholders, who should be protected from managerial shirking by law, are not receiving sufficient legal protection due to the competitive dynamics, and this in turn leads to inefficient outcomes in terms of incentives for shareholders to invest, which in turn will negatively affect the overall level of investment in public companies, the cost of capital for firms, the liquidity and efficiency of capital markets, and so on. This overall inefficient result is labelled the race to the bottom.[29]

Proponents of regulatory competition, however, argued that the disciplining effect of financial markets would prevent management from expropriating the interest of shareholders by taking the company into an inefficient management friendly jurisdiction.[30] This argument holds that managers who do not take due account of shareholders' interests will face an adverse response from shareholders, who can decide to exit their investment in the firm, and look for better performing management to trust their investment with. This means that the price of shares in these companies will drop, to account for the shirking of management, which of course translates into a higher cost of capital for these managers to finance their projects. Under this line of argumentation, managers are actually constrained by the financial market, and are compelled to act in the best interests of shareholders. Therefore, this view holds, any managerial decisions as to which state to incorporate in, even if the rules are less stringent with managers, are ultimately in the best interest of shareholders (for example by allowing more managerial discretion, better business decisions can be made, creating higher returns, and so on).

---

29 Cary (1974); Bebchuk, L.A. and Ferrell, A. (1999), 'Federalism and Corporate Law: The Race to Protect Managers from Takeovers', *Columbia Law Review*, vol. 99, p. 1168.

30 Such as Winter, R. (1977), 'State Law, Shareholder Protection and the Theory of the Corporation', *Journal of Legal Studies*, vol. 6, p. 251; Easterbrook, F.H. and Fischel, D.R. (1991), *The Economic Structure of Corporate Law* (Cambridge, MA: Harvard University Press); Romano, R. (1985), 'Law as a Product: Some Pieces of the Incorporation Puzzle', *Journal of Law, Economics and Organization*, vol. 1, pp. 225–244; Romano, R. (1993), *The Genius of American Corporate Law* (Washington: AEI Press).

The two camps, proponents and critics, differ on some crucial assumptions, such as whether financial markets can control management's behaviour and align it with the interests of shareholders or not.[31]

Later the debate took a more nuanced approach towards regulatory competition, and instead of arguing for an overall race to the top or race to the bottom, scholars turned to examine the details of competitive interactions and their impact on various stakeholder groups and legal actors.

2.4 The European Context: Identifying the Main Differentiating Features

The issue of regulatory competition in European company law has been relatively well explored in the literature: examining the concept of free choice of law in the context of company law;[32] describing the prerequisites for the emergence of regulatory competition with free choice;[33] exploring the possibility of the emergence of a race to the bottom;[34] looking at the developments of European case law;[35] and examining how regulatory competition shapes national legislation.[36] In the European literature, just like in its US counterpart, there have been scholars arguing in favour and against competitive settings. As the literature is based on US models, it is appropriate to start with an overview of the main differences between the two jurisdictions and their corporate environment. As the literature already points out, in Europe the ownership structure of firms is more concentrated than in the US.[37] Also, European countries' finance structures are less centred on stock exchanges and

---

[31] See Subramanian, G. (2002), 'The Influence of Antitakeover Statutes on Incorporation', *University of Pennsylvania Law Review*, vol. 150, no. 6, p. 1795.

[32] Tröger, T.H. (2005), 'Choice of Jurisdiction in European Corporate Law – Perspectives of European Corporate Governance', *European Business Organization Law Review*, vol. 6, pp. 3–64.

[33] Lombardo, S. (2002), *Regulatory Competition in Company Law in the European Community: Prerequisites and Limits* (Frankfurt: Peter Lang).

[34] McCahery, J.A. and Vermeulen, E.P.M. (2005), 'Does the European Company Prevent the Delaware Effect?' TILEC Discussion Paper; Enriques, L. (2004), 'EC Company Law and the Fears of a European Delaware', *European Business Law Review*, vol. 15, no. 6, pp. 1259–1274.

[35] Kirchner et al. (2004), 'Regulatory Competition in European Corporate Law after Inspire Art: Unbundling Delaware's Product for Europe', University of Illinois Law and Economics Working Paper no. LE04-001.

[36] Ventoruzzo (2006).

[37] See Barca and Becht (2002).

more reliant on bank financing. European Union, as well as member state policies, often aim to promote small and medium-sized enterprises as the main source of employment, even if these firms tend to stay away from international trade and are often less productive than transnational enterprises. It appears also that the turnover in EU top firms is slower than in the US, perhaps related to the fact that start-ups in Europe do not tend to have such a successful mechanism of financing as in the US, where venture capital has been flourishing for a long time.[38]

3. THE CHANNELS OF COMPETITIVE INTERACTION

Most studies on regulatory competition start by describing the conditions of mobility for firms. Here this issue is taken in a somewhat broader perspective. This section will examine which channels of competitive interaction are open for legal actors of company law to engage in competition.

3.1 Scope for Yardstick Competition

As introduced already in Chapter 1, rules that determine the potential scope for yardstick competition can be international, European, or part of the domestic institutional design. Rules that govern the legal actors' interaction as well as their activities and incentives (including their appointment, remuneration and other incentive mechanisms, observability and comparability of their performance, and so on) may all be relevant here. In the field of company law, there is no legally binding international or EU level governance set-up that would ensure better comparability and benchmarking among national policies.

As for governance mechanisms, in a neighbouring field, labour law, it is worth mentioning the existing open method of coordination that aims to align the policies of different Member States through non-binding means, by allowing them to coordinate among themselves, with the involvement of the European level.[39]

---

[38] See, e.g. McCahery, J.A. and Vermeulen, E.P.M. (2006), 'Corporate Governance and Innovation – Venture Capital, Joint Ventures, and Family Businesses', ECGI – Law Working Paper No. 65/2006. Available at SSRN: http://ssrn.com/abstract=894785 or http://dx.doi.org/10.2139/ssrn.894785

[39] See Kerber, W. and Eckardt, M. (2007), 'Policy Learning in Europe: The Open Method of Coordination and Laboratory Federalism', *Journal of European Public Policy*, vol. 14, no. 2, pp. 227–247.

> [The open method of coordination] seeks to establish a set of autonomous national decision-making arenas, coordinated by jointly produced best practice models. It attempts the best of all worlds: combining decentralisation of policy formulation and decision-making with re-integration at the EU level. As such it would seem to attempt the aggregation of preferences approach of Scharpf, but also has appeal to those of the Joerges' school of thought who like preference transformation. [...] This process can take place at least at two levels: the OMC can contribute to a common discourse, a common language and a common identification of a particular problem and the diffusion of shared beliefs, the acceptance of common problems and shared beliefs as to what is 'good policy' and what is 'bad policy'. At another level it can lead to the convergence of policies and policy transfer by identifying and praising 'good performance' and criticising and condemning 'bad performance'.[40]

However, as noted above, labour law will not be examined in detail here. Within what can be considered European company law, there is no institutional governance design that would aim to promote yardstick competition specifically, other than the establishment of the European Corporate Governance Forum,[41] the role of which 'shall be, in the light of developing corporate governance practices in the Member States, to enhance the convergence of national codes of corporate governance and to provide strategic advice to the Commission, either at the Commission's request or on its own initiative, on policy issues in the field of corporate governance'.[42] This Forum meets twice a year and puts forward one or two statements on issues that are central to corporate governance in Europe, but where harmonisation has not taken place yet (such as proportionality between ownership and control, executive remuneration, and empty voting).

Besides, there is a private, mainly academic, initiative – the European Corporate Governance Institute. This is an 'international scientific nonprofit association [providing] a forum for debate and dialogue between academics, legislators and practitioners, focusing on major corporate governance issues and thereby promoting best practice'.[43] This Institute organises events where academics and legal experts can exchange views, it collects and makes available academic publications on comparative

---

[40] Szyszczak, E. (2006), 'Experimental Governance: The Open Method of Coordination', *European Law Journal*, vol. 12, no. 4, pp. 486–502.

[41] Commission Decision establishing the European Corporate Governance Forum, 15 October 2004, (2004/706/EC), OJ L 321/53 22.10.2004.

[42] Ibid. Art. 2.

[43] See the ECGI mission statement at http://www.ecgi.org/organisation/overview.htm (last accessed: 14 February 2012).

corporate governance, and has a collection of national corporate governance codes translated into English. Both these initiatives help in comparing information about national legal solutions and initiate reflection about how to improve them.

Finally, in the field of corporate governance, the European legislator often resorts either to no legislative action at all, or soft law measures. This is the case, for example, for remuneration practices in non-financial companies, or for independent directors on corporate boards, where the Commission issued a Recommendation.[44] Norms that are not mandated by binding standards often take the form of a 'comply or explain' system, under which market participants are allowed to deviate from the solution put forward as best practice, but they are obliged to explain to other market players why they deviate. This solution not only raises costs for any non-recommended market practices, but it also raises information availability and facilitates surveillance by transacting business partners. Also, the Commission often examines the take-up and effectiveness of soft law instruments,[45] which again provide more transparency to legal actors across jurisdictions, raising the possibility of yardstick competition.

3.2 International Trade

The legal framework for international trade openness is fixed by non-field specific rules at the EU and at international levels. This means that the description of the legal situation provided below is valid for all three legal fields examined in this book.

At the international level the WTO rules or bilateral trade agreements with third countries will be determinative. At the European level, trade among Member States is liberalised and governed by the free movement of goods provision of the Treaty. Article 34 TFEU states that 'Quantitative restrictions on imports and all measures having equivalent effect shall be prohibited between Member States'. The European Court of Justice has interpreted this provision on several occasions and developed in its case law the mutual recognition principle, which means that a Member State is obliged to grant access to its markets if the goods in

---

44 Commission Recommendation on the role of non-executive or supervisory directors of listed companies and on the committees of the (supervisory) board, 15 February 2005, (2005/162/EC) OJ L 52/51, 25.2.2005.

45 See, e.g. Report on the application by Member States of the EU of the Commission 2009/384/EC and Recommendation on remuneration policies in the financial services sector, Brussels, 2.6.2010 COM(2010) 286 final.

question have been lawfully produced or marketed in another Member State. The only statutory exemption from this principle is laid down in Article 36 TFEU, allowing certain national measures that restrain trade, and the case law of the Court has further identified reasons of general public interest (such as environmental and consumer protection) to suspend the applicability of Article 34 TFEU.

For the sake of complicity the freedom of trade in services should also be mentioned, as a smaller but non-negligible part of international trade in products. At the international level services trade liberalisation is governed by the General Agreement on Trade in Services (GATS), while at a European level it is Article 56 TFEU that prescribes market integration in services trade. This provision is undeniably in close relation to Article 49 TFEU, the freedom of establishment. However, in the current context of examining international trade as one of the potential channels of inter-jurisdictional competition, the freedom of establishment is not relevant for the moment. It will however be examined under mobility of regulatees, as another potential channel of competition.

This European legal framework guarantees a significant level of market openness within the European Union implying a high amount of cross-border trade. When compared to the US, the picture is somewhat less bright, as Europe seems to have more non-legal barriers to trade, such as language and cultural differences, which render it less integrated than the US.

But the international framework of the WTO is potentially equally relevant when assessing the channels of competition among EU Member States, in the sense that such trade competition with a third (non-EU) jurisdiction could in theory drive changes in regulation within the Member State, affecting in turn the other EU countries in tight trade relations with this one Member State.

3.3 Cross-border Capital Flows and Mobility of Workers

With regard to this channel of potential competition, the legal framework is again fixed by EU level rules that are not specific to company law, and thus what is said here is applicable to all three legal fields examined here.

Capital mobility is one of the freedoms provided for by the EU Treaty. Article 63 of the Treaty provides that 'all restrictions on the movement of capital between Member States shall be prohibited'. Article 65 provides statutory exemptions in limited cases, and the case law of the Court of Justice allows for further exemptions from the application of Article 63 in this field as well as on the grounds of general public interest. This legal framework opens the way for a largely free circulation of capital within the EU. At the international level, the free movement of capital is laid down in several multilateral agreements, among them the IMF Articles of Agreement, the GATS and the OECD's Codes of Liberalization of Capital Movements.

As a result of this well-developed legal framework there is high capital mobility internationally, and even more within the European Union.[46]

With regard to the mobility of workers, the situation is quite different. Although the Treaty grants free movement to workers in its Article 45, and this right has been further clarified by the ECJ as well as the European Commission, mainly in Directive 2004/38/EC on the right to reside and Regulation 1612/68 on freedom of movement for workers within the Community, in reality the mobility of workers is naturally limited. The flow of workers across borders is blocked by personal preferences and family ties as well as language and cultural barriers, none of which can be qualified as a legal barrier. As a result, the current level of labour mobility is quite low in Europe: low enough not to contribute to optimal equilibrium outcomes in economic models assuming mobility of workers.

Labour mobility, enshrined in Article 45 TFEU, is a further, although less relevant, aspect of institutional competition both through the channel of production factor mobility and through choice or mobility of regulated firms. On this issue it is worth mentioning the 2007 decision of the European Court of Justice (Laval), which interpreted the posted workers directive,[47] the Treaty freedom on provision of services (posting of workers to a construction site) and the right of workers' unions to take collective action. Interestingly this case, although it has been interpreted more extensively from the angle of labour standards and collective rights,[48] also contains an element of free movement of (posted) workers. In the regulatory competition setting, this decision meant that the freedom of service provision, but also the access of posted workers to another Member State's labour markets, should not be disproportionately limited by collective action, which is a method of ensuring employees rights and employment standards.

---

[46] See Pelkmans, J. (2006), *European Integration: Methods and Economic Analysis*, 3rd edition (New York: Pearson Education Ltd).

[47] Case C–341/05, *Laval un Partneri Ltd* v *Svenska Byggnadsarbetareförbundet*, Judgment of 18 December 2007.

[48] See, e.g. Deakin, S. (2008), 'Regulatory Competition in Europe after Laval', University of Cambridge, Center for Business Research Working Paper no. 364.

3.4 Choice or Mobility of Regulated Firms: The Current Legal Framework

With regard to *mobility or choice of regulatees*, in the development of company law in Europe, the main actors creating the possibility of *mobility for firms* have been the European legislator and the European Court of Justice. Currently there is a shared competence between the European and national legislators on company law.

3.4.1 Scope for choice or mobility under the case law of the Court of Justice

Although the Treaty called on Member States to settle among themselves the question of recognition of corporate forms,[49] it was first the European Court of Justice, and then the European legislator that created a scope of mobility for European firms, to give effect to the freedom of establishment principle of the Treaty. This right of mobility is thus the only channel currently available to firms for choosing or changing the applicable legal regime.

In considering to what extent companies in Europe can change their governing legal regime either through choice or mobility, this section reviews the case law of the European Court of Justice on the interpretation of the freedom of establishment, as well as European secondary legislation that provides a broader scope for corporate mobility on the one hand, and sets its limits on the other hand.

In the case law of the Court, two directions are distinguishable: one opening the way to free movement and another setting limits to it. Indeed, the ECJ decisions are the most dynamic tools of company law harmonisation, developing a body of case law on the interpretation of the freedom of establishment that tackles national legal barriers to cross-border corporate mobility. This section presents the improvement of corporate mobility achieved by the ECJ in its decisions in the Centros,[50]

---

[49] Ex Art. 220 of the EC Treaty: 'Member States shall, so far as is necessary, enter into negotiations with each other with a view to securing for the benefit of their nationals: … the mutual recognition of companies or firms within the meaning of the second paragraph of Article 48, the retention of legal personality in the event of transfer of their seat from one country to another, and the possibility of mergers between companies or firms governed by the laws of different countries.'

[50] Case C-212/97 *Centros Ltd* v *Erhvervs-og Selskabsstyrelsen* [1999] ECR I-1459.

Überseering,[51] Inspire Art,[52] and Cartesio[53] cases. Then the analysis turns to assessing the limits of the protection of free establishment when interpreting the Daily Mail[54] case, together with its reading in the Überseering and Cartesio decisions. A conclusion at the end of the section assesses the effect of the present level of corporate mobility on possible regulatory competition in Europe.

In its Centros decision the ECJ has interpreted what is now Article 49 TFEU (on the freedom of establishment) to prohibit national measures that impede the practice of this fundamental freedom. The case was brought against the Danish authorities who had imposed additional capital requirements on a UK registered company that did not perform any activities in the UK, only in Denmark.

The ECJ held that it was contrary to the freedom of establishment to impose such additional requirements. But since both the UK and Denmark acknowledged the law of incorporation as the governing law of companies, the interpretation of the decision was subject to scholarly debate. The narrow reading of Centros would not have implications for the 'real seat' doctrine, while the broad reading would declare it to be contrary to the Treaty freedom of establishment. In between these two extreme positions was a 'weak interpretation of the real seat doctrine' that substantially narrowed the scope of application of the doctrine,[55] even though it did not entirely end the use of it.[56]

Later decisions of the ECJ further clarified the exact requirements of the freedom of establishment and its implications for the real seat doctrine. In Überseering, a Dutch company was denied legal standing before German courts, on the basis of not being incorporated in Germany. Under German law, the fact that German nationals hold all of the company's shares triggered the non-rebuttable presumption that the administrative office of the company was in fact transferred to Germany (in Überseering two German nationals acquired all of its shares in 1994).

---

[51] Case C-208/00 *Überseering BV* v *Nordic Construction Company Baumanagement GmbH* (NCC). [2002] ECR I-09919.

[52] Case C-167/01 *Kamer van Koophandel* v *Inspire Art* [2003] ECR I-0000.

[53] Case C-210/06 CARTESIO, 2006/C 165/31.

[54] Case 81/87 *The Queen* v *Treasury and Commissioners of Inland Revenue, ex parte Daily Mail and General Trust* [1988] ECR 5483.

[55] Wymeersch, E. (1999), 'Centros: A Landmark Decision in European Company Law', Financial Law Institute Working Paper 1999-15.

[56] McCahery, J.A. and Vermeulen, E.P.M. (2004), 'The Evolution of Closely Held Business Forms in Europe', in McCahery, J.A. et al. (eds) *The Governance of Close Corporations and Partnerships: US and European Perspectives* (Oxford: Oxford University Press).

Since Germany applied the real seat doctrine, the seat transfer required that German law be applicable to the company. Therefore, the authorities wanted to force Überseering to reincorporate in Germany in order to have legal standing. The Court established that once, under the law of the member state, a company is deemed to have moved its place of central administration to that member state, the company's capacity to bring legal proceedings could not be restricted, irrespective of the fact that the country follows the real seat doctrine. Thus the ECJ declared the requirement of re-incorporation to be contrary to the freedom of establishment, although it admitted that companies exist only by virtue of the national legislation that determines their incorporation and functioning. Thus, the Court made it clear that the real seat doctrine cannot be applied in such a way that it impedes corporate mobility in the form of mutual recognition. In other words this means that the transfer of corporate seat cannot imply a change of governing law.

In the subsequent Inspire Art case, the Court addressed the extent to which a national regulator can impose additional requirements on a company that has been formed under a foreign jurisdiction, in which the required capital is located, but where no business activity is carried out. In this case, Dutch legislation required Inspire Art, a UK limited company, to comply with the Dutch act on foreign companies, which included registration as a formally foreign company, meeting the Dutch minimum capital requirements and joint and several liability of the directors. The Court held that such additional requirements of the national law are inconsistent with the freedom of establishment laid down in the Treaty, and thus the decision in Inspire Art confirmed the freedom of companies to transfer their real seat into an incorporation doctrine jurisdiction while being established under the laws of another incorporation doctrine country, without having to meet additional legal requirements of this host state.

This line of case law thus points gradually towards a break-up in the real seat doctrine. There are, however, limits to the freedom of seat transfer that the Court did not eliminate in its decisions, creating apparent contradictions between the two sets of cases. These are reviewed below.

3.4.2 ECJ setting the limits to choice or mobility

There are still barriers to seat transfer under EU law, as the interpretation of the Centros and Überseering decisions, read together with an earlier decision in the Daily Mail case shows. The reason behind this is that the ECJ decided to deal with the issue of immigration of firms separately, and also differently, from the issue of emigration, leaving it to the discretion of national legislators to govern a field that is essential to corporate mobility: the issue of liquidation upon cross-border seat transfer.

In the Daily Mail case, a UK company wished to transfer its central administration to the Netherlands in order to qualify for Dutch tax law and escape UK capital gains tax on a certain transaction. Since both the Netherlands and the United Kingdom follow the incorporation doctrine, transferring the seat in this case did not change the governing company law of the corporation; the aim of the seat transfer was merely to opt into a more favourable tax regime.

UK tax law,[57] however, required the consent of the Treasury for transferring the company's seat (and tax residence) abroad while maintaining its legal personality and its status as a UK company. Daily Mail argued that the freedom of establishment gave it the right to transfer its central management either without prior consent or with the right to obtain such consent unconditionally.

The ECJ held that the (back then EC) Treaty does not grant the right of such seat transfer unless national law allows for it. Thus the ECJ left it to the national legislation under which the company is incorporated to decide about liquidation at the time of emigration, tolerating national rules that create impediments to corporate emigration within Europe.

The Court underscored, however, that 'the rights guaranteed by Articles 52 *et seq.* (EC Treaty) would be rendered meaningless if the Member State of origin could prohibit undertakings from leaving in order to establish themselves in another Member State'.[58] Then the Court continued to explain that the UK regulation applied in cases where the company wished to transfer its seat while maintaining a UK company status, and in such cases the national legislation may freely impose conditions, such as obtaining consent of the Treasury. The Court decision thus allows for national legislation to set either liquidation requirements or, while retaining the legal personality of the company, to set further legal (or tax) requirements to seat transfer.

In the Überseering case, the Court confirmed the Daily Mail judgment, distinguishing between the freedom of movement concerning immigration (meaning the transfer of seat into the territory of the country without changing the governing law, in which case member states cannot impose any additional requirements), and emigration (which is completely in the

---

[57] Section 482(1)(a) of the Income and Corporation Taxes Act 1970.

[58] Case 81/87 *The Queen* v *Treasury and Commissioners of Inland Revenue, ex parte Daily Mail and General Trust* [1988] ECR 5483 paragraph 16.

discretion of the national legislator, the laws of which govern the company).

The uncertainty of the interpretation of the Daily Mail and Überseering decisions lies in the fact that they do not hold explicitly that member states can set rules governing the companies incorporated under their laws without limits. Furthermore, the Daily Mail case is an example of tax arbitrage not regulatory arbitrage and this distinction might provide a better explanation for the Court's decision not to ban limitation of free movement between tax jurisdictions.

Finally, in Cartesio, the ECJ made two declarations that go both in the direction of liberalisation and in the direction of restriction. In this case, a Hungarian company wanted to transfer its registered office to Italy, while keeping its Hungarian legal status and continuing to be governed by Hungarian law.

Indeed, the distinction between changing the governing law or not appears to be the decisive element in this case.

> Nevertheless, the situation where the seat of a company incorporated under the law of one Member State is transferred to another Member State with no change as regards the law which governs that company fails to be distinguished from the situation where a company governed by the law of one Member State moves to another Member State with an attendant change as regards the national law applicable, since in the latter situation the company is converted into a form of company which is governed by the law of the Member State to which it has moved.[59]

One possible terminology to consistently distinguish between the two scenarios is that change of seat without changing the applicable law refers to the situation of moving the head office of a firm. Transferring the seat together with the applicable law then means the transfer of the registered office.

The head office is the central place of administration, and does not trigger the application of the law of the state where it is located. Changing the state of the head office only means relocating the headquarters, but does not change the applicable company law rules. The registered office is always in the state of governing law: transferring the registered office triggers the change of applicable company law.

In Cartesio, the Court has, on the one hand, set a firm limit to the transfer of a company's head office in cases where the governing law of

---

[59] Para 111 of the Cartesio decision.

the company stays the same.[60] On the other hand, it also established that if a company wishes to transfer its registered office to another Member State and wishes to be governed by the law of that other state, such transformation should be allowed and cannot be restricted by the home Member State requiring winding-up or liquidation of the firm.[61] There may be limits imposed by the host Member State, however, as to whether such transfer of registered office is allowed under its national law or not. It is this latter condition that will determine the scope for mobility in the future. It is easy to envisage questions arising concerning for example the avoidance of the co-decision regime by way of transferring the seat of a company from Germany to the UK.

The Cartesio decision of the Court allows for the transfer of the registered office changing the applicable law, but it clearly sets out that transfer of the head office, without changing the applicable law, is not a right of European firms granted by EU law. The practical implications of this decision are yet to be seen. It appears however that it has opened up the scope of mobility of companies, despite the fact that the case at hand

---

[60] Para 110 of the decision says:

> Thus a Member State has the power to define both the connecting factor required of a company if it is to be regarded as incorporated under the law of that Member State and, as such, capable of enjoying the right of establishment, and that required if the company is to be able subsequently to maintain that status. That power includes the possibility for that Member State not to permit a company governed by its law to retain that status if the company intends to reorganise itself in another Member State by moving its seat to the territory of the latter, thereby breaking the connecting factor required under the national law of the Member State of incorporation.

[61] Paras 112 and 113 of the decision refer back to the transfer of the registered office, which changes the applicable law of the company:

> In fact, in that latter case, the power referred to in paragraph 110 above, far from implying that national legislation on the incorporation and winding-up of companies enjoys any form of immunity from the rules of the EC Treaty on freedom of establishment, cannot, in particular, justify the Member State of incorporation, by requiring the winding-up or liquidation of the company, in preventing that company from converting itself into a company governed by the law of the other Member State, to the extent that it is permitted under that law to do so.
>
> Such a barrier to the actual conversion of such a company, without prior winding-up or liquidation, into a company governed by the law of the Member State to which it wishes to relocate constitutes a restriction on the freedom of establishment of the company concerned which, unless it serves overriding requirements in the public interest, is prohibited under Article 43 EC (see, to that effect, inter alia, *CaixaBank France*, paragraphs 11 and 17).

was decided in the negative (as the firm wanted to transfer its head office, keeping its governing law).

To summarise the case law of the Court on the freedom of establishment, as it currently appears, is to distinguish between the following scenarios:

1. When a firm wants to exit
   a. but stay the national of its Member State of original establishment
      - Member State of origin can require the firm to become a national of the new state (*Cartesio*)
      - Member State of origin can make exit conditional or taxable[62] (*Daily Mail*)
   b. and become national of its destination state
      - Member State of origin cannot require liquidation or winding up (*Cartesio*)
2. When, keeping its original governing law, a firm wants to enter
   a. into an incorporation state
      - the destination state cannot impose additional requirements (*Centros, Inspire Art*)
   b. into a real seat state
      - the destination state cannot impose additional requirements (*Überseering*)
      - the destination state cannot require the firm to reincorporate (*Überseering*)
3. When, changing its governing law, the firm wants to enter
   a. into either an incorporation or a real seat state
      - the destination state can define the conditions of entry (*Cartesio*).

As this analysis demonstrates, the possibility of transferring the registered office of a company is presently still defined by the case law of the European Court of Justice. Reading together the cases relating to the free movement of firms across jurisdictions, we can conclude that the Court has made it relatively easy to move between two incorporation countries, or from an incorporation to a real seat country. Such relocation may be taxed or made conditional upon consent, but liquidation, reincorporation or any additional requirements cannot be imposed. Exiting from real seat countries is much more difficult. In these cases the Member State of destination defines the requirements for the relocating firm, and it may be

[62] Exit tax case law developments are a related line of case law.

required by its former home state to change its nationality, but no liquidation can be imposed upon it.

3.4.3 EU legislation enhancing mobility

The concepts of harmonisation and regulatory competition are usually considered as opposite, or at least conflicting, regulatory approaches. This is not necessarily true for harmonisation that is trying to reduce entry barriers, and a very good example of this is European company law, where harmonisation has been used also as the tool opening up the way for regulatory competition by creating mobility for companies. It is important to distinguish between harmonisation that eliminates the diversity of regulations, limiting the discretion of national regulators to provide more competitive norms and harmonisation that is necessary to enhance corporate mobility to give effect to the freedom of establishment. Indeed, there are also certain limits to harmonisation. In the case of the European Company Statute (or Societas Europea), the current Article 115 TFEU was not an adequate legal basis for the instrument, therefore Article 352 TFEU was used.

In the context of company law in Europe the fundamental difference between the incorporation and the real seat doctrine made it an overly complex and unattractive option for companies to change their governing legal regime and to move their main seat across countries. But harmonisation in such a diverse legal environment is hard to achieve, especially if the differences are deeply rooted not only in legal culture but also in political and socio-economic contexts.

Legislative developments over the past decade, such as the Societas Europea Regulation or the cross-border merger directive have brought about a higher level of corporate mobility. However, as the analysis of these legislative actions will show, in some respects there are still barriers to free establishment within the EU.

Currently, at the European level, the following instruments facilitate the mobility of firms across borders in an indirect manner:

- The tenth directive on cross-border mergers;
- the EEIG;
- the Societas Europea;
- the Societas Privata Europea.

The tenth directive on cross-border mergers is intended to assist SMEs and aims to substantially reduce legal and economic barriers that presently have a hindering effect on employment and competitiveness of enterprises. However, the harmonised rules for cross-border mergers also contain limitations in relation to special rights of employees. The protection of labour rights is established in Directive 2001/23/EC[63] (safeguarding employees' rights in the event of transfers of undertakings), Directive 2002/14/EC[64] (establishing a general framework for informing and consulting employees in the European Community) and Directives 94/45/EC and 97/74/EC (concerning the establishment of a European works council and the informing and consulting of employees). These provisions make sure that a merger resulting in a change of employer does not affect the contract or employment relationship in force at the time of the merger, but that it is automatically transferred to the new owner.

The European Economic Interest Grouping (EEIG),[65] the Societas Europea (SE),[66] and the European Private Company (SPE)[67] also aim to facilitate the cross-border transactions and activities of firms. The EEIG Regulation introduced the possibility of firms from different Member States developing joint activities without having to merge or set up jointly-owned subsidiaries.

Under the SE Regulation, firms operating in two or more Member States may form a European Company. The limits to this freedom are set by certain formation requirements. The law governing the company will be the law of the Member State where the SE is registered. The SE also offers more mobility for companies in terms of cross-border transfer of seat.[68] The Directive on Involvement of Employees[69] puts certain restrictions on the free choice of legal arrangements of national laws: a firm cannot reorganise as an SE and choose another Member State's company law as applicable without the consent of its unions if originally the

---

[63] Council Directive 2001/23/EC of 12 March 2001.

[64] Directive 2002/14/EC of the European Parliament and of the Council of 11 March 2002.

[65] Council Regulation 2137/85 on the European Economic Interest Grouping (EEIG) [1985] OJ L199/1.

[66] Council Regulation EC no.2157/2001

[67] Proposal for a Council Regulation on the Statute for a European private company presented by the Commission{SEC(2008) 2098}{SEC(2008) 2099}.

[68] 'The registered office of an SE may be transferred to another Member State [...]. Such a transfer shall not result in the winding up of the SE or in the creation of a new legal person.' Council Regulation (EC) No 2157/2001 of 8 October 2001 on the Statute for a European company (SE) OJ L 294, 10/11/2001, 0001-21. Art. 8, paragraph 1.

[69] Council Directive 2001/86/EC of 8 October 2001 supplementing the Statute for a European company with regard to the involvement of employees OJ L 294, 10.11.2001, pp. 22–32.

governing corporate governance regime prescribed labour representation rules for the company.

The SPE introduces a regime similar to that of the SE, but for private companies.

The European Commission considered preparing a proposal for a directive on the transfer of registered offices that might have ended Member States' powers in setting liquidation requirements before seat transfer.[70] However, in the light of the, then, still forthcoming legal developments in 2008 (ECJ decision on Cartesio), the proposal was shelved. Although the European Parliament called on the Commission to submit a proposal on the issue.[71] The Parliament gave a detailed proposal as to the content of the proposal to be submitted, including the following issues:

> Cross-border transfers of registered offices shall not give rise to the winding-up of the company concerned or to any interruption or loss of its legal personality; consequently, the company shall retain its legal identity and all its assets, liabilities and contractual relations shall remain unaffected. Furthermore, the transfer shall not circumvent legal, social and fiscal conditions. The transfer shall take effect on the date of registration in the host Member State.

The Commission has so far not come forward with the proposal again, thus the limits of national discretion in setting registration requirements are today still governed by the principles established by the Court of Justice, leaving the question open whether action from the European legislator will be needed.

---

[70] [A] company formed in a Member State may decide (i) to transfer its registered office to another Member State in order to acquire legal personality there in place of the legal personality of its home Member State and (ii) to modify its memorandum and articles of association as required; it may do so without losing its original legal personality before acquiring legal personality in the Member State to which it wishes to move; and the company concerned may be registered in the new Member State as a legal person under national law without further incorporation formalities being necessary provided it meets the substantive and formal requirements for companies to be recognised under national law.

Public Consultation of the European Commission on the proposed Directive on transfer of registered office. See also: MEMO/03/112.

[71] See: European Parliament resolution of 10 March 2009 with recommendations to the Commission on the cross-border transfer of the registered office of a company (2008/2196(INI)).

3.4.4 EU harmonisation setting limits to national diversity

Beside the intention of the European legislator to create some corporate forms that facilitate the cross-border mobility of firms, there is also considerable legislation at the European level that constrains regulatory competition by harmonising the substantive rules of national company laws across Europe. These harmonising measures were introduced before the adoption of the stream of legislation creating mobility.

Indeed, European company law directives can be divided into four generations, each reflecting a different approach to harmonisation. The first generation of directives, affected by the fear of a 'race to the bottom', aimed at total harmonisation, leaving no discretion for national regulators in the implementation of directives.[72] The diverse national rules of company law, however, made it virtually impossible to achieve a compromise in various fields of the regulation, and the tools of total harmonisation could not eliminate the basic differences between different company law systems in the EU, also referred to as the outsider and the insider system. Throughout the second and third generation of directives, more flexibility was introduced into regulation, and a new approach to harmonisation was followed in line with the aim of the single market and the Single European Act.[73] Finally, the fourth generation of directives was mainly based on reflexive law-making and the articulation of general principles, also stimulating self-regulatory mechanisms.

The first company law directive has harmonised certain rules in relation to the protection of third parties dealing with both public and private limited companies, such as nullity of the company, the validity of transactions of the company and the disclosure of documents and particulars of persons authorised to bind the company.

The second company law directive lays down rules that relate to the formation, maintenance, and reduction or increase of capital of public companies.

Two directives (the third and tenth company law directives) deal with the merger of public limited companies, covering national and cross-border mergers respectively, and a separate directive (sixth) addresses the division of companies.

The fourth and the seventh directives deal with corporate accounts and consolidated accounts of groups of public and private companies, in order to create a more comparable and thus more integrated system

---

[72] For an analysis of the reasons for total harmonisation and the effect of the fears from a race to the bottom in regulatory competition situations see, e.g. Edwards, V. (1999), *EC Company Law* (Oxford: Oxford University Press).

[73] Single European Act, OJ L 169, 29.6.1987.

within Europe. The eighth directive in turn addresses mandatory requirements for auditors.

The eleventh directive extends the mandatory requirements laid down in the first, fourth, seventh and eight company law directives to branches of companies.

The twelfth directive deals with single member private limited companies, aimed at balancing appropriate creditor protection with freedom of establishment for individuals under limited liability.

The takeover bids directive[74] was adopted with several optional provisions from which Member States could choose. The directive originally aimed at harmonising rules on hostile takeover bids and the availability of takeover defences on the part of the board of target companies. However due to a lack of political agreement, the final version of the Directive contains several compromises in the form of opt-outs and opt-ins for Member States, as well as for firms.

The area of corporate governance structure of companies (fifth directive) and groups of companies (ninth directive) was left unregulated due to the lack of political agreement, similarly to the area of transfer of registered office, mentioned above.

4. CURRENT FORMS OF COMPETITIVE INTERACTION IN EUROPEAN COMPANY LAW

The current pattern of regulatory competition will be examined here through the analysis of recent legal developments over time. In order to get an overview of different angles of competition, various legal areas are reviewed here. The specific cases selected for this inquiry are:

- reform of private limited liability companies that exhibit features of competition over 'price' that is, costs of establishing a company and maintaining it;
- reform of public listed firms that do not appear to take either the direction of lower costs, nor the direction of higher standards;
- employee participation regimes' protection in cases of cross-border reorganisations;
- the Directive on Hostile Takeover Bids, in order to trace the potential drivers behind a failure to harmonise and enact better rules.

---

[74] Directive 2004/25/EC of the European Parliament and of the Council of 21 April 2004 on takeover bids. This instrument aimed to harmonise cross-border hostile takeover bids, which qualifies as free movement of capital.

4.1 The Case of Private Limited Companies – Price Competition

The rules relating to private firms are the obvious place to start exploring competitive interactions in company law. The literature refers to this field as the most prominent example of an emerging regulatory competition pattern in European company law. Indeed, the legal developments in Member States (accompanied by the actual statistics on cross-border mobility of firms), show that there is a tendency towards speedier incorporation services, lower costs of establishing firms coupled with lower legal capital requirements. The examples of a number of European jurisdictions are briefly presented in Table 2.1.

Table 2.1 Comparative table on time, costs and minimum capital requirements for establishing a private company

	Time	Costs	Min. capital
France	3 weeks	£3060	€1
Germany	11–12 weeks	£3290	€25,000
Austria	N/A	N/A	€35,000
UK	1 day	£120	none
Ireland	3–5 days	£540	€100
Netherlands	3 weeks		€18,000
CZ	2 weeks	£1860	€7,600
Italy	2 weeks	£6500	€10,000
Spain	2 weeks	£1740	€3,000

Source: http://www.formacompany.com/en/home

In Germany, there is a minimum capital requirement of €25,000 for private companies, with the exception of small companies with a maximum three shareholders. The so-called *Unternehmergesellschaft* (entrepreneurial company) does not require a minimum capital at its establishment, but there is a mandatory requirement to save up profits until a minimum level of capital has been reached. Small firms, however, (with a maximum of three shareholders) can use the model articles of association without the need for a notarial deed. These solutions speeded up the incorporation of firms and reduced their costs compared to the earlier legal setting.

France lowered its minimum capital requirement to €1 in 2003, whereas the Netherlands, despite the number of firms attracted to the UK, kept its €18,000 minimum capital.

In the Netherlands, the law streamlines the buy-out and valuation procedure in private firms and allows temporary injunctions, both of which address the minority/majority shareholder agency problem. In the assessment of Bratton et al., 'it is questionable, however, whether these changes are fundamental enough to attract foreign companies or prevent domestic firms from migrating to other jurisdictions'.[75]

Denmark also introduced more fast track formation procedures but without altering, in effect, the minimum capital requirements. Bratton et al. show in their research that there is actually a fall in the use of the UK Limited company form as a result of national reforms in the case of Denmark.[76] Indeed the data on foreign incorporations collected by Becht et al.[77] shows an interesting sudden increase in the use of 'UK Limited' by Danish firms[78] between 2001 and 2002. In 2001, 299 such companies were counted, whereas in 2002 this figure jumped to 1131. By comparison it is worth recalling that the judgment of the European Court of Justice in the Centros case, concerning a UK incorporated Danish firm was handed down in 1999.[79] Interestingly, as of 2004, there is a sharp drop in the number of UK incorporations, from 1484 companies in 2003 to 239 firms in 2004.

The trend in the Netherlands was relatively stable until 2003, with around 500 firms incorporated in the UK each year, whereas in 2004 there was a steep increase to 1571 companies, further rising to 2192 firms in 2005. Unfortunately, the latest year covered by Becht et al. is 2006, still a peak with 2156 UK incorporated Dutch firms.

Another big contributor to firms' immigration to the UK is Germany, where the increase of firms incorporating outside seems to have increased in several waves: largely doubling each year between 2001 and 2003;

---

[75] Bratton et al. (2008).

[76] Ibid.

[77] Becht, M. et al. (2008), 'Where Do Firms Incorporate? Deregulation and the Cost of Entry', *Journal of Corporate Finance*, vol. 14, no. 3.

[78] Foreign incorporated firms are identified as firms with a majority of directors residing in a foreign jurisdiction (in this case Denmark), with an activity only in another Member State (Denmark), but incorporated as 'UK Ltd' form.

[79] A slight increase occurs already in the figures between the years 2000 and 2001, the number of UK incorporated Danish firms climbing from 163 to 299, but the real flood of firms takes place in 2002.

more than tripling in 2004; and growing further until 2006. Overall, from 717 firms in 2001, UK incorporated German companies peak at 16 438 in 2006.[80]

There are further interesting fluctuations, such as a one-year peak in Irish firms incorporating in the UK in 2003 (1914 firms, as opposed to some four or five hundred firms in the years before and after that).

Becht et al conclude that the ECJ rulings have had a dramatic effect on the legal geography of new company formation, as the number of private limited companies from all Member States incorporating in the UK per year has increased from 4,400 firms pre-Centros to 28,000 firms post-Centros. Between 1997 and 2006 almost 120,000 of these foreign private limited companies were incorporated in the UK.[81]

As to what drives companies' appetite for the UK rules, they find that

> minimum capital requirements specific to the individual Member States directly influence the flow of companies from that country to the U.K. In particular, using a cross-sectional model we find that much of the variation in the change between pre- and post-Centros flows of firms from Member States to the U.K. is explained by direct and indirect costs of national incorporation procedures. The stronger enforcement and disclosure standards in the U.K. as well as potential legal uncertainty and language barriers seem to be unimportant in comparison for the large numbers of firms utilizing the freedom of incorporation within Europe provided by the ECJ rulings.

Besides minimum capital requirements and costs, other considerations could also drive companies' choice, such as requirements for employee representation (discussed below) or the obligation to set up a supervisory board. While in Germany a supervisory board is obligatory over 500 employees, in Austria this obligation is more restrictive and firms are required to set up supervisory boards if there are more than 300 employees. In Italy the limit is set even lower (meaning yet stricter requirements): having more than 100 employees triggers the obligation to have a supervisory board. However Becht et al. note that 'Corporate mobility is mostly confined to the smallest companies. Paradoxically, it is therefore companies with a largely domestic outlook in their real activities that choose to be internationally mobile'. This finding suggests

---

[80] Again, the data set of Becht et al runs until 2006.

[81] Becht et al. (2008). They add also that 'Germany alone accounts for 48,000 firms, where aggressive marketing by registration agents continues to emphasize the comparative benefits of incorporation in the U.K'. By this, the authors acknowledge the strong role of lawyers and legal counsel in the choice of governing law for newly established firms.

that firms that incorporate abroad do not have a high number of employees, so requirements for setting up a supervisory board or granting employee representation do not seem to be likely drivers of UK incorporations.

As for the type of firm incorporating abroad, Bratton et al. add that: 'Amongst the economically active companies, the most popular sectors employing the UK private limited companies in the Netherlands are: wholesalers (20%), service providers (19%), retail companies (10%) construction and transport firms (10%) and IT and software (9%).'[82] They note that there is about a one third survival rate among them.

McCahery and Vermeulen[83] analyse the legal changes with regard to private companies in Germany and the Netherlands. They reveal that legal reforms are not showing the signs of active competition by attracting companies from other jurisdictions, but merely a reactive attitude in order to retain national firms within the borders. The legal reforms are mainly imitation or follow-up to the features and offerings of UK law.

Indeed the reforms relate mainly to the reduction of costs and time for incorporations, which was argued above to be a decisive factor attracting private companies.

4.2 The Case of Public Listed Firms – No Clear Competition on Quality

The assessment of the regulatory changes in France, Germany and Italy shows that the protection of minority shareholders has increased in the law on the books. Enriques and Volpin[84] analyse the major legislative reforms concerning collective redress, shareholder empowerment and internal governance reforms between 1990 and 2005 in France, Germany and Italy. Although the legal changes they list over this period of 15 years seem to point in the direction of improved corporate governance framework and more effective shareholder rights, they conclude that:

> Too little has been done to resolve the problem of related-party transactions, which is the most common form of self-dealing for dominant shareholders in Europe. Germany has done nothing to improve its law on this matter. France

---

[82] Bratton et al (2008).

[83] McCahery, J.A. and Vermeulen, E.P.M. (2004), 'The Evolution of Closely Held Business Forms in Europe', in McCahery, J.A. et al. (eds) *The Governance of Close Corporations and Partnerships: US and European Perspectives* (Oxford: Oxford University Press).

[84] Enriques and Volpin (2007).

> and Italy have introduced stricter rules on such transactions but have not done enough to strengthen private enforcement, which is an absolute necessity for giving these rules 'teeth', making them effective in the real world, not just in the statute books. In other words, there is a serious risk that these rules will be better only on paper.

Indeed Enriques demonstrates in an earlier paper how the judiciary can alter the law on the books and steer it in a direction not foreseen by the legislator.[85] The three country reviews also revealed potential flaws arising from the application and interpretation of these new rules by the courts.[86]

As for the effects of the amendments, European reforms have been to a great extent modelled on US corporate and securities law. The literature on legal transplants shows how borrowing from other legal systems may not achieve the desired effect.[87] Bratton and McCahery argue that the convergence of corporate governance systems is limited, due to the different function of different legal institutions in one system or the other.[88] The fundamental differences in ownership structure between Europe and the US referred to above mean that emulating laws whose focus is on curbing managerial opportunism may not be an appropriate way to prevent self-dealing by controlling shareholders.

This point is made by Enriques and Volpin as well.

> Indeed, to be cynical one might observe that politically it may be a kind of 'path of least resistance' for European policymakers to adopt US-style solutions designed to tackle managerial agency problems. This way, they can appear to be doing something to reform corporate governance while actually leaving the rents of dominant shareholders perfectly intact.[89]

To conclude, it does not appear either from the data on corporate mobility patterns or from legislative changes that there are active competitive dynamics in European corporate governance for listed public companies that effectively alter the balance of power between the constituencies of the firm. The legislative changes over time indicate

---

[85] Enriques, L. (2002), 'Do Corporate Law Judges Matter? Some Evidence from Milan', *European Business Organizational Law Review*, vol. 3, pp. 765–821.

[86] Enriques, L. and Volpin, P. (2007), 'Corporate Governance Reforms in Continental Europe', *Journal of Economic Perspectives*, vol. 21, no. 1, pp. 117–140.

[87] See, e.g. Berkowitz et al. (2003).

[88] Bratton and McCahery (1999).

[89] Enriques and Volpin (2007).

some movement in the direction of what is perhaps perceived as a modernised corporate governance regime. However, this development is not triggered by regulatory arbitrage but, rather, by policy emulation or yardstick competition among legislators.

The lack of correct implementation by courts also implies that we cannot speak of a regulatory race, at least not in the countries examined above. If anything, there is more sign of regulatory resistance, as a form of intra-jurisdictional competitive interaction between legislators and courts, in which courts do not actively advance the legislator's intent.

4.3 Employee Participation: Protectionism or Competition?

In the case of employee representation on the Board, the increased scope for corporate mobility within Europe gave rise to concerns that firms would opt into legal regimes without employee participation schemes. Although this issue is often referred to in the context of the German co-determination regime, labour representation on boards is much more widespread across Europe.

The fear of mobile companies evading worker participation obligations has been addressed at European level through mandating the maintenance of participation in cases where the firms originally had such legal requirements.

The Directive on Involvement of Employees[90] puts restrictions on the free choice of legal arrangements of national laws; a firm cannot reorganise as an SE and choose another Member State's company law as applicable without the consent of its unions if, originally, the governing corporate governance regime prescribed labour representation rules for the company. The EU level measures ensure that the same level of employee representation is maintained in the new governing legal regime as under the old one. The SPE introduces a regime similar to that of the SE, but for private companies.

Recitals (13) and (14) of the Cross-Border Merger Directive state that:

> If employees have participation rights in one of the merging companies under the circumstances set out in this Directive and, if the national law of the Member State in which the company resulting from the cross-border merger has its registered office does not provide for the same level of participation as operated in the relevant merging companies, including in committees of the

---

[90] Council Directive 2001/86/EC of 8 October 2001 supplementing the Statute for a European company with regard to the involvement of employees OJ L 294, 10.11.2001, pp. 22–32.

> supervisory board that have decision-making powers, or does not provide for the same entitlement to exercise rights for employees of establishments resulting from the cross-border merger, the participation of employees in the company resulting from the cross-border merger and their involvement in the definition of such rights are to be regulated. To that end, the principles and procedures [...] are to be taken as a basis, subject, however, to modifications that are deemed necessary because the resulting company will be subject to the national laws of the Member State where it has its registered office. A prompt start to negotiations under Article 16 of this Directive, with a view to not unnecessarily delaying mergers, may be ensured by Member States in accordance with Article 3(2)(b) of Directive 2001/86/EC.
>
> For the purpose of determining the level of employee participation operated in the relevant merging companies, account should also be taken of the proportion of employee representatives amongst the members of the management group, which covers the profit units of the companies, subject to employee participation.

Furthermore, the choice of applicable legal regime is not granted to management or shareholders solely: all concerned constituencies have to be consulted.

It was stated above that different theories exist as to what is an efficient corporate governance system. It would seem obvious that, in so far as both theories base their arguments on efficiency, the market should pick the winner through a natural selection process. Such a Darwinian 'survival of the fittest' is one of the positive features of regulatory competition. It could be asked then why labour participation is exempted from free law shopping.

However the interpretation of the European legal solution is not necessarily that employee participation is safeguarded and cannot be subject to competition. Indeed, what the current legal rules achieve is a legal certainty for stakeholders such as employees that the rights under which they entered into a contract with the firm will not be changed later unilaterally. This type of legal rule enables firms to make a credible commitment towards their constituencies, in much the same way as contracting parties do under contract law. Thus prohibiting existing firms to change applicable corporate governance rules to the detriment of those who benefited from a certain protection of their interests under the old regime might very well be a justified choice from an economic perspective.[91]

---

[91] Incentives and behaviour would change if the rules were easy to evade and, in extreme circumstances, could lead to a situation where co-decision regimes would no longer be able to grant reliable rights to employees.

What this means in practice is that arbitrage with free choice is available at incorporation stage. At later stages of the company's life the choice of legal regime is shared among all constituencies that had a role in corporate governance originally. Also, the different legal regimes are still in competition through international trade with one another.

Theoretically, it is also possible that different corporate governance systems will be optimal for different types of firms. Stakeholder theory predicts that specific investments by employees will be important drivers of efficiency. This may hold true for some industries and services more than others. Or, it may simply be more important under certain conditions of competition, product differentiation, and so on.

Finally the question may be asked: What if the co-decision regimes are not necessarily more efficient, as viewed from an overall cost-benefit perspective and as priced by market mechanisms, but they still represent the preference of a society? We can imagine a society that cares about the well-being of employees and would like to uphold the system of co-decision even at the expense of a loss in productive efficiency and thus higher prices (measured in monetary terms without taking full account of utilities). If we entertain this hypothesis for a moment, we will realise that, in the current legal and economic environment, international trade is too intrusive and production networks are too complex for consumers to be readily informed about which product to buy in order to support employees. This resembles a market failure, where information asymmetries do not allow for the correct selection process. It is easy to see that in such a situation (in an extreme case, again, to demonstrate otherwise probably very marginal effects) firms with labour representation regimes would soon end up losing the product market competition. They would close down if they were not allowed to leave the jurisdiction and if they could not find a good solution to address the information asymmetry (such as labelling, see, for example, biological products, fair trade, ecological labels, or even national products, and so on).

In this case, however, Member States will be able to 'buy' the corporate governance regime preferred by society by offering tax advantages, other public goods or specific advantages of the national market to firms that are willing to take on the additional burdens (if we presume that stakeholder theory is wrong about the value added of employee participation and that firms cannot use signalling towards consumers) of operating under a co-decision regime. Taxpayers' preferences would be achieved at the cost of the taxpayers, solving an example of a market failure through public intervention.

4.4 Takeovers: The Incentives of National Legal Actors Matter

The European legislator adopted the directive on takeover bids in 2004 with the aim of achieving a more convergent approach in the field of takeover transactions. The intended result was an increased integration of European capital markets by creating favourable conditions for the emergence of a European market for corporate control: efficient takeover mechanisms; a common regulatory framework; and strong rights for shareholders, including minority shareholders.[92] The main provisions helping to achieve this were the board neutrality and breakthrough rules.[93] Due to the lack of political support, the directive was adopted with the significant compromise of making some of its most relevant provisions (among them board neutrality and the breakthrough rule) optional, rather than mandatory. Thus, the Member States had freedom to decide, under the directive, whether they want to apply these rules.

> Member States are allowed to choose between imposing these rules or not. However, if a Member State decides not to make them mandatory, it cannot prevent companies from applying these rules on a voluntary basis. The decision on voluntary application of the rules in turn has to be adopted by the general meeting and can be reversed in the same way. A further element of the final compromise is the so-called reciprocity exception, which allows Member States to permit companies applying one or both of these rules to disapply them, and thus to 'retaliate' against a bidder who is not subject to the same rules. The reciprocating power can be used only if it is authorised by both the Member State and the general meeting of the target company.[94]

An implementation report completed in 2007 shows that the actual result of the adoption of the directive has been to worsen the original divergent and, on average, board-friendly national legal landscape. According to the findings of the report, only Malta introduced the board neutrality rules as a result of the directive, while 17 other Member States already had such a provision in their national law (thus, in total, 18 Member States impose board neutrality). Five of these Member States, however,

---

[92] European Commission 'Report on the implementation of the Directive on Takeover Bids', Commission staff working document SEC (2007) 268.

[93] Board neutrality means that the board cannot frustrate a bid unless shareholders authorise it. The breakthrough rule ensures that voting restrictions, or other mechanisms that are in place and could thwart off a potential bidder, are not applicable once a takeover bid has been made.

[94] Ibid, 268.

introduced as a new element the reciprocity exception,[95] which was not in their national law before the adoption of the directive. On balance, this means on the one hand that national laws did not converge, and they even protect the board somewhat more than before the adoption of the directive, which is exactly contrary to the intended effects.

Similarly, with regard to the provision on the breakthrough rule, the directive achieved unexpected results. It emerged that the vast majority of Member States have not imposed the breakthrough rule, but have instead made it optional for companies. Imposition of the breakthrough rule was only considered by the Baltic States, which cover only 1 per cent of listed companies in the EU. Besides, Hungary originally had a partial breakthrough rule, which it eliminated with the transposition of the directive.

Given that only a few Member States intend to impose the application of the rule, its takeover-facilitating effect will depend almost exclusively on whether or not companies will apply the rule on a voluntary basis. As the Commission's report on the implementation of the takeover bids directive explains:

> Voluntary application of the breakthrough rule is made conditional upon the approval of those benefiting from disproportionate or special rights or of a large proportion of shareholders in certain Member States. This makes the application of the rule on a voluntary basis more difficult.
>
> If a company decides to apply the breakthrough rule on a voluntary basis, such decision can immediately be reversed as soon as the bidder becomes a target. The reversibility of the company's decision may even create confusion on the market.[96]

The explanation of this outcome can be twofold. One possibility is that the Member States have a different theory of efficiencies of takeovers and the defence measures applied by target boards.

Another, more likely, scenario is that even though Member States have quite similar theories about efficiencies, in line with the reasoning of the Commission, which would dictate the adoption of the breakthrough rule and board neutrality, they still ended up not adopting these 'best rules' because they played a non-cooperative game which lead to a lower overall welfare than a cooperative outcome.

---

[95] The reciprocity exception allows companies not to apply the board neutrality and breakthrough rules *if* the bidder company is not subject to these rules either.

[96] Commission Staff Working Document, Report on the implementation of the Directive on Takeover Bids SEC (2007) 268 Brussels, 21.02.2007.

The comment of McCreevy, Commissioner for the Internal Market at the time of adoption, reflects this latter interpretation:

> Too many Member States are reluctant to lift existing barriers, and some are even giving companies yet more power to thwart bids. The protectionist attitude of a few *seems to have had a knock-on effect on others*. If this trend continues, then there is a real risk that companies launching a takeover bid will face more barriers, not fewer. That goes completely against the whole idea of the Directive.[97]

The fact that Member States changed their national rules at the time of the implementation of the directive and not earlier, also seems to imply that these legal changes granting more protection to the board are not coming from independent national considerations, but are the impact of the introduction of the directive.

Given that European law would not allow discrimination in the treatment of domestic and foreign bidders, Member States are forced to adopt the same rules for both situations. But the aim of increasing national welfare (or perhaps just the welfare of certain lobby groups) through protectionism may be stronger than the goal of maximising national welfare through adopting the most efficient rules on takeovers. This in turn will imply that states will want to ensure foreign firms can be fended off. Due to the market opening provisions of EU law they are thus forced to extend this provision also to their national firms. In other words, there is a double failure in the aims of the legal instruments: first at the level of the takeover bids directive, then, indirectly and in this specific situation, at the level of EU law opening up markets through non-discrimination provisions.

4.5 Which Legal Actors Enter the Arena of Competition?

This section gives an overview of the legal actors that are involved in shaping the rules of company law in Europe, assessing their incentives in their respective activity and whether they enter into competition with each other. In the European context, a brief examination of the various legal actors may help in understanding the nature of their involvement in shaping the law and entering into competition with each other, or refraining from doing so.

---

[97] McCreevy, Ch. (2007), 'Corporate Governance: Member States Reluctant to Give a Greater say to Shareholders in the Context of Takeover Bids, says Commission Report', European Commission Press release IP/07/251, issued on 27 February 2007.

4.5.1 The legislator

With regard to the European legislator, in a comparative assessment Enriques and Volpin note that: 'The US central government has long played a much more important role in regulating corporate governance than the European Community on the other side of the Ocean.'

At the national level, company law is the domain of the respective national legislators, the rules being interpreted and applied by the national courts, with relatively significant leeway in shaping the applicable norms.[98]

In the example of American corporate law, the revenues from incorporation franchise fees can be identified as the most relevant incentive for Delaware to attract incorporations. In Europe, however, there are no similar franchise fees imposed on incorporating companies.[99] Thus European member states lack the most plausible incentive to engage in competitive law-making.

The benefits derived by the judiciary and the bar as the providers of legal services should be mentioned as further incentives on the Member States to engage in competitive law-making.[100] But it is questionable whether these alone would provide sufficient incentives for the states to start competing. Indeed, it is often argued that the legal advisors and public notaries rather than the judges may be the winners of a regulatory arbitrage scenario. The legislator may favour these groups and decide to create a legal environment that is attractive to firms.

Another important aspect for the legislator is the tax consideration. Tax competition is not examined in this study as the comparison of tax competition and regulatory competition would require a separate extensive discussion. However, a few words need to be said about this aspect and its interplay with regulatory competition.

---

[98] Enriques, L. (2002), 'Do Corporate Law Judges Matter? Some Evidence From Milan', *European Business Organization Law Review*, vol. 3, no. 4, pp. 756–821.

[99] Some authors argue that franchise taxes levied by the state of jurisdiction on corporations having their headquarters outside of the jurisdiction governing the company are not allowed under European corporate tax rules. See Keininger, E.M. (2004), 'The Legal Framework for Regulatory Competition Based on Company Mobility: EU and US Compared', *German Law Journal*, vol. 6, no. 4, p. 747. Also, Dammann, J. (2003), *The US Concept of Granting Corporations Free Choice among State Corporate Law Regimes as a Model for the European Community*, available at: http://ssrn.com/abstract=418660.

[100] Macey, J.R. and Miller, G.P. (1987), 'Toward an Interest-Group Theory of Delaware Corporate Law', *Texas Law Review*, vol. 65, no. 3, p. 469.

Within Europe, the tradition of the real seat doctrine continues to exert its influence and, as explained above, company law jurisdiction is therefore often linked to tax jurisdiction over corporate income. Taxation rights over corporations will certainly also provide an incentive for states to attract incorporations, however the competition for foreign direct investments will imply a tendency to reduce corporate income taxes rather than increasing them as a 'price' for the state's corporate governance regime as a product. Therefore, as studies on tax competition conclude, this model of competitive law-making will most probably lead to a fall in tax rates, linked to the competition for foreign direct investments. In other words, if corporate mobility is tied to the real seat doctrine, a tax competition scenario will very likely remain to outweigh regulatory competition, as long as taxation is decentralised.

4.5.2 The private regulator

Another look at the legal area of takeover regulation reveals more about the significance of legal actors' incentives, its impact on the rules they produce, and ultimately on regulatory competition itself. Armour and Skeel[101] compare the regulatory institutional set-up in the UK and the US, in order to find a possible explanation for the divergence in the two jurisdictions with regard to the stance on the permissibility of a takeover defence. In the US, takeover defence mechanisms are permitted but the UK prohibits defence by the board. The two jurisdictions, being both part of the Anglo-Saxon legal family, have a lot in common in the field of corporate governance as well as corporate ownership patterns. It is thus all the more surprising that they would diverge so sharply over the takeover issue.

Armour and Skeel show that the person of the legislator (and its incentives) is determinative of the outcome. In the US, federal legislation occupied the field of securities law and state legislators took the role of setting rules for the permissibility of takeover defences. In the UK, on the other hand, it was the industry that initiated a private regulatory approach to takeovers.[102] The City Code on takeovers is developed by a panel

[101] Armour, J. and Skeel, D.A. Jr. (2007), 'Who Writes the Rules for Hostile Takeovers, and Why? The Peculiar Divergence of US and UK Takeover Regulation', *Georgetown Law Journal*, vol. 95, p. 1727.

[102] This pattern of private regulation was changed by the Directive on hostile takeover bids that required Member State action. The UK decided, therefore, to introduce an ex-post legislative recognition of the private regulatory outcome, which basically keeps the private regulation touch of UK takeovers – within the limits set by the Directive.

whose members are industry representatives (from investment banks, pension funds, and so on).[103] The interests of this private regulatory body were aligned and clearly called for a regulation in favour of a lively market for corporate control, in contrast to the American model, where Delaware's legislator and judiciary serve a market for incorporations.[104]

This example demonstrates that the person of the legal actor, and its incentives, are determinative of the legal outcome. Indeed, continental European legal regimes, where the rule-makers are national legislators like in the US, mostly follow the pattern also observed in the US of allowing defensive measures against hostile bids by the board.

Without entering into the question of which outcome is more efficient, two questions should be addressed here: what is the likely legal outcome of competitive models of private regulation, and what outcome could be expected if a model similar to that in the UK were introduced in continental Europe?

With regard to the first question, competition among private regulators is an interesting set-up, where arguably the private regulators being mainly financial institutions and also shareholders themselves, will have aligned incentives with one constituency within firms: shareholders. Introducing competition among these private regulators would probably force them to take better account of the interests of those constituencies that have a strong influence on the choice of applicable law. Here, it was concluded that it is ultimately shareholders and managers who choose jurisdiction. But since the original interests of private regulators are so closely aligned with those of shareholders, it is unlikely that competition among them would lead any jurisdiction to introduce overtly management friendly rules – unless a specific pay-off structure is in place, such as high charter fees, and so on. Competition among private regulators with shareholder aligned incentives may thus be envisaged as a form of competition that puts limits on both side's extreme solutions: on favouring only shareholder interests and on favouring only management. The specific design of competitive interaction, especially factors that may

---

[103] Note that the introduction of the Takeover Bids Directive required Member States to legislate in this area. The solution adopted in the UK was to introduce an ex-post recognition of the Code. Since then the regulatory model in place is ex-post recognised private regulation.

[104] Again, the welfare implications of the two solutions can only be measured through empirical analysis or by following one theory of efficiencies. Here the main point is that depending on who writes the rules the outcome may be different.

influence the pay-off structure of legal actors is an extremely relevant determinant of the final outcome, however.

Also, the above hypothetical example leads us to conclude that competition between private regulators (as a group of legal actors with homogeneous interests across jurisdictions) will presumably lead to different legal outcomes from regulatory competition among private and public legal actors (or any other two groups of legal actors with heterogeneous interests). If we imagine that the UK private regulator is in direct competition with continental European legislators and judiciary, it is predictable that with a high mobility of firms (with relatively low costs) and choice being allocated mainly to management,[105] companies would easily migrate from the UK to jurisdictions with more management friendly rules, ones that legislators or judges are likely to create as soon as they have the incentive to do so.[106]

Finally, let us address the question of what the introduction of a UK-style private regulatory model would result in, in a continental Europe context. It can be expected that setting up private regulation with the respective continental European counter-parts to the British institutions would result in similar rules to the UK, that is, shareholder-friendly rules on board passivity.

It should be recalled at this juncture, however, that the ownership structure of UK and continental European companies is different. Therefore, the practical impact and consequently the welfare implications may also change. In the UK, shareholder-friendly rules are introduced in a more dispersed ownership environment but in continental Europe, some controlling shareholders already have a say in directing corporate affairs, including takeovers, which for them means selling out not only their shares but also their control over the company.

In the continental European case, therefore, what is of much more relevant concern is the situation of minority shareholders, who may be suffering damage in the form of opportunity costs as they cannot grasp opportunities offered to them by takeover bidders.

---

[105] This assumption can of course be debated. Under concentrated ownership structures, such as that of continental European countries, it is likely that strong shareholder groups will be able to exert substantial influence over managers.

[106] This incentive may be anything from monetary benefits, such as in the case of Delaware, to welfare considerations of democratically elected legislators, the own agenda of the national judiciary, etc.

4.5.3 The judiciary

A growing literature shows that the law on the books in a jurisdiction can be 'as good as' in the best performing countries and yet their effect may be minimal.[107] A significant factor in the quality of the law and its actual impact is enforcement by the national courts.

The significance of the judiciary (and the Bar) in shaping Delaware's corporate law has been extensively analysed in the American literature.[108] In Europe, the role of the judiciary with regard to regulatory competition is also affected by the European legal context.

The approach of the German and Austrian courts is a good example of this. The decision of the Austrian Supreme Court, based on the ECJ's decision in Centros, established that Austrian law had to acknowledge the existence of a company incorporated in the UK but carrying out its commercial activity in Austria,[109] and similar decisions have been reached also in Germany.[110] Such early opening towards immigrant companies implies that – at least for start-up firms – there is scope for a regulatory arbitrage that companies can take advantage of through a certain degree of mobility.

This arbitrage is opened up by the interpretative work of judges, since at this stage most member states' national legislation contains substantial impediments to the recognition of foreign established companies operating within the country.

When national courts refer questions to the European Court of Justice for a preliminary ruling, this is also a sign of cooperative behaviour with the European judges. The examples for this are the cases forming the basis of the ECJ's case law in the follow-up to Centros. As the European

---

[107] See Pistor, K. et al. (2000), 'Law and Finance in Transition Economies', *Economics of Transition*, vol. 8, no. 2, pp. 325–368. See Black, B. et al. (1999), 'Russian Privatisation and Corporate Governance: What Went Wrong', *Stanford Law Review*, vol. 52, p. 1731 (recognising that even Russian law, designed under the advice of Professors Black and Kraakman as a 'self-enforcing' model of corporate law, was absolutely irrelevant, due to the extreme weakness of the Russian enforcement system and especially of the courts). Enriques, L. (2002), 'Do Corporate Law Judges Matter? Some Evidence From Milan', *European Business Organization Law Review*, vol. 3, no. 4, pp. 756–821.

[108] See, e.g. Romano, R. (1993), *The Genius of American Corporate Law* (Washington: AEI Press).

[109] Oberster Gerichthof (OGH) decision of 7/15/1999 Österreichisches Recht der Wirtschaft (RdW) 719 (1999). Analysed by: Kieninger, E.M. (2004), 'The Legal Framework for Regulatory Competition Based on Company Mobility: EU and US Compared', *German Law Journal*, vol. 6, no. 4, at p. 746.

[110] Ibid., p. 747.

Court has been the leading actor in opening up freedom of establishment to European companies, national courts interpretation in accordance with the ECJ case law also signals an opening up.

By enhancing mobility, courts can create regulatory arbitrage in their case law that makes the law of a certain jurisdiction more attractive to regulatees. However, it is important to point out that there is no direct monetary incentive for the courts in this activity that can be linked to regulatory competition as clearly as in the case of Delaware.

With regard to other incentives, it was argued in Chapter 1 that the national courts may have an incentive to cooperate with the European court and legislator in order to enhance their legitimacy, as well as independence from the national legislator. However, courts may also have an incentive to emulate the best legal standard as a way of enhancing their authority. Any of these incentives may result in decisions enhancing free choice of law or mobility by firms. On the other hand, an increase in the number of companies within the jurisdiction also means an increased workload. This may be a disincentive in jurisdictions where, unlike in Delaware, the company incorporations do not finance the judges.

The question is, what would be the incentive of the national court to achieve free choice or mobility in the first place under a legal environment where these are originally restricted, and where the competitive pressure of international trade mainly dominates? As the analysis of the European legal framework on legal harmonisation pointed out, one of the main goals of the Treaty on the Functioning of the European Union is to achieve market integration through free movement of goods, services, persons and capital. Pursuing this goal, the European Court of Justice interpreted the provisions of the Treaty on free movements as providing mobility to European firms. National courts follow this reasoning when they open up their own national systems. Their incentive to follow the line of the ECJ case law may be twofold. From one perspective, they are under legal obligation to follow the decisions of the ECJ. From a less legally focused perspective, they may want to enhance their authority and independence by keeping their national discretionary powers as broad as possible.

Thus, in order for a well-functioning system of regulatory competition to arise, there is a necessary first step for legal actors in enhancing mobility, and a second step to develop national law. Theory provides that courts may have incentives to perform both functions sequentially, although it is not clear whether the two require the same incentives or, if not, whether the judiciary's incentives would change along with the change in the legal environment and competitive pressures.

At the same time, with regard to changes in substantive rules, the judiciary may have an incentive to develop the existing rules even if mobility or choice are not present. The competitive pressure arising from international trade and capital mobility may be sufficient to trigger concern for national firms' international competitiveness, especially if judges' policy agenda involves a concept of effectiveness or efficiency.[111]

In Italy, for example, the case law of the Milanese court points in the direction of interpreting recent legal amendments in a restrictive manner, thereby delaying the intended impact of new legislation. A study by Enriquies[112] reveals that the Italian courts are not readily adapting a minority shareholder protection approach in their interpretation of the law.

In Germany in the 1980s and 1990s, the case law of the courts was aiming for greater shareholder protection and inferred fiduciary duties for directors towards shareholders. This change, introduced by the courts, significantly alters the 'value' of German corporate governance standards for shareholders *vis-à-vis* other jurisdictions and, as companies have growing mobility and freedom of choice, such decisions will arguably affect incorporation decisions.

The fact that, under international trade competition and competition through mobility models, the incentives of the judiciary may coincide can potentially ensure that both the necessary preconditions for regulatory competition – the opening of the legal systems, and the development of national rules – will occur.

While the assessment of the role of the judiciary in the US shows the positive role of judges in shaping Delaware's corporate law to make it more attractive to companies, the European scenery shows a slightly different picture. In Europe, the institutional framework reveals a much more mandatory character with more barriers than in the US. The most obvious example is the mandatory rule on the place of litigation,

---

[111] It should be noted here that the notion of efficiency does not necessarily have only one form. Efficiency considerations may drive decisions of a seemingly social character, depending on the theory of the firm one adopts, and presumptions about the relevance of various constituencies of the firm in the success of the enterprise as a whole.

[112] Enriques, L. (2003),'Off the Books, but on the Record: Evidence from Italy on the Relevance of Judges to the Quality of Corporate Law', in Milhaupt, C.J. (ed.) *Global Markets, Domestic Institutions: Corporate Law and Governance in a New Era of Cross-Border Deals* (New York: Columbia University Press).

prescribing that corporations cannot litigate certain subject matters outside the state of establishment. The European Council Regulation on Jurisdiction[113] provides that where the subject matter of the litigation is the validity of the constitution of a company, the nullity or the dissolution thereof, or the validity of the decisions brought by the company's organs, the courts of the Member State of establishment have exclusive jurisdiction. Authors argue that this binding norm creates substantial costs for companies in Europe, also due to the language barriers.[114] But this feature of the European institutional framework gives further emphasis to the argument that the judicial system plays an essential role and is not negligible if a state is to engage in regulatory competition.

Under the Überseering doctrine, in all other matters the courts of the Member State where the company is litigating have to apply the law of the state of formation and have to acknowledge the legal personality of the company. However, due to the institutional set-up of national courts in European countries, litigation in front of a national court requiring the application of foreign law is also very costly and can be a deterrent to corporations considering out-of-state incorporation. Therefore, the conclusion from the American example, that the quality of the judicial system is one of the main driving forces of foreign incorporations is less convincing in Europe, due to the language barriers that place additional difficulties and financial barriers before out-of-state establishments.[115] A similar language barrier argument can be put forward as an impediment of choice of foreign law as well as foreign forum.

With regard to litigation involving external affairs, the corporations can be sued in their state of establishment as well as in other states that have jurisdiction over the matter in question. Thus there is no specific European rule that would impose limitation on litigation in external matters of the corporation, and the state of establishment is not determinant or exclusive in such matters.

---

[113] Council Regulation 44–2001 of 22 December 2000, on jurisdiction and the recognition and enforcement of judgments in civil and commercial matters, 2001, O.J. (L 12), 1. 8.

[114] Dammann, J. (2003), *The US Concept of Granting Corporations Free Choice among State Corporate Law Regimes as a Model for the European Community* available at: http://ssrn.com/abstract=418660.

[115] Tröger, T. (2004), *Choice of Jurisdiction in European Corporate Law: Perspectives of European Corporate Governance* available at: http://ssrn.com/abstract=568782; Dammann, J. (2003), *The US Concept of Granting Corporations Free Choice among State Corporate Law Regimes as a Model for the European Community* available at: http://ssrn.com/abstract=418660.

Corporations thus face the above legal constraints when considering choice of foreign law with special regard to choice of forum. As for the possible gains from choice of forum, considerations such as the speed of litigation and the expertise of the judiciary might play an important role, and differences among countries in these respects might be an additional element in regulatory competition.

4.5.4 Lawyers

As for the role of lawyers, and legal services in general, the same can be said in the European context as in the American example, with the exception that European lawyers are not trained yet in another (winner) legal system so that they can easily provide legal services to companies that wish to use that other jurisdiction as their governing law. This is, however, due to the fact that within Europe no clear 'winner' of the competition for incorporations has emerged yet, although there is some evidence pointing to the UK as the most internationally-oriented jurisdiction.[116] But should a preferred legal system be identified, there is no practical obstacle to quick adoption by lawyers in other jurisdictions, acquiring skills in the corporate law of the winner state. This aspect of the institutional set-up is greatly determined by the network externalities described in the previous sections, and is a focal point of regulatory competition due to the central role of the institutional framework in creating and maintaining market leading position of states in the market for incorporations.[117]

Therefore if a European state wishes to engage in competitive law-making, its main investments have to be put into developing a strong institutional framework supporting the substantive corporate governance rules. This is necessary not only because of the network externalities mentioned above, but also because of the possibility of other states copying the substantive rules of the leading jurisdiction. If a state tried to establish its leading position as the provider of corporate rules based only on its innovation in substantive corporate governance rules, it could easily be challenged by other jurisdictions, which, even without being inventive or offering additional advantages in their legal system, could copy the legislation of the innovator state.[118]

---

[116] Wymeersch, E. (2003), 'Corporate Law in a Turmoil and the Way to "Global Company Practice"', *Journal of Corporate Law Studies*, vol. 3, p. 283.

[117] See the analysis of US corporate law above, and in general Bebchuk and Hamdani (2002) cited above.

[118] There is evidence that states in the US follow the lead of Delaware in updating their corporate governance codes. See Romano, R. (2005), 'Is Regulatory Competition a Problem or Irrelevant for Corporate Governance?' ECGI

Such copying would arguably be sufficient to retain domestic incorporations and prevent the flight of companies to another jurisdiction, because out of state incorporations are costly for companies (due to legal and other structural barriers, as explained above). They therefore naturally prefer to stay in their domestic jurisdiction. If substantive norms are the only 'products' a foreign state competes on, and these rules can – without major delays – be transposed into the domestic legal system, the costs of opting for the foreign jurisdiction will probably be greater than the benefits the foreign state can provide for companies.

5. A THEORETICAL INQUIRY: HOW WOULD DIFFERENT FORMS OF REGULATORY COMPETITION WORK IN COMPANY LAW?

This section will examine the externalities arising from different legal rules across stakeholder groups and across borders, and it will analyse the potential welfare implications of regulatory competition in a simplified theoretical setting.[119]

5.1 What is an Externality?

Externalities arise when someone benefits or suffers loss from an activity or transaction by others, where the cost or benefit to the third party is not priced into the activity or transaction. We can thus talk about external costs or external benefits. In the first case, the activity or transaction would be performed too much (over-production), whereas in the latter case it would be performed too little (under-production), compared to the optimal state. Simple as it sounds, it is not always easy to tell who imposes an external effect on whom, and how that situation should be resolved. Therefore, the starting point of the analysis matters, since

Working Paper no. 26/2005, Available at: http://ssrn.com/abstract=693484. This provides further support for the argument that it is much more the system of litigation rather than the substantive rules that companies 'buy' when incorporating in Delaware, and underlines the importance of the institutional framework in shaping regulatory competition.

[119] The aim of this analysis is to identify the potential effects of competitive law-making, not to explore and determine the actual welfare outcomes. For a precise determination of overall welfare implications, very accurate values on individual utility gains and losses would be necessary. Instead parties who win and lose can be identified in a simple example.

externalities without a pre-existing legal framework can go both ways: if a certain action takes place, A suffers an externality; if it does not take place, B suffers a negative effect. It is most often legal norms that assign property rights or set up rules governing the activities that cause external effects, and we can interpret the direction of external effects as a function of these legal rules.

In some cases the legal rules themselves may create externalities, or reverse the direction of external effects. Economics tells us that the most efficient outcome is a world without externalities, where all actors fully internalise the costs and benefits of their activities and transactions. In a decentralised legal framework the different jurisdictions may impose externalities on one another with their different legal regimes.

5.2 The Example of Legal Capital Rules and the Limitations of this Exercise

It has been described above how the European rules shape the mobility of firms and set the limits of divergence of company laws across the EU. The current forms and outcomes of regulatory competition have also been reviewed above. Here, the analysis takes a step back and looks at a hypothetical example of the interaction of different legal regimes. It aims to highlight in a general manner some of the main drivers behind the dynamics of competitive law-making as well as the positive and negative impacts on different groups of actors. This hypothetical example will also serve as the basis for examining the welfare implications of regulatory competition, pointing out the different assumptions behind any welfare judgment. Finally, the main aim of this section is to reach conclusions on whether competitive interactions could be maintained in European company law under either the current, or different, arrangements of competence allocation and governance.

Therefore, we use here a simplified framework with some illustrative figures that help in following the direction (but not the exact magnitude) of externalities and welfare effects.[120] The chosen methodology therefore does not aim to accurately describe the exact welfare results of regulatory competition, nor is it intended to give a precise cost-benefit analysis.

---

[120] A simplified and non-exhaustive list of affected parties is used in the analysis, in which only the most significantly and directly affected constituencies are examined. Then the gains and losses of each of these parties are assigned a fictive value.

The analysis will focus on the question of how different theories of efficiency determine the welfare implications of different legal solutions and thus the welfare outcome of regulatory competition.

The subject selected for the analysis is the rules on minimum capital requirements. The area chosen represents conflict of interest and agency problems within the firm between creditors and management or owners. Other fields of regulation would imply different agency problems and different outcomes.

5.3 The Regulated Actors and Beneficiaries

From a law and economics perspective, the creditors of a firm can be grouped into two categories: adjusting and non-adjusting creditors. Adjusting creditors are those that have sufficient economic power to amend the terms of credit according to the situation of the firm they contract with to provide credit (typically banks). Non-adjusting creditors on the other hand cannot change the terms of contract (if a contract exists) to achieve an optimal legal environment tailored to the credit risk of the firm they 'lend' to. Usual non-adjusting creditors are tort creditors, trade creditors, consumers and the state (for unpaid tax liabilities).[121]

With regard to adjusting creditors, theory states out that they are able to contract optimally for themselves. For this class of creditors, the legal capital rules could only have a limited impact on optimal contracting. Legal rules will not be able to substitute creditors' scrutiny and negotiation, because each borrower firm has a different debtor that needs specific covenants. There is no one single optimal solution, or any economies of scale, that would require regulation to take on the role of standardising contracts, thereby reducing transaction costs.

Protecting non-adjusting creditors, however, who are not able to contract optimally for themselves, may well be justified on efficiency grounds.

As for trade creditors, some may have bargaining power and thus be able to mend the terms of contract. Others, however, are likely to be small suppliers or retailers who are 'forced' to enter into contract with the economically more powerful counterparty without being able to negotiate and optimise the terms of contract.

---

[121] See Armour, J. (2006), 'Legal Capital Requirements: An Outdated Concept?' *European Business Organization Law Review*, vol. 7, no. 1, p. 5.

In the case of non-adjusting creditors there are two potential market failures: one is information asymmetry; the other is market power.[122]

Involuntary (tort) creditors are virtually always unable to adjust the terms of becoming creditors of the firm, as they do not even have the choice over becoming so. They suffer damage due to the activity of the firm without necessarily being able to avoid such a situation. Looking at it from the perspective of equity, it needs little explanation why tort creditors should be protected from firms pursuing hazardous activities with virtually no capitalisation. The question here is: will legal capital rules, introduced to address the problem of tort creditors have more benefits than costs?[123] Or would the policy maker be ready to trade-off some economic advantages for more equitable distributive outcomes?

Existing literature examines the effectiveness and efficiency of existing legal capital rules. Here the analysis will launch a simple theoretical inquiry: Can legal capital rules be designed in such a way that they achieve their goal, even under decentralised competences with at least two different sets of legal rules and free choice or mobility between them?

The affected constituencies are:

- *Start-up firms' shareholders and managers (*shareholders and managers of start-ups are assumed to be either the same persons, or to be affected in the same way): start-up firms will bear the costs of legal capital rules, as access to limited liability becomes more expensive. Depending on the exact amount mandated, some entrepreneurs may find these costs prohibitive and refrain from establishing a new firm. The creation of start-ups benefits the economy through higher innovation and entrepreneurship; losing start-up firms is thus a cost to the economy. Those firms that do incorporate regardless of capital rules will bear the monetary costs of the rule.

---

[122] It can be argued of course that trade creditors also have freedom of contracting and so even if they cannot amend the terms, they always have the freedom not to enter into a contract. But if competition is fierce enough at the level of suppliers, while the customer is enjoying considerable market power, competitor suppliers will take the business opportunities from suppliers. They are thus forced to enter into sub-optimal contracts on which they may well lose out, decreasing their profit margins for the gain of the contractual counter party with market power.

[123] It should be noted that here the definition of utilities is determinative of the result. If utilities are understood to include equity for example, the answer to this question will be different from the case of measuring mere monetary benefits.

- *Shareholders of established firms*: shareholders are assumed to be affected negatively, since (effective) capital maintenance rules will imply that certain distributions cannot be made to shareholders.
- *Adjusting creditors*: As explained above, theory tells us that adjusting creditors do not benefit but probably they remain largely unaffected by legal capital rules.
- *Non-adjusting creditors*: This group benefits from legal capital provisions, as they cannot themselves contract optimally. It is possible to speculate about further distinctions between non-adjusting creditors of big firms and smaller start-ups (for example, in terms of hazardous activities, established firms are more likely to inflict damage and they are likely to inflict greater damage than start-ups), but for the purposes of this analysis these differences will not be considered. However the amount of capital mandated will be a crucial determinant of the magnitude of benefits for non-adjusting creditors. In a cost-benefit analysis this aspect would require probably the most attention.[124] The aim here however is not to carry out a cost-benefit analysis of a given jurisdiction's applicable legal capital rules, but instead to look at the potential effects of competitive interactions between two hypothetical jurisdictions.

5.4 Two Jurisdictions with Different Rules

There are different potential reasons why two jurisdictions would set different legal capital rules.

Scenario 1: One possibility is that country A has more creditors, and country B has more entrepreneurs. Country A will therefore set higher creditor protection rules, whereas country B will try to enhance its firms' competitiveness, and will thus impose negative external impacts, if its firms have foreign creditors from country A, through international trade or secondary establishment. This scenario may sound highly hypothesised, and yet the Centros case of the Court of Justice discussed this issue.

---

[124] The extent of the benefits flowing to non-adjusting creditors will of course depend on the actual design of the rules and the amount of minimum capital and capital to be retained. Similarly the extent of costs borne by the above two constituencies will be determined by the very same legal design. The trade-off is thus between more entrepreneurship and higher promise of innovation on the one hand and a higher level of creditor protection on the other hand.

Scenario 2: Another possible cause of different regulations is the heterogeneity of regulatees between the two jurisdictions. If the utilities of creditors derived from legal capital protection is lower in B than in A, the latter will optimally set lower capital requirements. But firms' negative utility from capital rules may also be different. Such differences may derive from market features, such as the ease of financing start-ups, or from the different preferences of society with regard to the state's role in protecting individuals participating in markets.

Scenario 3: A reason behind regulatory differences may also come from regulators' different perceptions or motivations, that ultimately lead to different outputs, even if the markets (creditor/entrepreneur balance) and regulatees' utilities are exactly the same in the two countries. This can happen if there are information problems or lobby influence on decision-makers. In this case, it is likely that at least one, but maybe both, legal rules are suboptimal. This latter scenario may also arise when decentralised legal actors engage in parallel experimentation, and identify different theories of efficiency to explain and guide their policies. It was already noted earlier that there are different theories of corporate governance, and no one theory has been ultimately proclaimed as the only valid or most efficient framework.

Let us assume that two jurisdictions set the following rules: (A) a given level of legal capital rules; (B) no legal capital rules. The jurisdiction with capital rules sees the following costs and benefits accruing for different stakeholder groups from its introduction of minimum capital requirements and capital maintenance rules:[125]

- Start-ups (including costs to society as some firms will not be established at all):[126] –10

---

[125] Values assigned to each stakeholder group's losses and benefits are merely fictive examples in order to allow us to follow what changes under different scenarios.

[126] Assigning a real value to constrained or facilitated entrepreneurship is an exercise that not only involves a debate on measuring utilities and making interpersonal comparisons, but also requires the assessment of a quite complex sequence of indirect impacts.

- Established firms' shareholders: –5
- Non-adjusting creditors: +20.

The benefits to non-adjusting creditors, as well as the opportunity costs to society for giving up some start-up firms, are hard to measure in monetary terms, and indeed all of the assigned values depend on which one of the above three scenarios we follow.

Under the first scenario, where one jurisdiction has more creditors and the other has more entrepreneurs, the overall costs and benefits may differ simply because of the higher number of individuals (respectively creditors or entrepreneurs) in each jurisdiction. That means that individual creditors' utilities are the same in country A and country B, but the total of their utilities will be higher in A than in B.

Under the second scenario, however, it is individual creditors' and entrepreneurs' utilities[127] that are different in the two jurisdictions, not necessarily their numbers. In a jurisdiction with a preference for creditor protection, the assessed benefits for creditors may well be higher than the perceived costs for firms and their stakeholders.

However, under scenario three, the actual utilities (of entrepreneurs and of creditors respectively) are the same across the two jurisdictions, but the regulator does not perceive them as such. In this latter scenario, both regulators think that the assigned values (costs and benefits) are correct, but they do not agree on these values.

Let us now assume that jurisdiction B (under any of the above three scenarios) would perceive the following costs and benefits from the rules A introduced:

- Start-ups: –15
- Established firms' shareholders: –5
- Non-adjusting creditors: +10

It is clear then that jurisdiction B will set a different level of minimum capital requirements than those optimal in A, perhaps even abolish minimum capital rules altogether. The optimal policy choice for the two jurisdictions will be different. The (perceived) optimal legal capital rule

---

[127] More precisely, it is the aggregate or average utilities of the two groups that differ across jurisdictions, depending on how the decision-maker within each jurisdiction measures and aggregates utilities – see discussion about the measurement of welfare in Chapter 1.

for jurisdiction A is 'a given level of legal capital' whereas the (perceived) optimal rules in B are no legal capital rules at all.[128] As scenario three presumes that the regulator does not always have perfect information, and can therefore be wrong about the exact utilities, we should add the adjective 'perceived' to all values and optimal rules discussed here, when thinking about the possibility of scenario three. This will not be done in each and every case, but the reader is invited to keep this in mind throughout this example.

The distributional effects of their choices are displayed in Table 2.2.

Table 2.2 Optimal legal capital rules in two jurisdictions with different preferences

Jurisdiction A – Creditor Protection Preference – Given X Level of Legal Capital Rules			
Benefits		**Costs**	
Non-adjusting creditors	+ 20	Start-ups	–10
		Established firms' shareholders	–5
Jurisdiction B – Entrepreneurship Preference – No Legal Capital Rules			
Benefits		**Costs**	
Start-ups*	15	Non-adjusting creditors	–15
Established firms' shareholders	5		

Note: *Here the benefits from start-ups are valued higher than in jurisdiction A, and thus the figure is higher (15) than in the other jurisdiction's table (–10).

[128] For the sake of simplicity, it is assumed here that B will not introduce any legal capital rules at all. It would also be reasonable to assume that B simply introduces a lower level of (less stringent) legal capital provisions. The impact on the *direction* of costs and benefits (externalities across stakeholder groups) would be comparable. However, such a solution would risk being ineffective in its aim of protecting creditors, and thus it may be reasonable to ask whether the remaining lower level of obligations is worth maintaining at all as it imposes costs on firms, while it does little to protect creditors. Indeed, a detailed cost benefit analysis may show that such rules are only effective at either of the two ends of the scale: with a high degree of capital rules, achieving real creditor protection; or at a zero level of capital rules, achieving stimulation of entrepreneurship.

5.5 Can Free Choice of Regimes Work?

This section will briefly analyse the efficiency of a theoretical free choice of law setting. Let us assume that both jurisdictions described above grant free choice of law to companies.

Under the first and third scenarios of the causes of legal differences, regulatory arbitrage may emerge, whereas, under Scenario 2, the preferences or utilities of firms in the two jurisdictions are different, and so are consumers' preferences, which may mean that the different rules represent an equilibrium (or at least that fewer firms would opt out of its original regime).

In order to know where the legal arbitrage of firms would lead to, we would have to know also whether there is a possibility of signalling quality to creditors, or whether creditors are ultimately and clearly in an inferior bargaining position.

If we acknowledge the possibility of signalling and the heterogeneity of regulatees with regard to their preferences in each jurisdiction, then hypothetically we would observe three types of legal arbitrage:

1. Those who opt into lower capital requirements because they do not have any non-adjusting trade or tort creditors (because they have a different business model and conduct a non-hazardous activity). These firms might trigger a race to lower requirements (race in laxity) among legal actors, but without imposing externalities, thus this is optimal, no race to the bottom.
2. Those that opt for higher capital requirements to signal to business partners/consumers their ability to compensation for possible damages (signalling). These firms may start a race in stringency among legal actors, leading to optimal welfare outcomes, that is, a race to the top
3. Those that opt into lower capital requirements, regardless of the fact that they have potential future non-adjusting creditors. These firms are externalising costs on these creditors, which may then lead a race to the bottom (a race not only towards laxity but also towards lower overall welfare implications).[129]

Without discussing in detail why a firm may want to signal creditworthiness to *non-adjusting* creditors, a few examples should be mentioned.

[129] As always overall welfare measures necessitate a correct measurement of welfare with interpersonal comparisons of utility, which will not be detailed further in this study.

First, potential reasons may be linked to product market competition. Fierce competition in the market might mean that firms can find their niche in the market by offering reliable after sales service to consumers backed by (legally enforceable) minimum capital pledge in case of the firm's bankruptcy (for example, reparation of long endurance goods with high service costs included in the sales price). Corporate social responsibility in the case of hazardous activities is another channel through which firms may be induced to use signalling of such kind. Finally, trade creditors as non-adjusting creditors may trust certain legal forms more than others if those provide for minimum capital requirements. The same rationale can also imply that trade creditors may distrust certain foreign incorporated businesses even in Member States where minimum capital rules are in place. This attitude is rational if the information costs about the foreign business form are high. In other words, a trade creditor would be less willing to do business with a foreign legal form business, for example, as long as its national law protects him and he cannot get or cannot afford to get information about the foreign legal provisions governing the firm. This effect may limit the incentives of firms to incorporate in a low legal capital regime, and may increase the power of signalling.[130]

However, if there is no quality signalling and non-adjusting creditors cannot (as the name of this category of actors already suggests) identify and avoid the firms that impose externalities on them, these firms will be able to conduct a race to the bottom, opting into the rules that are at lowest cost to them due to externalising part of the costs. The free choice regime of regulatory competition will thus lead to a suboptimal welfare outcome where the jurisdiction with preference for creditor protection cannot have such rules effectively in place.

A couple of clarifications are of course called for here. First, it is implicit that firms opting into one jurisdiction's legal regime can (continue to) conduct their business in the other country. Secondly, a

---

130 The issue of signalling to creditors is close to the discussion about who should be entitled to choose the applicable legal regime by way of choice or mobility. If creditors are empowered to choose, the outcome of regulatory competition will of course be completely different, than if choice is put into the hands of firms. It would be rational for non-adjusting creditors to do business with highly capitalised firms obliged by law to maintain their legal capital, unless the efficiency of production in that firm is negatively affected and the non-adjusting creditor bears the ultimate costs of that (e.g. consumers, or trade creditors who are in a vertical chain and whose profits may depend on the competitiveness of the firm they trade with).

distinction has to be drawn between actors who are disadvantaged by the rules and overall negative welfare implications. Creditors may be disadvantaged, for example, in the second jurisdiction where society overall has a preference for entrepreneurship, and thus capital rules are abolished, without necessarily compensating the creditors for this in practice, even if overall welfare is increased within the society (distributional impacts). Overall negative implications for welfare may occur in the first jurisdiction where compensating creditors is more relevant than entrepreneurship (be it due to preferences, a higher number of creditors, and so on).[131]

Also, the potential arbitrage of firms is only a first step towards a competitive framework. In a dynamic setting, jurisdictions will respond to the changing market reality. Indeed, there are cases in which a jurisdiction having a preference for creditor protection will decide to abolish minimum capital rules in the face of regulatory competition acting through the mobility of firms. Under conditions of no choice or mobility across jurisdictions the policy maker in such a jurisdiction should opt to introduce the right level of legal capital provisions.

But there are two ways in which this policy choice may be altered by opening up borders to firms: first, if the group benefiting from attracting more firms into the jurisdiction gains more than creditors lose by not having legal capital rules in place; and secondly, if there is a competitor jurisdiction that has already abolished minimum capital requirements. In the former case, attracting firms may benefit the domestic legal professions, such as lawyers and legal advisors, notaries, the incorporations house, and so on.[132] As Table 2.3 shows, the policy makers in such a case would face a situation where simply adding up costs and benefits would prompt them to abandon minimum capital requirements.

---

[131] It is worth noting here that externalities and negative welfare outcomes can arise not only due to different preferences (such as political orientation towards a social or liberal model), but also as a result of differences in certain features among jurisdictions, such as the number and relative weight of creditors versus firms. It is possible to imagine that in a small open market economy a relatively small number of creditors and firms are present, but these few firms may be active in foreign markets and thus 'create' creditors there. By abolishing minimum capital rules, the home country may externalise the negative impacts on other jurisdictions' creditors.

[132] 'Realising' that there are benefits to these groups can also turn into regulatory capture by these interest groups, as a result of which the decision-maker will assign higher value to their gains when balancing it against losses to other stakeholder groups.

Table 2.3 Optimal legal capital rules where there is cross-border competition

Jurisdiction B – Creditor Protection Preference + Costs/Benefits on Legal Actors – No Legal Capital Rules			
Benefits		**Costs**	
Start-ups	+10	Non-adjusting creditors	–20
Established firms' shareholders	+5		
Legal advisors (attracting foreign firms)	+6		

If the legal advisors' gains are indeed higher than the difference, there is no capture. It is, from an overall welfare perspective, more efficient not to have legal capital rules.[133] However, there are clear distributive impacts that the national policy maker should deal with.[134] An additional gain on the side of the legal advisors may thus flip the decision in favour of abolishing or not adopting measures on capital. However, if the gain by legal advisors is less, and does not compensate for the difference between creditor loss and start-up and shareholder gain, abolishing the legal capital rules would be the result of regulatory capture, rather than an optimalised policy decision.

[133] Here we are talking about Kaldor-Hicks efficiency. Whether the creditors can be compensated for their loss, and whether they should be, is not discussed here. In any case, Pareto optimality (someone is better off without anyone being worse off) cannot be defined here, as the starting point is not defined – on purpose – in this hypothetical exercise. The reason behind that choice is that the current legal rules necessarily reflect an earlier policy choice. If a country has provisions on legal capital and then considers abolishing them under the principle of not making anyone worse off, this will hardly be possible. However, if we look back even further in history to the time when there were no legal capital rules, the same principle will mean that the policy maker would have been prevented from introducing legal capital rules in the first place, as it makes start-ups less likely (and through them society as a whole somewhat worse off).

[134] The magnitude of costs and benefits is not examined here as the figures are merely illustrative, but it is likely that the benefits derived by legal advisors in any jurisdiction can only outweigh otherwise significant benefits to creditors if there are few creditors within the country and/or there are a lot of legal advisors with a large capacity to attract large numbers of foreign firms. It is often argued in regulatory and tax competition literature that small states can more easily become competitive as they can externalise costs to bigger countries with masses of losing stakeholders, such as creditors in this case.

A second reason why jurisdictions with a creditor protection preference may change their optimal policy choice under regulatory competition is the presence of a competitor jurisdiction with laxer, or no, legal capital rules. If jurisdiction B is already offering a regime without capital rules (as the section above predicts) and firms from A are free to switch governing law, A will have – in the extreme case of assuming no transaction costs for changing legal regime, no signalling incentives for firms, and rational behaviour – a payoff structure within its borders that will be the same as if it abolished its own rules, since firms will, under such assumptions, leave the jurisdiction. At this point, the decision-maker in A may want to consider the costs or benefits accruing to its own national legal advisors and, perhaps, the advantage for local creditors of reduced transaction costs if they can contract with firms governed by national law (language, court system's familiarity with the rules, enforcement, and so on). Decision-maker A might consider actually repealing its capital rules and trying to retain domestic firms (prevent their incorporation under another law).[135] The following cost/ benefit table will apply.

Table 2.4 Costs and benefits of a jurisdiction with creditor protection preference choosing not to introduce minimum capital requirements

Jurisdiction A – Creditor Protection Preference + Costs/Benefits on Other Legal Actors in a Dynamic Setting – No Legal Capital Rules			
Benefits		**Costs**	
Start-ups	+ 10	Non-adjusting creditors	–20
Established firms' shareholders	+ 5		
Legal advisors (retaining domestic firms)	+ 1		

[135] Note that under this scenario, the state would be better off with higher standard rules on legal capital, were it not for the competitive pressure coming from the other Member State (a dynamic scenario of regulatory competition). However that solution is no longer possible due to competitive pressures, which ultimately leads to a race to the bottom (lower overall welfare than without competition).

It is clear from the example that here the costs outweigh the benefits, but the only alternative for jurisdiction A would be to introduce the legal capital rules but without any of its benefits, as according to our assumption all firms will migrate to B. Thus, the only difference in the above figures would be the loss of what domestic legal advisors could gain from retaining home companies (in the example this is equal to 1).

In other words, introducing costless mobility or choice for firms will render the otherwise optimal policy choice of jurisdiction A ineffective. B will impose an overall negative externality on A, which consists of a positive externality of 15 for A's start-ups and shareholders, and a negative externality of 20 for A's non-adjusting creditors. The response of state A, to abolish its own legal capital rules, will in return mean that B is losing some benefits from its rule as A retains its home companies.[136]

This demonstrates also the differences in the pay-offs for countries that aim to actively attract incorporations and those considering legislative amendments in order to retain companies.

It is also important, however, to point out that once mobility of firms, and thus the possibility of competition for incorporations, is introduced, the choice to abolish minimum capital requirements is efficient under the definition of Kaldor-Hicks efficiency, although it clearly hurts tort creditors, therefore not being Pareto superior to the scenario of no regulatory competition.

6. CONCLUSIONS

6.1 Factors Influencing the Emergence, Dynamics and Welfare Implications of Regulatory Competition

As this chapter argued, the analysis of the emergence, dynamics and welfare implications of regulatory competition in the field of company law in Europe requires the assessment of the specific European legal features that determine the framework for competition, and distinguish it from the one observed in the case of American corporate law.

---

[136] At this point of course if all Member States abolish their capital rules, B may no longer have any benefit from having no capital rules, but will no longer have real possibility to introduce them, which is a sort of race to the bottom, sub-optimal regulatory outcome. However for such situations to arise the pay-off structure of jurisdictions has to be very specific.

In the European system of corporate governance, where dispersed shareholders control the firm over the continental European system of corporate governance,[137] the limits of cross-referencing across the two systems[138] also means that, even if one system moves away from legal solutions that are considered to be welfare enhancing in the other system, it does not necessarily signal a welfare-destroying race to the bottom.

Arguably, another main feature distinguishing the welfare implications of the European model of regulatory competition from that in the US is *legal and cultural/linguistic diversity*. The different cultural, social and political backgrounds of the European Member States result in greater diversity in preferences for what constitutes optimal regulation. Based on the predictions of the original Tiebout model, this higher divergence of preferences will therefore increase the benefits from regulatory competition that leads to perfect sorting. Thus, regulatory competition in Europe might yield even higher benefits than in the United States.[139]

6.2 The Behaviour of Different Legal Actors

It has been argued in this section that the incentives of legal actors are determinative of the outcome. The various legal actors that are present in company law regulation arguably have different incentives and thus they decide the question on design of mobility – as a pre-determinant of regulatory competition – in different ways. In company law the two most involved actors are the courts and legislators, both at European and at national level; but the role of the private regulator is also an interesting question in this context.

6.2.1 Courts

Currently, the decision as to which norms are excluded from competition under the imperative public policy exemption lies with the courts: the national courts and, ultimately, the ECJ are the actors who can determine whether a given issue constitutes imperative public policy and is therefore sheltered from regulatory competition, or not. Therefore, the national courts and ultimately the ECJ play a crucial role in setting the limits of competitive interaction.

---

[137] La Porta, R. et al. (2000), 'Investor Protection and Corporate Governance', *Journal of Financial Economics*, vol. 58, no. 1–2, pp. 3–27.

[138] See Bratton and McCahery (1999).

[139] Dammann, J. (2003), *The US Concept of Granting Corporations Free Choice among State Corporate Law Regimes as a Model for the European Community* available at: http://ssrn.com/abstract=418660.

The national courts may have an incentive to establish a very broad, European welfare concept in their case law and become the leaders in open system legal thinking, or they may have an incentive to increase their independence and develop a strong stance on the national features of their jurisdictions' rules. Thus they could theoretically take both the position of market opening and cooperation with the ECJ and the position of strengthening their autonomy by defending the national legal system from external influences. There are examples of both attitudes.

The European Court of Justice can be characterised as the most significant driver of market opening in this field. The Court has been exerting its influence in waves, alternating opening decisions with slow-down checks on the liberalisation process. The latest Cartesio decision displays both features of liberalisation and of setting limits to law shopping. The ECJ's place at the top of the legal hierarchy in deciding the institutional design of regulatory competition would seem to indicate a strong liberalisation direction.

6.2.2 The legislators

The national legislators are by nature responsible to their national electorate and, under different theoretical assumptions, they will act either in the best interest of their constituencies (in a perfect democratic decision-making situation), in the interest of the strongest national interest group (in a capture situation), or perhaps the agency problems created by the bureaucracy will impede them from pursuing either of the above goals effectively.

The European legislator can however occupy the field and prescribe precisely what falls out of the scope of national competences. The European Commission has a power of initiative, but it is ultimately the Council and the Parliament that has the final say on the scope of liberalisation in the corporate field. Although market opening is in no way the only mandate the EU legislator has, the creation of the Internal Market is the most often used legal basis for legislative action in this field.

Thus, in conclusion, it seems that two major legal actors are the final decision-makers for the institutional frame of regulatory competition: the European Court of Justice and the European legislator, with different policy agendas with regard to market opening and the scope for regulatory competition.

6.2.3 Private regulator

It is observed in the UK that private regulation (without free choice among governing legal regimes) produced a different outcome from public regulation in the US under the forces of regulatory competition through choice of law. Especially since the two jurisdictions have rather similar models of corporate ownership, this led authors to conclude that private regulators' incentives were radically different from that of public regulators. Indeed, if we look at the channels of competitive interaction, the UK private regulatory body (the financial industry) was mainly concerned by the international flow of capital, and aimed at creating an efficient investment market or market for corporate control from the perspective of investors. The US saw a different development, where public legal actors competed over attracting regulated companies. It is also worth recalling at this point that there are different theories concerning the efficiency of corporate governance solutions. Under the managerial and stakeholder theory allocating more discretion to management is a positive development, whereas shareholder theory considers this welfare destructing. Depending on the starting point one takes with regard to these theories, the welfare outcome of regulatory competition changes.

6.2.4 Interaction among legal actors

The above analysis also extended to the potential interaction of different types of legal actors. It was observed that the competition among private regulators (as a group of legal actors with homogeneous interests across different jurisdictions) will presumably lead to different legal outcomes than regulatory competition among private regulators on the one hand and public legal actors on the other (or any other two groups of legal actors with heterogeneous interests). In a horizontal setting there is some legal change that indicates competition among national legislators (summarised in the sub-section below), and in the vertical setting the European legislator introduced legal forms for public as well as private companies that firms can opt for, creating an alternative to their national regime.

6.3 Recent Legal Changes as Trends in Competition

A look at the direction of legal change in recent years allows for some preliminary conclusions on the presence/absence and the direction of regulatory competition. In the case of private companies, the traces of price competition emerge. Public companies' regulation is less obvious, and it would seem that there is no competition in any clear direction – at least not through mobility, since for these firms mobility is probably too expensive (not so much in monetary terms but organisationally, as well as in terms of public opinion that a potential move would trigger, and so on). But a further possible explanation is that for these big firms the additional gains are marginal compared to what is at stake in terms of taxation policies, labour cost differences, and so on.

We saw also through the example of employee participation regimes that certain basic institutions that exist in some Member States, but not in others, are safeguarded, either by carve-outs or by special provisions in the legal norm that was finally adopted.

Finally, an example of the takeover regulation represents a legal outcome contrary to the European Commission's original intention. National actors were given certain options that, without coordination, naturally led to taking a defensive position, protecting national firms from takeovers by granting management wider powers to frustrate bids.

6.4 Hypothetical Competition and its Welfare Implications

Some hypothetical examples of competitive interaction among jurisdictions showed that there are circumstances under which even the perfect democratic decision-making model would fail to achieve optimal (welfare maximising) outcomes, either due to cross-border externalities and the lack of a European welfare concept at national level (national legislators remaining with national welfare concerns), or due to a dynamic interaction among Member States that eventually leads to a solution in which the welfare of all states, as well as the individual Member State, is reduced.

With regard to overall welfare implications, this chapter observed that there are different theories of efficiency in corporate governance. The methodology chosen here to deal with these differences was to observe both theories and reach conclusions about the welfare implications from the perspective of both sides. Comparing welfare effects or external effects among Member States necessitates either a choice between theories of efficiency, or accepting that different jurisdictions may adopt different theories. This study has tried to follow the second approach and observe potential differences in Member States' approaches to regulation, with possible different underlying theories on efficiency.

It was also pointed out that transplanting a legal outcome from a jurisdiction following one approach into a jurisdiction with a different approach (where legal differences are coupled with different market outcomes, such as different share ownership structures) will not necessarily achieve the same market outcome, and therefore its welfare implications are also questionable.

3. Regulatory competition in European securities law

1. INTRODUCTION

This chapter examines regulatory competition within European securities law. It starts by looking at the theory of regulation. Starting with a simplified description of what securities markets are, it explores the most common market failures that call for regulatory intervention. Different theories are described as regards these market failures and the optimal regulatory intervention to correct them (Section 2). The competent legal actors are identified in Section 3, with a discussion of the new supervisory authority, ESMA, the comitology decision-making under the Lisbon Treaty, as well as private regulatory functions, among others. Section 4 looks into the current scope for regulatory divergence under the prospectus and market abuse regimes (including reference to the latest amendments and Commission proposals), the Transparency Directive and the Takeover Bids Directive. Section 5 reviews the available channels of competition, elaborating on the choice of law regime of securities law that allows for the accumulation of the features of all applicable regimes, and where issuers and investors (as well as intermediaries) all have some scope of choice. After the review of the current state of play, Section 6 offers a theoretical inquiry into what could be called optimal legal design in terms of arbitrage possibilities and in terms of (competitive or cooperative) regulatory interaction. Section 7 concludes.

2. WHAT ARE SECURITIES MARKETS AND WHY REGULATE THEM?

2.1 A Simplified Description of Securities Markets

Securities markets are the aggregation of transactions between issuers of securities and investors. Investors pay to buy the debt or the equity of a firm. By the nature of the legal design of debt and equity, the risk of the investment and the potential gains are different for debt holders and shareholders. While the risk-taking of both types of investor is capped,[1] the opportunities for gains make all the difference. Debt holders contract for a specified interest rate in return for their money, while shareholders contract for the residual gains of the enterprise.[2]

But investors can be distinguished also along another, perhaps even more relevant, axis: their sophistication in finance. Institutional investors (such as financial institutions, firms, rich individuals who can pay for sophisticated and reliable financial advice) will have the means both to collect information about the investment they are considering, and to process that information to make an informed investment decision. Unsophisticated investors on the other hand (mainly households, small firms, and so on) are not well-equipped either for information gathering or detailed and precise interpretation. Institutional investors have the advantage of economies of scale, both in terms of their investment power and in terms of accumulated institutional knowledge in information processing. What is only a marginal cost to a sophisticated investor, would cost private individuals acting alone a lot of time and money, even if it could be done at all.

It is indeed difficult to speak of securities markets in the strict sense, without taking account of the features of the broader financial markets. This is because securities transactions are not so simple. Retail investors can delegate the task of gathering information, comparing investment possibilities and choosing the best investments to so-called financial intermediaries. These can be retail banks, individual financial advisors, investment firms, broker houses, and so on. Obviously, trading between institutional investors does not require financial intermediaries to assess, explain or even choose the best-suited products. Institutional actors are often engaged instead not only in the buying and selling simple securities, but in trading financial products derived from simple equities and bonds, packaged into more complex products with different features such as maturity, risk exposure, and so on. Due to these derived and packaged products, the number of participants in the financial value chain is much

---

1 The maximum amount they can lose is the amount they invest, with priorities given to debt holders in case of bankruptcy.

2 The most relevant implication of this difference is that the incentives of the two groups can become misaligned. While shareholders should rationally have a tendency to higher risk taking as they can possibly benefit from the eventual success of a high-risk-high-return venture, creditors cannot gain anything by it, but they might lose out if the venture fails. A further difference is that shareholders receive voting rights (control rights) over the firm, while debt holders cannot take part to the same extent in corporate decision-making.

bigger than in a simple model of investors and issuers interacting on the securities markets.

Securities markets bring together issuers and investors in a common market place, where individual transactions are aggregated into a large market, which has the advantages of market mechanisms for processing information about price discovery, execution, liquidity, and so on.

Securities markets are subject to market failures, however. The challenge from the regulatory perspective is to decide whether and how to address those failures in order to achieve optimal outcomes in these markets.

The market failures surrounding transactions in securities are summarised in section 2.2, and the role of financial markets is presented in section 2.3. Finally, the different theories of financial structures and efficient regulatory intervention within the economy are reviewed in sections 2.4 and 2.5.

2.2 Market Failures Surrounding Transactions in Securities

2.2.1 The nature of financial transactions

The products offered in financial markets are greatly diversified. An important feature of securities markets is that there is constant product innovation. Investors can chose to invest directly into a single type of share or debt instrument, but they can also put their money into more complex derivative instruments. Besides, investors can decide to invest their money into one or more funds. These different types of financial products are often in direct competition with each other from the investor's perspective. While direct investment into a single share, for example, implies a contractual relationship between the shareholder and the company, more often money is put into more complex structures, often after a process of intermediation between the investor and the issuer of these financial products.

Both simple and complex financial transactions can be thought of as incomplete contracts, the value of which is partly determined by the behaviour of the supplier after the point of purchase.[3] This raises two problems. First, the issuer of the financial product or the financial intermediary has an incentive for opportunistic behaviour after selling the

[3] 'Two obvious examples are where an investment manager (e.g. a pension fund) turns out to be incompetent or even corrupt, and where a financial institution becomes insolvent while having fiduciary commitments to its customers.' Llewellyn, D. (1999), 'The Economic Rationale for Financial Regulation', *FSA Occasional Papers in Financial Regulation*, at p. 37.

product. Secondly, related to this opportunism, the consumer is unable to predict what the behaviour of the issuer/financial intermediary will be, and hence what the value of the offered contract is.

Due to these informational problems in financial contracts, and the uncertainties deriving from them, the consumer incurs the following transaction costs (assuming away existing facilitative legal rules):

- search costs (to find alternative products, and identify which one is suitable);
- bargaining and decision costs (agreeing on the terms of the contract);
- monitoring and verification costs (when the value of the contract depends on the post-contract behaviour of the supplier, the buyer has to monitor his behaviour in order to determine the ultimate value of the contract; information disclosure also needs to be verified);
- enforcement costs (to ensure correct delivery on the contract);
- redress costs (if there is no correct delivery).[4]

Due to the high transaction costs, consumers are not able to obtain full information on competing products in the market and, therefore, competition will be limited due to these information problems. Moreover, consumers, with their uninformed choice, may be locked in to contracts with potentially high switching costs. These problems are described below in more detail.

2.2.2 The nature of financial products and services

According to the categorisation created by Nelson,[5] goods can be divided into three kinds according to the transaction costs they impose on consumers. We can distinguish between: *search goods*, the quality of which consumers can promptly identify at low cost before purchase; and *experience goods*, which includes goods that consumers buy frequently so that they experience their quality through use. Tirole[6] identifies the incentives of firms to supply higher quality to be the main determinant in describing how the market for experience goods functions. Finally a further category of *credence goods*, reveal their quality only after or over

---

[4] Llewellyn (1999) at p. 35.

[5] Nelson, P. (1970), 'Information and Consumer Behaviour', *Journal of Political Economy*, vol. 78, no. 2.

[6] Tirole, J. (1988), *The Theory of Industrial Organisation* (Cambridge, MA: MIT Press).

a long time period, or imply substantial costs to ascertain their quality *ex ante*. Financial services in most cases and for most consumers belong to this category of credence goods.

2.2.3 Monitoring problems

As already referred to above, investors face significant monitoring problems, when buying financial products. To obtain and assess the information necessary for an ongoing monitoring activity, each investor would have to become a financial expert and spend time on information gathering and processing continuously throughout the time of their investment. Since there are (at least in retail markets) several investors buying the same product, significant economies of scale can arise from centralising monitoring activities in the hands of a single person or entity, saving each individual consumer from an unnecessary duplication of this work.

In this sense, centralised monitoring saves costs, but it also necessarily raises an agency problem between the monitor and the investors. This agency problem will vary according to the monitoring arrangement in place, the person or entity performing the task and their relationship with the investors, the issuer of the financial products in question, and other market participants.

2.2.4 Adverse selection and moral hazard

Firms complying with stricter requirements have higher compliance costs. But since consumers cannot reliably assess the quality of products, financial firms are in competition with other firms based solely on product or service prices. This raises the problem of adverse selection, because consumers will select the products with the lowest price, driving firms with high legal compliance costs out of the market despite their better quality.

In anticipation of adverse selection, a moral hazard problem will also present itself. This means that firms will have an incentive to lower prices even at the expense of safety and soundness, in order to stay in competition,[7] or, in other words, they will not have incentives to invest into the quality of the product if that increases their costs but does not gain them a bigger market share or investor base. This has an impact on competition in the market.

---

[7] Goodhart argues, for example, that adverse selection and moral hazard can occur for example in the banking sector as competitive conditions may induce banks to excessive risk taking: Goodhart, C. et al. (1998), *Financial Regulation: Why, How and Where Now?* (London: Routledge).

For example, since consumers have asymmetric information, firms offering financial products or services will typically compete on prices rather than quality. Financial intermediaries cannot, given the information problems described above, signal the quality of their services (through the prudence of the firm) to consumers. On the one hand, firms might be reluctant to disclose information but, on the other hand, even when they disclose it, consumers might not be able to interpret it correctly.

2.2.5 Investor confidence – 'lemons problem'

In a market for financial products where consumers face unmitigated informational and monitoring problems, the risk of bad (uninformed) choice and firm failure will necessarily undermine consumer confidence and lead to lower demand in the market. Lost consumer confidence and the resulting drop in demand is viewed as a clear cost. But it is also commonly accepted, that the 'lemons problem'[8] damages issuers and financial intermediaries as well through its negative effect on consumer demand, thus implying overall sub-optimal welfare effects for the entire economy and all stakeholders.

2.2.6 Interconnected markets and systemic risk

A brief account of major market features has to make reference to systemic risks, as a very specific feature of financial markets, which can have a strong impact on the external effects of regulatory competition. Only a few major characteristics of financial transactions have been listed above, at a very abstract, theoretical level. It would be wrong to claim that these features taken together, will lead straight to interconnected markets with systemic risks. The aim here is not to enter into a detailed analysis of the economics of complex international financial markets and give a detailed account of how risk can spread, and the difference between individual and systemic risk. This would be beyond the reach of this book, as it would require much lengthier analysis and discussion.[9]

Without going into the specific details of what causes systemic risks, we can establish that these risks will indeed arise from the interconnected nature of financial transactions and financial market actors. Products sold and bought carry in them inherent risks of default of counterparties,

---

[8] 'Lemons' originally referred to second-hand car markets, where purchasers discovered defaults only after the transaction.

[9] For an overview of the recent financial crisis and suggested reforms see e.g. Acharya, V.V. et al. (2009), 'Regulating Systemic Risk', in Acharya, V.V. and Richardson, M. (eds) *Restoring Financial Stability: How to Repair a Failed System* (Hoboken, NJ: Wiley), p. 283.

actors whose solvency itself depends on further actor's ability to perform. In a multiple web of counterparty risks, it becomes very difficult to predict what effect the default of any single actor will have on the other actors and how this effect will spiral down to further actors, ultimately affecting the entire market.

2.3 The Efficient Market Theory Underpinning Regulation, its Limits and its Critics

2.3.1 The role of financial markets and theories of information efficiency

Before considering what kind of regulation would best address the problems described above, we should first explore the economic theories describing the efficiency or failure of markets.

The role of financial markets is to facilitate the processing of information by individual parties otherwise not being able to price financial products precisely. Information efficiency theories need to be briefly recalled here to explain the role and potential of securities markets but only a brief summary is presented of what is a substantial and complex economic and legal literature.

There are three forms of market efficiency in financial markets: *allocative efficiency*, which ensures that funds flow to the highest return (risk-adjusted) projects; *operational efficiency*, that means transactions are timely and cost effective; and *information efficiency,* which ensures that the market price reflects all the relevant information for the pricing of a security. Here, the latter aspect, information efficiency[10] will be further examined, as this is one of the underlying determinants of the theory of regulation in this area.

> Primarily, the term 'efficiency' is used to describe a market in which relevant information is impounded into the price of financial assets ... The weak form efficient market hypothesis claims that prices fully reflect the information implicit in the sequence of past prices. This means that by looking at historical data only, no one can make investments with abnormal returns. The semi-strong form market efficiency of the hypothesis asserts that prices reflect all relevant information that is publicly available, meaning that based on publicly available information, no investor can beat the market and earn consistently higher than average profits.

---

[10] Fama, Eugene F. (1970), 'Efficient Capital Markets: A Review of Theory and Empirical Work', *The Journal of Finance*, vol. 25, no. 2, pp. 383–417.

> Finally the strong form of market efficiency asserts that all information known to any market participant is reflected in market prices.[11]

This means that no one, not even an insider, can earn abnormal returns based on any private information. The efficient market hypothesis predicts that even if information is *not* immediately and freely available to all market participants, the market will act *as if* it were.[12]

The theory of market efficiency is a starting point for normative regulatory design. Strong form market efficiency would mean that even uninformed investors could rely on the price information of the securities they buy. The semi-strong form of market efficiency means that investors in general, and unsophisticated investors in particular, may not be informed of certain, insider-type information. The weak form of market efficiency is even more irrelevant in terms of investor-issuer information asymmetries, and does not have major implications for the reduction of this information gap.

Academic and empirical research has not so far managed to establish with certainty what category describes our financial markets best. It is most likely that the semi-strong market efficiency theory is closest to the truth, at least in the case of the most developed financial markets, such as that of the US or the UK. In the EU context, there are no clear labels either, but less developed financial markets (for example, those of Central-Eastern European countries) are likely to be less efficient than those of Western Europe. What we can conclude from this brief overview is, first, that we cannot measure market efficiency with absolute precision, and secondly, that the choice of a desired level of market efficiency may also have implications for the appropriate level of regulatory intervention in addressing information asymmetries – and thus determine how competition among regulators is evaluated.

2.3.2 Efficient markets do not equal investor protection

Although increased market efficiency undoubtedly brings benefits, it is worth restating what those benefits are and considering whether a fully efficient financial market (if that could be achieved at all) would solve all the problems investors currently face in this area. Indeed, one of the main limitations on what efficient markets can deliver lies with human beings acting on these financial markets with sometimes (or often) irrational

---

[11] Dimson, E. and Mussavian, M. (1998), 'A Brief History of Market Efficiency', *European Financial Management*, vol. 4. no. 1, p. 91.

[12] Gilson, R.J. and Kraakman, R.H. (1984), 'The Mechanisms of Market Efficiency', *Virginia Law Review*, vol. 70, p. 549.

pricing behaviour. If the stocks are not priced according to their strictly calculated fundamental value (discounted future earnings) but according to individuals' perceptions about how others do and will value the stock, (expected price changes in the future), the information efficiency of financial markets cannot deliver huge benefits. Critiques of the efficient market as an ultimate policy objective argue that there is evidence for irrational pricing behaviour, which explains for example speculative bubbles and over-volatility.[13] Considering the above, Stout concludes that 'prices that are a timely index of psychological phenomena contribute nothing to the quest for the more efficient allocation of resources'.[14]

A further warning attached to the pursuit of efficient financial markets is that information efficiency prevents anyone from consistently beating the market. This means that those investors who are less strategic in their investment choice cannot be consistently 'beaten by the market'. But this does not mean that investors cannot lose money on an investment. Investments, by definition, contain some risk, and investors need to understand the risks they take. Also, financial markets are not simple product markets. Investors need to understand the products they buy. Often they need to call on expert third parties to provide them with objective advice on what to buy. Financial intermediation is an essential tool for boosting market confidence and efficient resource allocation.

In this complex world, efficient financial markets will not mean that investors will not lose money due to poor choice of product or poor timing of buy and sale. Indeed consumer protection rules are most often defined as a much higher standard than protecting ignorant investors from being *consistently* beaten by the market.

Stout even points out that unsophisticated retail investors do not benefit much from efficient markets as long as inefficiency does not lead to higher market volatility or reduced average returns. This is because, in an inefficient market, on average the investor will just as often find himself buying an overvalued stock as an undervalued one.[15] On the other hand, in such inefficient markets, some of the more sophisticated traders may

---

[13] See Stout, L.A. (1988) 'The Unimportance of Being Efficient: An Economic Analysis of Stock Market Pricing and Securities Regulation', *Michigan Law Review*, vol. 87, no. 3, pp. 613–709, referring to Schiller, R.J. (1981), 'Do Stock Prices Move too Much to be Justified by Subsequent Changes in Dividends?', *American Economic Review*, vol. 71, p. 421.

[14] Stout (1988), p. 198.

[15] Stout (1988) p. 700; quoting in part Benston (1973), 'Required Disclosure and the Stock Market: An Evaluation of the Securities Exchange Act of 1934', *American Economic Review*, vol. 63, p. 132.

be able to exploit their advantages and select the undervalued stocks – which leaves the retail investor with more probability of buying an overvalued stock than an undervalued one. Nonetheless, Stout's point about the difference between market inefficiency and inappropriate retail investor choices is worth keeping in mind.

These reminders are a warning that the goal of informational efficiency should not be understood as a panacea for the sources of other types of market failure (such as irrational behaviour) and that it should not be confused with consumer/investor protection, if the latter is defined as a higher standard than merely assuring fair play markets.

2.3.3 Rational actor theories questioning efficient markets

With the financial crisis starting out in 2007–08, many academics started to question the efficient market hypothesis, or, to be more precise, contesters of the hypothesis gained more voice after the crisis. These critical theories question the efficient market hypothesis, or at least reject its 'automaticism' in which competition delivers the right price or markets exert their own self-discipline. Under some rational actor models for example, it is financial intermediaries (both to retail clients and institutional investors) that stand in the way of efficient markets. They are described as acting with adverse incentives towards their ill-informed principals, the ultimate investors. These intermediaries furthermore have a limited liability,[16] which the theory predicts gives rise to moral hazard.

In a financial world of constant innovation, this setting is then predicted to result in failures when the intermediary exerts no, or not enough, effort to ascertain the robustness of a new financial product. Instead, the agent observes the product's market performance and relies on his belief that it is robust if he observes that it creates momentum. The problem with this is that such innovations may lead to bubbles, since 'one of the unusual features of a momentum strategy is that it is reinforced, rather than exhausted, by widespread adoption unlike strategies based on convergence to some stable value'.[17]

The specific theory quoted above, just like other critical theories, questions some of the basic assumptions of economics working with the concept of efficient financial markets. One such surprising tenet is that

---

16 Either legally or through a pay-off mechanism of sharing profits but not losses.

17 Woolley, P. (2011), 'Why are Financial Markets so Inefficient and Exploitative – and a Suggested Remedy', in *The Future of Finance and the Theory that Underpins it* (London: London School of Economics).

liquidity is not as desirable as under the efficient market hypothesis.[18] It is worth recalling that classical economic and policy thinking holds that liquidity is actually a good way to further efficient markets. It is thus clear that this theory, when it comes to policy implications, may be in dire conflict with the incumbent economic theory of financial markets.

2.3.4 Behavioural economic approaches to financial regulation

Behavioural economics questions the 'rationality' of actors in the classical sense, in that it does not assume perfect decisions in all circumstances. A lot of behavioural economic research explores the financial markets both at the level of agents' or intermediaries' actions[19] and at the level of consumer decision-making.[20] Recent policy initiatives start to take account of behavioural patterns, for example in the UK[21] as well as at a European level.[22] There is however no overarching theory that behavioural economics could offer to policy making, other than examining the behavioural aspects of each market, all its participants, on a case-by-case basis. Some of the established behavioural biases will be extended to new fields of financial markets, such as herding for example. But a complete theory that would describe the markets and give clear directions on their regulation has not emerged yet.[23]

---

[18] In brief, arguments are put forward that short-term oriented investment strategies make frequent trades and exchanges of assets, which, overall, do not create value, only momentum. These trades are costly, and they actually damage the end investors, benefiting only the multiple layers of counterparties and intermediaries involved in these trades. Ibid.

[19] Such as herding. See, e.g. Baddeley, M. et al. (2007), 'Herding and Social Pressure in Trading Tasks: A Behavioural Analysis', Cambridge Working Papers in Economics CWPE no. 0730.

[20] Dowling, M. and Lucey, B.M. (2005), 'The Role of Feelings in Investor Decision-Making', *Journal of Economic Surveys*, vol. 19, no. 2, pp. 211–237; Spindler, G. (2011), 'Behavioural Finance and Investor Protection Regulations', *Journal of Consumer Policy*, vol. 34, pp. 315–336.

[21] See for example Henley Center Ltd (2005), 'Towards Understanding Consumers' Needs', report prepared for the Financial Services Authority, available at: http://www.fsa.gov.uk/pubs/consumer-research/crpr35.pdf (last accessed: 6 January 2012).

[22] IFF Research and Yougov (2009), 'UCITS Disclosure Testing Research Report', report prepared for the European Commission, June 2009, available at: http://ec.europa.eu/internal_market/investment/studies_en.htm (last accessed: 6 January 2012).

[23] Murno, A (2009), *Bounded Rationality and Public Policy: A Perspective from Behavioural Economics* (Dordrecht: Springer).

The aim of the above overview is not to advocate one or another theory, but to show the multitude of theoretical perspectives on the role of financial markets, something that is fundamental to any regulatory design. An interesting aspect of legal actors' interaction is whether they follow a particular economic theory in their regulatory activity. The spread of new economic thinking can signal innovation and a learning process among legal actors along the axis of the theoretical underpinnings of policies.[24] It is often after retain shocks, such as a crisis, that so-called paradigm shifts take place. These are fundamental changes in policy and in the theory it builds on. Observing changes in policymakers' reliance on behavioural economics, or other economic theories that question the efficient market hypothesis in the wake of the financial crisis, would be an interesting exercise in this respect.

2.4 Why Regulate and How? Policy Implications of Economic Theory

Why do we need regulation? Despite the above warnings on the limits of efficient financial markets, most jurisdictions agree on the principle of striving for greater market efficiency, coupled with a notion of investor protection, even if there may be divergence as to the exact interpretation of these goals. But agreement on the principle does not always mean agreement on the details. There are several proposals about how efficient financial markets should be, and what solutions are adequate and acceptable for achieving a given level of information efficiency. The same is true for investor protection. Finally, crisis response is an interesting challenge to achieving agreement between policy makers, given that action is needed, indeed is politically expected of the most democratically accountable legal actors, but a common understanding of the roots of the problem, and how to address them, may not yet have emerged.[25]

---

[24] Dow, Sh. (2008), 'Mainstream Methodology, Financial Markets and Global Political Economy', *Contributions to Political Economy*, vol. 27, no. 1, pp. 13–29.

[25] When it comes to financial stability, there is a common understanding that action is necessary, but different solutions are possible. What makes financial stability a special concern, is that the extent of externalities is huge, the impacts of a potential financial crisis are devastating, and policy makers – as well as the general public, their electorate – are very aware of this after the crisis of 2008. Different jurisdictions have to act in a concerted manner in order to prevent loopholes that allow for risks to come through the back door. Given the unpredictable nature of systemic risks, where actors do not know where the crisis will hit hardest, but all of them are likely to be hit, incentives for coordinated

In the following section, a broad overview of the theoretical debate is given with alternative approaches to financial regulation in a number of policy areas, starting with macro-level questions on the optimal financial architecture, and going on to meso- and micro-level issues on how best to govern financial markets.

On the issue of market efficiency, there are different ways in which regulatory interventions can occur to help optimal outcomes. If strong form efficient markets do not arise spontaneously, regulation can target:

- alternative ways to develop efficient financing within the economy;
- the creation of strong form efficiency in securities markets;
- the information asymmetries that less than strong form efficient markets do not clear.

This section explores these options by (1) describing alternative theories of finance structures, (2) analysing whether and how strong form efficiency can be achieved and (3) describing contrasting theories about whether regulatory intervention should correct inefficient (less than strong-form efficient) markets by introducing mandatory rules on information disclosure.

2.4.1 Which financial structure to follow? The bank-based and market-based system debate

There are different theories of efficiency with regard to the financial structure of the economy. The two contrasting theories are the bank-based and the market-based models. The *market-based theory* of finance predicts that capital markets aggregate information and effectively transmit this information to investors, with beneficial implications for firm financing and economic performance.[26] Thus, proponents of the market-based view claim that competitive capital markets enhance economic growth and will reduce the inherent inefficiencies associated with banks.

---

action are likely to be stronger than in the case of financial market efficiency or investor protection. Note however, that the goals of efficiency and investor protection are not fully replaced, rather they are supplemented by the aim of strengthened financial stability – even if in some cases trade-offs are necessary among these goals. Proof of supplementary objectives can be found in recent explanatory memoranda to legislative texts and impact assessment objectives. See, e.g. short selling, MiFID, etc.

[26] Boot, A.W. and Thakor, A.V. (1997), 'Financial System Architecture', *Review of Financial Studies*, vol. 10, pp. 693–733; Allen, F. and Gale, D. (1999), *Comparing Financial Systems* (Cambridge, MA: MIT Press).

The market-based model also provides greater incentives to market participants to research firms, since it is easier to profit from this information by trading in big, liquid markets.[27] Besides, this system enhances corporate governance through a lively market for corporate control.[28] It provides a criticism of the bank-based model, by claiming that powerful banks with few regulatory restrictions on their activities may collude with firm managers against other creditors and impede efficient corporate governance.[29]

The *bank-based view* of financial structures holds that banks should be at the centre of the financing system because they are best placed to:

- acquire information about firms and managers, thereby improving capital allocation and corporate governance;[30]
- manage cross-sectional, inter-temporal, and liquidity risk, thereby enhancing investment efficiency and economic growth;[31]
- mobilise capital to exploit economies of scale.[32]

According to this view, banks form long-run relationships with firms and do not reveal information immediately in public markets. Also, banks – as coordinated coalitions of investors – are better than uncoordinated markets at monitoring firms and reducing post-lending moral hazard (asset substitution).[33] Proponents of the bank-based model also point out that liquid markets create a myopic investor climate, where investors can

---

27 Holmstrom, B. and Tirole, J. (1993), 'Market Liquidity and Performance Monitoring', *Journal of Political Economics*, vol. 101, pp. 678–709.

28 Jensen, M.C. and Murphy, K.J. (1990), 'Performance Pay and Top-management Incentives', *Journal of Political Economics*, vol. 98, pp. 225–264.

29 Wenger, E. and Kaserer, C. (1998), 'The German System of Corporate Governance: A Model which should not be Imitated', in Black, S.W. and Moersch, M. (eds), *Competition and Convergence in Financial Markets: The German and Anglo-American Models* (New York: North-Holland Press), pp. 41–78.

30 Ramakrishnan, R.T.S. and Thakor, A.V. (1984), 'Information Reliability and a Theory of Financial Intermediation', *Review of Financial Studies*, vol. 51, pp. 415–432.

31 Allen, F. and Gale, D. (1999), *Comparing Financial Systems* (Cambridge, MA: MIT Press).

32 Sirri, E.R. and Tufano, P. (1995), 'The Economics of Pooling', in Crane, D.B. et al. (eds) *The Global Financial System: A Functional Approach* (Cambridge, MA: Harvard Business School Press), pp. 81–128.

33 Boot and Thakor (1997).

inexpensively sell their shares, so that they have fewer incentives to exert rigorous corporate control.[34]

It is also argued that powerful banks can more effectively force firms to re-pay their debts than atomistic markets, especially in countries with weak contract enforcement capabilities. Thus, according to the bank-based view, greater market development may hinder corporate control and economic growth. The bank-based view holds that banks can exploit scale economies in information processing, ameliorate moral hazard through effective monitoring, and form long-run relationships with firms to ease asymmetric information distortions.[35]

2.4.2 How to make finance structures more efficient? The financial services view and the law and finance theory

Instead of clear evidence about the efficiency of one system over the other, a third policy proposal emerged to argue that whatever finance structure the economy may have (bank-based or market-based), the efficiency of the accompanying financial service provision is what matters.[36] The *financial services view* stresses that financial arrangements – contracts, markets, and intermediaries – serve to address market imperfections and provide financial services.

> Financial arrangements arise to assess potential investment opportunities, exert corporate control, facilitate risk management, enhance liquidity, and ease savings mobilization. By providing these financial services more or less effectively, different financial systems promote economic growth to a greater or lesser degree. According to this view … the issue is creating an environment in which intermediaries *and* markets provide sound financial services. Conceptually, the financial services view is fully consistent with both the bank-based and market-based views.[37]

The focus is on how to create better functioning banks and markets.

---

[34] Bhide, A. (1993), 'The Hidden Costs of Stock Market Liquidity', *Journal of Financial Intermediation*, vol. 34, pp. 1–51.

[35] Levine, R. (2002), 'Bank Based or Market Based Financial System: Which is Better?', *Journal of Financial Intermediation*, vol. 11, no. 4, pp. 398–428.

[36] Merton, R.C. and Bodie, Z. (1995), 'A Conceptual Framework for Analyzing the Financial Environment', in Crane, D.B. et al. (eds) *The Global Financial System: A Functional Perspective* (Cambridge, MA: Harvard University Press); and Levine, R. and Zervos, S. (1998), 'Stock Markets, Banks, and Economic Growth', *American Economic Review*, vol. 88, pp. 537–558.

[37] Levine (2002).

Finally, La Porta et al. proposed the *law and finance theory* of efficiencies in finance and suggested that 'bank versus market-centeredness is not an especially useful way to distinguish financial systems'.[38] Indeed, even if it were established that one model is more efficient than the other, the practical policy implications would be meager, given that it is hard to change the system of finance within a country without major negative implications on its economy. Instead, in the view of the law and finance theory, the legal system's efficiency is determinative of the efficiency of financial structures, since finance is a set of contracts. These contracts are defined – and made more or less effective – by legal rights and enforcement mechanisms.

2.5 What Information Inefficiencies Should Regulation Correct and How?

Within the broad topic of information inefficiencies, selected aspects of the functioning of securities markets will be examined, emphasising the differences in policy implications of starting from different economic and theoretical assumptions. As this area is mainly dependent on the efficient dissemination of information, the selected issues include insider trading and transparency, the latter being broken down into three different fields: transparency of trading platforms (as a more macro-level inquiry); mandatory disclosure of information for listed securities in general; and disclosure to retail investors.

2.5.1 Mandatory disclosure rules and their efficiency

Investors need information about the firms and financial instruments[39] they invest in. The two main types of information they will be looking for are: information at the beginning of the investor-investment relationship, and information on an ongoing basis throughout this relationship.

In theory, during the individual negotiation process between a firm and an investor, an optimal point can be reached where the firm will disclose the exact amount of information the investor requires to make their investment decision. In reality, however, investors often do not find it

---

[38] Laporta, R., Lopez-de-Silanes, F., Shleifer, A. and Vishny, R.W. (1998), 'Law and Finance', *Journal of Political Economy*, vol. 106, pp. 1113–1155.

[39] Here, a relatively simple example of corporate shares is taken to demonstrate the role of information in investment decisions. In the case of more complex and derivative financial products, information disclosure is equally important – only the assessment of such information becomes even more complex.

possible, or worthwhile, to negotiate for disclosure and thoroughly inspect the information they receive. Issuing companies disclose a certain level of information to the public and potential investors then decide whether to invest or not.[40]

In the theory of law and economics, regulatory intervention should only take place in cases of market failure (such as information problems, externalities, and so on) that can be corrected or mitigated through legal means. In this case, the market failure can be identified as information asymmetries between issuers and investors. The longer-term risk of such opportunistic dealing on the side of individual firms is that investors will lose their confidence in the markets and refrain from investing. The higher the disclosure standards are, the better informed investors will be and the more willing they will be to invest in securities, creating higher demand and higher volume of trading, which translates into lower costs of capital for firms. However, mandatory rules cannot set the level of disclosure at the highest possible level, because there are certain trade-offs to high disclosure. On the one hand, these trade-offs appear in the form of costs for the disclosing companies but, on the other hand, higher than optimal disclosure arguably increases market volatility.

The economic debate about efficient disclosure regimes (mandatory vs. optional) for publicly listed securities started in the 1960s.[41] A more recent follow-up to this debate was sparked by Romano[42] as well as Choi and Guzman,[43] arguing that disclosure should not be mandated, as market forces could provide sufficient incentives for issuers to disclose, and that such a system would be optimal overall. Other scholars have argued, however, that disclosure at will is not the best solution: disclosure rules have to be mandated.[44]

---

40 This was the case on securities markets *before* the introduction of mandatory disclosure rules.

41 In the US, mandatory disclosure rules were introduced by the Securities Act of 1933 and the Securities Exchange Act of 1934. The academic literature has examined the efficiency of these mandatory rules since their introduction, but they were questioned more seriously only in the 1960s.

42 Romano (2001).

43 Choi, S.J. and Guzman, A.T. (1997), 'Portable Reciprocity: Rethinking the International Reach of Securities Regulation', available at SSRN abstract no.10701. In the European context, see Enriques, L. and Troger, T.H. (2008), 'Issuer Choice in Europe', *Cambridge Law Journal*, vol. 67, pp. 521–559.

44 Coffee, J.C. (2002), 'Competition Among Securities Markets: A Path Dependent Perspective', Columbia Law and Economics Working Paper No. 192; Easterbrook, F.H. and Fischel, D.R. (1984), 'Mandatory Disclosure and Protection of Investors', *Vanderbilt Law Review*, vol. 70, p. 669.

Optional disclosure allows choice of disclosure regime for firms, which opens the way for regulatory competition. The race to the top predictions of those advocating freedom of choice divide further into two groups. One argument is that issuers, once they are granted free choice, will opt for the rules of a stricter jurisdiction to signal their quality, as long as it is bringing them more benefits than costs. This will lead jurisdictions to introduce strict standards and will ultimately increase the welfare of all.[45]

Another, more refined and perhaps more realistic, prediction is that a separating equilibrium would arise with some jurisdictions introducing stricter disclosure regimes and others relaxing their rules. This dual track will then lead to an overall increase in welfare, since firms can choose the jurisdiction that is the best fit for them. Firms with only smaller local market financing needs need not comply with high disclosure standards, while other firms may have aspirations to reach deep capital markets and may find incurring the higher cost of compliance worthwhile.[46]

At the same time, scholars sceptical of the relaxation of mandatory disclosure rules argue that such policies would lead to a race to the bottom (meaning an overall reduction in welfare, through laxer standards). This may occur either through political pressure on regulators to reduce disclosure standards to increase trading volume,[47] or through externalities among the choosers of the rules and the rest of corporate and social actors,[48] or through showing that low transparency dealers are capable of out-performing more transparent competitors.[49]

Commentators in the opposing camps have a slightly different starting hypothesis and thus they examine the problem from different angles. The starting point in the analysis of efficient disclosure regimes is the identification of the actors who decide on the level of disclosure[50] or, in a regulatory competition context, who choose the applicable rules.

---

[45] See Romano (2001).

[46] See Choi and Guzman (1997).

[47] Fox, M.B. (1997), 'Securities Disclosure in a Globalizing Market: Who Should Regulate Whom?', *Michigan Law Review*, pp. 2626–2627.

[48] Fox, M.B. (1999), 'Retaining Mandatory Securities Disclosure: Why Issuer Choice is not Investor Empowerment', *Virginia Law Review*, vol. 85, pp. 1335–1419.

[49] Bloomfield, R. and O'Hara, M. (2000), 'Can Transparent Markets Survive?', *Journal of Financial Economics*, vol. 55, no. 3, pp. 425–459.

[50] In a negotiation process the party with the greater economic power can be considered as the one influencing the final outcome.

Supporters of the mandatory disclosure regime most often take the view that it is the issuer's managers who will exercise this choice.

Fox shows that disclosure's costs to issuers are greater than its social costs and disclosure's benefits to them are lower than its social benefits. The two drivers of the divergence between social and private costs and benefits of disclosure are the agency relationship between managers and shareholders, and the so-called inter-firm costs. These are defined as a negative impact on the firm from the fact that, with broader disclosure, their competitors will know more about their business activity. These inter-firm costs are burdensome for the disclosing firm but are overall beneficial for society, as they open the way for tougher competition in the given product market, thus accumulating as benefits for consumers. Therefore, he argues, if we leave free choice of disclosure regime to issuers, each issuer will choose a socially sub-optimal level of disclosure.[51]

The second significant driver of the divergence between private and social costs is the *agency relationship* between shareholders and managers. This is due to the fact that periodic disclosure increases the effectiveness of shareholder control through wider information provision to shareholders. However, higher levels of periodic disclosure can also increase the threat of hostile takeover. Both of these mechanisms limit the ability of managers to deviate from acting in the shareholders' best interests. Therefore, higher periodic disclosure standards impose a cost on managers, who would prefer to pursue their personal goals under as few constraints as possible. As long as it is managers who choose the applicable legal regime on disclosures, it is argued that they will choose a regime with lower than optimal standards.

In order for voluntary disclosure to achieve the socially optimal level, it would be necessary for the issuer's share price to fully reflect the

[51] Fox also reports that 'the extensive presence of interfirm costs was one of the main factors that drove adoption of mandatory disclosure in the first place. One of the major categories of information required by the Exchange Act that was not provided by many corporations prior to its enactment in 1934 was sales and cost of sales.' In the annual reports of major corporations in 1930, 47 per cent of the firms omitted their net sales figures. Kaplan and Reaugh suggested that this result could be explained by the existence of inter-firm costs: 'The usual reason given for refusing to disclose sales and cost of sales figures is the creation of consumer resistance where the gross profit margin is wide and that its publication invites competition or gives an advantage to existing competitors, especially where the competitors' figures remain undisclosed.' See Kaplan, M.C. and Reaugh, D.M. (1939), 'Accounting, Reports to Stockholders, and the SEC', *Yale Law Journal*, vol. 48, p. 935.

social benefits of the disclosure level that has been chosen. A further precondition is that the persons making the disclosure choice – the issuer's managers – should fully enjoy this share price improvement. Fox argues that this is not the case:

> An issuer's increased disclosure will result in three kinds of social benefits that will, at least in some situations, not be fully captured by its managers:
>
> (1) the reduction in the portfolio risk for the issuer's less than fully diversified shareholders;
> (2) the improvement in quality of real investment projects chosen to be implemented in our economy; and
> (3) the reduction in the agency costs of management.

For the last-named, Fox argues that a fall in share prices, which indicates the switch between rules, will not restrain management sufficiently, as 'even if the price decline were as great as the decline in value, the managers would often find that the increased freedom, especially the freedom resulting from the reduced threat of takeovers, would be worth the price decline'.

In other words, Fox, as a representative of the camp opposing free choice of law in the securities field, starts with the premise that the choice of disclosure regime would be allocated to managers and the assumption that agency problems between issuers and managers remain unmitigated by the financial markets as a disciplining mechanism.

On the other hand, academics arguing for regulatory competition with free choice in securities law, such as Romano, assume *fully diversified investors* (hence benefits flowing to non-fully diversified investors from more accurate pricing is not accounted for) and *no agency problems* between managers and shareholders (thus the benefit from reduced agency problems is non-existent). Finally the third benefit mentioned by Fox, a better selection of investment projects, is also acknowledged by Romano, but she concludes that empirical evidence does not show that this channel of potential benefits actually materialises in reality.

In fact, empirical tests would seem like an easy way to decide which camp is right but unfortunately they are difficult to design in a way that offers reliable answers.[52]

---

[52] With regard to empirical evidence as to which theory (mandated disclosure or free choice) is optimal, Gilson and Kraakman note that '... The proponents of relaxing mandatory disclosure do not argue that deregulation will increase the informational efficiency of prices; rather, they argue only that it will decrease issuer filing costs while leaving the amount and quality of information

The debate described above demonstrates well how different assumptions and starting points in theory lead to different policy prescriptions. Today, regulatory actors largely concur that disclosure should be mandated in some form, even if they do not always agree what the right amount and format of that disclosure should be. The existing European legal norms will be examined in later sections for specific types of disclosure, and legal actors' competences will be mapped out in these fields.

Before moving on to the current legal landscape, we should try to distinguish the theoretical debates in the US and the EU, by identifying potential differences in the European market, that can lead to different welfare results of regulation and regulatory competition in the European context.

The most important parameters that emerged as relevant to measuring the overall welfare implications of mandated disclosure rules were the diversification of investors and agency problems between shareholders and managers. It is interesting to note that the resolution of the management-shareholder conflict will also determine who is considered to be the chooser of the norms. It does not come as a surprise then that theory arrives at different conclusions depending on these two variables.

In European Member States the diversification of investors is expected to be lower than in the US, due to the somewhat less significant role of stock markets. From the US debate it appears investors who are not fully diversified are one of the beneficiaries of mandated disclosure. Thus, mandatory disclosure may be expected to have stronger positive effects in the EU than in the US.

With regard to the shareholder-manager agency problem, the previous chapter on company law has already explained that in the European context this problem is less relevant due to the presence of blockholder owners, who can arguably monitor management better than the dispersed shareholders common in the US. This means that the potential benefits of mandatory disclosure rules reducing shareholder-manager agency costs is less likely to accrue in Europe as much as in the US. In terms of minority and majority shareholder agency relationships, the mandated disclosure

---

largely unaffected. […] This conclusion is extremely difficult to evaluate, not only because of the empirical uncertainties surrounding the costs and benefits of 1934 Act disclosure, but also because these variables themselves depend on the particular disclosure that is required.' Gilson and Kraakman (1984), 'The Mechanisms of Market Efficiency', *Vanderbilt Law Review*, vol. 70, pp. 549–644.

rules may still be relevant, perhaps somewhat less than in the case of shareholder-management agency problems.

Overall this means that mandated disclosure is more likely to yield benefits for one side (to non-fully diversified investors) but is less likely to deliver positive impacts to the other (reducing agency costs for shareholders). Moreover, the choosers of the disclosure regime are more likely to be the managers and controlling owners of the firms, as in Europe such controlling ownership is more frequent than in the US.

The literature does not seem to indicate which of these impacts are more relevant and it is also difficult to guess to what extent the differences between the US and Europe may influence the extent of materialised benefits from mandatory disclosure.

2.5.2 Regulation of insider trading

The phenomenon of insider trading is an issue that law and economics literature has long been exploring.[53] Scholars arguing for a prohibition on insider trading point out that such rules would protect the market for managerial services, reduce conflict of interests among managers and shareholders, and therefore increase the value of the firm. The first argument holds that shareholders contracting with managers should be able to foresee what they contract for. Allowing managers to trade on insider information would be an open contract, the value of which is hard to identify. Besides, the behaviour of managers themselves will determine how much inside information is created that can be traded upon. The second argument points to the conflicts of interest that arise if insider trading is contractually permitted.

Dyer[54] lists six types of such conflict. The first is indifference to corporate losses, since insiders can avoid personal loss by trading on inside information. Further conflicts arise from: the incentive to create rumours; the incentive to spend resources spying to gain access to inside information that is not needed for corporate purposes; the temptation to delay internal disclosures of information to colleagues in the firm, who need it for corporate purposes, until the insider has traded on it; the lack of incentive to take business opportunities that do not produce a sufficient gap in time that allows the insider to trade; the incentive to delay a

---

[53] The early discussion pointed to the controversial questions under law and economics, e.g. Bainbridge, S. (1986), 'The Insider Trading Prohibition: A Legal and Economic Enigma', *University of Florida Law Review*, vol. 38.

[54] Dyer, B.K. (1992), 'Economic Analysis, Insider Trading and Game Markets', *Utah Law Review*, vol. 1, pp. 1–66.

corporate transaction until trade is completed.[55] It is argued by the proponents of a prohibition that the elimination of the above concerns will increase the value of the firm.

On the other side, academics argue that permitting insiders to trade on the information they have creates the potential for performance-related remuneration (thus reducing agency costs that arise from other forms of remuneration), it allocates property rights in information efficiently under the Coaseian transaction cost theory, and it has the potential to convey information to the market and thus increase informational efficiency. The first argument, a remuneration mechanism with lower agency cost, is the mirror image of the first argument of the proponents of a prohibition. To counter the second claim it is pointed out that insider information cannot be 'allocated' like other resources. With regard to the claim that insider trading signals to the markets valuable information, thus contributing to informational efficiency, the counter argument is that market participants cannot know whether trading is by insiders or not; and most importantly they cannot distinguish insiders from 'noise traders'.[56]

A further proposition[57] is that inside information should be allocated to analysts, as they are more efficient at signalling through their trades to the market, while they do not face the same conflict of interests problem as insiders themselves do.

In Europe, especially in continental Europe, securities markets are less liquid and deep; trading is therefore more concentrated than in the US. The pricing efficiency of the markets is supposedly lower,[58] which means that improvement is perhaps more needed and brings a greater value added than in the US. However, it is also due to the lower efficiency of

---

[55] The details of these arguments and their potential criticism, e.g. how remuneration could be balanced with other mechanisms, are not discussed further here.

[56] Noise traders refer to those investors who buy or sell securities based not on correct inside information but instead on untrue information spread among them, so-called 'noise'; see Dyer (1992). The author lists further objections to the claim that insider trading increases pricing efficiency, none of which will be discussed here.

[57] Goshen, Z. and Parchomovsky, G. (2001), 'On Insider Trading, Markets, and "Negative" Property Rights in Information', *Virginia Law Review*, vol. 87, p. 1229.

[58] Chordia et al. find empirical evidence that more liquid markets process price information faster and more effectively. See Chordia, T. et al. (2008), 'Liquidity and Market Efficiency', *Journal of Financial Economics*, vol. 87, no. 2, pp. 249–268.

markets that insider trading is less likely to be an effective mechanism to transmit information to the market.

European public firms most often have a controlling owner, and therefore the agency relationship between managers and shareholders is reduced. The contracting issue is less relevant in the European context, which implies that allowing insider trading will not be to the detriment of shareholders to the extent it would be in the US – or, under the theory of those promoting insider trading, it would not convey so much benefit.

In Europe the manager-shareholder agency problem is replaced by the majority-minority owner issue. Prohibition of insider trading will have an impact on this relationship, rather than on the one between managers and shareholders. Arguably, the claims of either side would hold for the EU case, the only difference being that, in Europe, majority-minority shareholder conflicts are more frequent but shareholder-manager conflicts are less widespread than in the US.

In reality insider trading is prohibited today in all major developed financial markets. Differences among jurisdictions may exist, not so much in the objective of the legal norms, but rather in their precise form and in their enforcement.

2.5.3 Investor protection measures in retail markets

As noted above, market efficiency, even if accepted without reservations and even if achieved to its fullest extent, does not necessarily guarantee retail investor protection in itself. Retail investors also have access to securities, (such as through a broker), but more often they invest into products specifically targeted at them.[59] Therefore, securities disclosures are designed to ensure market efficiency and investor protection, and the disclosure rules for retail investment products, such as mutual funds, are even more centred on the needs of non-sophisticated buyers.

Retail investors, who are not experts on financial matters, need to be well informed in order to make optimal investment decisions. Behavioural economic research warns that merely disclosing all correct and relevant information will not always achieve a correct interpretation, let alone an optimal investment decision. Whereas the rules should not patronise citizens as retail investors by trying to make the 'right' choices for them, it may be good to ensure people understand the implications of their investment choices. Disclosure documents written with brevity in a

---

[59] For the simple reason that investing in funds, for example, increases portfolio diversification and therefore lowers the risks.

plain and comprehensible language, emphasising important points, are likely to improve investment decisions.

Whereas legal and economic research, as well as policy measures, focused for a long time on the problems that so called 'rational' actors faced in financial markets, today policy and academic research put more and more emphasis on the problems real retail market actors face.

At the same time, behavioural economics is often criticised for its piecemeal approach. Whereas neoclassical economics can build economic models that describe and predict an entire system of actors, behavioural economics cannot offer a comprehensive model that would describe and predict outcomes with reasonable validity across fields and actors. But the piecemeal research seems to inform policy, nonetheless.

3. IDENTIFYING THE LEGAL ACTORS – ALLOCATION OF COMPETENCES

The numerous legal actors involved in shaping the rules around securities markets can be distinguished along the vertical dimension of European and national competences, as well as along the horizontal dimension of legislative, regulatory, supervisory and enforcement bodies. Most of these legal actors are public bodies, but some private regulation also occurs.

In securities law, there is multi-level regulation with respect to the regulatory bodies involved, where the tasks of regulators and supervisory bodies are often allocated to the same actor. This section looks at the legislative and regulatory process at the European level, examines the mandate of the EU level supervisory authority, and lists the national legal actors with competence.

3.1 Decision-Making at EU Level: Comitology from Lamfalussy to Lisbon

The regulatory process for European securities and financial markets is based on a multi-level decision-making process. The current set-up dates from 2011, and is based strongly on the previous institutional setting, the Lamfalussy Committees, which, due to its ten years of existence is relevant to our analysis, since much of the current financial legislation was adopted under the 'old' Lamfalussy structure.

A 'Committee of Wise Men' set up by the European Commission in 2000 put forward proposals to make regulation more efficient.[60] Among their recommendations they proposed to distinguish high-level European legislation from lower-level industry-related implementation, in a process based on consultation with the national regulators and supervisors. This comitology process was labelled the 'Lamfalussy approach', and consisted of four levels, of which the first two concerned EU level legislative and executive powers.

At the first level, the European Parliament and the European Council adopted directives on the initiative of the European Commission. All political decisions were brought to this first level, and this legislation only defined framework principles in order to ensure that detailed technicalities did not hold up the decision-making process.

The implementing powers were delegated to the European Commission at the second level, which could enact directives and regulations, after consultation with the European Securities Committee (ESC). The European Securities Committee was set up by Commission Decision 2001/528/EC, consisting of high-level representatives of Member State securities regulators and chaired by the European Commission. An independent advisory group had also been established, the Committee of European Securities Regulators (CESR),[61] consisting of senior representatives of national supervisory authorities, giving technical advice to the European Commission, which decided on the final implementation measures together with the ESC.

The ESC was a classical regulatory committee under the Commission's comitology procedures, as defined by a Decision of the European Council.[62] The Commission was obliged to submit its proposal to the ESC, which delivered its opinion, and the Commission could only adopt the measure if it was in line with the Committee's opinion. Otherwise, the Commission had to send the proposal to the Council and notify the Parliament. The Parliament could notify the Council if it considered the Commission's proposal was outside its regulatory powers. Finally, the Council could decide on the proposal within three months. If the Council

---

[60] Final Report of the Committee of Wise Men on the Regulation of European Securities Markets. Brussels, 15 Feb 2001.

[61] Commission Decision 2001/527/EC.

[62] Council Decision 1999/468/EC, of 28 June 1999, replacing the original Comitology Decision of the Council of 1987. This Comitology Decision distinguished between three types of comitology procedures: management, regulatory and advisory procedures. A further amendment added regulatory procedures with scrutiny in 2006.

did not make a decision within this period of time, the Commission could adopt the measure. This procedure therefore ensured that the opinion of the ESC was of great relevance in the decision-making procedure.

This structure of decision-making was amended by the Lisbon Treaty on comitology, under which regulatory powers given to the Commission are divided into two categories: delegated powers (delegated acts), in the case of far-reaching powers, and implementing powers (implementing acts), which lay down more technical details. The procedures and power of scrutiny by Council and Parliament are different under the two categories of acts.

In the case of delegated acts, Member States have no voting power on the Commission drafts and there is no obligation but only a power for the European Commission to consult experts from Member States informally. This is a substantial change compared to the previous comitology procedure under which the ESC had real influence. A Common Understanding on delegated acts specifies however that the Commission will consult the committees during their adoption. At the same time, the Lisbon Treaty specifies that the delegation of powers to the Commission can be revoked at any time by either the Council or the Parliament. Besides, the two institutions are also given the right to oppose the delegated acts proposed by the Commission.

With regard to implementing acts of the Commission, the ESC has to be consulted[63] under the examination procedure, where it is provided that the Commission cannot adopt the draft implementing act if no opinion is delivered by the ESC. If there is a negative ESC opinion, the Commission can either submit a new draft proposal or refer the original draft to the appeal committee. If the latter delivers a negative opinion the draft measure cannot be adopted. If there is no opinion it can be adopted by the Commission. The Council and the Parliament have scrutiny powers to ensure the Commission does not go beyond its mandate.[64]

The most relevant development in the EU level decision-making procedure is the ability of the Commission to adopt measures which are immediately applicable. This arguably enables the European level regulator to react swiftly to new market developments in a fast-changing environment, but it re-shapes the balance of power *vis-à-vis* other EU as well as national institutions.

---

[63] Art. 3 (3) of Regulation No 182/2011 of the European Parliament and of the Council of 16 February 2011 laying down the rules and general principles concerning mechanisms for control by Member States of the Commission's exercise of implementing powers OJ L 55/13.

[64] Art. 11 of Regulation 182/2011.

3.2 The European Securities and Markets Authority (ESMA)

Until 2011, at the third level of the Lamfalussy process, an enhanced cooperation took place among national securities regulators to ensure consistency in the transposition of European legislation into national laws. At this level various tasks were entrusted to the CESR. This is relevant to an analysis of the competitive interactions of legal actors, since it aimed to achieve consistency and a certain convergence in the implementation of European measures. The prevention of 'gold-plating' was a major goal of this institutional design, which in turn had implications for the scope of regulatory competition among Member States.

The final, fourth level of the Lamfalussy process concerned enforcement, which, under the lead of the European Commission, involved the authorities of the Member States as well as the private sector.

Set up in 2011,[65] the European Securities and Markets Authority (ESMA) is the child of post-crisis financial reform, which aimed to further strengthen financial stability in Europe. As it is a relatively new institutional set-up, its composition, independence, powers and functioning is analysed here in greater detail.

As for its composition, the Regulation establishing ESMA sets up the following bodies:

- a Board of Supervisors;
- a Management Board;
- a Chairperson;
- an Executive Director; and
- a Board of Appeal.

The Management Board comprises of seven members[66] of the Board of Supervisors and the Chairperson of ESMA.[67] The Board of Supervisors is composed of the Heads of the 27 national supervisory authorities as voting members, and some other important stakeholders (EU bodies, other agencies) as observers.[68] This set-up is quite unusual, when

---

[65] Regulation (EU) No 1093/2010.

[66] The first set-up of the Management Board as of 2011 includes Estonia, Austria, Spain, Luxembourg, Portugal, the UK and Germany.

[67] Currently this position is filled by the financial authority of the Netherlands.

[68] The Commission, the ECB and the two other ESA's have non-voting membership. The Chairperson of the Board has no vote either.

compared to the two-tier board structures of companies, since the oversight body is broader in its composition than the management body. Under corporate governance logic, the two boards would be made up of different people (at least in part). In the case of ESMA however, it seems that the role of the Supervisory Board is not solely the independent control of quality, as in corporate governance, but also the safeguard of neutrality and the balance of national interests, as in a supra-national governance model.

The Board of Supervisors is designated to frame and oversee the functioning of the Management Board. It adopts the work programme and the budget and, importantly, it appoints[69] and exercises 'disciplinary authority over the Chairperson and the Executive Director and may remove them from office …'.[70] To ESMA's working methods, the Board of Supervisors takes all policy decisions, voting with qualified majority for guidelines and technical standards, and voting with a simple majority otherwise, where each member has one vote.[71]

The Chairperson represents the authority, while the Executive Director[72] manages it. The Chairperson prepares the work of the Board of Supervisors and chairs the meetings of the Board of Supervisors and the Management Board. He is appointed for a five year period, renewable once. With regard to his independence, two further important provisions are in place. 'Without prejudice to the role of the Board of Supervisors in relation to the tasks of the Chairperson, the Chairperson shall neither seek nor take instructions from the Union institutions or bodies, from any government of a Member State or from any other public or private body.'[73] Similar duties are placed on Member States and EU bodies to refrain from influencing the Chairperson.[74]

The Executive Director's tasks include facilitating the more specific implementation of the authority's tasks, and managing staff matters within ESMA. Her term in office and her independence are similarly regulated as in the case of the Chairperson. With regard to the staff, ESMA comprises of delegates from national authorities and own staff.

---

[69] The Executive director is appointed with the approval of the European Parliament. It is interesting that for his removal there is no need for EP approval, whereas the Chairperson is appointed by the Supervisory Board acting alone, but can only be removed with the approval of the EP.

[70] Art. 43 (8).

[71] Art. 44 (1).

[72] This position is currently filled by the UK FSA.

[73] Art. 49.

[74] Ibid.

The tasks and powers of ESMA are broader than those of CESR under the previous supervisory framework. ESMA is empowered to develop draft regulatory technical standards, which the European Commission can endorse, leaving a one-month period for the European Parliament and the Council to object (extensible by another month). If the European Commission deviates from the draft proposed by ESMA, the deadlines for Parliament and Council extend to three months, extensible by another three months.

In addition, ESMA is empowered to develop draft implementing technical standards, with quite similar rules to the above, the difference being that implementing technical standards should not imply policy choices, but merely the application of the main act(s).

The independence of ESMA is a further interesting angle to explore in the light of regulatory interactions. Its independence (based on rules governing its financing, nomination and the removal of key people, and so on) has to be interpreted as independence both from the Commission and from Member States' regulators (ministries) and supervisory authorities.

Very importantly, ESMA has direct supervisory powers over credit-rating agencies, and can theoretically receive further powers of supervision under EU law.

ESMA can also issue guidelines and recommendations addressed to competent authorities or financial market participants. In this capacity, the authority has a free hand (apart from stakeholder consultations and seeking the opinion of the Securities and Markets Stakeholder Group). And although guidelines and recommendations are not binding, the national authorities and market participants have to explain any non-compliance, which provides an additional source of peer pressure to apply harmonised rules. Certainly, comply or explain is not the same as binding rules, but the actual effect of this system of governance should be measured a few years after its entry into force. In addition, in the case of national authorities' non-compliance, ESMA has to report to the European Parliament and the Council on how it plans to achieve full compliance for the future.

From the regulatory competition perspective it is of course interesting to see where the ESMA regulation calls for explicit harmonisation. One such instance is investor protection, where the Authority is entrusted with the task of contributing to the development of common disclosure rules. Another example is the use of guidelines and recommendations to promote the safety and soundness of markets and the convergence of regulatory practices.[75] The latter provision seems to mean that regulatory convergence is an aim in itself, which can justify the issue of new guidelines and recommendations, even in the absence of threats to the safety and soundness of markets.[76]

Further powers of ESMA include enforcement. Where national authorities do not apply correctly the relevant legislation, ESMA has the power to investigate non-compliance, on its own initiative or upon the initiative of other actors,[77] and issue a recommendation to remedy the breach. The next step is the European Commission's action in the form of an opinion, it can also launch an infringement procedure, and finally, ESMA can adopt individual decisions applicable to market actors, if certain conditions are fulfilled.[78]

Finally, ESMA has a dispute settlement role and tasks with regard to supervisory colleges. In dispute settlement, the Authority first acts as a mediator, setting a conciliation deadline for the national authorities in disagreement. However at a second stage, if the national authorities fail to agree on a solution, ESMA can bring a decision binding on the national authorities. In case the latter would not comply with this decision, ESMA can also bring decisions addressed to and binding on individual market participants in the jurisdiction of the non-complying authority, thereby overriding the national authority's 'non-conform' action.

With regard to supervisory colleges, ESMA has a facilitative and coordination role, enforced with the mediation role described above, and power to:

- request further deliberation of the college when it considers that the college's decision does not conform with EU law; and

---

[75] ESMA regulation Art. 9 (2).

[76] Compare with Art. 16 (1) where the use of guidelines is envisaged for 'ensuring the common, uniform and consistent application of Union law'. This wording seems weaker in terms of harmonisation, since it restricts the scope of ESMA's action to the application of Union law, whereas Art. 9 (2), referred to above, did not contain such a restriction in scope, referring to the convergence of regulatory practices in general.

[77] These are the European Commission, the European Parliament, the Council or the Securities and Markets Stakeholder Group.

[78] Where it is necessary to remedy in a timely manner such non compliance in order to maintain or restore neutral conditions of competition in the market or in order to ensure the orderly functioning and integrity of the financial system, provided that the requirements are directly applicable to the financial market.

- propose draft regulatory or implementing technical standards to promote convergence in supervisory functioning.

Besides these tasks, ESMA has also a coordinating/facilitative role in emergency situations, but this is not considered here in detail, as emergencies should be the exception rather than the rule for legal actors' interaction.

To conclude, we can observe that the new architecture set up close cooperation between the national supervisors and the European Authorities, strengthened by information sharing obligations. Overall, this new supervisory framework aims to create further centralisation of certain rule-making powers and will also enhance cooperation within the financial services regulatory arena.

ESMA has stronger powers than its predecessor, CESR, which would at first sight suggest that the centralisation element in EU regulation and supervision has been substantially strengthened. However, the composition and independence of the Authority is not that much different from the previous CESR set-up, which means that the actors that take the key decisions with these increased powers are still the representatives of national supervisory authorities. This implies a decision-making structure with 27 national interests in mind, rather than one single European vision. In other words ESMA has a clear mandate to think European, but, it is not fully clear to what extent and how this will be achieved in practice, given the composition of its decision-making bodies.

Some commentators argue that although the crisis was of immense impact and there was political pressure on policy makers to make radical changes, the final form of the new European supervisory authorities is not that revolutionary when compared to the previous Lamfalussy Committees.[79] It is too early to assess the impact of ESMA on the implementation and application of European securities law,[80] so at this stage only predictions can be made about how this institution will shape the competitive or cooperative interaction among legal actors.

3.3 National Legal Actors

At the national level, there are legal actors in charge of national legislation and regulation (the national parliaments and ministries), national supervisory authorities, and the national system of judiciary.

---

79 See, e.g. Schammo (2011).

80 An evaluation of the ESAs by the Commission is scheduled for 2013.

3.3.1 Regulators and supervisory authorities

The way in which ESMA and the framework of EU level decision-making involves national regulators and supervisory authorities in that decision-making and in implementation has already been described. Regulators are represented in the ESC, which is consulted on the Commission's draft implementing and delegated acts. National supervisory authorities are represented in ESMA, the new European supervisory authority, which has the role of direct supervision (of credit rating agencies), coordination, policy development and enforcement, as described above. Regulators and supervisory authorities also have some leeway in implementing European legislation as well as their own national powers to regulate (although the recent trend points in the direction of greater harmonisation). The substantive EU rules and scope for national divergences will be discussed in Section 4.

3.3.2 Judiciary and alternative dispute settlement

The issue of enforcement of securities law in general can also raise the question of institutional design in a multi-level setting. First of all, should enforcement occur at the European or the national level? Which legal actors should be the most involved in it: supervisory authorities, which might be closest to the field and reveal infringements; courts, which have a traditional role in applying the law and enforcing rights and obligations; or alternative dispute resolution bodies, which can alleviate court workloads and offer advantages in speed and specialised knowledge?

The design of the system of enforcement is ultimately the task of the legislator, as it can adopt rules to set the framework for enforcement within its jurisdiction. Legal actors can also try to develop enforcement activities without the help of legislative norms, but clearly in these cases the efficiency of legal institutions supporting enforcement might suffer. When examining intra-jurisdictional interactions of legal actors, it is interesting to observe how the legislator facilitates, impedes or stays passive *vis-à-vis* the potential role of different actors of enforcement.

Besides the legal actors, we should also look at the role of private actors that use the legal system, since their activity will ultimately define the robustness of enforcement mechanisms in cases where enforcement is not fully *ex officio*, that is, not fully reliant on the infringement monitoring and enforcement response of public bodies but also dependent on private actors' initiative.

Within the current legal framework, enforcement mainly takes place at national level. The EU level actors – ECJ, Commission, ESMA – mainly look after the correct transposition and application of the rules by national public bodies, but they do not typically engage in enforcement action against private parties as market participants. As noted above, ESMA has the power to issue decisions addressed to private actors in case of deficient cooperation by a national supervisory authority. However, the main role in enforcement does not lie with the EU level.

At national level, then, supervisory authorities do discover and remedy infringements in certain cases. A good example of this is the market abuse directive, where breaches are in some cases followed-up by criminal sanctions. National supervisory authorities currently have divergent enforcement powers, which is why the European legislator proposes to enhance and approximate their powers.[81] But, in general, national supervisors will have some scope to take enforcement action, and to refer cases to the national courts. Market participants that are subject to such enforcement proceedings typically have a right to appeal to a court or tribunal.[82]

National courts could in principle play a major role in enforcing securities laws, as there is already an example of an active court system in the US.[83]

However, in the case of European courts, the procedural framework that would facilitate collective action had been absent or under-developed in the past. Recently, legislative changes have allowed for different forms of collective action that can facilitate enforcement in cases where a wider, dispersed group suffers damage.

In Germany, for example, a special procedure is available for capital investors to pursue collective action.[84] Under this procedure, the Higher Regional Court can decide a common factual or legal question in several cases, which will be binding upon the plaintiffs in choosing the test case. The other pending cases on the same issue are suspended until the decision on the test case is reached and the parties involved are bound by that decision once the proceedings are resumed.

---

81 Commission Communication, 'Reinforcing sanctioning regimes in the financial sector', 8 December 2010, COM(2010) 716.

82 See, e.g. the Upper Tribunal in the case of FSA enforcement actions in the UK.

83 Besides the well-established case law in corporate governance, studies in the case of the US derivative markets also point to shifts in legal interpretation showing a clear trend in the development of derivatives regulation: Partnoy, F. (2002), ISDA, NASD, CFMA and SDNY: 'The Four Horsemen of Derivatives Regulation?' Public Law and Legal Theory Working Paper no. 39, University of San Diego School of Law, available at: http://ssrn.com/abstract_id=293085.

84 *Kapitalanleger-Musterverfharen*. The *KapMug* has been in force since 1 November 2005.

But courts in Germany reportedly began accepting and adjudicating more cases even before the introduction of the test case procedure by the legislator. The best example for this is the landmark decision of the German Federal Supreme Court recognising a cause of action against directors for deliberate misstatements under a provision of the Civil Code,[85] providing that wilful or unconscionable causation of damage to another party constitutes a tort and triggers liability for damages.[86] This decision developed the securities liability system and provided a broader scope for investor protection.

Non-legal actors also play an important role in kick-starting the available enforcement mechanisms. Consumer protection bodies can do a lot to coordinate retail investors who may have suffered damage, and in certain cases they can even bring an action on their behalf. They enable individual investors to litigate claims that otherwise would be too costly, in terms of time, money, and information costs. These bodies are organised at Member State or regional levels.

Alternative dispute resolution (ADR) systems play a further important role in enforcement. At EU level, there is a network of alternative dispute settlement, called Fin Net, comprising of national mediators and ombudsmen in the field of financial services. The network's main targets are cross-border financial services disputes, but it can also provide useful information to claimants regarding the competent national dispute settlement organisation for their individual case. An interesting by-product of the existence of this network is that the annual reports of its members are easily accessible, which provides more information and comparability across Member States in terms of ADR activities.

3.3.3 Private regulation

Private regulation occurs in securities law in at least two contexts: financial markets set rules for listed firms, and regulated markets set rules for non-regulated markets (alternative trading venues).

As for the former, the requirements of each market upon admission to trading can be more or less stringent for the issuers, and this form of conditionality in accessing the market deserves to be labelled private regulation as it has potentially far-reaching effects. For example, European harmonisation of legal norms stops at setting certain rules for listed

---

[85] § 826 Bürgerliches Gesetzbuch (German Civil Code, BGB).

[86] Reidenbach, D. (2004), 'Executives' Liability for Incorrect Ad Hoc Announcements – A Comment on the Decision of the German Federal Court of Justice (BGH) in In re Infomatec AG, BGH II ZR 217/03, 218/03 and 402/02 of 19 July 2004', *German Law Journal*, vol. 5, no. 9.

firms, leaving it to national legal actors to set further requirements if they wish to do so. Stock exchanges, as private actors, have set further listing rules which in some cases further harmonise and thus facilitate market access to firms across Europe. One such example is provided by Euronext:

> Although the Euronext business model is built upon the mutual recognition principle that is at the core of EC securities harmonization legislation, Euronext has proceeded beyond the minimum harmonization aspect of EC securities legislation and sought to create a unified set of listing and trading rules for Euronext exchanges.[87]

Clearly, the advantage of leaving this rule-setting capacity with the stock exchanges themselves has the advantage of allowing parallel experimentation among several private actors, and competence allocation to the actors that are best placed to follow up on what the latest market developments may require in terms of changes in these listing conditions. They can also change these rules relatively quickly – compared to the legislative procedures at European and even national levels.

Stock exchanges went through a wave of demutualisation. From the 1990s to today they transformed from non-profit mutual organisations into for-profit listed entities. The listing of stock exchanges poses a further issue of self-regulation: '... demutualization and listing of exchanges creates a new challenge for exchanges as self-regulating institutions: managing the conflicts that may arise between the owners and those who transact on the exchange.'[88]

With regard to the powers of regulated markets to organise alternative trading venues (so-called non-regulated markets), recent proposals for legislative amendments are likely to reallocate regulatory powers from private actors to public ones. The proposed amendments to the MiFID[89] – if accepted by Parliament and Council without major amendments – will

---

[87] Shipp, B.T. (2010), 'Filling Gaps in European Union Securities Law: Contractually Organized Supervision & the College of Euronext Regulators', *American University International Law Review*, vol. 23, no. 2, pp. 387–450.

[88] Aggrawal, R. and Dahiya, S. (2006), 'Demutualization and Public Offerings of Financial Exchanges', *Journal of Applied Corporate Finance*, vol. 18, no. 3, pp. 96–106.

[89] Proposal for a Directive of the European Parliament and of the Council on markets in financial instruments repealing Directive 2004/39/EC of the European Parliament and of the Council (Recast) SEC(2011) 1226 and SEC(2011) 1227.

end their relative freedom in organising such alternative trading venues, and will have these venues covered by public regulation.

The reasons behind this shift of regulatory powers from private to public bodies are the perceived need for more transparency and a level playing field among trading venues. This legal development seems to be one example of a trend to shift regulatory focus towards investor protection and financial stability.[90] As the latter is a particular example of large potential cross-border externalities, it is perhaps the need to take such external effects into account that may justify a move from decentralised private rule setting to a centralised public one.

4. THE SCOPE FOR DIVERGENCE IN THE CURRENT REGULATORY LANDSCAPE

Due to the multiple level decision-making process, there is a possibility of regulatory divergence at different levels, which can lead to regulatory arbitrage possibilities for regulatees.

The first scope for difference arises at the level of national implementation of the rules. This can be broken down to the acts of the national legislator or regulator, as the case might be, and further regulatory functions are often delegated to the national supervisory authority.[91]

Private regulatory powers may be exercised by the markets themselves over firms that are listed on a given market. Since usually within one jurisdiction there is only one regulated market, regulatory arbitrage and freedom of choice can only arise internationally or in the context of competition between regulated and non-regulated markets.

Further, the choice of supervision is also attached to national regulation (there is one supervisor within one jurisdiction for one aspect of regulation). As for the national courts of the Member States, the choice of forum is not a decisive factor in the choice of jurisdiction to list, but

---

[90] Another example of reducing the scope of private regulation under the pursuit of financial stability goals is the recent regulation of credit rating agencies Regulation (EC) No 1060/2009 of the European Parliament and of the Council of 16 September 2009 on credit rating agencies OJ L302. Investor protection as another goal in this specific case goes even beyond retail investor protection and links to financial stability, as regulatory intervention questions sophisticated investors' ability and incentives to assess risks correctly, taking potential systemic impacts into account.

[91] See Grunbishler, A. and Darlap, P. (2003), 'Integration of EU Financial Markets Supervision: Harmonisation or Unification?', Consultation Document of the FMA, Finanzmarktausicht, Austria.

there can be a separate forum shopping consideration, and arbitration is also commonly used in securities dispute settlements. Although, in the context of the Member States of the European Union, there is no comprehensive analysis of the role of courts in creating legal arbitrage, there is arguably substantial scope for such arbitrage due to the range of differently evolving legal interpretations, which in the case of the EU, with several different jurisdictions, will probably gain high importance.

The competition model in which regulators compete over norms to attract regulatees can be defined in the context of securities regulation in different ways when looking at which rule-making bodies are active and who are the regulatees.

This analysis does not aim to carry out a comprehensive comparative analysis of the national rules. In its place, certain specific aspects are examined across a number of EU countries, and the scope for legal divergence at the European level is described. The specific legal rules examined in this section are: the rules on market microstructure; insider trading; disclosure requirements; and the rules governing takeover bids.

4.1 The Market Microstructure

Pre- and post-trade transparency of price information is an important concern that is closely connected to the market microstructure of the exchanges. But, since market microstructures were traditionally different across Member States and the choice between the broker-dealer and auction systems was viewed as internal matter for the market, attempts to introduce one single European model have failed. Therefore, the harmonisation initiative left determining the structure and functioning of the market to the national authorities or the stock exchanges themselves, but transparency requirements were to be harmonised throughout Europe.

With this solution, the issue at stake was the competitiveness of broker-dealer markets in the face of the more transparent electronic auction markets. The regulatory outcome was a compromise solution that allowed for substantial deviation between the two types of markets in post-trade price transparency.

The example of price transparency regulation showed that, at the EU level, harmonisation could not be swiftly achieved. But more importantly, it demonstrated that the competition between exchanges had led to a convergence towards a more efficient market structure even without regulatory intervention, witnessed by the introduction of the electronic trading system model at the London Stock Exchange shortly after the debate,[92] or Deutsche Borse's move from IBIS (an electronic inter-dealer-broker system) to XETRA, a pure electronic order-driven system.[93] The decision was made by the Exchange Council of the Frankfurt Stock Exchange, so a private industry initiative, rather than public intervention, achieved more harmonised market microstructures.

Such spontaneous convergence at national level shows the relevance of market dynamics in regulatory decisions. National stock exchanges were under pressure from investors to adopt better systems, and responded effectively to this pressure. There is also some competitive element to this specific change in market microstructures, as in the 1990s institutional investors became not only more important but also more and more international. Cross border investments were rising, and so arguably markets had to offer the best available trading environment to attract them.

4.2 Disclosure

As explored above, one important theme that has called for regulation in financial markets is information disclosure. Within this category, two types of relevant information provision can be distinguished: a duty of listed companies to disclose to the primary markets where their securities are listed (disclosure in the prospectus), and the duty of traded companies to ensure disclosure in the secondary markets in the form of continuous disclosure obligations (ongoing transparency obligations).[94]

---

[92] In the 1990s institutional investors' presence and weight increased in the European markets. Surveys showed that institutional investors were concerned by execution costs that could negatively impact their portfolios' performance, and were willing to sacrifice immediate execution if that resulted in lower trading costs. See Schwartz R.A. and Steil, B. (1996) 'Equity Trading: Institutional Investors' Trading Practices and Preferences', in Steil, B. (ed.) *The European Equity Markets* (London: Royal Institute of International Affairs). In response to this, exchanges designed their trading mechanisms to offer a choice between immediate execution and delayed execution. 'The London Stock Exchange, for instance, has emphasized that one purpose of SETS (a new order-driven market [...]) is to reduce trading costs by offering the opportunity of trading patiently, with limit orders, to investors.' Demarchi, M. and Foucault, Th. (2000), 'Equity Trading Systems in Europe: A Survey of Recent Changes', *Analyse d'Economie et de Statistique*, vol. 60, pp. 73–115.

[93] This still ran parallel though with floor trading on the eight German stock exchanges of the time. See Demarchi and Foucault (2000).

[94] Once these instruments start trading, however, there is a third type of information that becomes very relevant, but not immediately available, to

4.2.1 Prospectus Directive: applicable law and arbitrage possibilities

The Prospectus Directive (PD)[95] designates the supervisory authority for securities issues. For derivatives and bonds and that are denominated above €1000, the directive allows the supervisory authority to be chosen out of: those jurisdictions where the issuing firm is incorporated; the place of its listing; and the place where an offer is made to the public. In the case of shares, or bonds that are denominated below €1000, the home Member State is the state where the issuer has its registered office.

The latest proposal from the European Commission proposed to eliminate this distinction and broaden the scope of choice to all debt securities, whatever their denomination.[96] The logic behind this was to create more competition. As Luxembourg and London are regarded as the centres of bond issuance activities, issuers are likely to choose an authority that is experienced in the issue of bonds or derivatives. The Commission proposal wanted thus to leave room for choice of supervisory authority to allow for efficiencies flowing from positive network externalities.[97] The proposal was not accepted, even if, in reality, the minimum threshold may not have a substantial impact on the market. On the one hand, bond issues are easily modifiable to denominations above €1000 and, on the other hand, retail investors do have access to such bonds. But, as Schammo describes, the €1000 denomination threshold has an interesting negotiation history.[98] There was a compromise under which the choice of home state (and, along with that, the choice of supervisory authority) was made possible with a very low limit of €1000, in exchange for further tightening of the scope for private regulation.

---

investors and supervisory authorities: trading data. This third type of information disclosure is trade transparency, closely linked with the market microstructure discussed above.

[95] Directive 2010/73/EU of the European Parliament and of the Council of 24 November 2010 amending Directives 2003/71/EC on the prospectus to be published when securities are offered to the public or admitted to trading and 2004/109/EC on the harmonisation of transparency requirements in relation to information about issuers whose securities are admitted to trading on a regulated market (2010) OJ L 327/1.

[96] See http://ec.europa.eu/internal_market/securities/prospectus/index_en.htm

[97] See Enriques and Troger (2008); Ferran, E. (2004), *Building and EU Securities Market* (Cambridge: Cambridge University Press), p. 56.

[98] Schammo, P. (2011), *New Perspectives on Regulatory Competition in Securities Markets* (Cambridge: Cambridge University Press).

As for the distinction between retail and sophisticated institutional investors, the recent amendment of the PD lifted the threshold of €50,000, which previously defined transactions that qualified as non-retail. The new threshold is set at €100,000.[99]

Scope for divergence in the implementation of EU level legislation (the Prospectus Directive) occurs in areas such as the *translation requirements, the publishing requirements, and the definition of 'public offer'*.[100] The *enforcement regime and sanctions* attached to the breach of provisions used to be a further source of divergence, currently under harmonisation.[101] Although for the time being the harmonisation of sanctioning regimes goes no further than harmonising the powers of competent authorities and introducing a minimum amount for maximum fines, this already brings national systems more in line, and carries the promise (or threat) of further action at EU level if it is deemed necessary.

4.2.2 Transparency Directive

The Transparency Directive,[102] similarly to the prospectus directive, assigns the administrative competences to the authority of the state of incorporation for share issuers, while issuers of debt securities above €1000 can choose among the same regimes as under the Prospectus Directive.[103] Wholesale markets, debt instruments with a denomination

---

[99] Art. 1 (3) of the amending act, modifying Art. 3 (2)c of the Prospectus Directive.

[100] This source for divergence is subject to review in 2016, according to Art. 4 of the amendment, which asks for the Commission to consider whether the definition of public offer should be modified. The preamble of the same amendment states that '(11) In order to allow for the efficient application of [the Prospectus, Transparency and Market Abuse Directives] and to clarify underlying problems of differentiation and overlaps, the Commission should put forward a definition for each of the terms "primary market", "secondary market" and "public offer".'

[101] See the Sanctions Communication and its implementation in EU legislation, such as the MAD, PD, etc. Communication from the Commission to the European Parliament, the Council, the European Economic and Social Committee and the Committee of the Regions 'Reinforcing sanctioning regimes in the financial services sector' Brussels, 8.12.2010 COM(2010) 716 final.

[102] Directive 2004/109/EC of the European Parliament and of the Council of 15 December 2004 on the harmonisation of transparency requirements in relation to information about issuers whose securities are admitted to trading on a regulated market and amending Directive 2001/34/EC.

[103] See Art. (2) h of the directive. Here the amendments to delete the differentiation between low and high denomination debt securities have not been proposed yet.

above €50,000 are excluded from the mandatory disclosure rules, and similarly to the Prospectus Directive's new increased threshold for a wholesale disclosure regime, the Commission is now proposing to increase this to €100,000.[104]

The Transparency Directive lays down minimum duties on firms to publish annual financial reports as well as half-yearly interim financial reports. It also requires the disclosure of major shareholdings (acquiring or disposing of blocks of shares). The national laws may prescribe *stricter requirements*, which leaves scope for relevant divergence across Member States. However the current Commission proposal to amend the Transparency Directive aims to curb Member States' powers. It would allow issuers to voluntarily disclose more than is legally expected of them but it would not permit Member States to prescribe stricter requirements.[105] This is an interesting development from the perspective of regulatory competition since, so far, investor protection has been a frequent excuse for stricter binding national standards. The current trend towards a single rule book and greater harmonisation seems to channel this towards uniform rules at European and Member State level. It is interesting to note, however, that private actors may continue to comply with higher standards if they wish to do so. In this respect, if markets require more disclosure, issuers can satisfy them; but under the new approach to financial market regulation at EU level, it should no longer be Member States that decide to impose these rules. This signals a transfer of regulatory power from national public regulators to private parties.

Under the Transparency regime, there are, nevertheless, issues that fall entirely under national regulatory competence that are not touched upon in the current proposal to amend the Directive. The private law *liability for false statements, public enforcement* of the disclosure obligations and *criminal sanctions* are all up to Member State legal actors to define.

---

[104] Proposal for a Directive of the European Parliament and of the Council amending Directive 2004/109/EC on the harmonisation of transparency requirements in relation to information about issuers whose securities are admitted to trading on a regulated market and Commission Directive 2007/14/EC. Brussels, 25.10.2011 COM(2011) 683 final.

[105] See, e.g., the proposal to abolish quarterly reports and interim management statements.

4.3 Insider Trading

The Market Abuse Directive (MAD) deals with insider trading and market manipulation. For insider trading rules, the applicable law is either the law of the Member State where the financial instruments are (or where they have requested they be admitted to) trading, or the state where the relevant action is carried out.[106] In practical terms this means the law(s) of the Member State(s) where the securities of the firm are admitted to trading (thus the more markets a firm accesses, the more legal regimes it needs to comply with), and very probably the law of the headquarters of the firm.[107] The issue of compliance with the rules of multiple jurisdictions is increased in cases where the corporate headquarter is placed in a Member State other than the country of listing, and in cases of multiple listings.

The MAD originally laid down minimum rules on both issues. However, in the Lamfalussy process, at level three these minimum rules were virtually turned into maximum harmonisation,[108] leaving little scope for divergence across Member States.

The fields where countries have substantial discretion today in working out their own national rules are the *liability* and the *enforcement regimes*. However, new rules on enforcement are currently proposed by the European Commission. Market abuse (insider dealing and market manipulation), as well as inciting, aiding and abetting such breaches have to be accompanied by the possibility of criminal sanctions, for which the proposal prescribes a minimum, that they have to be effective, proportionate and dissuasive.[109] Moreover, the criminal sanctions should also be applicable to legal persons.

---

[106] Art. 10(b) of the Market Abuse Directive. Enriques and Troger (2008) note that this connecting factor resembles the classical *lex loci commissi delicti*, which acknowledged that certain activities or failures to act can be tracked more efficiently by the competent authorities at the location of their occurrence. Enriques, L. and Troger, T.H. (2008), 'Issuer Choice in Europe', *Cambridge Law Journal*, vol. 67, pp. 521–559.

[107] The headquarters of the firm is usually the place where statements are made, which establishes the applicability of the law on market manipulation. With regard to insider trading, the headquarters is the location of the insiders, even if in practice this does not necessarily mean that they trade on that given market.

[108] Enriques and Troeger (2008).

[109] Proposal for a Directive of the European Parliament and of the Council on criminal sanctions for insider dealing and market manipulation Brussels, 20.10.2011 COM(2011) 654 final.

The proposal's Explanatory Memorandum explains that, 'One of the problems identified in the impact assessment is the fact that the sanctions currently in place to fight market abuse offences are lacking impact and are insufficiently dissuasive, which results in ineffective enforcement of the Directive'.[110] The UK authority, for example, reported 11 criminal convictions for market abuse between 2009 and 2011, and at the end of 2011 there were 15 further individuals under investigation,[111] whereas other EU Member States do not have criminal sanctions foreseen for such breaches.

Further modifications to the Market Abuse Directive are also proposed, in the form of a regulation.

4.4 Takeover Bids Directive

The Takeover Bids Directive lays down rules governing the situation of hostile takeover bids, leaving a significant scope of discretion to Member States in implementing it. The divergence in the rules across countries extends to the percentage of holding at which a mandatory bid should be launched, which makes sense if countries have different ownership structures. It also has provisions prescribing the duties of the Board of Directors (allowing or prohibiting them to actively defend against a hostile bid *without shareholder approval*) and a rule suspending transfer restrictions and voting caps in case of hostile takeover situations (the breakthrough rule).

These divergences may lead to substantial differences in the outcome of a takeover bid and, thus, over time they might impact the corporate governance and ownership structure of that jurisdiction as a whole.

Looking first at the issue of the percentage at which a mandatory bid should be launched, we can observe that given the different ownership structures in different countries, it may be desirable to have different thresholds in place for example in the UK compared to Germany.

The governing law is the law of the registered office of the (target) company for the threshold for the mandatory bid rule and exemptions from it, and for the neutrality or permissible defensive tactics of the Board, as well as for providing information on the target company's employees.[112] However, the governing law is the law of the Member State where securities are admitted to trading for *transparency issues,*

---

110 Ibid.

111 FSA announcement available at: http://www.fsa.gov.uk/pages/Library/Communication/PR/2011/114.shtml

112 See Art. 4 (2)e; and Art. 5 (3).

procedural duties under the Takeover Bids Directive, and the *price for the mandatory bid.*[113]

For companies that have multiple listings (for the issues listed above as governed by the rules of the country of listing) the governing law is:

1. the target company's home state (where it is registered), if its shares are listed also on this home market; or
2. it is the country where the shares were first admitted to trading in case they are not listed in the home country's market; or
3. the companies have the choice of governing law on the first day of trading if trading commenced simultaneously in several markets.

5. CHANNELS OF COMPETITION PRESENT IN EU SECURITIES LAW

5.1 Free Choice of Law or Mobility

5.1.1 The governing law, scope for and allocation of choice

The previous section explained the governing legal rules and the scope for divergent national rules in the main areas of securities regulation. To summarise the applicable laws in a cross-border context, Figure 3.1 demonstrates the applicable law and competent authorities for shares and bonds below €1000.

With regard to issues under the rules of the state of incorporation, firms need to reincorporate in order to change the applicable regime. However, for issues governed by the market of trading, they need to change markets or enter the market of the legal regime of their choice. There is a clear difference between the two types of mobility: mobility through incorporation and mobility across markets. As for the former, out of state incorporation is not an option in all Member States, and reincorporation is costly. A firm can clearly not be incorporated in two Member States at the same time. Whereas, in the case of mobility across markets, listing on another jurisdiction's market is feasible and it is possible to cross-list on several stock exchanges at the same time.

5.1.2 Cumulative regulatory features

Whilst such cross-listing will not result in a duplication of legal requirements concerning public regulators' rules (given a clear definition

[113] See Enriques and Troger (2008), p. 20.

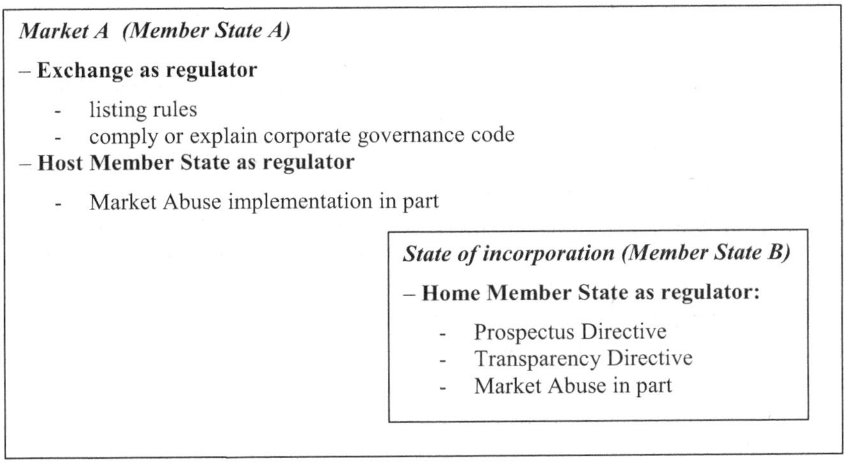

Figure 3.1 Applicable law for different securities laws

of a single applicable legal regime and mutual recognition),[114] private regulatory requirements may apply in each individual market. In these cases, the strictest legal regime will determine the stringency of regulation in all markets, irrespective of other jurisdictions' comparatively lax standards. This is because the subject of the parallel regulations is the same entity that issued the listed financial instrument, that is, the same issuer has to comply with rules of varying stringency. This can lead to an accumulation of regulatory requirements on the issuer and result in an accumulated high stringency of listing requirements (for example, in corporate governance standards to follow within the listed firm).

This accumulative feature of parallel regulations is very important as it can influence the strategy of legal actors and regulates *vis-à-vis* regulatory arbitrage. One possible strategy is for issuers to list on the market where standards are highest, while they stay listed on markets where standards are lower. The result will be a compliance with the strictest requirements in all markets, which may translate into benefits for the issuer as long as investors perceive it as optimal or at least preferable over laxer regimes. Whether the issuer will be able to signal its superior

[114] An exemption from this is the Market Abuse Directive (proposed Market Abuse Regulation), where more than one single jurisdiction's rules may apply at the same time, as applicable law is defined according to where the infringing activity took place or had its effects.

'product quality' to the investors in markets with lower regulatory standards is an issue that will be discussed later.

Another potential arbitrage strategy arises when the issuer wants to opt for lower standards. Under regulatory feature accumulation it would have to opt into (that is, list on) a market with a laxer regime, and de-list from all other stringent regime markets.

The above cases of cumulative regulatory features should be distinguished from the scenario where the applicable legal regime is linked to the home supervisory authority, coupled with mutual recognition when entering other jurisdictions. Under this legal design of applicable law, one market participant can have only one set of rules applicable and therefore accumulation of legal features cannot occur.

Another market access design is host-country control, where the regulatee has to comply with each jurisdiction's rules where he is physically or economically present. Here, no regulatory feature accumulation takes place because the subject of regulation is not the regulatee itself, but rather his activity, or product offered, within each market. This design of market access means that the products or activities are no longer going to be homogeneous (similarly regulated) in all jurisdictions. In other words regulation by stricter jurisdictions will not have any impact on the activity or products offered in jurisdictions with laxer standards. When a market participant enters two or more different markets with different regulatory standards, these will not add up, but instead different rules will apply to the products, contractual relationships, and so on in the different jurisdictions. This means that the output (product, contract, legal relationship) and its legal features will be differentiated. No accumulation of legal features from different jurisdictions is possible, even if the regulatee is present in several markets and complies with several jursidictions' rules. The legal rules in this case target the product or conduct of the regulatee in a given market, without that having any effect on the products or conduct of the same regulatee in other markets.

In other words, regulation can achieve the following results in terms of rules or standards:

- A single European standard (through harmonisation);
- A single national standard (through mutual recognition);
- Standard accumulation (through host country control of a business entity or its Europe-wide activities);
- Standard fragmentation (through host country control of local products or local activities).

The scope for regulatory arbitrage, and thus regulatees' strategies, will be different under the different legal solutions listed above.

5.1.3 Choice of law in securities law: who has the choice?

In the context of securities rules, it is not merely the issuers who have some leeway to choose which rules should be applicable to them. Investors have significant mobility across European markets, and can relatively easily avoid governing laws they do not consider to be good enough. If we differentiate between institutional and retail investors, there is perhaps more cross-border choice for the institutional actors, given their size and direct access to international platforms. But retail investors also have a substantial cross-border investment opportunity, not only in the form of direct share purchases, but also in the field of other retail investment products. The problem retail investors face is rather that of information asymmetries.[115]

As for issuers, the section above described the scope of legal arbitrage left open by European level regulation. But who exactly are the choosers of norms and what kind of legal arbitrage takes place? The choice of an issuer can be interpreted as the choice of the firm's management and owners, since the latter need to approve this choice of law. For firms that issue securities for the first time in an IPO, the choice of applicable legal regime will be granted to the parties who have the right of decision under the constitution of the firm or under the venture capital contract.

In the case of public companies, issuing new securities (be it shares or debt securities) will be the choice of management under strict rules of shareholder approval. In many of the public companies in Europe however there are controlling shareholders, who we can think of as the ultimate decision-makers for the choice of legal regime.

5.1.4 Legal arbitrage

As to what type of legal arbitrage takes place, we can observe four interesting trends.

First, issuers of bonds as well as fund managers seem to have preferred governing jurisdictions.

Secondly, in the area of equities, more recent European securities regulation has led to choice of regimes through a different channel than under the original regulatory structure. Originally, the aim was to help issuers cross-list and launch pan-European offerings. But, after the

---

115 See below the discussion on the possibilities of signalling.

introduction of the European passport of trading markets by the Investment Services Directive,[116] the situation changed. Issuers do not have incentives to cross-list, since they can easily sell their home-country listed securities to investors outside of their home country. Indeed equity markets are much better developed in the Member States, giving more opportunity for issuers to exploit their home market without having to go abroad to raise equity capital. Also, issuers may not offer cross-border issues very often because it is more costly for the investors to obtain information about the issuer (which is crucial to assess the quality of the financial product).[117]

Arbitrage could exist also in the case of private placements, as these are exempted from the detailed and costly disclosure requirements that public offerings have to comply with. Opting for a private placement means lower costs for disclosure, but it does not yield all the advantages of a public offer, as the products cannot be sold on to the wider public without due disclosure. In this sense the choice between public or private offer is a choice (free movement) between different markets. The Prospectus Directive established the criteria for private placement exemptions from disclosure as:

> The obligation to publish a prospectus shall not apply to the following types of offer:
>
> (a) an offer of securities addressed solely to qualified investors; and/or
> (b) an offer of securities addressed to fewer than 150 natural or legal persons per Member State, other than qualified investors; and/or
> (c) an offer of securities addressed to investors who acquire securities for a total consideration of at least EUR 100 000 per investor, for each separate offer; and/or
> (d) an offer of securities whose denomination per unit amounts to at least EUR 100 000; and/or
> (e) an offer of securities with a total consideration in the Union of less than EUR 100 000, which shall be calculated over a period of 12 months.

[116] Directive 93/22/EEC of 10/05/1993, EC Official Journal N L141 of 11/06/1993.

[117] CSES report refers to other corporate law and tax reasons: 'Even though passports are not used as often as they might be (especially for equity securities), this is often due to business considerations which are influenced by factors outside the scope of the current directive (e.g. market developments, other areas of corporate/tax law).'

Finally, within a very limited scope, there is also some choice among different markets and legal regimes for IPOs.[118]

5.1.5 Legal actors' competition for mobile regulatees

With relatively easy choice on both the demand and supply sides of the market (investors and issuers), legal actors compete not only for listings, but also for investors and investment. A benchmark often quoted is the stock of investments in financial products. European Commission reports, when looking at the competitiveness of EU financial markets and comparing them to the US, often take market turnover figures, nominal size of markets, or market volume to GDP in order to arrive at figures that are comparable and take account of differences in national economies.[119]

In terms of the direction of regulatory competition, it is argued that the UK attracts issuers with its high regulatory standards, while Ireland features as a jurisdiction with lax standards in its implementation of the Prospectus Directive.[120] This indicates that both directions, race in laxity and race in stringency, can be observed within the same regulatory field, which is an interesting insight from practice into the theoretical debates over regulatory competition.

Scholars also warn that regulatory competition in laxity is often the attribute of small jurisdictions, which do not have a substantial domestic investor base, and can therefore afford to introduce laxer standards for consumer protection. However, this can be seen as an overall welfare reducing race to the bottom only if sorting of firms and investors with different preferences is imperfect.

The outcome of regulatory competition, as it appears from the empirical evidence available, signals that there are presumably two types of firm. One type prefers stringent rules and high regulatory standards to signal to its investors the quality of the financial product it offers, while the other type of firm prefers less stringent standards and less burden on

---

[118] See interactions between company and securities laws at IPO stage discussed in the previous chapter.

[119] See, e.g., European Commission (2007), European Financial Integration Report, p. 33. The focus and language of publications after the 2007/2008 events in financial markets changed from competitiveness to financial stability, so more recent reports at national level for example do not contain highlighted references to the size of markets. Instead, in line with the argument put forward here that there is a shift of regulatory focus towards financial stability, they speak of the regulatory objectives of financial stability and consumer protection.

[120] CSES Report (2008).

the firm as to disclosure and other costly requirements. For these firms, the aim is to disclose only as much as is necessary and they assume target investors who have alternative means of obtaining information about them.

To conclude, the case of disclosure requirements, and more precisely the Prospectus Directive, shows an interesting trend of two-way regulatory competition, both in the direction of stringency and in the direction of laxity, occurring at the same time. From a welfare perspective it is hard to tell what the implications of such competition are exactly. But one feasible explanation for the phenomenon may be that there are different types of firms with different needs and different groups of investors with correspondingly different requirements. If this is the case, it can easily be imagined that competition among markets, and regulatory competition leaving space for their divergent regulation, can achieve perfect sorting of the issuers into jurisdictions of their preference, as well as investors into their preferred regulatory markets. This is another specific feature of securities regulation, that both the issuers (regulatees) and, to a great extent, investors (parties protected by the regulation) are mobile or have the freedom of choice of governing law (through choice of markets in which to invest). Whether this can lead to perfect sorting will be examined in Section 6.

5.2 Competition through Mobility of Capital, International Trade and Yardstick Competition

In the field of securities regulation, the choice of investor is basically equal to mobility of capital. In this sense, competition through capital mobility will be the other side of the coin to competition for regulatees (that is issuers) examined above.

International trade competition in financial market regulation (and securities regulation more specifically) can be interpreted in different ways. Here we look at the question whether international trade in goods and services within a country's entire economy (rather than only its financial services industry) could benefit from better financial market regulation – and whether this can motivate legal actors to regulate more efficiently. A vast body of literature discusses the link between financial structures and economic performance,[121] or financial regulation and

[121] See Section 1.4.1 above.

economic performance,[122] but some point out that the link between the two is not so direct.

Surely, even if strong financial markets do not directly translate into higher economic productivity (as there are several other factors that influence a country's total factor productivity), easier access to finance can be positive for economic development and can bring international trade advantages. This may be a motivation for certain legal actors to develop financial markets in order to create a more competitive economy.

Finally, yardstick competition is a field that is so far largely unexplored in the literature. The decision-making described above and governance mechanisms that are in place both facilitate information exchange, which is favourable to the emergence of yardstick competition. This form of competition can occur among legal actors who are not or not necessarily in direct competition with each other for production factors, regulatees or own resources. Yardstick competition is not excluded even in cases where other competitive channels are open (factor competition or competition for regulatees with choice or mobility), as long as legal actors' incentives to engage in these other forms of competition are not stronger than under yardstick pressure.

5.3 Conclusions: What Forms of Competition Take Place Today?

This overview of the relevant legal instruments at EU level, and the scope they offer for divergence at national implementation, indicates that there is some scope for differences in rules across Member States, although recent regulatory intervention at EU level generally narrows the scope for it. The rules determining the applicable law also show the scope for legal arbitrage that is available to issuers. The question is how attractive this legal arbitrage opportunity is to firms in the face of the costs of relocating the company's seat or changing the country/market of listing.

Enriques and Troger[123] warn that with the level of corporate mobility remaining rather low, there is a danger of double compliance costs, captive firms (firms in inefficient regulatory regimes not able to move to more efficient regimes) and thus a lack of incentive on the side of regulators to offer more attractive rules. They also point out that the regulator in the state where the company is registered may not have

---

122 See the discussion in Section 1.4.2 above.

123 Enriques and Troger (2008).

sufficient incentives to properly monitor firms that are listed only on a foreign market and have solely foreign shareholders.[124]

Mobility across markets (in cases where the competence and applicable law is established by the place of listing) entails accepting not only the rules (lax or strict) but also the market reality that these rules imply (illiquid or liquid, less deep or deep markets, and so on). However under the directives' rules it is possible for issuers in certain cases to change their markets without changing the applicable laws.

As for the substantive provisions of the above examined directives, there is no extensive scope for divergence among Member States' public legal actors on the main regulatory issues. Private actors, such as regulated markets and alternative trading facilities, compete on the market within the limits of their discretion on how to organise and regulate trading in their respective venues. We have also seen that this competition is a product market competition where market participants offer their services and compete for clients. But this market competition also means that there is a potential choice for investors, and also for issuers, that already resembles regulatory competition with choice.

International trade competition may be a motivation for certain legal actors to develop financial markets in order to create a more competitive economy. But they may have other incentives to do so, which are stronger and more direct than international competitive pressures. The regulatory competition examined above, with its choice of issuers and investors, can be one such stronger incentive for those legal actors that directly benefit from a bigger and thriving financial industry. The supervisory authority – with certain regulatory powers – would likely qualify as being one such legal actor.

Schammo argues[125] that regulatory competition was supported by Member States (and legal actors) that had as their mission the promotion of competitiveness. Whereas other Member States' regulatory approach was aiming at investor protection, rather than the enhancement of financial markets, and so they tried to prevent competition among national actors. An interesting development in this respect, since the financial crisis, is that most legal actors (certainly national legislators, regulators, and supervisors, as well as the EU legislator and regulatory bodies (that is, the European Commission and ESMA)) seem to show a shift towards financial stability and investor protection in their goals and

---

[124] Referring to Ferran, E. (2004), *Building and EU Securities Market* (Cambridge: Cambridge University Press), p. 152.

[125] Schammo (2010).

regulatory focus. Of course some weight is still placed on competitiveness, and not all jurisdictions and legal actors are concerned by such an apparent shift. But such changes in goals, however slight, as well as post-crisis institutional changes,[126] reinforce legal actors' incentives towards cooperative, rather than competitive, interactions. Therefore, as argued above, there is less and less scope for national divergence, which means there is less and less scope for both competition and cooperation – with centralisation replacing these.

6. A THEORETICAL INQUIRY: WHAT IS THE OPTIMAL DESIGN OF REGULATORY COMPETITION IN SECURITIES LAW?

As referred to above, different theories emerged about the potential welfare implications of regulatory competition in securities regulation. Here, we will first examine information asymmetries and signalling, as one issue that is decisive of the outcome of any form of regulatory competition. The analysis then turns to examine the embeddedness of legal rules in non-legal institutions and asks what scope remains to change the rules and what the impact of any isolated change would be. The existing regulatory framework of conflict of laws rules (determining the applicable law) is also analysed for the incentives and externalities it creates. Finally, the analysis closes with an assessment of the predicted outcome of regulatory competition both in terms of stringency or laxity, and in terms of overall welfare implications.

6.1 Identifying the Market Failure

It has already been pointed out that the welfare implications of regulatory competition will depend on the ability of investors to perceive and evaluate quality differences among different financial products, and, when regulation comes into the picture, among different legal regimes.[127]

---

[126] Both at EU level (e.g. the set up of the European supervisory authorities) and at national levels (such as the restructuring of FSA competences in the UK).

[127] See, e.g. Trachtman, J.P. (2001), 'Regulatory Competition and Regulatory Jurisdiction in International Securities Regulation', in Esty, D.C. and Geradin, D. (eds) *Regulatory Competition and Economic Integration: Comparative Perspectives* (Oxford: Oxford University Press), pp. 289, 293–294; Enriques and Troger (2008).

6.1.1 Can investors differentiate between financial products? Three theoretical scenarios

There are two theories concerning the efficiency of information disclosure and processing in markets without any regulation at all.

The first theory predicts imperfect information processing on the side of investors. In this case, higher voluntary disclosure would not be perceived by investors, but would cause higher costs for firms. In an open market, no firm would have an incentive to adopt higher disclosure standards than other firms, and disclosure is likely to stay below the optimal level. Presumably, under this scenario of imperfect information processing, the same holds true for decentralised regulation at Member State level: no state would adopt higher disclosure standards in an open EU market. Arguably, this is especially true for small Member States that could easily export the regulatory externalities, that is investor detriment, because most of the investors in the firms would be from foreign jurisdictions, while their national issuers would enjoy the benefits of low cost disclosure, liability, and so on. This scenario thus leads to a race to the bottom, both in terms of race in laxity and in terms of lower overall welfare.

Under the second scenario, investors process information better, there are signalling possibilities within the market, and branding can take place across jurisdictions. If investors can observe quality differences between firms' governing securities laws, some jurisdictions could emerge with high regulatory standards. This would either lead to an incentive for all Member States to follow the example and raise their own standards, or result in a two-way equilibrium with some states strengthening their regimes and others having a low level of regulatory intervention. The regulation and financial products offered would depend on investors' preferences, and in an open choice of law setting, both issuers and investors would be able to choose their preferred disclosure regime.

The scenario does not predict an overall race in stringency, because it allows for different preferences of both firms and investors. Given that disclosure is costly, the theory assumes that those firms and investors that prefer to assure quality and the matching of their preferences in different ways from mandatory disclosure rules would both be better off in a light-touch regulatory regime.

This scenario is argued to lead to a two-way separating equilibrium, under which all investors find the right match of investments, and all issuers find the right match of regulatory regimes. The result is thus perfect sorting, with positive welfare outcomes.

These two scenarios thus distinguish between two settings of investors' information processing capabilities (high and low), and allow for different preferences for both issuer firms and investors in terms of disclosures (high and low). The second scenario presumes heterogeneity of investors and issuers in terms of their preferences. However, both scenarios consider investors to be a homogeneous group in terms of information processing capacities. Either all investors are assumed to perceive high quality or none are. If we consider for a moment that some investors may be able to perceive quality while others are not, we arrive at a third potential scenario, under which the two way separating equilibrium is less than perfect, since low standards of disclosure may attract investors with preferences for such a regime, as well as investors that are not capable of perceiving quality differences among disclosure regimes. Let us call this possibility the third, alternative, scenario, with a two-way separating equilibrium that does not lead to perfect sorting.

6.1.2 Evidence to confirm or rebut these theories

What can we then learn from these theories? There are indications that issuers listing on different exchanges in Europe are driven by investor preference for these jurisdictions.[128] More research on this would certainly be welcome to clarify whether investors' or intermediaries' preferences drive the markets. Further, evidence exists in the empirical literature observing positive abnormal returns as a result of listing on high-quality exchanges.[129] Both these empirical observations seem to exclude a complete race in laxity (scenario one), and point in the direction of a separating equilibrium (scenarios two and three). Within that, however, it is not possible, based on the above observations alone, to decide whether scenario two (with positive welfare impacts and perfect sorting) or scenario three (with less than perfect sorting and mixed welfare outcomes) is more likely to occur in reality.

There are some practical examples of institutional investors warning about the consequences of a two-way separating equilibrium without sufficient distinction between the applicable legal regimes, that is, the

---

[128] At least this is what, in general, the financial media reported before, and even during, the financial crisis. See, e.g. *Financial Times*, 'Less risk, More Kudos on the Stock Exchange', 6 April 2008.

[129] See Enriques and Troger (2008). But the logic of most of these studies is somewhat backwards: first the high quality exchange is identified (by scholars), then it is tested whether the investors reflect the same thinking in their behaviour.

absence of an effective branding mechanism.[130] This signals that even sophisticated investors may find it challenging to distinguish the quality of disclosure regimes.

Besides, we should not forget that much of the investment into financial products goes through financial intermediaries. It is therefore not only individual (retail) investors that judge products' quality, but also financial intermediaries that may package and sell these to investors. If there is unresolved information or agency problems at the level of financial intermediation, we cannot expect a perfect match between investor needs and financial products. Both of these observations point in the direction of a less then perfect sorting under a two-way separating equilibrium, meaning that while some investors and issuers will opt into the regime of their preference, increasing overall welfare, some scope remains for certain investors to buy the products they do not correctly perceive the quality of, thus obtaining a less then perfect welfare outcome.

6.2 Target of Regulatory Intervention and Level of Harmonisation

Overall, it appears, then, that it is not possible to draw clear conclusions about whether investors are always able to measure the quality of the applicable legal regime, and if not, how often such mismatches of investment and investor preference occur. Therefore, to determine whether regulatory competition is ultimately welfare enhancing or welfare reducing would be premature. This may, even if only on a precautionary basis, call for establishing some minimum requirements to prevent the emergence of a two-way separating equilibrium where looser standards can actually cause investor harm and reduce overall economic efficiency. For optimal regulatory outcome empirical and behavioural economic studies could establish more precisely which markets, products and investors are yet to be better informed – and whether regulation can achieve positive welfare impacts. In markets involving high intermediation, retracing the incentives of intermediaries throughout the value chain is clearly a prerequisite to understanding what rules need to be mandated and at which level (private or public, European or national). A case-by-case analysis of markets seems to be thus the right way forward,

[130] Sophisticated investors complained about the secondary listings on the London Stock Exchange as not being divided perceivably enough to be distinguished, jeopardising the reputation of LSE as a market run by a high quality legal regime. See *Financial Times*, 'LSE to Act on Foreign IPO Concerns', 5 April 2007.

but this does not prejudge the search for the theory that describes and predicts markets best.

Since the financial crisis the EU legislator and regulator has introduced several reform measures to address information and agency problems effectively. Whether these rules will work out optimally and enable investors to perceive differences in product quality, or at least to rely on intermediaries, remains to be seen after the implementation of the full package of measures.[131] But, surely, the latest legal amendments point in a direction of centralisation and complete harmonisation (the pursuit of a Single Rulebook), leaving less and less scope for national differences.

6.3 Optimal Allocation of Competences

In order to determine the optimal allocation of competences, we should look at the incentives of the different legal actors. The existence, the intensity, and also the welfare implications of regulatory competition are dependent on these incentives. There are conflicting theories describing the public authority's behaviour. Conclusions range from benevolent regulators to self-interested maximisers. In the specific context of financial services, however, some general observations should be made.

On the one hand, financial services are a highly technical and complex field of regulation. This means that technical expertise within the regulating entity is needed, otherwise it could lend itself more easily to industry influence than other, simpler, regulatory fields. On the other hand, it is an extremely important area of regulation, because financing is a crucial element of economic growth and competitiveness. This means that any market or regulatory failures in finance can have potentially devastating consequences and contagion effects on other jurisdictions and the real economy. This feature of financial regulation may mean that political actors will want to assure themselves, perhaps over-assure themselves, against the political risks of a financial crisis. But these two features together (complexity and relevance) may also mean that, even with the best intentions of covering risks optimally, crucial fields will be left under-regulated, or unregulated, by politicians, if the issues are understood by neither political actors, nor their electorate.

---

[131] For example measures on consumer education would be an interesting terrain of (behavioural, empirical but also theoretical) research.

These specificities of financial markets make delegation to an independent regulatory agency an attractive option. Political decision-makers can thus commit to stay out of the influence of lobby groups and obtain the necessary technical expertise at the same time.

Regulatory agencies' ability to regulate optimally depends on a myriad of factors. Independence (from political actors) and in-house expertise (that is, independence from undue industry influence) are two crucial aspects. At the European level, the regulators are the European Commission and ESMA, with the ESC as a consultative body. Of these, the Commission, and to some extent ESMA, have some leeway to shape the regulatory landscape. ESMA, as a new agency, is independent under its statute, but still it is the Commission controlling its budget, and the national supervisory authorities constituting its membership and decision-making bodies.

At national level the legislator and government has less and less scope for action, and arguably the potential cross-border contagion effects of crises render national level regulation of contagion-capable issues[132] less optimal. As for national supervisory authorities, they are not only involved in ESMA, but also controlled by it in cases of defection from the coordinated strategies. There is, however, still some scope for different approaches to increase the effectiveness and efficiency of financial regulation. Authorities have their own culture and background, their own market context. It is not only their legal output but also their non-legal context that may render them different from each other. Such divergences are perceivable by market participants, and if these are worth the costs, they may trigger some arbitrage across jurisdictions. Even more important, the governance framework around supervisory authorities also makes differences or convergence among supervisory authorities perceivable to one another. Such information flows facilitate the emergence of yardstick competition. Interestingly, performance information may serve as yardsticks not only among supervisors, but also *vis-à-vis* other legal actors, such as the Commission (in a vertical setting) or private regulators and enforcement bodies (in an intra-jurisdictional setting).

---

[132] The current overview does not expand in detail on what areas of financial regulation are capable of posing cross-border contagion effects. An analysis of such nature would require much deeper inquiry into the details of actors' and legal rules' interactions. However in general disclosure rules are first and foremost an area targeting investor protection. Its potential contribution to contagion is usually not considered as a field calling for European level intervention for the main goal of crisis prevention.

Private regulatory actors have incentives to compete with one another, and under the current allocation of competences, they are left some scope to do so.[133] As they are market players, their regulatory competition is a product market competition, only they compete with rules and conditions set for other market actors.

Finally the judiciary is a legal actor that is historically used to performing the role of the ultimate enforcement and appeal body. However it is facing the same issues of technicality and complexity as political actors. Alternative dispute resolution bodies may have more specialised expertise.

6.4 Differences in Investment Patterns and Regulatory Missions

Member States currently differ in their choice of market structure and its accompanying legal rules, with regard to the target investor-type. In the UK, the relative significance of retail investors is negligible compared to institutional investors, whilst, in France for example, retail investors are more common. It could be argued that the differences between national markets (which may result from different rules but may also be the outcome of other – cultural, political, historical – determinants) would justify different rules to satisfy different demands. From this perspective, the disclosure rules for the French market should be different from disclosure rules in the UK.

The obvious question that arises, given the substantial integration of financial markets across Europe, is what types of externality are imposed on other jurisdictions. If the low disclosure regime targeting retail investors in the UK can reach retail clients in France, the aim of the French regime is potentially compromised. However, if uniform rules are introduced in all Member States, this one-size-fits-all approach may not satisfy preferences optimally if national markets are indeed different. The choice to be made is a trade-off between market integration and financial

[133] Stock exchanges have their own standards with regard to listing conditions, but it remains to be seen how the MiFID recast will regulate alternative trading venues. Recent amendments by the The European Parliament to the proposal tabled by the European Commission asked for stronger public regulation of trading venues. See Amendments adopted by the European Parliament on 26 October 2012 on the proposal for a directive of the European Parliament and of the Council on markets in financial instruments repealing Directive 2004/39/EC of the European Parliament and of the Council (recast) (COM(2011)0656 – C7-0382/2011 – 2011/0298(COD)). Available at: http://www.europarl.europa.eu/oeil/popups/ficheprocedure.do?reference=2011/0298%28COD%29 (last accessed: 11 November 2012).

stability on the one hand (two goals that can, in certain cases, already be in conflict with one another), and parallel experimentation to innovate and identify the best rules on the other.

7. CONCLUSIONS

7.1 Determinants of Competition with Mobility

7.1.1 Regulatees' preferences and information

To conclude, in the field of securities law, the regulated entity is most often the firm that issues securities. There are potentially other regulatees as well, such as persons holding inside information, markets and trading platforms, and so on. In those cases where the applicable rules allow for choice of law, the choosers of norms are mainly the issuer firms. But investors are also given the freedom to choose to invest in different products, with potentially different governing legal regimes. Nonetheless, minimum investor protection rules always apply in the investor's jurisdiction.

Looking at their preferences, issuer firms can arguably be categorised into three groups: one aiming for the highest mandated rules; another group going with the national rules, whatever those may be – either because they are medium quality issuers or due to transaction costs of opting into another, more suitable system; and finally a group of 'rogue issuers', who opt for the lowest quality mandated disclosure rules. We can also distinguish investors along differences in their sophistication in finance, which has direct implications on how much information disclosure they need and in what format. But investors also have different profiles according to their appetite for risk, or their attitude towards liquidity, for example. In an optimal world, investors would find the products best suited for their preferences.

This chapter recalled however that the welfare predictions of regulatory competition, where issuers can freely choose the applicable legal regime, are not unanimous. Some commentators predict a race to the top, either with a tendency towards more stringent disclosure standards and higher overall welfare,[134] or through a separating equilibrium with two different directions of legal change:[135] one towards more stringent rules

[134] See Romano (2001).

[135] Choi, S.J. and Guzman, A.T. (1997), 'National Laws, International Money: Regulation In A Global Capital Market', *Fordham Law Review*, vol. 65, p. 1855.

where firms can signal their quality; and another moving towards laxer standards for issuers who do not wish to avail themselves of such signalling mechanisms.[136] Other scholars predict a race to the bottom: laxer rules resulting in lower overall welfare.[137] Empirical results so far do not unambiguously resolve the debate over mandatory disclosure[138] but trends in cross-listing show that some firms opt into stricter regimes, which seem to exclude the absolute race to the bottom scenario, and suggests instead a separating equilibrium. This can be associated either with positive welfare outcomes,[139] or with mixed results, if investors are not all capable of perceiving the quality of disclosures and ultimately the quality of products. We can observe at least some instances of information problems where investors' preferences are not matched perfectly, but how often this occurs is not clear.

It seems therefore that the direction of competition in terms of overall welfare implications depends largely on the extent of information asymmetries between issuers and (sophisticated as well as retail) investors. If a 'lemons' market emerges, competition among systems may lead to a worse outcome than mandated uniform rules. This suggests that free choice of substantially different legal regimes could only deliver good results if investors were well informed. Information should not only be available, but it should also be clear and understandable without major effort or cost to investors. Legal competition could be spurred on by any innovation that creates a clearly distinguished regulatory 'brand' – a legal system of good quality norms that investors can appreciate and distinguish from legal regimes that do not serve their interest and preferences.

---

136 In this theory 'lower-quality legal regimes persist, typically as the law of regional exchanges catering to purely domestic issuers, because some firms have financing needs that do not warrant the costs of compliance with high-quality securities laws governing the world's principal exchanges'. Enriques and Troger (2008).

137 Fox, M.B. (1997), 'Securities Disclosure in a Globalizing Market: Who Should Regulate Whom?', *Michigan Law Review*, p. 2626 (arguing that political pressure will induce regulators to reduce disclosure standards to garner trading volume); Fox (1999) (purporting that issuers would 'choose a regime requiring a level of disclosure well below what is socially optimal for it').

138 Fox (1997).

139 Ribstien, L.E. (2004), 'Cross-listing and Regulatory Competition', *Review of Law and Economics*, vol. 1, no. 1; Coffee, J.C. (2002), 'Competition Among Securities Markets: A Path Dependent Perspective', Columbia Law and Economics Working Paper No.192.

7.1.2 Legal design of competence allocation and applicable law

Under the current legal landscape the scope for divergence across Member States is limited by European legislation, and further steps are being taken towards harmonisation, for example in the field of sanctions. Some possibilities for legal arbitrage occur in the choice of supervisory authority when offering bonds and derivatives, and issuers can choose to launch private placements instead of public offerings, but as it has been pointed out above, these target separate markets. For public offering of shares, locational decisions at IPO stage are relevant, as the competent supervisory authority is designated according to the place of the registered office. To change the seat of the company later on is arguably too cumbersome and also quite unusual in a company's life.

With regard to the supply side of norms, multiple legal actors were identified as having competence to set or apply rules within securities law. A recent development is the new supervisory framework, with more centralisation in both regulatory and supervisory powers. It is too early to test how ESMA reacts *vis-à-vis* other legal actors, but its institutional set-up suggests multi-lateral negotiated solutions, rather than legal outcomes invented by a truly European legal actor. But the governance framework allows for frequent interactions and information exchanges, which facilitates the emergence of yardstick competition. Choice of law (or mobility) is present in different forms for the various legal rules governing information disclosure around securities issuing and trading. Some areas of securities law are governed by the country of the issuer firm's registered office (for example, Prospectus Directive requirements for shares); other areas fall under the regime of the market of listing (for example, Prospectus Directive requirements for bonds). As for the design of legal regimes' interaction, we find mutual recognition (where the home state's national regime is recognised as valid governing law in any other Member State, such as the passporting of prospectuses), as well as host state control (where regulatees have to comply with the national requirements of each jurisdiction or market they are 'active' in, such as stock exchanges' requirements upon admission to trading).[140]

We noted that host state control can have two varieties. Certain features of regulation are cumulative, as long as the subject of regulation is the global activity of the regulatee (such as corporate governance standards of a firm listing on a stock exchange), rather than local

---

[140] Often mutual recognition has some limitations where host states can impose some of their national rules in the general interest. There is thus no sharp division line between home state and host state control.

activities (as, for example, an intermediary's dealings with local consumers). Such accumulation of regulatory features imply that in case of multiple applicable legal regimes, the regulatee complies with the highest standards or the most stringent rules not only when it deals with consumers or business partners from the most stringent jurisdiction, but also *vis-à-vis* any jurisdictions' actors. In other words, its presence in a stringent legal regime affects its stakeholders in all jurisdictions, making it possible for a 'race to the top' to emerge.

As for the second variety of host state control, regulatory compliance does not accumulate, because each Member State's law, if applicable, will only regulate local activities of the regulatee. It was argued that this creates regulatory feature or standard fragmentation, as well as compliance cost duplication (or even multiplication).

7.2 The Potential for Mobility and Yardstick Competition under Different Legal Designs

From a more forward-looking and normative perspective, it appears that regulatory competition could deliver positive welfare results in yardstick competition among national (as well as European) regulators to define disclosure standards and formats that work for a given market. Similarly, competitive rule-setting for intermediaries (conflict of interest, information disclosure, and so on) in different markets could also deliver positive results, and indeed the harmonisation efforts of the European legislator often looks to national experiences at the stage of preparing a proposal.[141] The recent financial crisis also spurred some debate about the hypotheses underlying the current regulatory framework. A potential paradigm shift in the overarching theory of how financial markets work would doubtlessly benefit from testing before introducing it on a larger scale and possibly at EU level. Yardstick competition among Member States is a form of parallel experimentation that could also perform this testing function.

But competition for mobile regulatees might also deliver different results, depending on the design of connecting norms (or international private law) that determine which jurisdiction's law applies to which situation. Under the legal design of host country control of local activities, competitive lawmaking for mobile regulatees may promote the

---

[141] See a number of impact assessment analyses in the field of financial services, available at: http://ec.europa.eu/governance/impact/ia_carried_out/ia_carried_out_en.htm.

rules of the biggest market, rather than the most efficient rules. Compliance cost duplication means that regulatees will only opt into a jurisdiction if the local market is worth the costs of compliance. Bigger countries would thus have an advantage in being an 'attractive' jurisdiction. Jurisdictions with small markets on the other hand are unlikely to attract high numbers of regulatees, even if they have the best rules, since these rules only apply within the borders and cannot be leveraged to other bigger markets.

However, competition for mobile regulatees with standard accumulation is a more promising scenario, since it prevents negative externalities from too lax legal regimes. As for its potential to reveal the best norms, we should consider whether stakeholders in all jurisdictions can fully appreciate any given Member State's rules. Small states will only have a real chance of becoming leading jurisdictions in a race in stringency or 'legal quality' if information about the quality of its legal regime is available to everyone, even outside the borders. In absence of such readily available knowledge of legal quality, it is again likely that bigger jurisdictions win the race, not solely on the basis of superior legal solution, but also because their rules are better known across borders.

As it emerged from the discussion above, information problems can inhibit the optimal functioning of regulatory sorting. Whether investors can fully understand the financial products and thus choose the product most suited to their preferences is a key condition to positive welfare effects. Therefore a mechanism controlling whether there is sufficient matching of investor preferences would be one possible way to address some pitfalls of competitive lawmaking.

Compared to competition for regulatees, yardstick competition on regulatory performance is more likely to work effectively even in the case of small jurisdictions. As the precondition of such competition is information exchange among legal actors, often associated with benchmarking, peer pressure or mutual evaluation, the size of markets and the knowledge of market players and citizens are not necessarily as important as in the case of competition for mobile regulatees.

Besides the dichotomy of big and small jurisdictions, the distinction between national and European level legal actors should not be forgotten either. Yardstick competition is a field where the European regulatory could (and to some extent already does) play an important role in facilitating information flows, performance comparisons, establishing benchmarks, and so on. Parallel experimentation does not mean that the role of the European legal actors is reduced to mere copying. It can define the best standards itself, as an active participant of this competition, or it can spark competition among national actors (for example, through a threat of intervention if a given field is not regulated well enough). But the theory of yardstick competition underlines the importance of looking at experiences of different jurisdictions. This is done to some extent already in impact assessments.[142]

Also, in securities law, we observe that mobility or choice, as a main channel of competitive interaction can be interpreted as mobility across markets. The definition of 'applicability of rules' results in a specific regulatory feature – portability – or, in other words, the stringent requirements of one jurisdiction accumulate with the strictest features of another jurisdiction's rules.

---

[142] See impact assessments on several issues concerning financial services and other areas, available at: http://ec.europa.eu/governance/impact/index_en.htm (last accessed: 14 November 2012).

4. Regulatory competition in EU competition law

1. INTRODUCTION: LEGAL FRAMEWORK AND REGULATORY COMPETITION IN COMPETITION LAW

This chapter examines systems competition in the field of competition law. Previous studies have addressed this issue[1] but an extensive inquiry with a comparative analysis has not yet been carried out in this field.

On the face of it, the field of competition policy does not lend itself easily to regulatory competition analysis, since the latter has mainly been understood as being the competition of legal actors and legal norms under free movement of regulatees. However, as described in Chapter 1, competition can take place in much broader forms than merely through mobile regulatees. This chapter will examine a considerable variety of these through the example of competition policy in the EU.

The framework of this chapter is the same as adopted earlier, starting with a general overview of the legal framework of competition law in Europe and a review of existing approaches to regulatory competition in antitrust law (Section 1). The analysis is then extended to the four models of regulatory competition based on different degrees of mobility. Section 2 examines whether there is scope for regulatory competition through different channels, such as: free choice of law or mobility of regulatees; international trade (the competitiveness of national firms and industry); mobility of capital; and yardstick competition. Section 3 looks into

[1] See, e.g. Head, K. and Ries, J. (1997), 'International Mergers and Welfare under Decentralized Competition Policy', *Canadian Journal of Economics*, vol. 30, no. 4, pp. 1104–1123; Barros, P.P. and Cabral, L. (1994), 'Merger Policy in Open Economies', *European Economic Review*, vol. 38, pp. 1041–1055; Smets, H. and Van Cayseele, P. (1995), 'Competing Merger Policies in a Common Agency Framework', *International Review of Law and Economics*, vol. 15, no. 4, pp. 425–441; Meessen, K.M. (1989), 'Competition of Competition Laws', *Northwestern Journal of International Law and Business*, vol. 10, pp. 17–30. The following sections provide a brief description of these approaches.

vertical and horizontal relationships between the various competition authorities under the framework of Regulation 1/2003. Here, the convergence of national competition laws is also examined, with a special focus on the provisions that were *not* subject to harmonisation by the Regulation (spontaneous policy convergence). To examine the drivers of such convergence, this section looks at the functioning of the European Competition Network and its impact on the competitive or cooperative strategy of national competition authorities, both in applying EU competition law, and in applying national competition rules.

In Section 4, the impact of private enforcement is assessed with regard to the role of national courts *vis-à-vis* national competition authorities and, horizontally, other national courts. The question posed is whether, and how, private enforcement could trigger a competitive reaction from national legislators, and what impact it would have if the European legislator left scope for divergence in procedural and other aspects.

Section 5 contains a hypothetical example of two jurisdictions with different competition policies and competitive law-making. Its purpose is to analyse the potential arbitrage strategies of firms and the strategic law-making of legal actors where the extraterritorial enforcement of competition law is imperfect. Section 6 offers conclusions on the drivers of competitive interactions within competition law, the areas where such competitive interactions occur, and the effect of the existing policy design on regulatory competition.

1.1 The Legal Framework: Actors Involved and Allocation of Competences

Competition law is a special legal field within the European Union legal framework because it is one of the few exclusive competences of the Union under Article 3(1) b of the Treaty on the Functioning of the European Union. According to Article 2 (1) TFEU:

> When the Treaties confer on the Union exclusive competence in a specific area, only the Union may legislate and adopt legally binding acts, the Member States being able to do so only if so empowered by the Union or for the implementation of Union acts.[2]

This legal framework already determines much of the allocation of competences in competition policy across Member States.

---

[2] Art. 2 (1) TFEU.

In practice, in the field of competition policy, dual layers of rules (European and national) co-exist. National competition law rules are set by the Member States' legislators, and national competition authorities act as regulators as well as enforcement agencies, with national courts also involved as enforcers.

European level competition law is set by the TFEU (Articles 101 and 102 on collusion and unilateral conduct, which this study will focus on) and secondary legislation may be adopted by the European legislator.

There is a European and a national level enforcement of the rules. At the EU level it is the European Commission (with recourse to the Court of First Instance (CFI) and the European Court of Justice (ECJ), as courts of appeal) and at the national level it is the national competition authorities (NCAs) that enforce the rules. In some Member States, national courts may be designated competition authorities,[3] and even where this is not the case, they may enforce competition rules in private actions for damages, and they may act as courts of judicial review and courts of appeal to decisions of national authorities. In cartel and unilateral conduct cases, both EU and national law can be applied simultaneously, provided that the application of national law does not prejudge EU law. In the field of merger control, European and national rules cannot be applied simultaneously and, according to the applicable regime, the enforcement agency is exclusively either the European Commission or the national competition authority.

With regard to the substantive rules of competition law, comparative studies have shown that a significant convergence among European and national laws has occurred.[4] Some Member States even abandoned their national competition law regime to adopt the EU rules.[5] This is a very interesting phenomenon in the context of competition between different regimes, and the reasons and implications of this apparent policy convergence will be examined in more detail.

1.2 Existing Typologies of Federalism and Regulatory Competition in Antitrust

Regulatory competition in competition policy has been described by legal, economic and political science scholars in various ways.

---

[3] This institutional arrangement was followed for example in Austria.

[4] See, e.g. Drahos, M. (2001), *Convergence of Competition Laws and Policies in the European Community: Germany, Austria, and the Netherlands* (The Hague: Kluwer Law International).

[5] This is the case, for example, in the Netherlands.

Economic models dealing with decentralised competition policy examine optimal competence allocation and the economics of federalism in merger control. One such model on competence allocation, worked out by Head and Ries, examines the externalities imposed by a merger control regime on another jurisdiction, under a decentralised system of merger control, as opposed to a centralised regime.[6] The externalities arising under this decentralised model stem from the difference in both the distribution of consumers and producers and the distribution of corporate headquarters among the hypothetical jurisdictions. They conclude that a centralised merger control system is warranted, given the existing negative external effects.

Other models show that a decentralised merger control that applies a territorial jurisdiction is inefficiently lax, whilst a decentralised regime with extraterritorial enforcement,[7] which applies a country's competition laws even to a foreign firm as soon as the firm's conduct has an effect on the market of that country, such as national competition laws in Europe, is inefficiently strict.[8] The conclusion of this model is, as for the one described above, that a centralised competition authority is the optimal solution as it will internalise all potential externalities.

Van den Bergh, Kerber and Budzinski respectively apply in their separate models the economics of federalism to antitrust policies. Further factors are examined in these federalism models beside externalities that may influence the welfare implications of decentralisation. Budzinski examines four criteria affecting the welfare outcome of decentralisation: cost savings; externalities; adaptability; and mutual learning.[9] The other analyses are generally extended to a cost efficiency analysis taking account of local preferences, restriction of the Leviathan state and competition as an innovation and learning process.

According to the approach followed by Meessen,[10] competition over competition laws is a rivalry about what the aim of antitrust policy should be. Scholars, enforcement officials and legal practitioners

---

[6] Head, K. and Ries, J. (1997), 'International Mergers and Welfare under Decentralized Competition Policy', *Canadian Journal of Economics*, vol. 30, no. 4, pp. 1104–1123.

[7] See the explanation of extraterritorial enforcement in Section 2.

[8] Barros, P.P. and Cabral, L. (1994), 'Merger Policy in Open Economies', *European Economic Review*, pp. 1041–1055.

[9] Budzinski (2006).

[10] Meessen, K.M. (1989), 'Competition of Competition Laws', *Northwestern Journal of International Law and Business*, vol. 10, pp. 17–30.

acknowledge that there has been disagreement about the goals of antitrust policy.[11]

Indeed these goals vary even today. In a study of 57 jurisdictions, Voigt notes that competition laws often contain stated purposes other than the promotion of competition. They may consist in furthering technological progress, improving international competitiveness, securing the survival of small and medium enterprises, or regional development concerns.[12] It is true, however, that the divergence of opinions is decreasing, and the various regimes get ever closer in the aims they pursue.[13]

The goals of antitrust law are also the starting point of the analysis in the work of Fox.[14] In her study, she asks, first, why antitrust laws are adopted increasingly in the various jurisdictions. Then she turns to analysing whether the mobility of firms allows for regulatory competition to attract investment and whether this competition leads to a race to the top or to the bottom. The framework of analysis also includes the phenomenon of jurisdictions aiming to export their antitrust rules, which Fox calls a 'race sideways'. Finally, she looks at the so-called 'regulatory disregard' of people and systems outside their respective jurisdictions by the various antitrust regimes, which is another way of describing externalities imposed on others, mostly unintentionally.

A different approach to competition about competition laws is taken by McChesney,[15] who examines, within the US, the competition of courts and the legislator *within* the same jurisdiction (*intra*-jurisdictional

---

[11] Ullrich, H. (1998), *Comparative Competition Law: Approaching an International System of Antitrust Law* (Baden-Baden: Nomos). The differences in the aims of intervention often correspond to the different efficiency theories about the virtues of competition. The documentation of different schools on competition policy has been carried out elsewhere and is not reviewed here in detail. (See for an overview: Budzinski, O. (2008), 'Monoculture versus Diversity in Competition Economics', *Cambridge Journal of Economics*, vol. 32, no. 2, pp. 295–324.) The fact that there are different competing theories about what is optimal competition policy is well-known, and this chapter – somewhat deviating from the structure of previous chapters – will not go into detail on the tenets of the different schools of thought.

[12] Voigt, S. (2006), 'The Economic Effects of Competition Policy – Cross-Country Evidence Using Four New Indicators', ICER Working Paper No. 20/2006.

[13] See the proceedings of the EUI RSCAS Competition Workshop held in June 2007.

[14] Fox, E. (2000), 'Antitrust and Regulatory Federalism: Races Up, Down and Sideways', *New York University Law Review*, vol. 75, pp. 1781–1807.

[15] McChesney, F.S. (2003), 'Talking 'bout My Antitrust Generation', *Emory Law Journal*, vol. 52, pp. 1401–1438.

competition). His study provides a detailed framework of analysis of 'competition for the field', by which he means the penetration of economics into law, and 'competition in the field', that is, the competitive interaction of courts in developing the law, once economic analysis has been accepted into antitrust policy thinking. Within the latter category, he describes competition with regard to the substance of the rules and with regard to their enforcement. He argues that competition in the field as to the substance of the norm takes place, for example, at the intersection of competition policy and intellectual property rights, where the courts are presently still looking for the best standard to be applied. An interesting extension of this line of research is Buzinski's work on the desirability of convergence or divergence in economic theory.[16]

Finally Kerber and Budzinski[17] analyse the four types of regulatory competition based on different degrees of mobility and economic openness in the field of antitrust policy: yardstick competition or mutual learning; regulatory competition via international trade; inter-jurisdictional competition through the mobility of production factors and firms; and, finally, regulatory competition through free choice of law. Kerber and Budzinski argue that, apart from mutual learning, all other types of competition in antitrust are likely to lead to a race to the bottom, that is, are detrimental to overall welfare due to externalities.

To conclude, the examination of competence allocation and regulatory 'competition in competition law' (that is, competition about the formulation of competition law rules) reveals several potential frameworks for analysis, all of which may be relevant to a final judgment on whether competitive interactions are desirable in this field. The following sections will explore how the four channels of competitive interaction do, or could, function in EU competition law.

---

16 Budzinski (2008).

17 Kerber and Budzinski (2004).

2. WHICH CHANNELS OF COMPETITIVE INTERACTION ARE AVAILABLE?

2.1 Choice or Mobility in Merger Control

In this section, the scope of physical mobility or mere choice of law by undertakings will be assessed briefly, in order to establish whether the first two forms of regulatory competition (competition with free choice of law and competition with physical mobility) can be expected to emerge in the field of antitrust policy under the current rules.

The jurisdictional rules of European and national competition regimes will be analysed below: first, with regard to merger control; then with regard to cartels and unilateral conduct. Both issues will be dealt with in the vertical setting first (European vs. national legal rules), followed by an analysis of the horizontal dimension (across different national regimes).

As a preliminary remark, it should be noted that the connecting factor that renders the law applicable and establishes jurisdiction over a given conduct or practice is 'participation in a given market'. Since even firms that are not present through either primary or secondary establishment can be caught, it is also referred to as extra-territorial enforcement. This is a distinctive feature of antitrust regimes, which *a priori* prevents choice or mobility. In theory, the only way to escape the applicability of a competition law regime is to avoid the market of that jurisdiction (a type of 'mobility across markets') which means not only the lack of a physical presence but also no exports into that market. However, the flaws in antitrust enforcement may diminish the effectiveness of this framework. A further interesting question is whether firms have choice of forum for enforcement.

2.1.1 Vertical dimension of merger control: EU or national regime?

In the field of merger regulation, national competition authorities apply national merger control rules, whilst the European Commission applies the European rules. Thus the forum is linked to the applicable law in the vertical context, while this is not the case for rules applying to unilateral conduct and cartels.

The jurisdictional rules of the Merger Regulation were originally based only on turnover thresholds. Later amendments introduced changes to these thresholds and new jurisdictional rules that, besides turnovers, also take account of the number of national competition authorities involved in determining whether EU law should apply.

Originally, EU legislation did not allow firms to choose the applicable law or forum but the 2004 amendment to the Merger Regulation introduced an interesting exception to that rule: pre-notification referrals.[18] This rule provides for the merging entities to request that their case be referred to the authority of their choice. This cannot, however, be considered a free choice of companies, since the competition authorities can refuse their request.

In the case of downward pre-notification referrals, firms may submit a request for their case to be assessed by the competition authority of a specific Member State if 'the concentration may significantly affect competition in a market within a Member State which presents all the characteristics of a distinct market and should therefore be examined, in whole or in part, by that Member State'.[19]

The case will not be allocated to the authority preferred by the firms if:

- the national competition authority requested by a firm expresses its disagreement within 15 days; and
- if the Commission does not refer the case to the requested jurisdiction.[20]

It should also be noted that the request for referral is notified to all Member States,[21] and even though they are not given any formal power to object to a referral, they may informally contact the Commission to prevent downward referral of the case.[22]

Similarly, the merging entities can request an upward referral, in cases where the concentration does not have a Community dimension but it is capable of being reviewed under the national competition laws of at least three Member States. In cases of upward referrals any of the concerned national competition authorities may object. The Commission may refer a case in its entirety, or make a partial referral.

---

18 Art. 5 (4) and (5) of the European Merger Regulation (ECMR). Council Regulation (EC) No 139/2004 of 20 January 2004 on the control of concentrations between undertakings OJ L 24, 29.01.2004, pp. 1–22.

19 Art. 4 (4) first indent.

20 Even if the criteria for the request are met, the Commission enjoys discretion in its decision to refer the case. However if the Commission does not act within 25 days, the case is deemed to be referred.

21 Art. 4 (4) second indent of the ECMR.

22 However, as the table below will show, refusals of referral requests are rare.

Table 4.1 shows the use of pre-notification referrals, together with their acceptance or refusal. The data shows, first, that upward pre-notification referrals are more popular than downward referrals (up to the end of 2011 there have been 67 requests for downward referrals and 227 requests for upward referrals). Secondly, the refusal of such requests is rare; only 5 (upward) referrals have so far been refused.

This indicates that firms do have some degree of discretion in choosing the competition authority and applicable law for their merger transactions, even if the criteria for requests leaves quite a narrow scope for their discretion. Whether the application of these rules leads to the circumvention of the competition rules depends on the scrutiny exercised by the Commission and the national competition authorities when deciding on the requests. It is unlikely however that this opportunity opens the way to what could be described as regulatory competition with free choice of law.

Table 4.1 Upward and downward pre-notification referrals by end 2011

	04	05	06	07	08	09	10	11	Total
Downward referral requests	2	14	13	5	9	6	6	10	65
Downward referrals	2	11	13	5	9	6	7	10	63
Partial downward referrals	0	0	0	1	0	0	0	1	2
Refusal of downward referral	0	0	0	0	0	0	0	0	0
Upward referral request	20	28	38	51	23	23	26	18	227
Upward referrals	16	24	39	50	22	25	24	17	217
Refusal of upward referral	2	0	0	2	0	0	1	0	5

Note: European Merger Control Council Regulation 139/2004 – Statistics.

Source: European Merger Control Statistics

2.1.2 Horizontal dimension: free choice or mobility among national merger control regimes

Under the regulatory competition model that has free choice or mobility in the horizontal setting, companies may have the freedom to choose the applicable law or to move to the jurisdiction of their preference. However, in the case of antitrust law, the scope of their choice or free movement is limited by the nature of antitrust laws, which use market shares as connecting factors to establish the applicability of the law to a given transaction. Most competition law regimes catch mergers that take place outside the country's borders between firms which are not seated or incorporated in the given jurisdiction, and have no branches or other assets there. This is simply by reason of their presence in the market for certain products. An overview of the 27 EU Member States' legal regimes reveals that the rules establishing jurisdiction over a merger are very similar across countries.[23] National laws usually establish jurisdiction over any merger that has an appreciable effect on the national market. They determine 'appreciable' on the basis of turnover thresholds, with the exception of Portugal, Slovenia and Spain, which apply a combined turnover and market share test, and the UK, which applies a combined turnover and share of supply test.

The Member States adopted an even more uniform approach to the applicability of merger control to foreign enterprises: all states, with the exception of Cyprus,[24] establish jurisdiction over foreign-to-foreign mergers through the jurisdictional rules (turnover or market share tests), regardless of whether the merging undertakings have subsidiaries or assets within that jurisdiction.[25]

From this assessment it appears that within the EU it is not possible for enterprises to opt out of a merger control regime by physical movement (that is, by way of transferring the corporate seat or re-incorporating in another country). Firms are bound by merger control regimes as long as they have a significant presence in the markets of those countries. Therefore, choice of law as well as mobility is restricted both in the horizontal and in the vertical context, and can only be practised as a form of mobility across markets.

---

[23] This main rule applies with minor qualifications. See, Davies, J. (consulting editor) (2007), 'Merger Control 2007, the International Regulation of Mergers and Joint Ventures in 61 Jurisdictions Worldwide', *Getting the Deal Through, Global Competition Review Special Report 2007* (London: Law Business Research).

[24] Merger control law of Cyprus applies only to companies incorporated there.

[25] Davies (2007).

2.2 Choice or Mobility with Regard to Rules on Cartels and Unilateral Conduct

With regard to rules on cartels[26] and unilateral conduct,[27] firms do not have a choice between the application of national or of EU law. If trade between Member States is affected,[28] European competition law will be applicable. Triggering the application of EU competition law is relatively easy, given that anti-competitive conduct covering a substantial part of one Member State's market, may already have an effect on intra-Community trade.[29] Nonetheless, certain national cartel cases of minor importance will fall outside the reach of EU competition law under the *de minimis* Notice,[30] or the block exemption regulations.[31]

---

[26] Art. 101 TFEU.

[27] Art. 102 TFEU.

[28] According to the definition laid down in Commission Notice 2004/C 101/7 Guidelines on the effect on trade concept contained in Articles 101 and 102 of the Treaty.

[29] See, e.g. C 359/01 P *British Sugar* v *Commission*, judgments of 29 April 2004, with the conclusion that where an agreement aims at restricting imports in order to prevent competitors from entering a national market, such agreement is capable of affecting trade between Member States. The actual effects do not have to be demonstrated, it is sufficient if the agreement is 'capable of having an effect' on trade.

[30] Notice of the European Commission on agreements of minor importance, which do not appreciably restrict competition under Art 81 (1) of the Treaty, OJ 2001 C-368/13. In this document the Commission set up some market share thresholds below which an agreement or concerted practice will not be deemed to have an appreciable effect on competition and therefore will not be investigated. Some, so-called, hardcore restrictions are not covered by this Notice, and these will thus fall under the scrutiny of the European Commission If any parties' contract contains any such restriction, it is unlikely to qualify for an exemption from the application of competition law rules. These are mainly price fixing, limiting production or sale, and market sharing.

[31] Block exemptions have been set by the European Commission for horizontal agreements, vertical agreements, transfer of technology and licensing agreements. Some sector-specific measures have also been adopted, e.g., for motor vehicles, agriculture, insurance, etc. It is interesting to note that some of these block exemptions are different in nature from the national competition law rules. For example, the Commission is currently reviewing the vertical block exemption regulation and is considering examining the market share of the buyer in addition to that of sellers. This may trigger additional interest in industry having their agreements reviewed under national competition law rather than under EU law.

A major difference from the Merger Regulation is that by triggering the application of EU competition law, firms do not escape national competition rules: European and national competition laws may be applicable simultaneously.[32] Under the Walt Wilhelm decision[33] of the ECJ, national competition law rules may be applied in cases where EU competition rules apply; however they cannot obstruct the effectiveness of EU law. In 2007, 23 Member States applied their national competition laws in parallel with the European provisions.[34]

2.2.1 Choice of law: the vertical context and the horizontal context

Companies' only way of avoiding the application of EU competition law to their conduct or agreement is to avoid affecting intra-Community trade. Their only option for avoiding the application of any national competition laws is not to participate (substantially) in that market.

Also, companies cannot choose merely between the applicability of two or more national competition laws for the simple reason that, once more than one national competition law regime were applicable to them, their conduct or agreement would almost certainly affect trade between Member States, which would trigger the (often parallel) application of EU competition law.

2.2.2 Choice of forum: the vertical context and the horizontal context

Beside the applicable law, the question of choice of enforcement authority (forum) may also be relevant in the regulatory competition context. Where a particular national competition law applies, there is no choice of forum; within that jurisdiction the designated national competition authority will be competent. However, there are different authorities that may be competent to apply EU competition law. Therefore, after establishing that EU competition law applies, the question is which authority should enforce EU rules?

Where EU law applies, both in the vertical (Commission or national authority) and in the horizontal (choice of national authority) context, the

---

[32] However, as will be discussed below, Regulation 1/2003 imposed certain restrictions on the decisions that can be reached under national competition law. Council Regulation 1/2003 of 16 December 2002 on the implementation of the rules on competition laid down in Articles 81 and 82 of the Treaty OJ 2003 L/1.

[33] Case 14/68, *Walt Wilhelm and Others* v *Bundeskartellamt*.

[34] See the May 2007 document of the ECN Working Group on Cooperation Issues, 'Results of Questionnaire on Convergence of National Competition Laws. Based on the answers received from the NCAs'. Formerly available at the website of the European Commission, DG Competition. On file with the author.

choice of forum for firms is excluded under Regulation 1/2003. The detailed rules of the Regulation will be discussed later; here it is sufficient to say that the Regulation does not leave scope for choice or physical mobility across the different enforcement agencies.

However, the picture is slightly different in cases of private enforcement. There is scope for choice, not for the regulatees (undertakings), but for the litigants to choose the national court to enforce EU competition law.[35] This aspect of choice of law and forum by the parties suffering damage in the domain of private enforcement will be analysed further below.

To conclude, it is unlikely that competition for regulatees could arise under choice or mobility models of regulatory competition. However, Member States may engage in other types of juridical competition without mobility: competition in international competitiveness of domestic firms; or yardstick competition with other jurisdictions. Exploring these types of competition among rule makers and enforcement agencies is the subject matter of the following sections.

2.3 Competition Through International Trade

As noted above, in the field of competition policy 'choice of law' and 'mobility' are defined as participation in (or withdrawal from) a market. As soon as firms' products reach a market (having an appreciable effect there), the jurisdiction's competition regime is applicable to them. It is, however, worthwhile pausing at international trade competition for a moment, and considering its implications in an international (EU and non-EU) context. With imperfect extraterritorial enforcement, different jurisdictions' competition laws may not always catch all firms that run up against their rules.

The applicable competition law regime of a country naturally influences its firms' international competitiveness. International trade competition and competition law have been the subject of scholarly analysis.[36] Here, the analysis will focus on two different hypothetical cases: competition in laxity and competition in stringency within international trade competition. The aim of this inquiry is to determine which of the two competitive strategies would be more likely to dominate if

---

[35] Indeed the distinction between the role of regulator and public enforcement agency is blurred in the case of NCAs.

[36] For a review of this issue, see Mitschke, A. (2008), *The Influence of National Competition Policy on the International Competitiveness of Nations* (Heidelberg: Physical Verlag).

jurisdictions had the freedom to design their domestic competition policies competitively.

2.4 Competition Through Mobility of Capital and Persons

The difference between this model of regulatory competition and the one described previously is that, under this model, workers and capital (of which clearly the latter is easier to relocate) should be mobile. Indeed capital mobility can take the form of foreign direct investment on the one hand (consisting of acquiring control of an already existing foreign enterprise or 'greenfield' investment, that is, setting up a new entity) and portfolio investment on the other hand (where the supply of money on financial markets is increased).

This model of competition in competition laws can be described as being similar to the previous channel of competition that assumed only mobility of goods (international trade) but no mobility of production factors. However, in this model, capital (and labour) are assumed to move into the jurisdiction that has more to offer them, working with two possibilities: either investors are looking for more stringent competition laws and enforcement, or they are seeking out laxity-oriented regimes.

Kerber and Budzinski argue that mobility of capital is not very different from mobility of firms as regulatees. They conclude that this model does not have broad practical implications, since the 'effects doctrine' (extraterritorial enforcement) would prevent firms from re-incorporating in a jurisdiction with lax competition rules and abuse their home market by exporting back the goods or services.

But there is a further possibility to consider under competition with capital mobility: when a *lax* or *strict* jurisdiction provides a more profitable investment opportunity, it may attract capital even without prospects to trade goods back to the jurisdiction of origin. In other words, there is a possibility that capital mobility may allow for a special type of competition for investment, that draws investment out of the country with one type of competition policy into a jurisdiction with the opposite, more profitable, policies. This capital will yield higher benefits not through trading with the jurisdiction of the capital investment's origin (which would trigger the applicability of that country's competition law), but through monopoly profits within the lax regime or through trade with third country jurisdictions.

2.5 Yardstick Competition: Experimenting and Mutual Learning

Yardstick competition is argued to be very relevant in the case of competition law.

> Economists and legal scholars influence the academic discussion on competition policy, and they may have large incentives for the innovation of new theories and arguments and/or for importing them into domestic academic discussions. Administrative officials, judges, and lawyers likewise have incentives to adopt new theories and to develop new arguments. The complex incentives and transmission mechanisms that might foster yardstick competition of competition laws merit detailed study.[37]

This section aims to identify whether yardstick competition may arise in antitrust law, and, if so, in what form it takes place.

The goals that competition law should pursue have always been heavily debated, and discussions continue even today, despite the considerable convergence that has taken place among EU Member States as well as world-wide.[38] There still remain some differences between the national regimes. The diverse goals of antitrust policies can satisfy diverse preferences within a given polity, or add value from a mutual learning from different systems. Clearly, uniformity has its advantages too, such as cost savings and efficiencies of scale (such as network effects of substantial case law, legal certainty, and better knowledge of the system).

Within the European Union, a change in the goals of antitrust policy has been discernable throughout the past decade. Whilst the aims of antitrust policy differed substantially across jurisdictions in the early 1990s, nowadays academics, regulators and practitioners agree that the goal of competition law is to maximise consumer (or overall) welfare.

Thus a clear convergence has taken place among the European countries in favour of the goal of enhancing welfare. But can this be described as an innovation and diffusion process? The major difficulty, which arises in convergence studies in general and regulatory innovation studies in particular, is that it is hard to prove what the exact causes of convergence are.

Similarly, in the area of substantive legal provisions on antitrust, there have been many instances identified of new solutions and of emulation. Convergence studies describe instances of policy convergence in national

---

[37] Kerber and Budzinski (2004).

[38] See the presentation held by Prof. Gerber and the following discussion at the 11th Competition Workshop, 2–3 June 2007, San Domenico.

competition laws within the European Union where there was no legal obligation to harmonise the national system.[39]

Procedural rules, jurisdictional thresholds, economic analysis and institutional set-up are examples of such convergence. For instance, the implementation of the European merger control regime had to be built on innovative solutions in order to make it work within the European 'federal' system.[40] Similarly the decentralisation of the enforcement of EU competition law rules on cartels and unilateral conduct may be described as innovation triggering changes at national level.

These examples also demonstrate the possibilities for yardstick competition. Regulatory innovation introduces a new legal solution, several legal solutions coexist, which is described as 'parallel experimentation' or 'laboratory federalism' and, finally, the best solutions will be taken over by other jurisdictions. If the process leads to complete convergence, the potential for further yardstick competition disappears. If, however, a new legal innovation arises, this process of parallel experimentation re-starts. The experimentation with different solutions and adoption of the best functioning rules can also result in legal divergence, for example when different rules serve better divergence preferences.

Yardstick competition in antitrust law could potentially be welfare enhancing in areas where optimal and efficiency-enhancing rules are still disputable. This is, or had been, the case in several areas, such as a number of exclusionary practices within the abuse of dominant position: predatory pricing; rebate schemes; and tying and bundling. But, it can also play a role in other areas, such as establishing the optimal balance between the protection of intellectual property rights (thereby incentivising innovation) and abuse of dominance provisions (granting access to protected intellectual property, enhancing competition). A further area that may need refinement in terms of a standard is private enforcement, where apart from the issues that the EU legislator will harmonise, all other procedural and substantive legal elements are to be defined at national level.

The question that arises, however, is whether parallel experimentation with different rules in these areas would increase or, instead, reduce

---

39 See, e.g. Drahos (2001).

40 Kerber and Budzinski (2004) suggest merger control as an example of vertical mutual learning. Merger control was introduced in Germany in the 1970s and existed in a few Member States before it would have been introduced at the EC level, which may be described as policy learning by the European level from the national level. Several examples have been observed in the opposite direction as well.

overall welfare. The answer to this question lies in two issues. The first concerns the architecture of the 'rules of the game'; that is, whether legal divergence is allowed in areas where externalities are important? The second question is: To whom are competences allocated and are there incentives for competent legal actors to compete or, rather, to cooperate?

The first question has been the main subject of our discussion up to now, with the conclusion that the main lines of competition policy in Europe are not open to legal divergence, preventing any potentially significant external effects arising from different competition strategies among Member States.

In what follows, the second question will be explored, with regard to the few areas where competition law regimes might diverge. We will be examining what incentives are given to legal actors through the applicable governance mechanism and competence allocation regime (Regulation 1/2003 and the European Competition Network). We will also explore what role private parties (beneficiaries of competition law rules) can play in choosing the forum of litigation in private enforcement, and what competitive effects, if any, this may introduce among actors both in an intra- and in an inter-jurisdictional setting.

To conclude, in competition law there are a number of open channels of competitive interaction. Yardstick competition promises to be relevant, as it is often very effective where the other channels of competition are not open. How this works in practice is analysed in Sections 3 and 4. International trade competition is strong by definition in the case of antitrust policies, and this was the main reason that a European level competition law was introduced. However, since the opportunities for applying competition laws in diverging or strategic ways are rather limited, this channel of competition is, in practice, often pre-empted by legal rules. How international trade competition would work is the subject of a hypothetical inquiry in Section 5. With regard to competition through choice or mobility, it was noted that firms cannot choose their preferred legal regimes, which are tied to the market where the firm is active or that its activity affects. Here, similarly to securities trading rules, a 'mobility across markets' exists. Market access is therefore conditional upon compliance with the relevant market's legal rules.

3. NETWORK GOVERNANCE AND LEGAL ACTORS' INTERACTION

This section examines the interaction of various legal actors (courts, regulatory agencies and legislators) along three dimensions (vertical, horizontal and intra-jurisdictional). It looks at the legal framework introduced by the Modernisation Regulation (Regulation 1/2003) and its impact on the interaction between the various legal actors. The section that follows deals with the role of courts in regulatory competitive or cooperative interaction with other legal actors. This is then explored in more depth through the specific case of private enforcement, assessing the interaction between courts and national competition authorities as well as the interaction among national legislators.

3.1 The Issues Raised by Decentralised Application of EU Law: The Modernisation Regulation

It has been noted that regulatory competition can arise not only among legislators, but also in relation to other legal actors. Furthermore, competition can take place not only horizontally, but also vertically (if the legal architecture allows for it). Therefore, a well-designed governance system has to take account of both the multitude of actors and the vertical and horizontal dimensions. The application of European competition law demonstrates this very well with the example of Regulation 1/2003. The legislator decided to decentralise the enforcement of EU competition law and introduced a governance framework to eliminate divergences across Member States. In regulating the interaction among the legal actors (the European and national legislator, regulator and courts) the Regulation indeed addresses both vertical and horizontal relationships, and aims to limit any scope for divergence in the practice of national competition authorities as well as national courts.

The main focus of the Regulation is to settle the allocation of competences vertically between national competition authorities and the Commission, and horizontally among national authorities. However, it also touches upon the application of EU competition law by national courts and the interaction of national and EU competition law through the practice of NCAs and the case law of courts. This section reviews the arrangements of this framework in order to assess what effects it might have had on convergence, both in terms of EU law enforcement (as intended) and in terms of convergence of national competition law regimes (as an unintended effect).

3.2 The Governance Framework

Several provisions of Regulation 1/2003 aim to ensure that decentralised enforcement of European competition law does not lead to inconsistency, thus excluding differentiation as well as forum shopping. Article 11 (3) and (4) require national competition authorities to inform the Commission in advance of their planned decision and provide a summary of the case. This provision is aimed at preventing divergent or inconsistent application of Arts 101 and 102 by the national authorities. Active monitoring of these decisions by the European Commission will have the potential to prevent non-uniform application.

A further provision aims to prevent national competition laws from interfering with EU competition law. Article 3 stipulates that national authorities are obliged to apply EU competition rules (should they be applicable to the case at hand) whenever they are applying national competition law rules.

Furthermore, although national competition law may be applied in parallel with European competition law, the application of national law cannot result in prohibition of agreements that are not caught by Article 101 or exempted under Article 101 (3) of the TFEU.[41] There is an exemption from this rather 'intrusive' rule where national competition policy pursues an objective different from that pursued by Articles 101 and 102 of the Treaty.[42]

There is not such prohibition, however, with regard to the application of national competition rules to unilateral conduct. These rules may be more stringent than EU law, and can prohibit conduct that would be allowed under Article 102.

Looking at the provisions of the Regulation, and the related Network Notice of the Commission,[43] interesting conclusions emerge for regulatory competition within competition law in Europe.

Table 4.2 provides an overview of the interaction of legal actors, under the applicable legal framework.

Under the modernisation regulation the enforcement of Article 101 and Article 102 is decentralised in such a way that the European Commission and national competition authorities have parallel competences. This means that both the European and the national authorities may enforce these rules. The main issue that arises under this system of parallel competences is case allocation, that is, who should apply the EU competition law rules in a given case? This question can be raised both in the vertical (European Commission-national competition authority) and in the horizontal context (which national authority).

---

[41] Art. 3(2) of Regulation 1/2003.

[42] Art 3. (3) of Regulation 1/2003.

[43] Commission Notice on cooperation within the Network of Competition Authorities (2004/C 101/03) text with EEA relevance.

Table 4.2 Overview of Regulation 1/2003 and its impact on scope for divergence[a]

	Interaction between actors	Issue	Legal source	Provision
Vertical	Between regulators at the EU and national level (COM–NCA)	Competences: case allocation	*Paras 14–15*	Effects in more than 3 Member States; application of other Community provision; new competition issue; ensuring effective enforcement
		Ensure uniformity: COM 'intervention'	Art. 11 (6); *Paras 50–57*	COM may act after case allocation to NCA to ensure effective and consistent application of EU law; relieves NCA[b] of competence
		Ensure uniformity: notification	Art. 11 (3) & (4); *Paras 43–49*	Inform COM in advance of planned decision & summary of case
	Between EU regulator and national courts (COM–NC)[c]	Ensure uniformity: notification	Art. 15	Notify decisions, COM may submit written observations
		Ensure uniformity: *stare decisis*	Art. 16	NC cannot arrive at decision contrary to previous COM decision; NC should consider staying the proceedings
	Between EU legislator/ regulator/ courts and national legislator (EC/COM/ECJ –national legislator)	Relationship between EC and national competition laws	Art. 3	Stricter national rules prohibited on concerted practices – exception of 'different goals'; stricter rules allowed on unilateral conduct

Table 4.2 continued

	Interaction between actors	Issue	Legal source	Provision
	Between national regulators (NCA–NCA)	Competences: case allocation	*Paras 5–13*	NCA commencing procedure; reallocation on 'well-placed' basis to single NCA; 2 or 3 NCAs
		Ensure uniformity: informing other NCAs		
Horizontal	Between national courts (NCA-NCA)	Ensure uniformity	Case law of ECJ on supremacy and the state liability doctrine	NC has duty to apply EC law; can be liable for damages for erroneous application
		Ensure uniformity: COM as central monitor	Art. 16 (see above)	NC cannot arrive to decision contrary to previous COM decision; NC should consider staying the proceedings

Notes:
[a] The Article numbers in the legal source column refer to Regulation 1/2003; paragraph numbers *in italics* refer to the Network Notice of the Commission.
[b] Including national courts acting as national competition authorities.
[c] Acting as fora of judicial review and private enforcement.

3.2.1 Vertical case allocation: competences of national authorities and the European Commission

Looking first at the vertical relationship between the Commission and national competition authorities, with regard to the allocation of cases to the Commission, paragraphs 14 and 15 of the Network Notice establish that the Commission is well placed to conduct the proceedings:

- If the agreement or practice affects more than three Member States;
- if the case is closely linked to other Community provisions which call for the action of the Commission in their application;

- when a new competition issue arises;
- or when the Commission has to ensure effective enforcement.

It is also worth noting that the Commission may decide a case only with regard to one Member State, even though it affects more than one Member State. Such a decision will constitute a 'lead case' for all national competition authorities, who will have competence to decide on the same infringement with regard to their jurisdiction in light of the Commission's decision.[44]

Parallel proceedings between the European Commission and a national authority may not take place and national competition authorities cannot commence proceedings once a case has been opened by the Commission. The reverse is possible, however. The Commission may start proceedings under Article 11 (6) even if a national competition authority is already acting on the case. In this case, however, the national competition authority or authorities dealing with the case will be relieved of their competence.

The Commission is entitled to start proceedings even after case allocation has taken place. The Network Notice further defines the criteria for such Commission action under Paragraphs 50–57. Thus the Commission may initiate proceedings after the allocation of a case if:

- the network members envisage different decisions;
- if the decision that NCAs want to make is obviously in conflict with previous case law;
- if the national authorities are unduly delaying the proceedings;
- when similar competition issue arises in several Member States which calls for development of Community competition policy or effective enforcement; and, finally,
- in any other case where the national authority in charge of the case does not object to yielding its competence to the European Commission.

The above provisions are a strong assurance that NCAs will not engage in divergent enforcement practices. However, up to 2010, the Commission has not initiated any proceedings to ensure coherence in decision-making (Article 11(6)).[45] The fact that the use of this interventionist

---

[44] Paragraph 14, Example 5 of the Network Notice.

[45] Commission Staff Working Paper accompanying the Report from the Commission on Competition Policy 2010 {COM(2011) 328 final} Commission Staff Working Paper (2010). Available at: http://ec.europa.eu/competition/publications/annual_report/2010/part2_en.pdf (last accessed: 6 February 2012).

procedure has not been necessary so far can be read as a sign of cooperative behaviour on the part of national competition authorities.

3.2.2 Horizontal case allocation: competences of national authorities

With regard to the horizontal dimension, the Network Notice envisages the allocation of a case to one or more (but, in any case, a maximum of three) national competition authorities.

Regulation 1/2003 and the Network Notice lay down rules for case allocation. Paragraphs 5 to 9 establish in general that the competition authority that commences a procedure *ex officio* or upon complaint shall in principle be in charge of the case. Re-allocation of cases should occur if this authority does not consider itself well placed, or where other authorities consider themselves well placed.

Paragraph 8 of the Network Notice sets out three cumulative criteria for determining which national authority is well placed to hear a case:

1. the agreement or practice has effect in, is implemented in, or originates in the jurisdiction;
2. the authority can bring the infringement to an end effectively and sanction it adequately;
3. the authority can gather the necessary evidence (possibly with the assistance of other competition authorities).

A national authority is considered well placed to deal with a case if the infringement substantially affects competition mainly within its territory[46] or, in cases where these substantial affects arise in more than one Member State's territory, the competition authority is well placed if its action is sufficient to bring the entire infringement to an end.[47] Finally, the Notice allows for a case to be allocated to two or three national competition authorities under parallel proceedings if the action of a single authority is not sufficient to bring the entire infringement to an end. In such parallel proceedings the NCAs are encouraged to designate a lead authority, which will coordinate the investigation.

The competence of any national competition authority or of the Commission is not pre-empted by the decision of another national authority. However, in such parallel or consecutive proceedings, the earlier decision may serve as sufficient basis for rejecting a linked case or to suspend the proceedings (in the case of national competition authorities).

---

[46] Paragraph 10 of the Network Notice.
[47] Paragraph 11 of the Network Notice.

3.2.3 The results of case allocation

Statistics on case allocation between the different national authorities and the European Commission reveal that enforcement is indeed decentralised in the vast majority of cases. As Table 4.3 also shows, in the period 2005–11, the yearly caseload of the Commission varied between 10 and 26, whereas national authorities dealt with a caseload of between 129 and 181 cases per year, the proportion of cases dealt with by the Commission relative to national authorities varied between 7 per cent and 19 per cent over these years.

A report by the European Commission reveals that disputes over which authority should be dealing with a case were rare.

> In 2010, there were once more very few instances where discussions on allocation of cases took place, and even fewer occasions where a case changed hands after initial allocation. A small number of complaints were re-allocated from the Commission to NCAs that were willing to follow up the matters raised. Collaboration on cases also took place through assistance by NCAs in respective national investigations under Article 22 of Regulation 1/2003, underscoring the ability of NCAs to deal with investigations involving cross-border aspects.[48]

Table 4.4 displays the allocation of cases across national authorities.

3.3 Legal Actors' Interaction

3.3.1 The activity of national legislators and patterns of cooperative interaction at EU level

In the context of vertical competition between the European Community and its Member States it is worth examining the impact of Regulation 1/2003 on the pattern of competition and cooperation. The modernisation Regulation introduced a decentralised enforcement system of European competition law, but did not prescribe harmonised rules for Member States at the national level. However, in practice the impact of the Regulation was predicted to be,[49] and in fact has been, a convergence of laws.

---

48 Commission Staff Working Paper (2010).

49 Larouche (2005), at p. 171: '... there is a fair chance that in the long run national authorities will focus their attention on the application of EC law, at the expense of national law'; Larouche, P. (2005), 'Coordination of European and Member State Regulatory Policy – Horizontal, Vertical and Transversal Aspects', in Geradin, D. and Petit, N. (eds), *Which Regulatory Authorities in Europe?* (Cheltenham, UK: Edward Elgar).

Table 4.3 Data on vertical case allocations

	Total Year 2004	Total Year 2005	Total Year 2006	Total year 2007	Total year 2008	Total year 2009	Total year 2010	Total Year 2011	January 2012
Total number of case investigations of which the Network has been informed	301	203	165	150	159	150	169	163	8
– of which COM cases	101	22	21	10	10	21	11	26	1
– of which NCA cases	200	181	144	140	149	129	158	137	7
Cases in which an envisaged decision has been submitted by NCAs during the period indicated	32	76	64	72	60	70	94	88	9

Source: European Commission (Available at: http://ec.europa.eu/competition/ecn/statistics.html).

Table 4.4 Data on horizontal case allocations among NCAs

Cases per Member State:		
Member State	New case	Envisaged case
Austria	35	6
Belgium	42	8
Bulgaria	15	4
Cyprus	3	1
Czech Republic	13	9
Denmark	69	37
Germany	148	74
Greece	35	27
Estonia	7	3
Finland	23	9
France	207	79
Hungary	84	21
Ireland	14	2
Italy	93	76
Latvia	13	4
Lithuania	17	12
Luxembourg	1	–
Malta	2	1
The Netherlands	85	40
Poland	25	11
Portugal	43	12
Romania	26	11
Slovakia	11	11
Slovenia	26	16
Spain	101	56
Sweden	39	17
United Kingdom	56	15
European Commission	214	*Not applicable*

Source: European Commission (Available at: http://ec.europa.eu/comm/competition/ecn/statistics.html#2).

The Regulation in Article 3 (1) prescribes the application of European competition law by national authorities wherever they apply national law and the applicability of EU law is triggered by the thresholds of the transaction.

Two official documents reliably demonstrate the actual impact of this, at first sight, rather innocent-looking provision. The first one is the Regulatory Impact Assessment document prepared before the adoption of legislative amendments implementing Regulation 1/2003 in the UK.[50] The other is a study carried out by the European Commission in 2008 on the convergence of national competition laws.

3.3.1.1 UK regulatory impact assessment on the implementation of Regulation 1/2003 In the case of the UK, after the entry into force of the Modernisation Regulation, the legislator decided to:

- remove the domestic notification system;
- harmonise the domestic maximum financial penalty with that applied under EU law and a number of national regimes;
- codify the practice in which the authorities can accept binding commitments;
- eliminate fast-track notification procedures for agreements falling outside a block exemption only marginally;
- introduce the requirement of taking into account the penalties levied in other member states when applying penalties subsequent to infringement decisions under EU law;
- require obtaining a warrant before searching domestic premises;
- give powers to the NCA to seal premises during investigations; and finally,
- remove exclusions for which there were no equivalent in EU law (for example the UK had exclusions for vertical agreements).

The UK implementing legislation's impact assessment suggests reasons for the legislative changes achieving greater similarity between UK and EU competition law and justifies amendments that are not required by the Regulation itself. The arguments of the UK legislator are twofold. On the one hand, it was feared that differences between national and European competition laws would unnecessarily overburden the national competition authority and the courts applying the two laws. On the other

[50] Regulatory Impact Assessment: Giving effect to Council Regulation 1/2003 (2004).

hand, businesses were also likely to be subject to excessive regulatory burdens by having to comply with two sets of rules, the situation being further aggravated by the uncertainty this approach would cause businesses trying to assess the applicability of one standard or the other. This, in the view of the UK legislator, was sufficient reason to introduce rules that converge on EU rules.

3.3.1.2 European Commission Study on the convergence of national competition laws The UK legislator was not alone in this conclusion. In 2008, the Commission launched a questionnaire to gather information about convergence of national competition laws. The results of this exercise also demonstrated that a majority of Member States chose to align their national legislations with EU law, despite not being required to do so under the Regulation.

The published results of the questionnaire contain the following caveat:

> For the purpose of this table, the term 'convergence' should be construed as referring to a voluntary process of approximation of national antitrust legislation to EC Regulation No 1/2003, and does not imply that such approximation is mandatory in respect of all the provisions of the Regulation referred to in the table. The table is not meant to express or reflect any view as to the compliance of national antitrust legislation with certain mandatory provisions of the Regulation 1/2003 and, more generally, may not be regarded as reflecting or stating an official position of the European Commission or any NCA.[51]

This questionnaire revealed, however, a growing trend of convergence toward EU law, and may even have exerted some influence on Member States that up to then had been hesitant to change their rules. The data collected through this questionnaire shows that, in 2006, the notification system had been abolished in 17 Member States, with three further states considering such amendments, and only six states maintaining their notification system regardless of the amendments made by Regulation 1/2003 to the European system.[52] In 2008, the number of Member States converging with the European solution was already 19, with three more

[51] ECN Working Group on Cooperation Issues Results of the questionnaire on the reform of Member States (MS) national competition laws after EC Regulation No. 1/2003 (as of April 14, 2008).

[52] The statistics show the 27 Member States, the figures here adding up to 26 only, as Portugal was reported to maintain a system that is partially convergent on this issue.

countries considering amendments and only four (Denmark, Greece, Italy and Latvia) staying with their original national solution.

There is greater divergence in national approaches to the power to impose structural remedies. Only 11 Member States have such provisions in their national competition laws, three others have similar, but not fully convergent solutions, while two countries are currently considering amendments in this direction. The other 10 Member States do not have, and are not considering adopting, provisions to empower national competition authorities to impose structural remedies under national competition law. There is also quite some divergence across Member States on the issue of specialised national courts – 20 Member states have responded that they do not have such specialised courts, while the remaining seven have specialised tribunals.

Note however that changing the court system and building up human, financial and institutional resources for specialised courts is not done as easily and as promptly as adopting and applying the above listed convergence amendments.

Overall, however, the overwhelming majority of Member States adhere to the EU level legal solutions. Only between one and four Member States diverge from the EU law solution. Of course, this information alone does not give us the full picture on the actual tendencies for convergence or divergence. It would take a comparison with the legislative situation before 2004 to confirm the degree of actual convergence of national laws with the European solution. However, a clear move towards greater alignment of national laws within the EU is observable.

3.3.2 National competition authorities' behaviour and cooperative interaction among themselves

In order to secure uniform application to the EU level competition law rules, Regulation 1/2003 required that the European Commission and the national competition authorities form a Network of national competition authorities.

In the assessment of competitive and cooperative interaction among legal actors, mention has to be made of this Network, and its impact on the behaviour of national competition authorities.

The case law of national competition authorities is observably converging,[53] and this trend was noticeable before 2004. The same is true for

[53] See, e.g. Hervé, D. and Jeunemaître, A. (1996), 'The Convergence of Competition Policies in Europe: Internal Dynamics and External Imposition', in Berger, S. and Dore, R. (eds) *National Diversity and Global Capitalism* (Ithaca,

competition policy in general as contained in the laws of the Member States. The question of what causes convergence has been extensively discussed in the literature.[54] This study examines two aspects that are relatively new to the convergence debate in antitrust issues: the role of independent regulatory agencies (often referred to as IRAs), and the role of the European Competition Network. It is difficult, however, to establish what causes convergence, and how much additional impetus an institution such as the ECN may give, in addition to convergence dynamics that already exist.

With regard to the influence of the ECN and the role and incentives of IRAs (such as national competition authorities), one interesting question to explore is who is driving policy convergence, the legislator or the NCAs (eventually the courts)? If it is the NCAs, that may be (partially) explained by their special incentives as independent agencies or by the existence and practice of the Network.

As discussed in the first chapter, the incentives of independent regulatory agencies, such as national competition authorities, may be to enhance their independence from political actors. The national authorities obtain more legitimacy (and therefore more independence from government actors) within the European Competition Network than by acting on their own. The trade-off may be less independence in shaping their own national competition policies and more dependence on the leadership of the European Commission and on other national agencies' practices. The setting up of the ECN may, therefore, have altered the previously competitive interaction between national competition authorities, introducing a cooperative strategy among them.

3.3.3 The activity of national courts and their interaction with other legal actors

National courts' obligation to decide cases in accordance with European law has long been established in EU law.[55] In the case of competition

---

NY: Cornell University Press), pp. 216–238; Gerber, D.J. (1998), *Law and Competition in Twentieth Century Europe: Protecting Prometheus* (Oxford: Clarendon Press); Drahos (2001).

[54] Drahos, M. and van Waarden, F. (2002), 'Courts and (Epistemic) Communities in the Convergence of Competition Policies', *Journal of European Public Policy*, vol. 9, no. 6, pp. 913–934. For an overview of the governance mechanism in place see: de Visser (2009).

[55] Art. 3a TEU (ex Art. 10 EC) lays down the principle of sincere cooperation, under which national courts are not to deviate from the EU legal outcomes when applying EU law. Regulation 1/2003 builds on this legal basis

law, the application of European competition rules by national courts may arise when:

- courts act as competition authorities;
- judicial review procedure is available against the decision of the national competition authority applying EU law;
- there is a private action,
  - o either as a follow-up to a previous national competition authority decision, or to a previous European Commission decision including its potential appeal to the European Courts,
  - o or when private parties bring an action before the national court without prior proceedings before competition authorities.

As for the application of Articles 101 and 102 TFEU by the national courts Article 15 (2) of Regulation 1/2003 provides that Member States should notify the Commission of national courts' decisions, and the Commission, as well as the respective national competition authority, may submit written observations to the courts throughout the proceedings. According to Article 16, national courts cannot arrive at decisions contrary to previous Commission decisions and, in case of parallel proceedings, they should proceed in the same way, giving consideration to staying the proceedings if necessary in order to wait for the Commission decision. These rules demonstrate the intention of leaving no scope for divergence in the application of the Treaty's competition provisions. Whether deviation nonetheless occurs is hard to tell without going through all decisions in detail. However, given the adversarial nature of court procedures, there is big chance that, if a decision deviates from EU law, either of the two litigants will be unhappy with the legal outcome, and report the case as infringing EU law.

Furthermore, there are also strict limits to divergence from the case law of the European Commission and ECJ case law. The case law on courts' liability for erroneous application of EU law is a further aspect that might influence courts' behaviour. In the Köbler case the ECJ declared that national courts – more precisely the state of these courts – are liable for damages if they breach EU law.

---

and defines the rules of cooperation of national courts with other legal actors, as further specified in the Commission Notice on the co-operation between the Commission and the courts of the EU Member States in the application of Articles 81 and 82 EC (2004/C 101/04) 27.4.2004.

> Member States are obliged to make good damage caused to individuals by infringements of Community law for which they are responsible where the rule of Community law infringed is intended to confer rights on individuals, the breach is sufficiently serious and there is a direct causal link between that breach and the loss or damage sustained by the injured parties. In order to determine whether the infringement is sufficiently serious when the infringement at issue stems from a decision of a court adjudicating at last instance, the competent national court must, taking into account the specific nature of the judicial function and the legitimate requirement of legal certainty, determine whether that infringement is manifest.[56]

Although the application of this case law before national courts is not absolutely predictable,[57] courts' liability may extend to the area of competition law enforcement, possibly covering not only the application of EU law contrary to former ECJ or CFI decisions, but also decisions not taking account of the Commission's practice. This area is without doubt an interesting issue that has not been clearly defined yet under the Regulation, but may be subject to interpretation by the ECJ in the future.

Besides these rules, there are also some softer instruments to direct courts towards the 'right' legal outcome. Regulation 1/2003[58] allows national judges to ask the Commission for any information in its possession or for an opinion on questions concerning the application of the EU competition rules, and this channel is sometimes by national courts.[59]

Also, the Commission is entitled to intervene in a 'soft' manner with an *amicus curiae* brief during the court procedure.[60] The Commission has used this possibility a number of times: in 2010 there were three such cases.

Finally, with regard to governance mechanisms, national courts are not organised into a network, in the way that competition authorities are.

---

[56] Case C-224/01 *Gerhard Köbler* v *Republik Österreich*, Judgment of 30 September 2003.

[57] In the UK, for example, the first damages claim based on the Köbler decision was dismissed in 2008. In *Cooper* v *Attorney-General* [2008] EWHC 2178, the Court of Appeal was alleged to have committed a manifestly serious breach when dismissing judicial review proceedings commenced by the applicant in October 1999. The judge hearing the case concluded that it fell 'far below the standard required to constitute a manifest infringement of the applicable law so as to give rise to a claim for damages', but granted permission to appeal.

[58] Art. 15 (1).

[59] In 2010 there were two such questions, from the Belgian and Spanish courts.

[60] Art. 15 (3) of Regulation 1/2003.

This would interfere with their institutional independence. Training for national judges is organised by the Commission, and Regulation 1/2003 and the Commission Notice on the cooperation of national courts lays down certain rules that all aim to ensure a uniform application of EU competition law, and may have a spill-over to the application of national competition laws as well. As discussed above, the Commission has mainly only soft tools to influence the courts.

Overall, the legal and governance frameworks around national courts' cooperation are weaker than in the case of national competition authorities, signalling a potential scope for legal deviation in cases where the European competition authority or the Court of Justice does not keep a close eye on legal developments.

3.3.4 Conclusions on impacts on legal actors' output

The decentralised application of European competition law rules by national courts may thus lead to some divergence in the application of the law. In the case of appeals against national competition authorities' decisions, in theory such differences may lead to competitive advantages through the competition channel of international trade – if the courts apply an EU competition law rule either in a more lenient or a stricter way than the national competition agencies. The Regulation leaves no real possibility of choice of forum or mobility across jurisdictions for firms. The jurisdiction of the forum for appeals is established according to which national (or perhaps the European) authority deals with the case. And the jurisdiction of the national authority is determined in line with the case allocation rules discussed above. A slight deviation from main stream European competition law can be feasible, therefore, potentially leading to minimal competitive advantages in international trade, but its scale is controllable under the carefully designed legal arrangements of Regulation 1/2003.

It appears that NCAs are better incentivised to adopt similar solutions to that of the EU actors: they are organised in a Network, there is quite high transparency as to their work, which creates some benchmarking and also peer pressure within the governance mechanism. Also, because independent regulatory authorities do not have the broad guarantees of institutional independence that courts traditionally have, they may be inclined to align their practices with the EU level actors, in order to gain more authority *vis-à-vis* the national legal actors above them in the legal hierarchy (for example ministries, but occasionally also national courts, and so on).

In terms of the institutional framework, it is important to note the difference between competition authorities' European governance and national courts' institutional setting. For courts, there is no such Network as for national competition authorities, as this would interfere with the independence of the judiciary. Some contact exists, however, among judges of different Member States in the form of cooperation in exchanging experience and establishing some 'best practices' in the application of EU competition rules at national level.[61] This strong institutional independence may thus leave more scope for competitive behaviour among national courts than among national competition authorities. Analysis of the hard and soft instruments, considered together, leads to the conclusion that a great divergence in the application of EU law is unlikely to occur but it would be interesting to see comparative studies on this as evidence of courts' full or partial cooperation, or perhaps partial competition.

The judiciary and the regulatory authorities also have different internal institutional set-ups, which influences their incentives differently. As referred to above, competition authorities enjoy fewer guarantees of their institutional independence but they may have a career system that sets individuals' incentives differently from the judiciary. At the same time, in certain jurisdictions high court judges are renowned and their decisions are cited by their name, which can give strong individual motivation to make a lasting contribution to the development of case law. Similar motivation mechanisms may not exist at all in competition authorities. It is not possible to reach conclusions on these questions in the absence of a significant set of institutional set-ups and comparative outputs. But, the point here is merely that the scope for a divergence that is defined by EU rules is not necessarily the only driver that would explain, in itself, the actual competitive or cooperative behaviour of a particular legal actor.

Finally, even if there is some minimal scope for unsanctioned and uncorrected divergence in legal output, this could only be interpreted as potential for international trade competition, given that there is no real possibility of choice of forum or mobility across jurisdictions for firms concerned. The jurisdiction of the forum for appeals is established according to which national (or perhaps the European) authority deals with the case. And the jurisdiction of the national authority is determined along the case allocation rules discussed above. Therefore, a slight deviation from mainstream European competition law may be feasible, potentially leading to minimal competitive advantages in international

---

[61] The Association of European Competition Law Judges (AECLJ) is one such network.

trade for domestic firms, but competition through mobility cannot occur in competition law enforcement, at least in public enforcement.

Besides, the fact that, in some Member States, information on court decisions is not provided to national authorities[62] reduces the potential for yardstick competition. In countries where information flows are unimpeded, NCAs and national courts have a clear picture of what the other actor is doing, and can learn from, or compete over, the best formulated rules.

A further potential aspect of yardstick competition in a decentralised enforcement setting is the scope for 'laboratory federalism' where national courts possibly contribute to finding the best solutions in applying European competition law, and regulatory agencies, even at the European level, may learn from their input. Whether this occurs already or will occur in the future would require an in-depth study of national case laws in parallel with the development of the national and European authority's output.

4. POTENTIAL COMPETITIVE PRESSURES IN PRIVATE ENFORCEMENT

Damages actions under EU competition law, also referred to as private enforcement of Arts 101 and 102, means that private parties who have suffered damages as a consequence of a breach of competition law may start proceedings in order to receive compensation.

Although private enforcement is mainly examined in the context of its function of enhancing the enforcement of norms, it has a potential impact on regulatory competition and cooperation as well, which is the subject of this section. In the latter respect, private enforcement strengthens the role of courts *vis-à-vis* other legal actors, thereby creating the opportunity for change in the original roles and relationships among legal actors. If private enforcement becomes feasible and is widely used in Europe, it may have an impact on the dynamics of competitive interaction.

Private enforcement raises the question of interaction between national courts and the European Commission and European courts in a vertical setting, as well as potential competitive interactions between different national courts (horizontal inter-jurisdictional setting), and the national

---

[62] See European Commission 'Overview of the application of the EC competition rules by national courts in 2006', available at: http://ec.europa.eu/competition/elojade/antitrust/nationalcourts/

courts and the national competition authority in one jurisdiction (intra-jurisdictional setting). These issues are reviewed in this section.

The potential impact of private actions on the role of the courts in regulatory competition depends on several factors. The two fundamental and interrelated questions are: whether there will be a wider uptake of private action in Europe; and whether national differences will motivate actors to engage in forum or law shopping. The European legislator has been exploring which elements of national legal systems and private solutions are to be clarified, approximated, or even harmonised, in order to make private enforcement work better than it has so far. This section looks at some of the national norms that can spur or discourage regulatory competition.

4.1 Current Legal Landscape for Damages Actions

The European Court of Justice ruled in Courage and Manfredi[63] that Articles 101 and 102 TFEU are directly applicable and private parties can rely on these provisions of the Treaty in front of national courts in order to recover damages caused by other market participants breaching these rules. The Court in its judgment in Courage clarified that the law of the national court shall be applicable for all procedural issues in such damages actions. Commentators argue, however, that it did not stipulate what the applicable substantive law ought to be.[64] Clearly, in these cases we are talking about the specific provisions of the Treaty (Articles 101 or 102), but to apply these and arrive at an award of damages, the national courts need to rely on further legal rules, ranging from the method of calculating such damages to the issue of fault requirements or the burden of proof.

At present, the law of obligations at EU level is not sufficiently developed,[65] and the current differences in national legal systems could only be resolved by the introduction of some form of conflict of law rules at EU level.

---

[63] Case C-453/99, *Courage* v *Crehan*, 2001 ECR I-6297; Joined Cases C-295/04 to C-298/04 Manfredi [2006] ECR I-6619.

[64] See analyses of the implications of the Courage judgment on damages actions by Basedow, J. (2007) 'Jurisdiction and Choice of Law in Private Enforcement of EC Competition Law', in Basedow, J. (ed.) *Private Enforcement of EC Competition Law* (Alphen aan den Rijn: Kluwer).

[65] Basedow (2007).

There is a long tradition of private international law rules resolving conflicts of laws in such ways. The Brussels I Regulation[66] lays down rules that determine which court has jurisdiction. On the question of applicable substantive law, it is the Rome I Regulation[67] that decides which law applies for contracts and Rome II[68] for torts.

4.1.1 Choice of forum – which court has jurisdiction to hear the case?

The jurisdiction of courts to hear private action cases against defendants domiciled in EU Member States is governed by Regulation 44/2001, the so-called 'Brussels I'. This regulation entered into force in March 2002 and established common EU wide rules on jurisdiction in civil and commercial matters. It clarifies which court is competent in a cross-border dispute and facilitates the recognition and enforcement of a judgment in one member state that has been issued by the courts in another EU member state. In the case of competition law breaches, the party suffering damages may well be in a contractual relationship with the breaching party. In these cases, the stipulation about the choice of court in their contract is valid also for the breach of European competition law rules, even if they opted for arbitration. If, however, the injured party is not in a contractual relationship with the party breaching competition rules, conflict of law rules under tort apply. These, as stipulated by Brussels I[69] and interpreted by the ECJ in Shevill[70] are:

- the place of the defendant's domicile;
- the place where anticompetitive acts were committed; or
- the place where loss was sustained.

---

66 Council Regulation 44/2001 of 22 December 2000 on jurisdiction and the recognition and enforcement of judgments in civil and commercial matters ('Brussels I', OJ 2001, L 12/1).

67 Regulation 593/2008 of the European Parliament and of the Council of 17 June 2008 on the law applicable to contractual obligations ('Rome I', OJ 2008, L 177/6).

68 Regulation 864/2007 of the European Parliament and of the Council of 11 July 2007 on the law applicable to non-contractual obligations ('Rome II', OJ 2007, L 199/40).

69 Art. 2 (1) and Art. 5 (3)

70 C-68/93 Judgment of 7 March 1995, Shevill and Others / Presse Alliance (C-68/93, ECR 1995 p. I-415).

The Commission has put forward a proposal for the amendment of the regulation,[71] which is currently under consideration by the European Parliament and the Council.[72]

However, this Regulation is not designed for collective damages actions, and few academics or lawyers agree that the Brussels I Regulation would be adequate in its current state for collective proceedings.

The public consultation conducted in 2011 revealed a perceived opportunity for forum shopping, which was regarded as potentially harmful. 'With regard to jurisdiction, collective redress havens and a race to the courts to be the first seized must be avoided.'[73]

What gives rise to such potential forum shopping is that there are multiple competent jurisdictions. A potential problem that arises under such a scenario is that there may be related cases pending in different fora, since courts are not coordinated across Member States when accepting cases.

4.1.2 Choice of law – which law will apply?

The European Commission explained the planned solution for limiting forum shopping in the White Paper[74] and Staff Working Paper[75] on private damages actions to address the currently divergent solutions across Member States. The legal instrument would make reference to the

---

71 Proposal for a Regulation of the European Parliament and of the Council on jurisdiction and the recognition and enforcement of judgments in civil and commercial matters (Recast) Brussels, 14.12.2010. COM(2010) 748 final; 2010/0383 (COD).

72 The European Parliament adopted its resolution on 20 November 2012. European Parliament legislative resolution of 20 November 2012 on the proposal for a regulation of the European Parliament and of the Council on jurisdiction and the recognition and enforcement of judgments in civil and commercial matters (recast) (COM(2010)0748 – C7–0433/2010 – 2010/0383(COD)). Available at: http://www.europarl.europa.eu/sides/getDoc.do?type=TA&reference=P7-TA-2012–0412&language=EN&ring=A7–2012–0320.

73 Feedback statement on the public consultation 'Towards a Coherent European Approach to Collective Redress', available at: http://ec.europa.eu/competition/antitrust/actionsdamages/index.html (last accessed: 12 February 2012) (Public Consultation 2011a).

74 White Paper on damages actions for breach of EC antitrust rules COM(2008) 165, 2.4.2008 (White Paper on damages actions).

75 Commission Staff Working Paper accompanying the White Paper on Damages actions for breach of the EC antitrust rules COM(2008) 165 final (Staff Working Paper 2008).

'Rome II' Regulation.[76] The Rome II Regulation sets the following rules for the applicable law for tort liability:

- where the market is, or is likely to be, affected;
- if this is the case in more than one country: the law of the court seised of the case, provided that the market in that Member State is directly and substantially affected.

According to Article 6(3) the law applicable to a non-contractual obligation arising out of a restriction of competition shall be the law of the country where the market is likely to be affected. In the case of Articles 101 and 102 violations, however, the market will usually be affected in more than one country. In these cases, the claimant may also choose to base his claim on the law of the Member State where he is bringing his claim. In order to limit forum shopping, the claimant can only choose that law when the market of that Member State is *directly and substantially* affected by the restriction of competition that gives rise to the damages claim.

The key question concerning the potential for forum shopping at this point is how the different national courts will interpret the condition of direct and substantial effect. The Commission in its Staff Working Paper notes that it:

> believes that Article 6(3) of Regulation 864/2007 contains an appropriate applicable law rule enabling claimants to effectively use their right to obtain antitrust damages in case of an infringement of the EU competition rules. In particular, these new rules, read together with the rules on jurisdiction, allow for procedural economy as they provide claimants with the option to have their case for antitrust damages heard by one court applying one single law, even in situations where more than one defendant is involved and where the damages occurred in several Member States. The Commission therefore does not consider it necessary to further address the issue of applicable law in the White Paper.[77]

Despite the Commission's conclusion that no further clarification is necessary with regard to the applicable law, public authorities 'urge the Commission to provide clear answers regarding the applicable law if

---

[76] Regulation 864/2007 of the European Parliament and of the Council of 11 July 2007 on the law applicable to non-contractual obligations ('Rome II', OJ 2007, L 199/40).

[77] White Paper on actions for damages.

mass damages are spread across several Member States'.[78] Similarly, businesses and legal experts called for amendment of Brussels I,[79] and some commentators note that one potential downside of the currently considered solution is the scope this leaves for so called 'torpedo claims'.[80] These are claims launched by one of the cartel members, or the dominant firm in a slower jurisdiction, in order to obtain a declaratory judgment of non-liability.

4.2 The Potential Impact of Damages Actions on Regulatory Competition

We should distinguish between two types of private enforcement action: follow-on and stand-alone actions or decisions. In the former case, the actions coming to the courts follow on from settled cases of national (or EU) competition authorities. Therefore, the role of the courts may not be highly relevant from a regulatory competition perspective, as they are asked to follow the case law of the authority.

Under the second scenario, private action claims raise situations that have not been dealt with by the EU or NCAs. Courts may thus have a much more active role to play. They will have the role of enforcers in parallel with national authorities. This position is expected to strengthen the competition between courts and national competition authorities in terms of: intellectual competition to develop the best rule; innovative solutions adopted; and divergence between the case law of courts and NCAs.

Even if the court decides not to award damages as a result of the legal or factual mistake of the competition authority in reaching its decision, the precedent case will presumably have a strong impact on the court's decision. This means that stand-alone actions before national courts have a greater potential to depart from the practice established by the (national or European) competition authority.

---

[78] Public Consultation 2011a.

[79] 'Most of the business representatives [...] considered that the Brussels I regulation needs to be modified. General competent jurisdiction shall be the place of business of the defendant in order to prevent forum and law shopping. Only a few business representatives submit that the Brussels I regulation works satisfactorily or, alternatively, that enforcement is a national matter.' Public Consultation 2011a.

[80] See the arguments of Basedow, referring to the example of torpedo actions brought by intellectual property infringers. Basedow (2007), p. 248.

This raises, of course, a threat to legal certainty. Realising this, France, for example, has already introduced a system of only permitting follow-on private enforcement, in order to prevent divergence (and potential competition) between national courts and the competition authority. Other Member States are likely to follow suit.

This following section discusses further whether claimants have an incentive to engage in forum or law shopping, whether national legal actors respond to any threat of competition, and what the welfare implications of competition may be.

4.3 Do Injured Private Parties have an Incentive to Shop around for the Best Forum?

It may be argued that the marginal differences between the jurisdictions would not be sufficient to trigger choice of courts for private action. However, divergence in the application of EU law may not only occur with regard to the application of substantive norms, but also in terms of length of litigation, procedural aspects, and use of easily accessible language.

Applicable law can trigger forum and law shopping. An example of this is the applicable standard of proof and other procedural rules. In Courage v. Crehan,[81] the ECJ recognised the scope for individuals to obtain damages for breach of Articles 101 and 102 TFEU. With regard to the procedural law applicable to obtaining such damages in front of national courts, the ECJ held that that 'it is for the domestic legal system of each Member State to designate the courts and tribunals having jurisdiction and to lay down the detailed procedural rules'. The Court in its case law set two limitations to national autonomy in designing procedural law: these are known as the principle of equivalence and the principle of effectiveness.

4.3.1 Standard of proof and costs of litigation

The differences in the standard of proof can, for example, give rise to incentives for forum shopping. Such differences are demonstrated by the following examples: in Cyprus, Ireland, Malta, Poland, and the UK the applicable standard is the balance of probabilities. In Denmark, a high degree of probability is required, while in Slovakia causation must be proven beyond reasonable or serious doubt. In Greece and Lithuania the

---

[81] Case C-453/99 *Courage Ltd* v *Bernard Crehan* and *Bernard Crehan* v *Courage Ltd and Others*.

proof must also be beyond reasonable doubt. Finally, in Slovenia certainty is required under national law as the standard of proof.[82]

Although the national legislator cannot reasonably be expected to change the general rules on the burden of proof in order to encourage private antitrust litigation, these differences may result in some differentiation between Member States in the use of private actions.

In an overview of 2007, a comparative report found substantial differences among the rules on fees applicable in Belgium, Germany and the UK. While in some jurisdictions claimants for each party bear their own lawyer's fees, irrespective of the outcome of the dispute, in others claimants have to pay an advance for the court fees, with the risk of bearing the defendant's lawyer's fees, in some cases amounting to more than €250 000 for each instance and for each defendant. Bearing the fees of the expert is another.[83]

However, these differences are not part of competition over the substance of competition law. Nevertheless, they may be crucial in establishing the leading jurisdiction, the courts of which would serve private action claimants. Such a preferred jurisdiction could then lead to developments in case law. However, it is also true that a single jurisdiction would also be easier for the European Courts to ensure it stays in line with EU case law.

4.3.2 Access to collective actions

One of the most important pre-conditions for damages actions to work in practice is private parties' having ready access to courts. Given that in antitrust actions for damages the injured parties are often widely dispersed consumers, each with a relatively small injury, procedural rules that allow a group of consumers to launch proceedings together, or a consumer association to launch a claim in the name of the group of injured consumers, is a crucial and interesting aspect of the national legal landscapes.

In trying to categorise such collective actions, different typologies can be set up. Here 'collective redress' is used as the overarching category of court proceedings subsuming more than one claimant into the same court procedure. Claimants may be represented by a single organisation in the dispute. This form of action is called representative action. Other procedural solutions may include collective actions where claimants can

---

[82] See Ashurst Report, pp. 52–55.

[83] Cartel Damages Claims 'Development of private antitrust enforcement in Europe' (CDC Services Sprl). On file with the author.

freely opt in if they are damaged by the same act under litigation (also called a group action), or collective actions where all persons concerned are *per se* party to the claim but may opt out if they wish (referred to as a 'class action'). Finally, there are also test case procedures (where a case is 'tested' and later claimants in the same matter may launch claims that will be dealt with in the same way).

According to reports in mid-2010,[84] 12 EU Member States did not have any collective redress mechanism in place. The test case procedure was available only in Austria and Germany, and representative action existed in nine jurisdictions. The group action was the most popular legal solution, with 13 Member States having such systems in place, and a further three proposing legislation to introduce it.[85]

Given the scattered availability of collective action, the European legislator is considering taking action at EU level to introduce access to justice in cases of dispersed claimants across Europe. In the White Paper of 2008, several options were discussed, and analysed in an impact assessment,[86] which found that among three legally binding alternative class actions – (1) opt-out class action, (2) opt-in collective action and representative action together, and (3) only representative action – it is the second, the coupling of opt-in collective action and representative action, that is the preferred option. The impact assessment acknowledged that the first option is the most effective in compensating as many victims of antitrust breaches as possible, but it called attention to the fact that 'in opt-out class actions, the very large group of victims included in the class may not always be able to control the lawyers acting for the class (principal-agent problem) and misalignment of their interests could lead to under-compensation'.[87]

Since then there have been further consultations but it is not yet clear what direction the future proposal will take.

---

[84] See BEUC (2010) 'Country survey of collective redress mechanisms: where does collective redress for individual damages exist?' (updated in July 2010) available at: http://www.groupaction4consumers.eu/docs/Country%20survey_Traffic%20Lights.pdf (last accessed: 11 February 2012).

[85] Note, however, that this overview covers all collective redress mechanisms, not only those specifically suited to antitrust damages claims.

[86] Commission staff working document accompanying the White Paper on Damages actions for breach of the EC antitrust rules Impact Assessment {COM(2008) 165 final} Brussels, 2.4.2008; SEC(2008) 405. (White Paper Impact Assessment).

[87] White Paper Impact Assessment.

4.4 Do Legal Actors Respond to Potential Demand Side Pressures?

4.4.1 Legislators' response to competitive pressure arising from private enforcement

As noted above, the opportunity for private enforcement in the form of collective redress is not equally well developed across all Member States. This feature of the legal system falls under shared competences: national legislators can develop this field further but the European legislator is also considering EU level intervention. This section examines whether national legislators are taking action to ensure that their respective jurisdictions become better performers,[88] or more attractive,[89] in processing damages actions.

If the national legislator considers it necessary, it can enact rules that are more favourable to private actions, thereby engaging in promoting damages actions within its jurisdiction as well as actively soliciting claims from the pool of cases with significant cross-border impacts. Alternatively, it may decide not to enhance private claims before domestic courts, by maintaining or enacting only limited opportunities for collective action or other significant procedural aspects. However, it is not only the legislator that can shape the national environment for collective actions. National competition authorities and national courts can also enhance the attractiveness of their jurisdiction. Here we focus on the legal standing of groups of litigants before the courts in a number of Member States and at EU level.[90]

---

[88] A more efficient system of collective redress will translate into efficiencies for the economy as a whole, which could be thought of as competition through trade or factor mobility. However, the actual difference may not be big enough to create tangible benefits for the legislator. Some studies claim nonetheless that an effective deterrence against abusing market power would yield over 1 per cent of GDP in benefits. See for an overview of macroeconomic benefits from enforcement: Camilli, E.L. et al. (2007), 'Making Antitrust Damages Actions more Effective in the EU: Welfare Impact and Potential Scenarios', Report for the European Commission, available at: http://ec.europa.eu/competition/antitrust/actionsdamages/files_white_paper/impact_study.pdf

[89] If claimants are allowed to choose between jurisdictions, competition with mobility may arise, provided that attracting litigation brings benefits to a jurisdiction.

[90] To restrict the length of the analysis here the assessment will be restricted to Germany, the UK, and the Netherlands; examples which are sufficiently illustrative to describe the issue that arises.

At the European level, the Commission Staff Working Paper on private action notes that 'in recent years, some Member States enacted legislation aimed at facilitating antitrust damages actions, even though not addressing all the issues identified in the Green Paper. There is no indication however that any sizeable number of other Member States is likely to introduce, in the foreseeable future, legislative changes that ensure an effective legal framework for damages actions of victims of antitrust infringements.'[91] In other words, the Commission predicted that national legislators would not engage in either competition for claimants, nor in yardstick competition to become better performers in antitrust enforcement.

But it is worth taking a closer look at the development of national legislation on this issue over time, in order to get a better idea of the dynamics of legal change. According to the report on the alternative remedies available to consumers,[92] prepared by a group of experts in 2007, collective action in Europe, even where available, was very diverse in its conditions and functioning. At that time, only 11 out of 27 EU jurisdictions provided for collective actions for damages and three further member countries had pending legislative proposals to introduce them. According to an overview of national legislations issued by BEUC in 2010, there were already 16 jurisdictions with collective action possibilities (not counting the Netherlands, where litigation is possible collectively, but damages have to be claimed in separate procedures), and one country had a pending legislative proposal to create one. Table 4.5 displays BEUC's findings. One year later, in 2011, Linklaters identified two further jurisdictions that have collective redress arrangements. No doubt the interpretations of authors differ as to what counts as readily available collective action. But clearly, more and more jurisdictions introduce such redress mechanisms, which can be interpreted as a reaction to a common problem, mutual learning, or even competitive lawmaking.

To determine which of the above is at play, the availability of a collective redress mechanism is not the only relevant issue. The features of these mechanisms can vary widely, and these may provide potential reasons for injured parties to seek out a jurisdiction that favours them. The legal solutions adopted by the UK, Germany, France and the Netherlands are reviewed here.

[91] Staff Working Paper (2008).

[92] Stuyck et al. (2007), 'An analysis and evaluation of alternative means of consumer redress other than redress through ordinary judicial proceedings – Final Report'.

Table 4.5 Availability of collective redress mechanisms in EEA Member States

Country	Collective redress for individual damage claims					No collective redress available
	Group action			Represent-ative Action	Test Case procedure	
	Proposed	In force	Collective ADR			
Austria	√			√	√	
Belgium	√					√
Bulgaria		√				
Cyprus						√
Czech Republic						√
Denmark		√	√	√		
Estonia						√
Finland		√		√		
France	√			√		
Germany		√*		√	√	
Greece		√				
Hungary						√
Iceland						√
Ireland						√
Italy		√		√		
Latvia						√
Lithunia		√				
Luxembourg						√
Malta						√
The Netherlands			√			
Norway		√				
Poland		√				
Portugal		√				
Romania				√		
Slovakia						√
Slovenia						√
Spain		√		√		
Sweden		√				
United Kingdom		√		√		

Note: * Capital investment.

Source: BEUC (2012).

In Germany, Section 10 of the 'UWG' (*Gesetz gegen Unlauteren Wettbewerb* – German Act Against Unfair Competition) provides a legal standing for representative organisations to bring action on behalf of injured parties for breaches of German competition law. The drawback to this procedure is that the damages are not paid to the injured parties or the representative body, but are collected by the Treasury.

In France the representative action (*action en représentation conjointe*) enables at least two consumers damaged by the same practice to mandate a licensed organisation to represent them in civil or criminal proceedings against the offender. The procedure requires however that each damaged individual supplies a personal mandate and be kept informed of progress personally, which makes the procedure overly burdensome and too often unsuccessful.[93]

Linklaters reported in 2011 that:

> [o]n 6 December 2007, claims for compensation brought by a consumer association on behalf of more than 12,000 individual consumers who suffered loss due to the anti-competitive behaviour of three French mobile phone providers were dismissed by the Paris Commercial Court on the basis that the claimants had not complied with the rules governing the joint representative action. […] The result of this decision is that, in practice, the consumer association may only bring a claim under the joint representative action procedure, including obtaining instructions from each claimant individually without being authorised to advertise for potential claimants.[94]

In the Netherlands, certain associations are empowered to bring legal action for the protection of other persons.[95] However, they cannot claim damages, which takes away their incentive to act. Under the Dutch system, injured parties need to file individual claims to recover damages. However the law on the collective settlement of widespread damages provides a settlement mechanism for victims of mass damage, negotiated by a representative organisation, and declared binding by the court for all victims. The individual victims can, however, opt out of the binding force of the judgment within a given time period. This procedure applies not only to consumers, but has been used for example in an investor

---

[93] According to the Stuyck Report (2007) there have been five cases in almost 15 years.

[94] Linklaters (2011) 'Collective Actions Across the Globe – A Review', available at: http://www.linklaters.com/pdfs/mkt/london/A13187695%20v0.0%201103_Collective%20actions.pdf (last accessed: 2 February 2012).

[95] Art. 3:305a-305c B.W.

protection case.[96] Since its entry into force in mid 2005 there have already been two applications under this procedure.[97]

In the UK, representative actions and opt-in group proceedings are both available, but mainly only the latter is in use. The disadvantage of this legal system is the high court fees, which need to be tackled through various financing mechanisms or agreements. Lawyers' fees may be determined on a 'no win no fee' basis, but contingency fees are not allowed. Within a group proceeding legal fees may be borne unequally by some parties to the claim, if the court so decides.

The above overview shows that the differences in collective action across Member States may provide incentives for injured persons to look for the most suitable jurisdiction to bring actions. This, or the threat of such law and forum shopping, can open up some regulatory competition in the enforcement of competition law. Not only does private enforcement enable the courts to enforce competition law rules more actively and thereby become a more relevant legal actor in the competition between legislator, regulator and judiciary (intra-jurisdictional competition), but it also implies competition between courts of different jurisdictions (inter-jurisdictional competition).

With EU level legislation in place, the national legal environments would be substantially approximated in terms of availability of courts. But it is unlikely that the EU legislator would harmonise all procedural rules around collective redress. This means that some scope for national divergence will remain and may still be the reason for choice of jurisdiction, motivating legal actors to compete.

Courts may create the competitive edge for themselves by interpreting procedural or substantive legal standards in a favourable way and handling cases in a timely and professional manner. For the judiciary, it may be in their interest to promote the use of their jurisdiction and competence (for example in order to increase the importance of the court in rendering the most significant decisions, gaining international recognition, and so on). The national legislator may have less direct interest in attracting lawsuits into its jurisdiction. Below, the case of the UK is analysed to see whether courts strive to gain cases.

---

96 *Dexia*, Court of Appeal, Amsterdam of 25 January 2007, *NJ* (2007), 427.

97 *DES*, Court of Appeal Amsterdam of 1 June 2006, *NJ* (2006), 461; and *Dexia*.

4.4.2 Courts' responsiveness to potential competition

On the face of it, the UK seems to be a litigation-friendly environment. Not only because of the language, but also because the court seems to establish its jurisdiction more easily than in France or in Germany, for example.

In a 2003 decision, the High Court in London held that private parties suffering injury by purchasing products Europe-wide, due to a cartel implemented in several Member States, among them in the UK, could press their claim in front of the English court. The question in the specific case was whether companies 'who have purchased cartel-affected products across Europe can choose to proceed against an English implementing subsidiary of a cartelist in respect of all European losses instead of having to pursue separate claims in multiple jurisdictions.'[98] The court held that, 'Where a subsidiary of a cartelist has, even if unknowingly, implemented a cartel in England, the English High Court has jurisdiction to hear claims by other European purchasers against the English subsidiary, even if there is no contractual relationship between the purchasing company and the English subsidiary'.[99]

More precisely, the court admitted the claim of a German plaintiff seeking damages against members of the Vitamins Cartel and their subsidiaries.[100] The factual element that allowed the British court to establish its jurisdiction was that one of the cartel members had a subsidiary in the UK, and the plaintiff could demonstrate that it would have bought vitamins from that subsidiary at a competitive price if there had been no cartel.

The other examples of private actions across Europe include the 2006 French decision by the Tribunal de Commerce de Nanterre (Arkopharma)[101] and the German version of the vitamins cartel case from 2004, rendered by the Landgericht Dortmund,[102] and further cases heard by the Mainz District Court.[103]

---

[98] See summary of the case at the website of the OFT http://www.oft.gov.uk/

[99] *Provimi Ltd.* v *Aventis Animal Nutrition & Others* [2003] EWHC 961 Comm.

[100] Ibid.

[101] Tribunal de commerce de Nanterre, judgment 'Arkopharma/Roche', 11 May 2006.

[102] LG Dortmund, Az. 13 O 55/02 Kart., *Vitaminkartell III*, [2004].

[103] Mainz District Court, decisions of January 15 2004, Cases 12 HK.O 52/02, 12 HK O 55/02 and 12 HK O 56/02, published in NJW-RR 2004, 478.

It is noteworthy that the French court rejected the claim of a purchaser against a French subsidiary of Hoffmann La Roche. The cause of the rejection was not that the subsidiary would not establish the court's jurisprudence, but that the claimant could not demonstrate that it was impossible to pass on these higher prices to the end consumers. With this strict interpretation of the 'pass-on' defence the court precluded the possibility of damages actions from many claimants that are not end consumers.[104]

Similarly, the German court took the view that the 'pass-on' defence precluded purchasers from bringing damages actions. Furthermore, the courts found that the price-fixing arrangements in question were targeted against all purchasers of the products, rather than against the plaintiffs specifically, which constituted another reason why the court would not accept the claims.[105]

A further look at the relevant case law in the UK is necessary to verify whether the prediction that the UK courts are aiming to render their jurisdiction attractive to litigants is true. Since the decision of the High Court of London, cited above, which dated from 2003, it is the Competition Appeal Tribunal that has competence to hear private actions for damages that are follow-on actions. The Competition Appeal Tribunal was created by the Enterprise Act 2002, s.12 and Sch.2, and came into force on 1 April 2003. Under s.47A of the Competition Act (inserted by s.18 of the Enterprise Act 2002), any person who has suffered loss or damage as a result of an infringement of either UK or European Union competition law may bring a claim for damages or for a sum of money before the Tribunal in respect of that loss or damage.

Such claims may only be brought in relation to loss or damage suffered as a result of infringement of either domestic or European competition law.

In general, claims may only be brought before the Tribunal when the relevant competition authority (namely the Office of Fair Trade (OFT), or sectoral regulator, or the European Commission) has made a decision establishing that one of the relevant prohibitions has been infringed, and any appeal from such decision has been finally determined.

Under s.47B of the Competition Act (inserted by s.19 of the Enterprise Act), claims under s.47A may be brought by certain specified bodies on behalf of consumers.

---

[104] A summary of the court decision in French is available at: http://www.economag.com/droit-de-la-concurrence/la-procedure-francaise-en-matiere-de-concurrence/procedures-judiciaires (last accessed: 12 February 2012).

[105] For a summary of the case in English see: http://www.internationallawoffice.com/newsletters/detail.aspx?g=d15558bb-bde4–42a1-a365–67736a457122 (last accessed: 12 February 2012).

Up to 2008, the Competition Appeal Tribunal has dealt with nine cases of monetary claims as follow-on cases: two cases arising out of the Vitamin cartel judgment of the Court of First Instance;[106] one case[107] based on a decision of the European Commission;[108] two cases[109] arising out of the national regulator's decision on the application of rail regulation; three cases[110] based on a decision of the national competition authority,[111] the OFT; and one case[112] based on a decision of the Tribunal itself on an appeal against the decision of the OFT (where parties reached out of court settlement). One of the above actions[113] for damages was launched by the Consumer Association. Table 4.6 below summarises the final outcome of these cases.

Looking at the details of these cases, it appears that the Tribunal's approach to claimants is not clearly competitive, or at least, that the court does not appear to satisfy damages claims at all costs.

For example, in the *Emerson Electric Co and others* v *Morgan Crucible Company plc,* the Tribunal took a cautious approach to the claims of the injured party. It found that

> the proceedings instituted by Schunk and Carbone Lorraine in the European Court of First Instance were challenging the scope of the infringement found by the Commission. In these circumstances, the ambit of the prior findings of infringement on which the claimants base their follow-on action and the extent of their alleged losses could differ from those originally found by the Commission. Until the European proceedings were determined, there was no sure foundation for the proposed claims.[114]

---

[106] Case T-15/02 *BASF AG* v *Commission* [2006] ECR II-497.

[107] 1077/5/7/07 *Emerson Electric Co and others* v *Morgan Crucible Company plc.*

[108] Decision of the European Commission (C(2003) 4457 in Case C.38359), adopted on 3 December 2003.

[109] 1105/5/7/08 (1) Freightliner Limited (2) *Freightliner Heavy Haul Limited* v *English Welsh & Scottish Railway Limited*; and 1106/5/7/08 *Enron Coal Services Limited (in liquidation)* v *English Welsh & Scottish Railway Limited.*

[110] 1108/5/7/08 *N J and D M Wilson* v *Lancing College Limited*; 1078/7/9/07 *The Consumers Association* v *JJB Sports PLC*; 1060/5/7/06 *Healthcare at Home* v *Genzyme Ltd.*

[111] One upheld on appeal.

[112] 1088/5/7/07 ME Burgess, *JJ Burgess and SJ Burgess (trading as JJ Burgess & Sons)* v *W Austin & Sons (Stevenage) Limited and Harwood Park Crematorium Limited.*

[113] 1078/7/9/07 *The Consumers Association* v *JJB Sports PLC.*

[114] See summary of judgment *Emerson Electric Co and others* v *Morgan Crucible Company plc*, published on 28 April 2008, available at: http://www.catribunal.org.uk/239–1911/Judgment-Permission.html

Table 4.6 Damages claims brought before the UK Competition Appeals Tribunal up to 2008

Case	Origin of claim	Final outcome
Lancing College	OFT decision	Settlement
Freightliner Ltd	ORR decision	Settlement
Grampian Country Food	CFI judgment (Vitamins cartel)	Dismissal of claim on limitation period
BCL Old Co Ltd	CFI judgment (Vitamins cartel)	Dismissal of claim based on limitation period
ME Burgess	OFT – appealed at CAT	Settlement
Emerson Electric	Commission Decision	Stay proceedings pending CFI appeal
Healthcare at Home	OFT decision	Settlement
Enron	ORR decision	Dismissal of claim based on lack of proof of causality
Consumer Association	OFT decision upheld by court	Settlement

Further damages claims against the defendants Schunk GmbH, Schunk Kohlenstofftechnik GmbH, SGL Carbon AG and Le Carbone Lorraine SA were denied by the Court, since the Court of First Instance judgments (Case T-73/04 Le Carbone Lorraine v Commission and Case T-68/04 SGL Carbon AG v Commission) were appealed and a decision of the ECJ was still pending. The President of the Tribunal therefore ordered the proceedings to be stayed until 21 days after the handing down of the judgments by the Court of Justice in both those cases.[115]

Two other claims[116] were refused based on the expiry of the limitation period. The CAT established a two-stage test. First, the claimant has to demonstrate a good reason for extending the limitation period. The second stage is a discretionary exercise involving value judgments, such as the balance of hardship.

The Tribunal held that while the claimants satisfied the requirements of stage one, 'the Tribunal has concluded unanimously that the BCL claimants should have taken at least some steps to establish and pursue

[115] Order of 2 April 2009.

[116] 1101/5/7/08 and 1098/5/7/08 [2009] CAT 29.

their claim during the period when they wrongly thought that they were precluded by s.47A from actually starting proceedings'.[117]

It is remarkable that there is no decision awarding damages among the above list of cases. Nonetheless, the activity of the court can be judged as quite successful if we take the number of out of court settlements as a sign of success for claimants in achieving compensation. Although the terms of these settlements are confidential, this may be a reasonable assumption. In five out of nine cases such settlements have been reached.

It is worth noting that the Competition Appeals Tribunal, although in principle only allowed to accept damages claims that follow decisions by other bodies, has already had the opportunity to decide one case of damages in its entirety, as the CAT is also the forum of appeal from the decisions of the UK competition authority, OFT. This is the ME Burgess case, which was based on an OFT decision that was appealed to the Tribunal by the claimants in the action. The CAT decided the case on substance and addressed the damages claim (although a final decision on damages was not made since the parties reached an out of court settlement). Thus, even in a system of only follow-on decisions, the competent court may shape the final legal outcome.

The Tribunal seems to have received a balanced mix of damages actions, both follow-on actions to domestic competition law cases (five cases) and to European competition cases (three cases). But research on 43 out of court settlements up to 2004 shows a slightly different, and more detailed, picture:

> 25.6% of these settlements were related to Article 81 EU Treaty, whereas 9.3% were based on Chapter 1 of the UK 1998 Competition Act (which prohibits anticompetitive agreements) and 7% were based on both provisions. As regards abuses, 4.7% of the settlements were based on an alleged infringement of Article 82 EU Treaty, 20.9% on an infringement of Chapter 2 of the Competition Act and 16.3% on both allegations. [...] Out of a total dataset of 43 settlements, 51.2% were concluded after commencement of court proceedings, with Article 81 cases being the most likely to settle after the commencement of trial, whereas Chapter 2 cases were the most likely to settle before a case is filed.[118]

This means that the ratio of claims based on domestic or EU competition law seems to depend on the nature of the infringement. Whilst cases concerning breaches of dominant position are mainly based on national law (given that dominance within the EU is harder to reach), cartel

---

[117] Paragraph 29 of the ruling.
[118] Camilli et al. (2007).

claims are mostly founded on EU provisions. But this does not necessarily indicate cross-border litigation. Another interesting fact is that only half of these settlements reach the court, indicating the significance of alternative dispute resolution mechanisms.

The analysis above has examined whether the judiciary in the UK adopted an 'expansionist' approach to determining its jurisdiction and awarding damages, as a step towards inter-jurisdictional competition with other courts. We saw that after a 2003 decision by the High Court of London in this direction, the CAT did not bring decisions indicating such an explicit agenda. Nevertheless, this court may still be an attractive forum for litigation.

With regard to intra-jurisdictional competition and the propensity of courts to adopt a position different from that of the competition authority in private action cases, a promising analysis would be to see whether private actions in the past resulted in decisions that departed from competition authorities' practice. Such studies would form a truly insightful contribution to the discussion of regulatory competition in competition law. In the future, private enforcement could raise the significance of potential departures between courts' case law and national competition authorities' practice. As noted above, some jurisdictions also limit the ability of national courts to hear damages actions as a stand-alone case. In France, for example, as well as in the UK, the courts are not supposed to take such cases: they can only hear follow-on cases, where they are less likely to deviate from the decision of the national competition authority. It is possible however, that the courts still have a major influence on the outcome of litigation if they are also the forum of appeal against the decisions of the national competition authority.

4.5 Welfare Effects of Competition Under Private Enforcement

The role private enforcement will play in the future greatly depends on the exact form of European action to facilitate and harmonise certain legal aspects.[119] Issues of great importance include: whether documentary

[119] National competition authorities are not necessarily in favour of harmonisation. In its response to the consultation on the Green Paper on private enforcement, the OFT stated: 'At this stage, the OFT is not in favour of the Commission adopting binding measures at Community level. It believes that it would be sufficient for the Commission to publish a summary of conclusions intended to inform and support advocacy efforts in the Member States. Several of the policy options set out in the Green Paper simply reflect features of the legal systems in a number of Member States.'

evidence collected in civil proceedings may be disclosed; the claimant's burden of proof; whether fault has to be proven in damages actions; whether damages in the case of horizontal cartel infringements should be doubled; and what method will be used for the calculation of the quantum of damages. Further important aspects are: whether the undertakings alleged to be infringing will have a pass-on defence or the indirect purchaser can sue for damages; and whether collective action will enable consumer organisations to bring damages actions – the success of which will, in turn, greatly depend on the way in which damages will be awarded (to the association or to its members). Finally, the success of the introduction of private actions also depends on whether the claimants will have to bear their own costs.[120]

Overall, it can be concluded that the introduction of private enforcement will strengthen the role of the courts *vis-à-vis* other actors. Whether harmonised rules are necessary to create an equal capacity for enforcement by each Member State's national courts is a further issue to be considered. By promoting private actions in this way, the intra-jurisdictional interaction between courts and competition agencies will be increased. Whether this interaction will be more cooperative or competitive remains to be seen. It should be noted, however, that in ensuring uniform application of EU competition law, the reach of the Commission does not extend to courts as much as to national authorities. At the same time, European law, through the established case law of the European courts, offers safeguards that EU law is properly applied by national courts. The scope for any divergence is thus determined by the effectiveness of this legal framework as applied to the field of antitrust private actions.

The case of private enforcement reveals an interesting form of regulatory competition through choice of law: the option of choice is located with the injured party, not with the regulated entity, as is often the case. The scope for choice between at least two jurisdictions' laws, as long as they are divergent to some extent, is likely to imply that the injured party will always choose the law that gives the highest possibility of recovering damages at the lowest relative costs. This will lead to more effective antitrust (private) enforcement, and thus to an increase in competition.

[120] See Green Paper on Private Enforcement.

5. A THEORETICAL INQUIRY: HOW WOULD REGULATORY COMPETITION WORK IN COMPETITION LAW?

In the field of competition policy we have seen that there is virtually no choice of applicable legal regime – apart from some choice for the injured parties for private enforcement. Also, there is little scope left open to any cross-border externality across jurisdictions when interacting through international trade. This section explores the potential impact of institutional competition through international trade and capital mobility, had legal rules not excluded this scenario.

5.1 Competition in Stringency

Under the impact of international trade, jurisdictions may choose to increase the international competitiveness of their domestic firms by increasing the stringency of their competition laws. The rationale behind such a strategy is to render the domestic firms fitter than firms that operate in less competitive environments. Clearly there is an advantage flowing from the competitive environment to firms and the industry in general in the form of increased innovativeness, as well as to consumers in the form of lower prices and better products.

The classical example[121] for the approach to increase the stringency of competition law is a jurisdiction that has relatively few producers and significantly more consumers. The enhancement of consumer welfare in such a jurisdiction would then be the rational welfare maximising reaction.

This example, however, does not take account of the potential externality that such a jurisdiction would impose on countries with more producers and fewer consumers, were it to enforce its competition law extraterritorially. The externality in this case stems from the difference in the definition of 'optimal competition policy', related to the different economic situations of the two countries. Were both endowed similarly with consumers and producers, they would have the same definition of 'good competition law,' that is the level of stringency of norms, and the increased stringency and extraterritorial enforcement in one jurisdiction would only mean positive externalities to the other.

Differences in consumer and producer density are not the only factor that can influence the concept of which competition rules are 'optimal'.

---

121 See, e.g. Kerber and Budzinski (2004).

Clearly, competition can also destroy some value, especially if intellectual property rights are not protected properly. Finding the right balance between competition law and the protection of intellectual property rights is the key to creating optimal incentives to firms' innovation. This balance is, however, not obvious, and different countries take different approaches to this issue. What is even more intriguing is that different legal actors within one jurisdiction may have different ideas about the role of intellectual property rights and the optimal level of competition, as it is documented by McChesney in the case of the US.[122]

Further issues that may divide opinions – or did so in the recent past – include the questions of how much weight consumer choice should have, what level of cultural diversity should be preserved, and whether Small and Medium-Sized Enterprises (SMEs) deserve special protection. Differences on these issues between jurisdictions can lead to divergence in their competition law regime, which is also interpreted by some scholars as a competitive discovery process, or competition over the goals of antitrust.[123]

Instead, it is argued that the strategy will be reinforced through inter-jurisdictional political competition, as both export oriented and import substituting firms (including their employees), or the dominating group of consumers, will benefit. On the other hand countries with more producers adopting lower standards will lose out as their citizens will be disadvantaged by having to finance foreign monopoly rents by consumers bearing higher prices, in order for the export-oriented firms to be able to compete in foreign markets, or because their import substituting firms will be challenged by foreign competitors.

5.2 Competition in Laxity

The exact opposite of the strategy previously described is to tolerate market power and lower the standards of competition law, thereby allowing firms to leverage their size or market strength into other markets. There are in fact three sub-categories that may explain the mechanism of this strategy.

5.2.1 Efficiencies on international markets

The first possibility is that domestic market power will create efficiencies on international markets. This possibility arises when there are certain

122 McChesney (2003).

123 See Meessen (1989).

economies of scale and scope. Kerber and Budzinski call this scenario the 'international competitiveness defence' and bring the example of the German E.ON/Ruhrgas merger case, in which the Ministry of Economics overruled the German competition authority to allow the merger to proceed, claiming efficiencies on the international markets.[124]

This case is also worth attention because the German competition authority and the court of appeal (the Dusseldorf Higher Regional Court) took a different opinion than the Ministry of Economics.

> After the Bundeskartellamt had issued a prohibition decision the companies concerned filed an appeal at the Düsseldorf Higher Regional Court and applied to the Federal Minister of Economics and Technology for a ministerial authorisation. On 5 July 2002 the ministerial authorisation was granted subject to obligations. The main reason the Ministry gave for the authorisation was that Ruhrgas' international competitiveness will be strengthened on the procurement side. According to the Ministry, the long-term purchase of inexpensive natural gas, particularly from Russia, will improve the security of supply in Germany. On 11 July 2002, following complaints filed by competitors of the participating companies against the ministerial authorisation, the Düsseldorf Higher Regional Court ruled that the authorisation was to be suspended. On 18 September 2002 the Ministry confirmed its authorisation subject to more rigid obligations. However, the Düsseldorf Higher Regional Court upheld its preliminary injunction in its ruling of 16 December 2002.[125]

Such a disagreement between two national legal actors is a good example of differences in preferences and potential intra-jurisdictional competition among the different actors. Even though the Ministry referred also to security of supply among the main reasons of allowing the merger to go forward, there is also an argument of international competitiveness. Such cases pose an interesting question: do different legal actors within the same jurisdiction have different incentives when it comes to competitive interactions with other domestic legal actors and with foreign jurisdictions? If so, what explains these differences? These questions, among other horizontal issues, will be analysed in the final comparative chapter of this book, Chapter 5.

5.2.2 Market power in international markets

The second possibility in the 'competition in laxity' setting is that companies are allowed to obtain market power in international markets.

---

[124] This categorisation is followed by Kerber and Budzinski (2004).

[125] Bundeskartellamt (2002), 'Our Activities in 2001–2002', available at: http://www.bundeskartellamt.de/wEnglisch/download/pdf/03_TB_Kurz-E.pdf (last accessed: 5 February 2012).

This is only realistic if there is no perfect enforcement of competition laws and firms that are not established in a given jurisdiction cannot be caught for infringements of that jurisdiction's antitrust rules. In such a case, the domestic competition authority may allow the merger or anticompetitive practice, as the negative effects of market power will be (mainly) felt by foreign consumers. Examples here include the promotion of R&D cooperations directed to international markets, the exemption of export cartels and the creation of 'domestic global players' and 'national champions'.

Under this scenario, the jurisdiction in question allows the acquisition and abuse of foreign market power but prohibits domestic anticompetitive practices. For example, a jurisdiction might allow a merger but maintain strict rules on abuse of a dominant position, only enforcing them for breaches that have effect within the borders.

5.2.3 Domestic market power and predation in international markets

The third scenario that may explain the toleration of market power and lax competition policies is where a domestic market power might allow a firm to be predatory on the international markets. The example offered by Kerber and Budzinski is the case of Deutsche Post, which enjoyed a monopoly in its home market for standard letters, and was expanding into international logistic markets in the US and Switzerland. They explain that the prices within Germany remained high while the newly acquired subsidiaries were cutting prices, which indicated a strategy of cross-subsidisation similar to the strategy of competition in laxity.

From an overall welfare perspective, Kerber and Budzinski argue that the first case may result in efficiency gains, but the last two cases are, overall, welfare reducing. They point out, however, referring to the work of Helpman, Krugman,[126] Guzman[127] and Kemp,[128] that 'national welfare gains … may be high enough to compensate the domestic losers – at least as long as the foreign jurisdictions do not engage in such strategies themselves'.[129] However, they conclude that

---

[126] Helpman, E. and Krugman, P. (1985), *Market Structure and Foreign Trade: Increasing Returns, Imperfect Competition, and the International Economy* (Cambridge, MA: MIT).

[127] Guzman, A.T. (1998), 'Is International Antitrust Possible?', *New York University Law Review*, vol. 73, pp. 1501–1548.

[128] Kemp, M.C. (2001), *International Trade and National Welfare* (London: Routledge).

[129] Kerber and Budzinski (2004).

> theoretically it remains unclear whether [the above described form of] regulatory competition improves competition laws (like in the competitive-advantage-through-domestic-competition case) or leads into prisoners' dilemmas with sub-optimal competition laws due to the dominance of strategic competition policies (implying deterioration of the protection of competition).[130]

With regard to practical implications, it is clear that the perfect application of the effects doctrine (extraterritorial application of competition laws) would render the pursuit of competition in laxity impossible. On the other hand, some cases of competition in stringency may be regarded as bad and wealth decreasing by some jurisdictions. In these cases, however, the extraterritoriality principle cannot prevent those stricter strategies, as only the more stringent systems can cancel the effects of laxer competition laws, and not the other way around. This observation would then suggest that, in a world of perfect international enforcement, competition can only lead to more and more stringent regimes, which, as noted above, can be suboptimal as well.[131]

It is also interesting to note that the competition in laxity scenarios cannot take place in the vertical setting between the Community and its Member States. Therefore vertical regulatory competition cannot arise with these strategies.[132] What the European framework does not prevent, however, is the reaping of EU wide or international efficiencies at the expense of national monopolies and the related inefficiencies.

5.3 Hypothetical Examples with Two Jurisdictions

5.3.1 Hypothetical competition through physical mobility and through international trade

This section explores the dynamics of competitive law-making with international trade as a transmission mechanism of competitive advantages and disadvantages. It provides a dynamic description of potential externalities stemming from divergent antitrust rules, under various potential scenarios and strategies. It first assumes away existing rules relating to extra-territorial enforcement of antitrust (the effects doctrine), and then extends the analysis to take account of it. Finally, it considers what the response of one jurisdiction would be to another's choice of

---

130 Ibid., at p. 20.

131 Barros and Cabral (1994), also show this.

132 See Fox (2000); Sinn, H-W. (2003), *The New Systems Competition* (Malden, MA: Blackwell Publishing).

antitrust regime. The aim is to discover what the implication of fully-fledged competition among legal actors would be in this field, to be able to assess whether the present institutional framework, which restricts competition, is optimal and justified or not.

Through a hypothetical example, this sub-section traces how regulatory competition works in a dynamic setting. The example allows for international trade and some mobility for firms and/or capital to establish subsidiaries abroad. It offers a dynamic forecast in the sense that firms and legal actors (enforcement agencies as well as legislators) of different jurisdictions are allowed to respond to each others' actions.

Let us work through the hypothetical case of two jurisdictions, one with a strict competition law regime (hereinafter called 'Strictland'), and another with a lax regime (labelled 'Laxland'). We can assume that the size of the markets is the same in both jurisdictions and demand is equal, with similar elasticities as consumer preferences are similar.

Within this hypothetical example, we can distinguish two cases: in the first, we assume that there is a national incumbent in the state of Laxland; in the second case we assume that there is no such national firm in that state.[133]

5.3.2 Hypothetical example with a national champion in lenient competition law jurisdiction

When there is an incumbent in Laxland, the presumption of international trade will imply that Laxland follows the strategy of competing (with lax norms applied to domestic firms) in any of the three ways described below: efficiencies on international markets; market power in international markets; domestic market power; and predation in international markets.

5.3.2.1 Efficiencies on international markets Under the first scenario, Laxland allows its incumbent firm to achieve international economies of scale, while Strictland does not allow its firms to do this. As a result, through international trade, the firm in Laxland will win market share from the firms in Strictland.

The fact that the firm resident in Laxland is not resident in Strictland but is selling in the market of Strictland would in practice trigger the application of antitrust laws in Strictland, due to the effects doctrine (the

[133] This may be a true description of developing countries where certain industries do not exist yet, but this example also describes countries with national firms that are inefficient and are not protected by the national legislator.

practice affects the domestic market in Strictland). To put the above theoretical case into the legal framework applicable in practice, this scenario can safely assume that Strictland will not prohibit the practice of the firm resident in Laxland. This would be the case if the activity of the firm domiciled in Laxland does not breach the antitrust rules of Strictland, for example because consumers in Strictland actually benefit from the fact that the firm achieves international efficiencies. But the laws of Strictland may not catch the practice of the firm from Laxland because the firm is not resident in Strictland and it is not selling in its market either. In this case Strictland may still suffer a disadvantage if its firms were to compete with the firm from Laxland in third countries' markets.[134]

5.3.2.2 Market power in international markets Similarly, if Laxland allows its firm to achieve international market power, Laxland wins market from Strictland.

In this case, however, it is very likely that in practice, under the existing rules in European Member States, Strictland will intervene regardless of the residence of the firm achieving market power, because its home market (and thus its consumers) is by definition affected by the Laxland firm obtaining international market power.[135]

This case is different from the previous one in that Laxland's incumbent will obtain market power in Strictland's market, while in the previous scenario this was not the case (even if the Laxland firm competed in Strictland's market, it was not necessarily dominant there, but instead had the advantage of economies of scale).

5.3.2.3 Domestic market power and predation in international markets Finally, under the third scenario, Laxland could allow its national champion to achieve dominance and leverage it to other jurisdictions – through cross-subsidisation of its activities across borders and

---

[134] It is worth noting however that, in the case of US antitrust law, the legal rules would actually be applicable in the latter scenario. In the US, the law catches practices that negatively affect US trade and commerce, which may be interpreted broadly, as to include prohibition of foreign rules that cause disadvantages to US companies selling abroad (competing with the firm from Laxland in a third market, in our example).

[135] For example, extraterritorially enforced merger control, or enforcing rules applying to dominant undertakings, as well as cartel rules applicable to firms colluding in the market of Laxland.

predatory behaviour in the market of Strictland. With such cross-subsidisation, Laxland's firm could exclude Strictland's firms from the market.

Again, as in the previous case, it is likely that the laws of Strictland would catch this practice and these laws would also be enforced against the misbehaving firm.[136]

5.3.3 Hypothetical example without a national incumbent in lenient competition law jurisdiction

When we take the example of Laxland having no incumbent or dominant firm at the outset, the expected result is that the firms in Strictland will in general be more competitive than firms in Laxland. This could trigger firms from Strictland exporting to Laxland at lower prices than firms in Laxland could charge. Theory tells us that these exporting firms would out-compete the domestic firms due to their superior efficiency achieved under more competitive pressure.

However the predicted effects do not stop here. Under such a scenario, the exporting firms from Strictland may try to form an export cartel, or achieve and abuse dominance in Laxland.

In practice, the laws of Laxland would not catch this and, therefore, extraterritorial enforcement would not stop this activity. On the other hand, Strictland has higher standards, and the activity of its firms would breach these rules. In practice, Strictland may or may not enforce its antitrust rules against an export cartel. The reason for enforcing would be consistency in applying the law, as in this case the competition authorities would be faced with a group of national firms forming a cartel. The reason for not enforcing, however, would be that no domestic consumers are suffering any damage.

If the domestic competition laws of Strictland were being enforced against the export cartel members, the firms of Strictland might choose to establish subsidiaries in Laxland, in which case the antitrust laws of Strictland would be even less likely to apply, since it is no longer a domestic firm (at least not directly) that breaches competition laws, and the damage does not occur on Strictland's domestic market either.

---

[136] The antitrust laws of Strictland could prohibit the practice of predation by the dominant firm from Strictland. Also, there are several examples of international trade disputes between the US and the EU that attack the subsidisation of certain industries. Having lax competition law standards in place achieves a very similar outcome on the foreign market as does subsidisation.

In this case, however, it should be noted that the subsidiary of the firm coming from Strictland and established in Laxland constitutes an incumbent company there, which, by starting to export back to Strictland, might lead us back to the scenarios considered above (where Laxland had an incumbent firm) that made it likely that Strictland would start enforcing its competition laws against Laxland's firm, due to the direct harm to Strictland's consumers.

In a dynamic setting, where jurisdictions are allowed to respond to each others' strategies, we can predict the following. If the choice is given to one jurisdiction in isolation from the rest of the world, the optimal choice is to introduce stringency rather than laxity in competition law. If, however, the choice is given to a jurisdiction that is in competition with several others through international trade, the individual jurisdiction's highest profit-yielding choice would be to be the only one with lax standards in a world of strict legal regimes. If, however, one opts for laxity, that will have negative externalities on others, and incentivise them to adopt similarly lax strategies. So far, this sounds like a prisoners' dilemma game. As a result of such situations, the final choice of all jurisdictions will be less optimal than if they all agreed on their strategies in advance in a credible manner. This would, therefore, suggest a call for harmonisation at EU and international level. However, if we introduce the possibility of extra-territorial enforcement (the effects doctrine), then any jurisdiction responding to a lax strategy could easily avoid negative externalities through such a broad enforcement of its own competition policies, and could therefore safely opt for a strict strategy, irrespective of others opting for a lax competition regime.

What should be kept in mind, however, is that the above rough explanation does not address the reasons behind a certain level of stringency or laxity. With a more nuanced approach it may be that relaxing the requirements of a regime yields benefits, and other jurisdictions enforcing stricter competition rules brings overall welfare loss. In these cases a move towards lower requirements (race in laxity) does not necessarily signal a negative overall welfare outcome (race to the bottom).

To conclude, the above considerations show that in the case of the 27 (soon to be 28) Member States, differences under national competition laws could trigger significant negative overall welfare implications. Therefore, it appears to be an optimal policy direction to

- apply the effects doctrine in national laws; and
- intervene at EU level, with EU rules, once trade between two (or more) Member States is affected.

It also seems reasonable, however, to keep the applicable national competition law parallel with EU rules, since the latter may have a different focus (bigger market, more scope for economies of scale, and so on).

Finally, divergences in national regimes should be kept, because

- markets are different in size, perhaps also in priorities, such as IPR (satisfying diverse preferences); and
- diversity allows for experimentation with different solutions and learning which works best (laboratory federalism).

The key to managing a system of decentralised competences is to control for the incentives and potential externalities.

6. CONCLUSIONS ON LEGAL COMPETITION IN COMPETITION LAW

This chapter analysed the scope and the model of systems competition in competition law in Europe. It found that models of competition based on the different degrees of mobility may not all be applicable to this field of law. Competition through free choice or mobility is not likely to emerge due to the legal rules defining jurisdiction and extra-territorial applicability, but also due to the legal rules connecting the applicable law to the markets. Such 'mobility across markets', similar to the one observed in securities regulation, does not make change of regimes feasible or economic. Apart from regulatory competition with mobility and through international trade, however, there is sufficient scope for yardstick competition.

This analysis of the competitive or cooperative interaction of legal actors assessed the impact of Regulation 1/2003 on the potential interaction between national competition authorities on the horizontal level, and with the European Commission on the vertical level. The analysis showed that while the vertical interaction is very carefully managed in such a way as to exclude any scope for competitive interactions, the relationship among national competition authorities is mandatorily cooperative only in the application of EU competition law, not in the field of applying national competition laws. In the latter case, there is some scope for competitive interaction under pressure of international trade (competitiveness), tamed by the extraterritorial enforcement of competition law.

The system of cooperation in the application of European competition law, even within the field of horizontal interactions among national competition authorities, is managed largely by the European Commission, observing potential divergences in the application of EU law rules. Also, the legal framework provides for a sharing of information, and thus a peer review system, that observably shifts the national competition authorities' strategy from competitive towards cooperative. This can also be observed in the example of the European Competition Network.

In comparison with securities law, the network governance in the field of competition is much more centralised. As for legislation and regulation, all powers are in the exclusive competence of the European legal actors. Enforcement used to lie with the European Commission and was subsequently decentralised to involve national competition authorities and, of course, national courts. So not only in its historical evolution but also in its current form of division of competences, network governance on competition displays a stronger element of centralisation.

The fact that national legal actors have enforcement but no regulatory powers, will arguably also contribute to the phenomenon of a greater convergence of enforcement practices than in the currently decentralised field of financial regulation. In newly emerging issues, national authorities can apply European competition law but the European Commission always has the power to intervene, should it not agree with the direction of the national decision.

The assessment of the courts as relevant legal actors of regulatory competition was carried out through the analysis of the system of private enforcement. This analysis showed that the legal framework promoting private enforcement may theoretically trigger a more competitive interaction of courts *vis-à-vis* the national competition authorities intra-jurisdictionally, and other national courts horizontally in an inter-jurisdictional setting.

However, a brief review of the UK cases did not reveal a clearly competitive approach in the Tribunal's case law, in any case not in the sense that the Tribunal would aim to satisfy damages claims *en masse*. In addition, jurisdictions may limit courts to hearing only follow-on actions.

The analysis of competition law as a field that is not a traditional subject for systems competition studies revealed numerous insights on the different channels and potential functioning of legal competition, as well as cooperative interaction of legal actors within this very peculiar European legal framework. The comparison of the observations made here with the previous two chapters describing company law and securities law reveals some interesting conclusions. These are described in the concluding comparative part, Chapter 5.

5. Regulatory competition in the Internal Market

1. INTRODUCTION

This book has looked at the driving forces of competition between legal actors and at the determinants of its welfare-enhancing or welfare-reducing effects. Starting from a broad interpretation of regulatory competition, including yardstick competition and international trade competition, it has identified a number of issues worth examining in this context. In order to see whether a given observation is relevant across different legal fields, the book has looked at three European policy fields. It has found that the emergence and outcome of regulatory competition is greatly influenced by:

- market failures and efficiency theories;
- channels of competitive interaction;
- regulatees' incentives and the allocation of choice of law (if any);
- competence allocation among legal actors;
- the incentive structures of legal actors (coming both from the internal 'organisational' and the external 'governance' context).

This chapter contains conclusions on general regulatory competition theory and on competitive lawmaking within the Internal Market context.

Earlier scholarly work has established that competitive interactions differ in different fields of law.[1] The different factors influencing the emergence, functioning and outcome of competition are gradually being explored in the literature, like the pieces of a puzzle.[2] The aim here is not only to describe the differences but to try to identify the causes of such

[1] See Bratton, W.W. et al. (eds) (1996), *International Regulatory Competition and Coordination* (Oxford: Clarendon Press).

[2] See Radaelli (2004).

differences, as well as certain common trends that can be observed across various legal fields.[3]

This chapter opens by reviewing the issues identified in Chapter 1 as potentially relevant drivers of competition or determinants of its outcome, with some remarks and observations as to how generally applicable the drivers proved to be, whether they could be systematically assessed throughout the three previous chapters, and how relevant they were. Section 2 looks at the role of regulatees in the emergence and functioning of competition. Section 3 continues with the analysis of legal actors' role in shaping regulatory competition. It compares the three previous chapters in order to verify four hypotheses concerning legal actors' behaviour and competition. The comparison reveals some interesting insights about how competition is shaped by different legal actors, and how legal actors' behaviour is determined by institutional settings and the channels of competitive interaction. Section 4 reaches conclusions on the outcome of competitive interactions.

Section 5 explores the relationship between the European legal framework and regulatory competition. It reviews interpretations of subsidiarity and proportionality, as the legal rules influencing competence allocation between the European and national levels, and looks at how these principles are, and can be, applied in practice. Section 6 continues with a review of the three policy fields described previously and summarises some of the recent emerging trends in regulation and regulatory competition within the Internal Market. Section 7 concludes the discussion, and sets a research agenda for the future on the issues that remain under-explored in the context of regulatory competition in Europe.

2. REGULATEES' ROLE IN REGULATORY COMPETITION

2.1 Introduction to the Theoretical Part of the Conclusions

The previous chapters reveal varying types of competitive interaction in different fields of law within Europe. The differences lie not only in the welfare implications, but also with regard to:

---

[3] This work does not aim to be generalisable to all legal fields simply on the basis of the three areas examined here, but it does claim that certain observations will be valid for other fields as well. Further, it is acknowledged that the framework of analysis and the choice of policy fields determine what conclusions will be reached and the list of drivers of competitive interactions is not intended as an exhaustive list.

- the drivers behind regulatory arbitrage;
- the drivers behind regulatory competition;
- the participating legal actors;
- the presence of cross-border and across-stakeholder externalities;
- the role of the federal level in mitigating externalities, and the consequent scope for regulatory divergence (such as level of harmonisation, competence allocation);
- the governance mechanisms in place to ensure uniformity in legal outcomes, or at least cooperation among legal actors, and so on.

Based on the analysis in the chapters above, this section sets out the conclusions on how the various pieces of the competition puzzle link with one another and influence the overall direction of regulatory competition. The aim is by no means to propose a complete model that would allow us to precisely calculate the likelihood of the emergence, the precise functioning and predicted welfare implications, of competition. But establishing links among the various drivers of competition can advance our understanding of when, how and why competition can, or cannot, work in various fields of law.

This and the following sections revisit the pieces of the puzzle described in Chapter 1 and examined in subsequent chapters. Building on the issues presented there, Sections 2 to 4 address the following questions:

1. Section 2: The regulatees:
   - Do regulatees have diverse preferences?
   - Do regulatees have free choice or mobility?
     - o Do regulates have perfect information?
     - o Regulatees' choice over bundled or tied legal norms
   - Do regulatees have incentives to engage in regulatory arbitrage?
     - o The allocation of choice or mobility among regulatees, beneficiaries and other affected parties
     - o Connecting the demand side (regulates) and the supply side (regulators)
2. Section 3: Legal actors:
   - Regulatory competition works differently in different legal fields
   - Different legal actors have different attitudes towards competition
   - The 'external' institutional setting matters
   - The 'internal' institutional set-up also matters

- Different legal actors react to different channels of competition
- Intra-jurisdictional coopetition shapes the final legal output.

3. Section 4: Measuring the outcome of competitive interactions:
   - The measures of welfare, the concept of efficiency and legal paradigms
   - Convergence and divergence, cross-referencing and legal paradigms.

These conclusions draw on examples from the three chapters describing legal competition in three different fields of law. They do not mirror the structure of Chapter 1, since not all aspects identified there resulted in relevant conclusions, or not with the same weight. Some further aspects that were not examined in Chapter 1 have also emerged through the analysis of the three fields, or did so at the stage they were compared. Conclusions on those issues are added to the list of research questions presented in Chapter 1.

2.2 Do Regulatees have Diverse Preferences?

Knowing your regulatees' (preferences) is not only important because it is the only way to respond to their needs, but also because different preferences will translate into different strategies in the face of regulation. It is ultimately regulatees' responses that will determine the impact of rules. Ignoring preferences and strategies of regulatees equals regulatory failures. In addition, diverse preferences among the regulated population can signal a potential for decentralised rule-making, which, if sorting can take place, can possibly satisfy these different preferences better than a uniform solution.

To observe whether preferences are different, one needs to look at the market transactions at hand. There is no guidance for systematically predicting whether preferences will diverge or not. Besides, it is difficult to measure the diversity of preferences. Looking at the existing rules and the preferences revealed among them by the choices that are made may be misleading, as competition among norms may be imperfect and not able to reveal all the preferences of regulatees.

We saw in the previous chapters that regulatees can have different strategies in choosing the applicable legal regime. This was observed for example in the case of securities law, where empirical evidence shows that some firms opt into stricter legal regimes, while others stay in their home market and home regulatory environment; again others search for quicker and lower cost regimes for their securities issues.

Regulatees may have different interests and business strategies and therefore they may respond to regulation differently. A famous example of this is the preference of incumbent firms for more regulation that can create a barrier to new market entrants. Also, some regulatees may be more mobile then others. This is true, for example, of big transnational companies, compared to SMEs. But, when talking about regulatees, we should not only think of the direct subjects of regulation but also the beneficiaries of a given legal norm.

The previous analysis also allowed for different preferences over the type of market and distributive outcomes that different jurisdictions wish to achieve. It is important to distinguish among the channels of competition and how diverse preferences of regulatees are distributed geographically across jurisdictions. Regulatory competition with mobility can lead to perfect sorting in case heterogeneous preferences are observed within each jurisdiction, whereas the other channels of competition cannot deliver such outcomes. If however diverse preferences occur only across jurisdictions (but there is homogeneity within each territorial unit), the other channels of competition can also deliver on satisfying diverse preferences.

2.3 Do Regulatees have Free Choice or Mobility?

Regulatory competition through mobility requires free choice of law, or a relatively easy mobility for regulatees across jurisdictions. In this channel of competitive interaction, it is the threat of exit, or actual migration of regulatees, that will eventually trigger a competitive response from legal actors. The other channels of competitive interaction – capital mobility, international trade or information flows – do not require mobility or choice of regulatees.

When assessing whether regulatees have choice or mobility, it is important to ask

- What are the costs of such mobility?
- Do regulatees have perfect information about their choice?
- Which party has the choice or final decision over governing law?
- Are legal norms where choice is offered bundled together with rules governing other aspects of regulatees' activity?

All of the above aspects are likely to influence regulatees' behaviour in terms of whether or not arbitrage occurs, and if so, in which direction. The previous chapters included examples of cost differentials among different legal regimes (such as actions for competition damages or the establishment of private companies). Cost savings are potential incentives for law shopping, as long as opting into another legal system does not come at the even higher cost of a more burdensome regulatory environment or less convenient legal rules. But another, equally important aspect of choice of law is information about available alternative legal regimes. For regulatees as well as transacting parties and beneficiaries of regulation, information about differences in governing law should be clear and understandable (as we saw in earlier chapters the example of retail investors and the format of disclosure, or creditors and foreign corporate forms).

2.3.1 Do regulatees have perfect information?

If regulatees have information asymmetries, these may impede perfect sorting and lead to less than optimal outcomes. If they can choose their preferred regime correctly, with full information being available for them, this will increase the chances for positive welfare implications. But acquiring information about their choice can be costly to regulatees. Information problems can thus also be regarded as another cost factor for regulatees. If the costs of law shopping exceed the expected gains, we cannot expect regulatees to react to legal differences among jurisdictions.

Another side of the coin is whether the business partners of regulatees have perfect information. If a foreign legal system is unknown to contracting partners, and the latter have the power to express their preferences when entering into transactions, regulatees may not wish to opt for such foreign laws. Such phenomena can be observed (or expected) for example in certain aspects of company law, and for certain transaction partners (adjusting creditors).

2.3.2 Regulatees' choice over bundled or tied legal norms

Legal norms are most often not stand-alone provisions, but are embedded in a given legal paradigm,[4] in the entire legal system, and in the institutional framework of the country (for example enforcement agencies, courts). When choice of law or mobility is granted to regulatees, this often means changing more than one set of rules, given that the applicable law is established by the same connecting legal norm for several legal areas. Typical connecting norms are: nationality or place of registration; the market where a given transaction takes place; the jurisdiction where effects of a certain activity occur, and so on. An example of a relatively 'unbundled' choice of law is the free choice of governing contract law, or the choice of dispute settlement for a particular contract. Changing the applicable company law regime by

[4] See Heine and Kerber (2002).

reincorporating, and thereby changing, for example, the applicable tax and accounting laws as well, is an example of a bundled choice.

As a result, regulated parties, even when they do have a choice, face decisions about a set of legal norms. The examples of company, securities and competition law analysed in the previous chapters all confirm this.

The result of the embeddedness of legal norms for the regulatee is that switching from one system to another becomes either more attractive or more costly. In terms of benefits, bundling can either increase or mitigate the expected advantages of switching. If all norms that are interlinked are more advantageous in one jurisdiction than in another, bundling will have a positive impact on switching incentives. If, however, only one or a few norms are worth changing regimes for, and the rest are equally or even less advantageous than the home regime, the switching costs for the regulatee may be too high compared to the expected benefits.

For this reason, the bundling of norms should be kept in mind when examining regulatees' incentives to engage in legal arbitrage. Although such tying of norms is in most cases perfectly justified, and therefore commonplace, this phenomenon can have an impact on the likelihood of the emergence, and the direction, of regulatory arbitrage and regulatory competition.

2.4 Do Regulatees have Incentives to Engage in Regulatory Arbitrage?

Once it is established that choice or mobility as a channel of potential competitive interaction is open to regulatees (within a given legal context (bundling) and with sufficient transparency), legal designers have to try to predict whether regulatees will have the incentive to engage in actual regulatory arbitrage. This conceptually boils down to a cost benefit analysis of the potential advantages of switching to another regime and its cost implications. Even when regulatees do not move across jurisdictions, it is relevant to ask whether they can pose a credible threat of exit. If they can, this may be sufficient to spur competition among legal actors.

Finally, the potential for regulatory arbitrage should also be examined in the context of the three other channels of competitive interaction, that is, international capital movements, trade, and information flows. Here regulatees may not have mobility across borders in the strict sense of the word. But their money and products can go across borders. In a sense, every legal rule that influences the investment climate within a country can be considered as regulation of the use of capital. From this functional perspective capital movements are similar to the movements of regulatees.

2.4.1 The allocation of choice or mobility among regulatees, beneficiaries and other affected parties

Inter-stakeholder externalities are important for redistributive considerations, but also when assessing overall welfare implications. Therefore, clearly identifying the affected parties is crucial for any welfare assessment. The welfare implications will vary, of course, according to the allocation of choice of law. Shifting this choice from one stakeholder group to another will result in completely different arbitrage outcomes and, therefore, different welfare implications.

The market failure that the legal intervention addresses can reveal some indications as to choosers' (regulatees or beneficiaries) agency problems and potential externalisation issues *vis-à-vis* other stakeholders.

Regulatees losing bargaining power may try to opt for less interventionist norms, while beneficiaries may opt for the highest possible level of protection. The literature describing the negative implications of regulatory competition often argues there will be a race to the bottom case when regulatees can chose legal norms. But reference is not so often made to the potential drawbacks of suboptimal high levels of protection for beneficiaries, when beneficiaries have choice of law.

While compliance lies with the regulated party in the narrow sense, enforcement may in some cases lie with the beneficiaries, and the overall welfare implications of certain norms, or regulatory competition as a whole, may ultimately be decided by the impact on other affected parties.

A further qualification should be added, however, to the observation above that regulatees, when allocated choice, will opt for laxer legal regimes. Even within a more homogeneous group of regulatees, there is often heterogeneity with regard to the strategy adopted. When new rules are introduced that impose restrictions on parties that originally had better bargaining power, some of these regulatees can decide to be the first mover, and make an advantage out of regulation. By being the first to adapt to changed legal requirements, firms can sometimes achieve significant economies of scale or avail themselves of network effects.

In a decentralised regime, market participants may find that the norms imposed on them are too burdensome, and may exit the market, as a strategy to respond to the new rules. If other jurisdictions do not impose the same rules, this may be a viable response. The threat of exit is greater in small markets, where business has lower expectations of market share gains and corresponding profits. Bigger markets can better afford to impose rules that curb firms' bargaining power with respect to their counterparts.

This brief observation is not meant to be a substitute for a full analysis of how regulatees can be expected to react, but calls attention to the fact that assuming homogeneity in reactions may be wrong.

2.4.2 Connecting the demand side (regulatees) and supply side (regulators)

It was argued above that the distinction between facilitative and interventionist norms can be useful in predicting the dynamics of legal arbitrage within a given field. The allocation of choice among the different parties and the predicted arbitrage strategy of choosers of norms should be added to this. Besides, taking into consideration the political weight (or lobby capacity) of the parties with choice takes us closer to understanding to what extent legal actors can be expected to react, and how they would respond, to regulatory arbitrage.[5] However, in order to appreciate the potential supply side reaction, certain determinants of legal actors' incentives need to be considered as well.

3. LEGAL ACTORS' ROLE IN SHAPING REGULATORY COMPETITION

Studies into regulatory competition often examine one legal field only, and their conclusions cannot therefore be applied across different legal fields. Nonetheless, authors of the few available comparative analyses warn that competitive interactions[6] and their welfare implications[7] will be different in different areas of law. This book reviewed three legal fields, posing similar questions across these fields, which makes it possible to compare some of the drivers and outcomes of regulatory competition across these areas.[8]

---

[5] For an interesting categorisation of regulatees' strategies and their impact on legal actors, see Murphy, D.D. (2004), *The Structure of Regulatory Competition: Corporations and Public Policies in a Global Economy* (Oxford: Oxford University Press).

[6] Gabor, B. (2010) *Institutional and Regulatory Competition in Europe: Connecting Some Pieces of the Puzzle on When, How and Why it can Work*, European University Institute Doctorate Thesis.

[7] Esty and Geradin (2001).

[8] It is important to note that the conclusions of such comparative analysis have the same limitations as the analysis itself. As noted above, the descriptive

Comparing the three fields is not a straightforward exercise, since sectors are different (such as externalities, cost effects of regulation on regulatees, trade effects of regulation) and legal institutions are different as well. When talking about institutions, a distinction is made between external legal rules (such as: Who are the competent actors?; What are the rules governing their interactions?) and internal institutional settings (taking account of the degree of independence of legal actors, its financing, accountability, composition, and so on).

Here the comparison of the legal areas examined above will test the following hypotheses with regard to the functioning of regulatory competition and the legal actors involved

1. Regulatory competition works differently in different legal fields.
2. Different legal actors have different attitudes towards competition.
3. The 'external' institutional setting (for example the governance mechanisms of interaction between legal actors) will influence legal actors' attitudes towards competitive forces and thus the final legal outcomes.
4. Besides external governance, the 'internal' institutional set-up of each legal actor (its independence, financing, nomination, composition, accountability, and regulatory mission) is also a determinant of how they react to competition.
5. Different legal actors also seem to react to certain channels of competition better than to others.
6. Finally, it is the interaction of legal actors within a given jurisdiction (intra-jurisdictional competition or cooperation) that shapes the final legal output, which might or might not be in competition with other jurisdictions' rules.

3.1 Regulatory Competition Works Differently in Different Legal Fields

The first question – whether competition works differently in different legal areas – is relatively easy to answer: 'Yes'. Earlier research,[9] as well

chapters show the main developments of certain legal issues through selected examples, and do not contain in-depth and exhaustive case law analysis of national courts or the regulatory activity of IRAs. Therefore, the conclusions drawn here are merely a first attempt to examine the dynamics of what drives competition. Further research and debate would be welcome on the competitive or cooperative attitudes of the various national legal actors in these fields.

[9] See, e.g. Bratton et al. (1996), or Esty and Geradin (2001).

as the previous chapters of this book, have shown that there are differences across legal fields. There are differences not only in the extent of existing regulatory competition (or the lack of it) and its welfare impacts in each field, but also in the potential functioning and welfare implications of such competition, had the legal framework allowed for it equally in all three legal fields.

In competition law, it is clear that there is no scope for competition for mobile regulatees, and even trade competition is limited. Yardstick competition could have a role in the future, provided that the governance tools that aim to exclude ruinous competitive behaviour allow for such positive forms of legal innovation and institutional learning. In contrast to this stands company law, where mobility across jurisdictions exists, and where legal rules are in direct competition with one another (at least for certain types of firms that can readily respond to regulatory arbitrage opportunities). In the middle, between these two models, we find securities law, where legal divergence and competition is not explicitly called for, but some scope is left to render a jurisdiction's market more attractive, and both parties to the transaction (issuers and investors, as well as their intermediaries) have some choice over the legal regime they want to cover their transaction.

An inquiry into the potential functioning of regulatory competition revealed differences across the three fields as well. In the case of competition law, negative externalities are likely to arise out of legal actors' competitive behaviour, were they allowed to compete over competition policy through international trade advantages. In the case of securities law, less than optimal outcomes can be expected from free choice of law if investors cannot fully and freely put a value on the quality of the governing law of issuers. Similarly, in company law, a free choice of regime can result in positive outcomes for adjusting creditors if they perceive the quality of legal regimes. But firm choice can impose costs on non-adjusting creditors. The differences between the three fields stem from many potential sources. Reasons for different outcomes include differences in the underlying market failures, the varying level of inter-stakeholder and cross-border externalities, and the different legal actors involved. To understand the role of legal actors in the emergence and functioning of regulatory competition, we need to ask further questions about their behaviour and its drivers.

3.2 Different Legal Actors Have Different Attitudes Towards Competition

The second question is whether different legal actors will respond differently to competitive forces. Indeed we observe fields where, for example, the legislator and the courts take different approaches to competitive interactions. It is not surprising that actors at a European and national level may also have different attitudes towards regulatory competition. In company law, for example, the ECJ opened the way to regulatory competition, while the EU legislator, up to that point at least, had mainly been harmonising in order to exclude a regulatory race. We observe that following an opening up of regulatory competition by the European Court of Justice, some jurisdictions moved towards a more attractive or, rather, less burdensome, regime for private firms. In the area of collective redress (relevant to all three legal fields examined here) we can also observe some developments towards better access to justice. Here, too, there has been a European Court ruling declaring that individuals can sue for damages in cases of a breach of EU competition law provisions, which opened the way for the courts, without limiting the choice of forum and law.

Strategic competition policy could yield potentially significant international trade advantages, had any given jurisdiction complete freedom in setting its norms. Were all European states free to regulate competition their own way, it is likely that a competitive outcome would result in overall lower welfare. This is the main reason why competition policy is the most centralised field (the exclusive competence of the European legislator). Even the enforcement of EU competition law, which has been decentralised, is filled with institutional guarantees that national competition authorities will not interpret and apply the otherwise uniform rules to the advantage of national constituencies at the cost of other Member States' constituencies. We observed also the incentives, and actual attempts, of the national regulator actively to create national champions. One example of this was the German postal sector's case. It is also interesting to note that the German courts have defended a different legal outcome: that of overall welfare under economic theory. In this case, therefore, it seems that the regulator is motivated by international trade advantages, as one channel of competition, whereas the courts are competing within their own jurisdiction against the regulator (intra-jurisdictional competition) to pursue the best rule and thus influence the final legal outcome.

But does this mean that a given type of legal actor, for example the courts, will always react similarly to competitive forces? Not necessarily.

Courts often have similar internal settings and an institutional freedom across different legal fields. And yet the French courts did not seem open to litigating antitrust damages cases, whereas the UK proved more welcoming to such actions. It appears that differences in the attitude to competition can exist not only across different types of legal actors, or within the same group of legal actors across different countries, but even within one jurisdiction. We saw that the High Court in London opened up a jurisdiction to hear antitrust damages actions. However, a new court with competence, the Competition Appeals Tribunal, has not (so far) made such a move to exert a greater influence on final legal outcomes. It is possible that we have to go beyond considering courts as one homogeneous group of actors. The question then, left for further research, is why there would be differences in the attitudes of a given group of legal actors even within one jurisdiction? Is there a real difference at all, or is it simply too early to see the pattern of the new competent court? Or are there differences in the internal institutional design and incentives of the old and the new court?

3.3 The 'External' Institutional Setting

The previous chapters observed that IRAs may be incentivised by certain governance structures to cooperate with IRAs of other jurisdictions, even if otherwise they would all have incentives to act strategically and engage in competition among themselves. This was observed in competition policy, but similar forces are detectable also in the case of securities regulation. The current European legal arrangements introduce, however, a framework within which these national actors have to cooperate. Their cooperation is not only mandated, but also facilitated and incentivised. Some of the external institutional elements, which were observed to promote cooperation, were transparency of legal outputs, potentially combined with additional cues for what the desired legal outcome is, and with oversight by a centralised actor. Cues for the desired direction of legal output can take various forms, including guidelines, mutual evaluation, benchmarking, 'naming and shaming', and so on.

In competition policy, the centralised actor is the European Commission; in securities law this is the Commission and ESMA, which we saw was not a 'pure' European actor, rather an EU body composed of national supervisors. This latter fact may in itself influence what scope ESMA will leave for regulatory divergence and competition. It is perhaps too early to predict how this will influence regulatory interactions, especially since there seem to be different national attitudes towards competition.

In any event, there is an obvious move towards centralisation and harmonisation in financial regulation at the EU level, as a consequence of the financial crisis. Without trying to over-interpret regulatory developments, it can be argued that the recent harmonisation at EU level is also a competitive move by the European legislator and regulator, in order to stay in the regulatory arena. If regulatory failure occurs, political accountability is a traditionally recognised disciplinary mechanism. In a regulatory space with multiple competent legal actors, however, the regulatory failure of one actor may mean losing the field. Another legal actor with competence (in this case national regulators) could step in and regulate 'better' than the failed actor did. This form of institutional competition should not be underestimated in the EU context, especially since there is a lively debate about democratic deficit and the right balance of competences under the principle of subsidiarity. The framework for exercising shared competences can be thought of as another external institutional setting that can shape legal actors' attitudes towards competition.

3.4 The 'Internal' Institutional Set-up

The first chapter of this book also introduced the subject of institutional set-up, a form of internal governance, of different legal actors. The existing literature revealed that there are different theories about what intrinsic motivations lie behind the decisions of judges, regulators, and so forth. Some authors argue that economic considerations drive discretional decisions, others point to altruistic motivations. One stream of literature looks beyond individual motives and argues that the institutional independence of any legal actor will influence the outcome of legal decisions. No doubt, the two, individuals' intrinsic motivations and institutions, interact. There is also likely to be an interaction between internal institutional set-up and the external governance mechanisms referred to above.

While a rigorous description and comparison of the internal institutional rules of different legal actors has not been carried out here, we observed, nonetheless, that legislation at the European level aims to establish institutional guarantees of independence. An example of this is ESMA, where legislation attempts to safeguard the independence of this European independent agency. As we observed, however, the composition of a legal actor is likely to matter also, and legal guarantees may work differently with different types of composition. In the case of ESMA, it is national supervisory authorities that make up the decision-making bodies, and much of the personnel. This stands in contrast to competition policy, where the European Commission is not only the regulator but also the most important enforcement agent, and the network of national competition authorities is subject to it. It is too early to see what the effect of this mix of composition, degree of institutional independence and external governance framework will be on the attitude of ESMA towards competition, but this could be an interesting subject of further research in the near future.

3.5 Different Legal Actors React to Different Channels of Competition

From the above analysis a further finding emerges. Whereas it would be tempting to say that courts embrace openness to competition more than other legal actors, such as the national legislator and independent regulatory agencies, this is not entirely true. In the Überseering case,[10] for example, it was a German court that did not accept the standing of the Dutch company, thereby refusing to recognise that companies can choose the governing law they wish. But it was also German courts[11] that did not follow the approach of the Ministry to applying competition policy strategically.

Thus it appears that courts are not necessarily responsive to competition, or at least, not to all types of competition. Observing the positive descriptions of competition in the three fields above, it seems that international trade competition does not seem to be the main driver of courts' behaviour. Often, however, courts seem to be sensitive to 'competition for the field', in other words, establishing their jurisdiction in order to enter the regulatory arena, or laying down a rule with final legal force.

Instead, courts are likely to enter into a 'competition for the field', that is often even intra-jurisdictional. This may or may not coincide with competition for regulatees. In the case of establishing jurisdiction for antitrust actions, the two seem indeed to coincide. International trade competition seems to motivate the competitive behaviour of the legislator or national regulator. Independent regulatory agencies may or may not engage in trade competition: this book has argued that their behaviour

---

[10] Case C-208/00 *Überseering BV* v *Nordic Construction Company Baumanagement GmbH* (NCC). [2002] ECR I-09919.

[11] Bundeskartellamt (2002) *Our Activities in 2001–2002*, available at: http://www.bundeskartellamt.de/wEnglisch/download/pdf/03_TB_Kurz-E.pdf (last accessed: 5 February 2012).

may be a function of their organisational set-up (for example, independence from the legislator or national regulator) and their external governance context.

3.6 Intra-jurisdictional Co-opetition Shapes the Final Legal Output

Legal actors with parallel competences within a jurisdiction can also interact with each other, and cooperate or compete for influence over a certain legal field. This form of intra-jurisdictional competition is also an element that has been addressed in the previous chapters. Organisation set-up is a relevant determinant of whether such competition can arise. If legal actors such as IRAs are independent enough to take decisions contrary to the rules made by the legislator or the courts, such competition within a jurisdiction can arise. One interesting example is competition law and the enforcement of the rules by courts and competition authorities with parallel competences.

A full account of intra-jurisdictional competition within the US is provided by McChesney.[12] Exploring in more depth the European variant of intra-jurisdictional competition would be an interesting research agenda. Here, intra-jurisdictional competition has been referred to mainly for its implications for inter-jurisdictional competition as it is proposed that the domestic interaction of legal actors will influence interaction at the international level. The proposition is that it may be one legal actor that opens the way to competitive interactions, and another that actually engages in competition. For example, the European Court of Justice opened up legal fields for competition in the field of company law, but never entered the competitive arena itself. At national level, courts may accept jurisdiction or render judgments that create competitive pressures not only for the judiciary but also (or mainly) for other domestic legal actors. Further research with a deeper analysis of the dynamics of intra-jurisdictional competition would be worth pursuing.

3.7 Conclusions

Regulatory competition works differently in different legal fields. The positive, descriptive conclusion is that in some fields there is scope for competition and competitive moves can be observed but, in other fields, legal rules leave no scope for divergence or competition. From the normative perspective, even if rules allowed for competition, this would

---

[12] McCheseny, F.S. (2003), 'Talking 'bout my antitrust generation', *Emory Law Journal*, vol. 52, no. 3, pp. 1401–1438.

not work always in the same way: in some cases it would lead to vigorous competition whilst, in others, no reaction would occur; in some cases it would be positive or neutral for welfare, whilst in others it would only ruin it. The reason for these diverse outcomes lies in the differences in the costs of arbitrage for regulatees, the availability of information about choice for regulatees, and the differences in potential externalities across different constituencies as well as across jurisdictions, and so on.

Different legal actors will react differently to institutional competition. But this statement implicitly means also that one given type of legal actor will always respond similarly, and this is not the case. We saw that courts across jurisdictions, and even courts within a single jurisdiction, can have different attitudes towards competition. This begs the question, What determines legal actors' reaction to competition? This analysis has tested for internal and external institutional designs as potential driving factors.

The external institutional settings (that is governance mechanisms of interaction) among legal actors will influence legal actors' attitude towards competitive forces and thus the final legal outcomes.

Besides external governance, the internal institutional set-up of each legal actor (independence, financing, nomination, composition, accountability, regulatory mission) is also a determinant of how they react to competition.

A further proposition emerges from the above analysis. Different external and internal institutional settings will render different legal actors more responsive to certain channels of competitive forces than to others. This means that the legislator (as well as the national regulator) is likely to respond to international trade competition more than other legal actors. Courts, above all, seem eager to enter the regulatory space and compete to make the best rule, often engaging in intra-jurisdictional competition with other national legal actors. The European level legal actors have different institutional limits and act differently in the face of competition. The European Court has shown itself most willing to open fields to competition. The European legislator and regulator is likely to be motivated to compete for the regulatory field in areas of shared competences, which can turn out to be a good disciplining mechanism to prevent or easily correct regulatory failures. Independent regulatory agencies are likely to respond to the channel of competition that is preferred by their internal and external institutional environment. If, for example, the legislator or the government has strong influence over the IRAs (weak independence), they may be driven by international trade competition, responding to the interests of legislators and regulators. If, however, there are stronger institutional guarantees of their independence, and if they are organised into an external governance mechanism that favours transparency and exchange among IRAs of various jurisdictions, they are likely to respond well to yardstick competition and act cooperatively from the perspective of international trade competition. Further analysis would be worth pursuing in order to explore these questions better.

Finally, this analysis proposes that the intra-jurisdictional interaction of legal actors can lead to competition domestically, and that these competitive interactions shape the final legal output of any given jurisdiction. Moreover, the field for competition may be opened up by a legal actor different from the one engaging in competition for regulatees, for example. Further research would be welcome also on the intra-jurisdictional aspect of regulatory competition.

4. THE OUTCOME OF REGULATORY COMPETITION

The main goal of this book is to explore what drives the differences in the emergence and direction of regulatory competition variants in different legal fields. Among the obvious drivers are differences in the underlying market failures, differences across the legal systems in which norms are embedded, differences among regulatees (as listed above, these may include different preferences or different strategies), and differences among legal actors (as discussed above, who they are, what their internal institutional set-up is, and governance mechanisms). Here two further issues are addressed with regard to the outcome of competition: how to measure welfare outcomes, and the extent to which legal solutions can mix or converge.

4.1 The Measures of Welfare, the Concept of Efficiency and Legal Paradigms

The previous three chapters reviewed different concepts of efficiency not so much in terms of theoretical discussions on the measure of welfare and efficiency, but in terms of economic theory governing a given legal solution within a jurisdiction. It emerges that there are competing economic explanations for whether the involvement of employees will deliver superior or inferior results, whether mandatory disclosure or a ban on insider dealing is good or bad, and whether competition should aim at preserving close-to-perfect competition in the markets, or should pursue other aims, to ensure diversity and choice for example. It is apparent that there can be differences among Member States concerning the theory of efficient regulatory intervention.

Efficiency debates are well known and have long and well-established roots. Much academic discussion has focused on resolving the issue of which solutions are more efficient. One attempt to answer this question was to measure the impact of trade competition among jurisdictions, using a GDP measure of welfare. La Porta et al. worked out a system to measure which legal system is more efficient. Their work suggests that legal solutions within a country will impact its economic and financial development, and that countries with an Anglo-Saxon legal origin consistently perform better than other legal systems. Although later critics question these conclusions,[13] what these studies actually aim to do is to verify the outcome of what in this book has labelled 'trade competition' among jurisdictions (the second channel of institutional competition). Given the complexity of issues that influence nations' competitiveness, proving the role of one single ingredient is not easy.

Here, the aim is not to resolve the debate, but to try to understand the place of this piece of the puzzle within the bigger picture of regulatory competition. Different legal solutions with different distributive impacts are not clearly distinguished in the current academic literature from different concepts of efficiency. Often, the underlying economic theory on welfare and the measure of optimal rules is not explained.

Indeed, the different solutions evolve around different institutional norms, embedded in the national (regional or European) legal context. This web of norms interacting and leading to a given outcome is described in the literature as different legal paradigms, along which norms in different jurisdictions evolve in different ways.[14]

The concept of efficiency, the distributive impacts of legal solutions and the functioning and evolution of legal paradigms are closely linked. It is a web of norms within a given legal system that will lead to certain welfare and distributive outcomes. The concept of efficiency is arguably just as linked to this legal paradigm as the accompanying institutional or legal norms. Thinking of efficiency outside its original legal paradigm context may therefore be misleading. One conclusion proposed here is

---

[13] See, e.g. Braendle, U.C. (2006), 'Shareholder Protection in the USA and Germany – On the Fallacy of LLSV', in German Working Papers in Law and Economics vol. 2006, no. 18; Deakin, S. and Seems, M. (2010), 'Comparative Law and Finance: Past, Present and Future Research', *Journal of Institutional and Theoretical Economics*, vol. 166, pp. 120–140; and Armour, J. et al. (2009), 'How Do Legal Rules Evolve? Evidence from a Cross-Country Comparison of Shareholder, Creditor, and Worker Protection', *American Journal of Comparative Law*, vol. 57, no. 3, pp. 579–629.

[14] See Heine and Kerber (2002).

that the measurement of efficiency should only be removed with caution from its original legal context.[15]

4.2 Convergence and Divergence, Cross-referencing and Legal Paradigms

A further question was whether the competition of legal actors can give birth to more efficient solutions, through either borrowing existing legal solutions from a more successful system, or inventing new ones. The answer to this question should be sought in research on path dependence and an evolutionary approach to legal change:[16] innovation is likely to emerge at the margins by making the existing legal system more cost effective, less time consuming, reducing administrative burdens, and so on. Innovative solutions that would entail a paradigm shift are less likely, since the existing norms are embedded in the context of the entire legal system of a given country. For the same reason, borrowing the efficient legal solution from other jurisdictions is not likely to be effective. Legal transplants can only work effectively in their optimal legal environment,[17] that is built along the same legal paradigm.[18] The concepts of legal paradigms and path dependence developed by Heine and Kerber are indeed the underlying explanation for different theories of efficiency in place. The legal systems, legal paradigms, have their own way of delivering results. Changing some spare parts in the system will not necessarily lead to better outcomes. On the contrary, they may have a negative impact on aspects of the system that the jurisdiction of their origin did not consider to be relevant at all. Cross-references to foreign jurisdictions' solutions thus have certain limits, in the international context, as has also been pointed out by Bratton and McCahery.[19]

---

[15] See the discussion on comparative law and economics, the conclusions of which go in a similar direction: e.g. Mattei, U. and Cafaggi, F. (1998), 'Comparative Law and Economics', in Newman, P. (ed.), *The New Palgrave Dictionary of Economics and the Law*, vol. 1, pp. 346–351.

[16] Deakin, S. and Carvalho, F. (2010), 'System and Evolution in Corporate Governance', ECGI – Law Working Paper No. 150/2010.

[17] See Berkowitz, D., Pistor, K. and Richard, J.F. (2003), 'The Transplant Effect', *The American Journal of Comparative Law*, vol. 51, no. 1, pp. 163–203.

[18] See Heine, K. and Kerber, W. (2002), 'European Corporate Laws, Regulatory Competition and Path Dependence', *European Journal of Law and Economics*, vol. 13, no. 1, pp. 47–71.

[19] Bratton, W.W. and McCahery, J.A. (1999), 'Comparative Corporate Governance and the Theory of the Firm: The Case Against Global Cross Reference', *Columbia Journal of Transnational Law*, vol. 38, no. 2, pp. 213–297.

A further conclusion is that the question above is linked with the modes of governance or the rules setting the framework for competitive interactions. Certain governance models may induce more legal innovation, while others incentivise actors to imitate each other. For example, benchmarking entails the selection of best practices against which the output of other jurisdictions is measured. Such exercises may lead to the imitation of the benchmark, rather than innovative legal solutions. Information about other jurisdictions' legal output, without any benchmarking or network governance, may spur competition, as information provision will increase the comparability of legal solutions both for legal actors and for regulatees (choosers of norms).

5. REGULATORY COMPETITION AND THE INTERNAL MARKET: THE LEGAL FRAMEWORK

A very important determinant of whether regulatory competition can emerge and, if so, what form it takes is the allocation of competences among legal actors at different levels (EU, national, regional) and with different (legislative, regulatory, judiciary, private regulatory) functions.

Competences between the EU and its member states are allocated by the Treaty. Besides a limited number of exclusive EU competences (such as competition policy), there is a wide range of shared competences. These are governed by the principles of subsidiarity and proportionality.

In economic literature, the European Union is often examined as a tool for achieving efficiency without much consideration being given to what the legal and political foundations of the Union are. But the EU being a legal institution, competence allocation rules determine when the EU is best placed to act, and when action should be taken by Member States.

Economic approaches to describing subsidiarity and proportionality take the approach of explaining these two principles from the perspective of an economic rationale for regulatory intervention.[20] Legal approaches follow the case law of the European Court of Justice in explaining the actual meaning of these principles. Here the Court's case law will be examined from the perspective of the economic rationale of decentralisation, to see what the relationship is between the legal approach and the economic approach.

[20] See Pelkmans, J. (2006), 'Testing for Subsidiarity' *Bruges European Economic Policy Briefings* no. 13, available at http://www.coleurop.eu/file/content/studyprogrammes/eco/publications/BEEPs/BEEP13.pdf. (accessed 19 January 2012); see also Van den Bergh (2000).

5.1 Conferral, Subsidiarity and Proportionality of EU Intervention

The governing treaties of the European Union, the TEU and TFEU, set out the framework of competence allocation among legal actors within the Union. First of all, they establish that the Union is only entitled to act within the powers conferred upon it by the Member States. Within Union powers, the TEU distinguishes between centralised (exclusive) and partially decentralised (shared) competences.[21]

As some form of decentralisation is needed for there to be regulatory competition within the EU, we are mainly interested in how the European legal framework governs shared competences, and the decision on what to harmonise and what to leave decentralised within these fields.[22] The governing principles of European intervention are conferral, subsidiarity and proportionality. There is a vast literature on the interpretation and application of these guiding principles in EU law but here only a brief overview is provided in order to frame the issue of regulatory competition better within the Internal Market.

Subsidiarity, according to the definition in the TEU, means that 'the Union shall act only if and in so far as the objectives of the proposed action cannot be sufficiently achieved by the Member States, either at central level or at regional and local level, but can rather, by reason of the scale or effects of the proposed action, be better achieved at Union level.'[23] This wording has been interpreted by the case law of the European Court of Justice, along with the second guiding principle, that of proportionality. 'Under the principle of proportionality, the content and form of Union action shall not exceed what is necessary to achieve the objectives of the Treaties.'[24]

It is clear that the principles of subsidiarity and proportionality aim to protect Member State competences from intrusive European level intervention. But where are the limits of the Union's power to regulate, both in terms of taking action (subsidiarity) and staying with the least interventionist solution (proportionality)? Under the Treaties, it is ultimately up to the European Court of Justice to interpret the meaning of

---

[21] Art. 5 TEU.

[22] Even though competition policy is an exclusive competence of the EU, the co-existence of national competition policies, as well as the decentralisation of enforcement of EU competition policy renders this area of law interesting from a regulatory competition perspective.

[23] Art. 5 (3) TEU.

[24] Art 5 (4) TEU.

these two guiding principles and to apply them in case Member States or private actors challenge the legality of European action.

The latest amendments under Lisbon also introduced national parliaments as safeguards of the limits of European legislative powers. The following sections will look first at the case law of the ECJ in interpreting subsidiarity and proportionality, then national parliaments' role in subsidiarity checks, and finally academic literature's propositions for how these principles should be interpreted and applied in practice.

5.1.1 The subsidiarity case law of the ECJ and the limits of harmonisation

The principles of subsidiarity and proportionality have been subject to interpretation by the ECJ on several occasions. As a result of this case law, we know that generally there are three parts to the subsidiarity test:

- the Community can act only if Member States cannot sufficiently achieve the objective;
- the Community can better achieve the objective due to scale or effects;
- Community action should not go beyond what is necessary.

There are also three questions that are asked under the proportionality test:

- Is the measure suitable to achieve the desired end?
- Is the measure necessary to achieve the desired goal?
- Are the burdens imposed on individuals not excessive *vis-à-vis* the pursued objective?

(This is proportionality in the strict sense. The third question is not always posed by the ECJ, or it is dealt with together with the second question about necessity.)

The European design of competence allocation assigns an important role to the European Court of Justice in interpreting the criteria for EU level intervention, and adjudicating whether a given legal act complies with the principles of conferral, subsidiarity and proportionality. Although some of the literature attached great hopes to the role of the ECJ in this respect,[25] more recent studies criticise the way in which the Court fulfils this task.[26]

---

25 Kumm (2006).

26 Weatherill, S. (2011), 'The Limits of Legislative Harmonization Ten Years after *Tobacco Advertising*: How the Court's Case Law has become a "Drafting Guide"', *German Law Journal*, vol. 12, no. 3, pp. 827–864.

Early case law of the Court of Justice, which sets aside an EU legislative act on the basis it went beyond its legislative competence, dates back to 1998 with the judgment on tobacco advertising ('Tobacco Advertising').[27] This case was followed by further tobacco-related cases, Imperial Tobacco[28] and Swedish Match.[29] A recent case where the ECJ has ruled on the questions of legal basis, subsidiarity and proportionality of EU legislative action is the Vodafone case,[30] which challenged European competence to introduce price ceilings for international roaming fees in mobile phone communications.

Any inquiry into whether the European legislator stayed within its legislative competence needs to address the inter-related questions of the legal basis, subsidiarity and proportionality. It may be that only the legal basis is called into question (this was so in the Tobacco Advertising case). In other cases, it is all three elements that are examined (for example in the Vodafone decision).

When the Court examines the appropriateness of a legal basis, it makes an inquiry into the adequacy of the given Treaty basis for EU action and the objectives of the legislative act, as well as its effects. This was done in Tobacco Advertising, where the Court annulled the Directive in question because it was not adequate to address the stated objective. The aim of the legislative measure was to establish and enhance the functioning of the single market, whereas it introduced minimum requirements on banning tobacco advertising, leaving some scope for Member States to introduce stricter prohibitions. The substance of the measure therefore achieved a health protection objective quite effectively but did not correspond to the logic of the establishment and safeguarding of the single market.

The Court found the following problems with the provisions of the Directive

1. Certain prohibitions of tobacco advertising could not be justified by the need to eliminate obstacles to the free movement of goods or services.[31]

---

27 Case C-376/98 *Germany* v *Parliament and Council*, 2000 E.C.R. I-8419.

28 Case C-491/01 *The Queen* v *Secretary of State for Health, ex parte British American Tobacco (Investments) Ltd and Imperial Tobacco Ltd*, 2002 ECR I-11453.

29 Case C-210/03 *Swedish Match AB and Swedish Match UK Ltd* v *Secretary of State for Health* 2004 ECR I-11893.

30 Case C-58/08 *Vodafone, O2 et al* v *Secretary of State*, 2010 ECR I-04999.

31 Tobacco Advertising, paragraphs 99 and 100.

2. The Directive did not ensure the free circulation of products that were in conformity with its provisions, since Member States retained the right to lay down stricter requirements.[32]
3. Distortions of competition were not found to be appreciable in cases where fewer restrictions in some Member States resulted in advantages to economic actors, because these advantages were not comparable to the distortions of competition caused by differences in production costs.[33]
4. In certain other cases, where distortions of competition might be appreciable, the Court used what seems to be a proportionality argument to hold: 'such distortions [...] are not such as to justify the use of [the current Article 114] for an outright prohibition of advertising'.[34]
5. Finally, the Court argued that a wide-ranging ban on advertising would level the playing field in the wrong direction, so to speak. Instead of removing distortions of competition, it would restrain the forms of competition among existing and new market players to mere price competition in all Member States.

Overall, while the Court agreed that adopting a directive with prohibitions of certain forms of tobacco advertising and sponsorship would have been possible under the internal market's legal basis, it considered that specific provisions of the legal act went beyond the legislator's competence under that legal basis. Therefore it annulled the Directive.

What is interesting in this case is not only the entire logic of the inquiry, but also some of its details. For example, the definition of appreciable distortion of competition is worthy of attention in the regulatory competition context. The court argues that distortion of competition is not to be considered appreciable as long as the effects of this distortion are not comparable to the distortive effects of differences in production prices. Clearly, competition among legal actors through the channel of international trade would involve regulatory changes that could provide advantages to firms competing outside the market of the home state. It appears that as soon as one or several Member States are successful at finding legal solutions that affect the production price within their territories, this would qualify in EU law terms as an appreciable distortion of competition within the Internal Market.

[32] Ibid., paragraphs 101–103.
[33] Ibid., paragraph 109.
[34] Ibid., paragraphs 110–111.

In further case law, the ECJ established the following criteria, more recently applied in the Vodafone case,[35] for accepting the internal market legal basis to be used

- The *object* of measures adopted on the basis of Article 95(1) EC[36] must *genuinely* be to improve the conditions for the *establishment and functioning* of the internal market.[37]
- A *mere* finding of *disparities* between national rules and the abstract risk of infringements of fundamental freedoms or distortion of competition is not sufficient. Differences between national rules have to be such as to obstruct the fundamental freedoms, thus having a *direct effect* on the functioning of the internal market,[38] or causing significant distortions of competition.[39]
- If the aim of the measure is to *prevent* the emergence of such obstacles to trade resulting from the divergent development of national laws, the emergence of such obstacles must be *likely* and the measure in question must be *designed to prevent* them.[40]
- Where, beside the internal market, there are further reasons for intervention, such as consumer protection, provided that the conditions for recourse to Article 95 as a legal basis are fulfilled, the Community legislature can rely on that legal basis on the ground that consumer protection is a decisive factor in the choices to be made.[41]
- 'Measures for the approximation' in Article 95 EC: the authors of the Treaty intended to confer on the Community legislature a discretion, depending on the general context and the specific circumstances of the matter to be harmonised, as regards the method of approximation most appropriate for achieving the desired result, in particular in fields with complex technical features.

35 Vodafone case. Case C-58/08 [2010] ECR I-04999.

36 Currently Art 114 TFEU.

37 Case C-491/01 British American Tobacco (Investments) and Imperial Tobacco [2002] ECR I-11453, paragraph 60.

38 Case C-380/03 *Germany* v *Parliament and Council* [2006] ECR I-11573, paragraph 37.

39 As established in Tobacco Advertising, see above.

40 *Germany* v *Parliament and Council*, paragraph 38.

41 *Germany* v *Parliament and Council*, paragraph 88.

Given that the Court of First Instance/Court of Justice has already overturned Commission decisions on the basis of flawed economic reasoning,[42] this criterion becomes of central importance. In theory the Court could open up an investigation into the economic reasoning contained in impact assessments, and consequently the preambles of legal acts. However, in the Vodafone case, the economic side of the inquiry, along the lines of criteria listed above, consisted mainly in looking at whether the preamble of the Regulation in question, as well as the impact assessment that was prepared at the stage of the regulatory proposal, claimed to comply with these conditions. The Court did not reopen the investigation into whether the preamble and the impact assessment were right in their detailed economic arguments and findings of fact. The fact that it has not done so yet, can be a sign of the complexity of such a task, but may not necessarily mean that the Court will refrain from entering into an in-depth review of economic reasoning in the future.

Also, on the issue of subsidiarity and proportionality, the Court has stated in Vodafone that judicial review of compliance with those conditions must allow the European legislator broad discretion in areas in which its action involves political, economic and social choices and in which it is called upon to undertake complex assessments and evaluations. 'Thus the criterion to be applied is not whether a measure adopted in such an area was the only or the best possible measure, since its legality can be affected only if the measure is manifestly inappropriate having regard to the objective which the competent institution is seeking to pursue.'[43] The test applied by the Court looks at the wording of the preamble and the impact assessment again, to check the box for compliance with the criteria of subsidiarity and proportionality, without opening up economic investigation into the matter, or defining new limits to the European legislator as a legal standard.

Some commentators regard this as watering down subsidiarity and proportionality.[44] It remains to be seen which legal actor will take into its

---

[42] In the field of competition policy the ECJ overturned several merger decisions of the European Commission on the basis that the economic reasoning was flawed. See Case T-3310/01 *Schneider Electric* v *Commission* [2002] ECR II-4071; Case T-5/02 *Tetra Laval* v *Commission* [2002] ECR II-4381; Case C-12/03 *Commission* v *Tetra Laval* [2005] ECR I-987; Case T-342/99 *Airtours* v *Commission* [2002] ECR II-2585; Case T-251/00 *Lagardère SCA and Canal+* v *Commission* [2002] ECR II-4825.

[43] Vodafone case paragraph 52, quoting Case C-189/01 Jippes and Others [2001] ECR I-5689, paragraphs 82 and 83.

[44] Weatherill (2011).

hands the ultimate control of the economic arguments, and whether the Court will go further in defining legal conditions for regulatory intervention by the European power.

5.1.2 National parliaments' role in subsidiarity checks

Under the Protocol to the Lisbon Treaty regarding the application of the principles of subsidiarity and proportionality,[45] certain transparency requirements have been imposed on the EU legislator. Article 5 of the new Protocol states:

> Draft legislative acts shall be justified with regard to the principles of subsidiarity and proportionality. Any draft legislative act should contain a detailed statement making it possible to appraise compliance with the principles of subsidiarity and proportionality. This statement should contain some assessment of the proposal's financial impact and, in the case of a directive, of its implications for the rules to be put in place by Member States, including, where necessary, the regional legislation. *The reasons for concluding that a Union objective can be better achieved at Union level shall be substantiated by qualitative and, wherever possible, quantitative indicators.* Draft legislative acts shall take account of the need for any burden, whether financial or administrative, falling upon the Union, national governments, regional or local authorities, economic operators and citizens, to be minimised and commensurate with the objective to be achieved.

It is interesting to note reference to possible quantitative indicators in proving that the subsidiarity principle's second requirement is fulfilled. This is quite a novel development, given that the Treaty itself does not speak of quantifications, nor does the interpretative case law of the Court of Justice (reviewed above).

Building on these information requirements, the Protocol then enables national parliaments to raise objections concerning the fulfilment of subsidiarity and proportionality requirements. Each national parliament is given two votes and if, within eight weeks, one third of the total votes express a negative opinion, the European Commission must review the draft proposal, and can maintain, amend or withdraw it. This is also labelled a 'yellow card', to describe the type of warning from national parliaments to the EU legal actors. For proposals falling under co-decision, a simple majority of all votes allocated to the national parliaments can trigger a mandatory review by the Commission, which is called an 'orange card'. In this case, the Commission can maintain, amend or withdraw the proposal.

---

[45] Lisbon Protocol No.2 on the Application of the Principles of Subsidiarity and Proportionality.

However, if it maintains it, it has to provide a reasoned opinion on why it thinks the proposal complies with subsidiarity. The European Parliament and Council shall decide, before the first reading of the draft is concluded, whether they are satisfied with the reasons provided. The European Parliament can reject the draft (on the basis of its non-compliance with subsidiarity) by a majority of votes cast, whereas the Council needs 55 per cent majority of its members to do so.

In practice this procedure does not give far-reaching powers to national parliaments, but it does definitely involve them in the formulation of a definition and practical test for subsidiarity and proportionality. Currently, most national parliaments are still preparing to implement their own internal subsidiarity check procedures.[46] Therefore, even if such checks have already taken place, it is still premature to draw any conclusions on what their outcomes are and what this means for the future. However, academic literature assessing this framework is not very optimistic with regard to its function and effects, not least because of the fact that the powers of parliaments do not extend to veto.[47]

From a regulatory competition perspective, what is interesting about this framework is the involvement of a new (legal) actor in the definition of competence allocation – and a decentralised (national) actor at that. From a legal perspective, this innovation raises the question of how potential conflicts between the ECJ case law and national parliaments' opinions (confirmed or rejected by the European Parliament and the Council) would be settled. This is all the more relevant, given the complex and not yet fully settled nature of the ECJ's interpretation of subsidiarity and proportionality.

5.1.3 Academic literature on the optimal interpretation of subsidiarity in the light of decentralisation benefits

Academic literature has interpreted the principles of subsidiarity and proportionality in different contexts, and from different perspectives. Here, examples of legal and economic interpretation are noted, to show what the literature currently understands by subsidiarity and proportionality as limits to EU legislative powers. Economic approaches to the interpretation of this concept deserve special attention, not only because this book treats the topic of regulatory competition, which is by definition an area where economic

---

[46] See 16th Bi-annual Report of COSAC, October 2011, available at: http://www.cosac.eu/en/documents/biannual/ (last accessed: 5 March 2012).

[47] See, e.g. Schutze, Robert (2009), 'Subsidiarity after Lisbon: Reinforcing the Safeguards of Federalism?', *Cambridge Law Journal*, vol. 68, no. 3. pp. 525–536.

principles matter, but also because of the Protocol to the Lisbon Treaty, quoted above, that calls for 'qualitative and, wherever possible, quantitative indicators' to prove that the principles (and in particular the second condition of subsidiarity) have been complied with.

To start with, from a legal and political perspective, Weatherill[48] criticises the case law of the Court, which has been quoted above, as being too superficial, and leaving too broad a scope for the European legal actors to justify their intervention. Indeed, the ECJ does not look into the substance of the arguments, and, Weatherill argues, it provides a checklist for legal drafters of EU institutions that is empty of meaning and not seriously controlled by the Court.

In a normative economic analysis of what subsidiarity should mean within the European context, Van den Bergh[49] puts together a checklist for the European legal actor to consider before deciding whether to harmonise or not. These considerations incorporate not only the potential benefits of regulatory competition and its limitations, but also other factors, such as possible cost savings from economies of scale if regulation is undertaken at EU rather than national level.

Box 5.1 displays this checklist.

BOX 5.1 INTEGRATED LAW AND ECONOMICS CHECKLIST FOR THE ALLOCATION OF COMPETENCES IN THE EUROPEAN UNION

1. Are preferences of firms and citizens with respect to the envisaged legislative action heterogeneous?
   - if yes: presumption in favour of decentralised governance, unless positive answer(s) to questions 3, 4 and/or 5.
   - if no: go to question 6.

2. Given heterogeneous preferences, is there a sufficiently large range of legal rules to choose between, is information on alternative legal rules easily available, and is there a sufficient degree of mobility, so that firms and citizens can move to the jurisdiction offering them their preferred set of laws?

---

48 Weatherill (2011).

49 Van den Bergh (2000). Note that the study dates back to a time when the EU counted only 15 Member States, hence the reference to a 16th regime, which today would be called a 28th regime (or, probably, after the accession of Croatia, the 29th regime).

- if yes: strengthen the competitive process by applying the rule of mutual recognition.
- if no: consider EC rules to enhance competition, such as adding a sixteenth option, measures of standardisation and harmonisation of rules on conflict of laws.

3. Given heterogeneous preferences, does decentralised governance imply significant interstate externalities?
- if yes: (1) consider Coasian solutions in the form of agreements between the states involved; (2) in cases of high transaction costs or strategic behaviour, consider harmonisation measures reflecting the degree of preferences diversity; (3) make sure that the solution chosen is well targeted at the problem at hand; (4) go to question 7.
- if no: harmonisation measures are not needed, unless there are positive answers to questions 4 and/or 5.

4. Given heterogeneous preferences, does competition between Member States' laws entail the risk of a 'race to the bottom'?
- if yes: (1) take measures of minimum harmonisation to guarantee a floor of rights; (2) go to question 7.
- if no: harmonisation measures are not needed unless positive answer to question 5

5. Given heterogeneous preferences, are there important economies of scale or significant savings on transaction costs when the competence is assigned to the European Union?
- if yes: (1) take harmonisation measures allowing the maximum degree of diversity; (2) go to question 7.
- if no: no harmonisation measures required.

6. Given homogeneous preferences, are there important scale economies or transaction cost savings to be achieved by centralised governance?
- if yes: (1) full harmonisation may be appropriate; (2) go to question 7.
- if no: no harmonisation.

7. If the answers to the above questions provide support for harmonisation measures, is the risk of political distortions (impact of pressure groups on policy making) minimised?

Does the decision-making process satisfy the requirements of independence, transparency and accountability?
- if yes: the harmonisation measure suggested by economic analysis (see questions 3–6) may be taken
- if no: no harmonisation.

Source: Van den Bergh (2000).

This list of questions is doubtlessly an important step towards understanding and implementing different aspects of regulatory competition in practice.

Another, also mainly economic, approach is proposed by Pelkmans, who argues that

> one important criterion to decide upon the degree of centralisation, once the need-to-act-in-common test is passed, is credibility. [...]As game theory teaches, simple and repetitive cooperative games lead to 'learning' and may eventually result in efficient bargaining. But non-repetitive cooperation is often difficult to agree upon, for instance when the number of interested parties is large, the range of policy alternatives is wide, the problem is complex, and when the (relative) gains and losses of players would be unevenly distributed. What really matters for economic agents in the market, however, is whether cooperation is credible, hence sustainable. Credibility of cooperation is low if information is highly imperfect or asymmetrically distributed, especially in complex policy areas, because this renders it impossible to monitor compliance. Credibility is also low when the incentives to cheat are strong and the ability or willingness to impose collective sanctions is perceived as minimal. If cooperation cannot come about, or it would not be credible, there is a case for centralisation.[50]

Based on the above observation, Pelkmans[51] proposes the test for subsidiarity in Box 5.2 below, that is, to decide whether the European or national legal actors should tackle a given problem:

BOX 5.2 PELKMANS' FIVE-STEP SUBSIDIARITY TEST TO JUSTIFY EU INTERVENTION

1. Identify whether a measure falls within the area of shared competences (if exclusive to the EU, the treaty test does not apply);
2. Apply the criteria (scale and externalities, Art. 5, EC, and possibly other criteria) – this is the 'need to act in common' test;
3. Verify whether credible cooperation is feasible;
4. If 1 and 2 are confirmed, and 3 denied, then the assignment is to the Union level;
5. Define to what extent (proportionality) implementation, monitoring and enforcement should also be assigned to the EC level, or, indeed, can be assigned to the Member States, perhaps in a common framework.

Source: Pelkmans (2006).

50 Pelkmans (2006).
51 Idem.

Besides these more economic approaches, there are academic interpretations that blend legal, economic and socio-political approaches. Kumm[52] proposes, for example, that instead of defining the scope for EU level intervention under subsidiarity and proportionality along the lines of distortions of competition or a race to the bottom, the Court should focus on the prevention of 'structural biases of the democratic process'. He defines this as systematic occurrence of strategic regulatory behaviour that imposes costs on the less mobile actors in its competition with other jurisdictions over the mobile actors. Kumm argues that: 'The idea of free and equal citizens governing themselves within the framework of democratic constitutions thus enjoys conceptual and normative priority over the idea [of] a competitive market for goods. As a matter of normative justification it is the former idea that guides thinking about the role and appropriate structure of markets, not the other way around.'

It is perhaps interesting to look to the other side of the Atlantic for the parallel multi-disciplinary discussion on federalism. In the US the Supreme Court outlined a test called the state action doctrine, whereby it sets out the limits to state autonomy. Inman and Rubinfeld[53] interpret the case law of the Supreme Court within a framework assigning value to political participation and economic efficiency of decentralisation, limited by cases of inter-state spill-overs. They argue that the Supreme Court, despite the flaws of its case law, is nonetheless the ideal legal actor to set the 'rules of the game', that is the allocation of competences, for a decentralised system.

Finally, within the EU context, there are also authors who argue that: 'The truth of the matter is that attempting to define *ex ante* criteria of a general and abstract character for the purpose of limiting central intervention stands little hope of success.'[54] The reason for this, according to Estella, is that there is a functional interconnection among policy fields, due to which 'it will always be possible to argue that due to close

---

[52] Kumm, M. (2006), 'Constitutionalising Subsidiarity in Integrated Markets: The Case of Tobacco Regulation in the European Union', *European Law Journal*, vol. 12, no. 4, pp. 503–533.

[53] Inman, R.P. and Rubinfeld, D.L. (1997), 'Making Sense of the Antitrust State-Action Doctrine: Balancing Political Participation and Economic Efficiency in Regulatory Federalism', *Texas Law Review*, vol. 75, no. 6, pp. 1203–1299.

[54] Estella, A. (2002), *The EU Principle of Subsidiarity and its Critique* (Oxford: Oxford University Press).

relationships between [certain regulatory areas] and the development of the single market, some Community intervention will always be necessary'.[55]

5.1.4 Current practice of the EU legislator

Indeed, currently there is no established test that would take systematic account of the economic pro's and con's of potential regulatory competition that the EU level legislator could follow in order to decide whether the subsidiarity principles' requirements are fulfilled for EU action to take place. Impact assessments and the explanatory memoranda of legislative acts explain the fulfilment of these principles, but rarely go into greater depth and detail about the potential benefits of decentralisation and the reasons why centralised action in any particular case is better, despite these advantages.

Perhaps impact assessments would be the ideal place to perform such in-depth inquiries. Indeed the Impact Assessment Board of the European Commission[56] called explicitly for a 'thorough subsidiarity analysis for initiatives extending the scope of EU intervention. This was the case for several initiatives adopted in the aftermath of the financial crisis – amendments to the Directives on Deposit Guarantee Schemes[57] and Investor Compensation Schemes,[58] an initiative on Short Selling and Credit Default Swaps,[59] and the White Paper on Insurance Guarantee Schemes.'[60]

The current requirements for the format of impact assessments (limits on length, a long list of compulsory elements other than subsidiarity and proportionality) do not easily lend themselves to thorough analyses of these issues. But, given the warnings of the Impact Assessment Board and increasing scrutiny from national parliaments, the emphasis of impact analysis may change in the future.[61]

---

[55] Idem.

[56] Report from the Commission on subsidiarity and proportionality (18th report on Better Lawmaking covering the year 2010) COM(2011) 344.

[57] COM(2010) 368.

[58] COM(2010) 371.

[59] COM(2010) 482.

[60] COM(2010) 370.

[61] It is also worth noting that the European Parliament has recently introduced its own impact assessment mechanism for certain important amendments. See, e.g.: http://www.europarl.europa.eu/document/activities/cont/201202/20120220ATT38592/20120220ATT38592EN.pdf (last accessed: 26 Novovember 2012).

5.2 Proportionality: *How* the EU Intervenes Will Also Shape Regulatory Competition

While the principles of subsidiarity and proportionality are in a close interaction, in general we can say that subsidiarity mainly determines the cases in which the European legal actors are entitled to act, whereas proportionality sets out the possible extent of that intervention. 'Subsidiarity is a guiding principle for defining the boundary between Member State and EU responsibilities – that is, *who should act*? [...] Proportionality is a guiding principle for determining how the Union should exercise its competences, both exclusive and shared – *what should be the form and nature of EU action?*'[62]

The elements of the proportionality test – suitability, necessity and proportionality in the strict sense – can refer to several aspects of regulation when applied in practice. They can refer to the appointment of the right legal actor (the legal actor with the right incentives or tools for intervention), to the level of decision-making (whether it should be national, regional or international legal actors who define further rules or enforce them), to the extent of harmonisation (minimum, maximum or total harmonisation), and so on. A legal intervention at European level could, in most cases, take different forms, depending on what regulatees are its targets, which legal actor regulates and enforces, whether it offers an incentive or imposes a ban, and so on. The various forms of governance design, under which a particular policy field is regulated, will also have to comply with the criteria of proportionality. Indeed it is this principle that obliges the European legal actor to create an effective and efficient legal environment.

Moreover, the different forms of legal intervention and governance are also crucial from the perspective of regulatory competition, as they may influence the likelihood of competitive interactions emerging among different legal actors.

The analysis carried out above already signals that governance may play an important role in changing legal actors' incentives, legal diversity, innovation, as well as cross-border externalities or regulatees' switching costs.

Once rule-making is separated from the rest of the governance cycle (that also includes monitoring or supervision and enforcement), and the roles are divided across different legal actors, governance mechanisms

---

[62] Definitions of the Report from the Commission on subsidiarity and proportionality (18th report on Better Lawmaking covering the year 2010).

are needed to coordinate this cycle of governance. If the segmentation is not only across different legal actors, but also across different levels of government (EU or national, sometimes also local), governance arrangements gain even more importance. The form of intervention and related governance mechanisms are therefore reviewed below when discussing influences on the emergence and legal outcome of regulatory competition.

5.3 Conclusions and Issues for Further Research

With regard to the legal framework governing the channels of competition, the treaty freedoms, clearly, ensure that at least two channels of competition – international trade and capital mobility – are open within Europe. But much deeper analysis would be necessary to determine how European law endorses or restricts yardstick competition and regulatory competition with mobility. The general principles of subsidiarity and proportionality are only the main guiding rules. In each policy field there is a myriad of norms that predetermine how new legal interventions can function. Rules that build the institutional context of any policy area may lock the legal actors into a path dependent situation or may be efficient. Either way, they steer new norms in a particular direction. The form of legal intervention then also has an effect on the incentives of legal actors, of regulatees, and on externalities across stakeholder groups or in a cross-border context, and so on.

Deeper research into other policy fields and broader comparisons across more fields would be welcome on this issue. Further specific questions to explore would include: the relationship of market integration and regulatory competition; the balance between a desirable level of legal competition, presuming the legal diversity and harmonisation necessary to create an internal market, and whether this balance is legally defined, or whether it can at least be deduced from the legal text; what market integration means in the ECJ case law on the legal basis of European measures; judicial competition and the European framework for judicial cooperation, and so on. All these issues would serve as useful research questions for further analysis.

6. REGULATORY COMPETITION WITHIN THE INTERNAL MARKET: SOME RECENT TRENDS AND GENERAL OBSERVATIONS

Based on the three chapters examining the models of regulatory competition in the legal fields of company, securities and competition law, this section will aim to draw some conclusions on what appear to be cross-cutting trends in this subject matter across these legal fields. These conclusions are by no means meant to predict what happens in other regulatory areas, although some of the observations are expected to be valid also in fields that have not been examined here.

6.1 Governance Mechanisms Used to Engineer Optimal Interaction Among Legal Actors

One clear trend, observable in recent European legal action, is that there is a move towards using legal tools and governance methods that are intended to trigger cooperation among national legal actors, but leave important competences and powers decentralised.

This is the case for competition law, where enforcement of EU competition rules has been decentralised since 2004. The more recent issues, where the Commission has proposed action, have often been tackled using a soft law approach, such as a recommendation, followed by a published Commission report that compares how Member States and market participants responded to the proposal. In the field of financial services and securities regulation, however, there has been some tightening of regulatory standards, and stricter rules are being introduced for previously non-regulated markets. The setting up of the European Supervisory Authorities is also a step towards greater, although not nearly complete, centralisation. Even with this tightening of the regulatory approach, there are certain competences that have been left at ESMA and national level.

From the perspective of yardstick competition, the important question to ask is whether there is scope for parallel experimentation and mutual learning, or whether actors are being directed towards centrally designed legal solutions.

Whilst this current review of these three legal fields has identified areas for parallel experimentation, an interesting extension of the research would be to look at these governance models in a dynamic setting over time, and analyse what scope they left for bottom-up solutions, and whether in practice these solutions did emerge and have a successful application.

6.2 Regulatory Convergence Towards Economic Rationale(s) for Intervention

In the field of competition law, the European Court of Justice originally imposed stricter requirements on the European Commission for economic analysis in overruling two merger cases. In response to this, the Commission set up a team of economists, lead by a chief economist, to establish whether the reasoning of the authority in the cases it decides is consistent with the latest economic theory. There is a trend in the US also towards more economic analysis in antitrust law, documented among others by McChesney.[63] Within the EU, national competition authorities are starting to apply economic analysis more rigorously, and they perform market monitoring exercises. Arguably, this trend is a mutual learning process, and it can be argued that a system of parallel experimentation could lead to discovering economic theories that describe markets better and guide legal interventions better. In particular, Budzinski argues for pluralism in competition policy and its economic rationales, and claims that competition economics should also be subject to competition and evolution over time, rather than any single theory being imposed on all actors centrally.[64]

But competition law is not the only policy field where the penetration of economic reasoning can be observed. In securities regulation, and in financial market regulation in general, economic analysis is gaining ground as well. There are two interesting areas of discovery recently in this respect. On the one hand, the regulation of retail financial services and products is being tested empirically with the tools of behavioural economics, not only at the European level, but also internationally, as well as in some EU Member States.

A further field in which new economic theories can gain a footing is financial market regulation in general. With the recent financial crisis, regulators are looking to find better economic explanations of the working of financial markets and the interaction of financial agents, in order to be better able to foresee and avoid similar events in the future.

At a much more general level, in several Member States the requirement to do an impact analysis (or cost-benefit analysis) before adopting

---

63 McCheseny (2003).

64 Budzinski, O. (2008), 'Monoculture versus diversity in competition economics', *Cambridge Journal of Economics*, vol. 32, pp. 295–324.

new legislation is being introduced. Impact analysis requires, among others, economic justification for a given policy action.

This consideration of an economic analysis of law, with normative recommendations for the policy maker, may warrant a brief explanation. Some, policy makers as well as academics, may not feel at ease with the idea of economics guiding (European or national) policies and, in some sense, rightly so. Economic analysis is not an exact science, but should be regarded as a continuous process of discovery. As such, it can inform policies, without claiming to take the ultimate decision-making from the democratically elected political actors. What this book has tried to reflect, as well, is that there are sometimes several economic theories that aim to describe a particular market and explain its regulatory issues, without any one being clearly rebutted or superseded. Although competing theories often have different implications in redistributive terms, and therefore they are more or less convenient for a certain political group, economic analysis can, and should, be used in a neutral way, without necessarily taking sides in political terms. In order to do this, underlying assumptions and limitations of any given economic theory should always be clearly explained.

6.3 Race to the Top and Race to the Bottom in an EU Context

Chapter 1 discussed how the interpretation of 'race to the bottom' is a reduction in overall welfare compared to a scenario of no competition, coordination or harmonisation. But this does not exclude inter-stakeholder or cross-border externalities. The interpretation of what is an 'optimal' welfare outcome may not be equal in all jurisdictions. So, establishing whether a race to the bottom occurs at a European level requires either a clear choice about the theory of efficiency to be applied, or acceptance of different theories in different member states. In the latter case, we will observe lower than optimal outcomes more often in cases of legal convergence, since it is rare that a given legal norm would satisfy two different efficiency criteria. This means that in a more diverse socio-political and legal context, such as the EU, there is likely to be more disagreement about what the efficient solution is. Competition among jurisdictions may deliver legal diversity or convergence; the latter can breach one or other efficiency criteria. This is not a contradiction of the wisdom of established literature that regulatory competition is expected to work better in diversity, because it can match the diverse preferences of citizens. Such diversity in the preferences of regulatees are satisfied better if regulatory competition results in legal divergence and either the regulatees are mobile across jurisdictions (competition through mobility) or if they are already grouped into different jurisdictions (for example, through yardstick competition).

Under such conditions of diverse political choices or economic theories concerning efficiency, the European decision-making process allows a simple or qualified majority to proceed with a measure that can impose external effects on some member states. In practice, however, it appears that EU players often negotiate policies up to (near) unanimity, taking account of several policy measures at the same time. This would suggest that decision-making is a repeated game.

Yet, protecting each Member States' interests during negotiations (and at the implementation stage) does not necessarily lead to a better overall regulatory outcome at EU level (see, for example, the Takeover Bids Directive). This would imply that EU decision-making cannot be thought of as coordination in repeated games, but analysing EU level decision-making and national implementation separately would probably explain the final legal outcome even better.

In all three policy fields examined above, different approaches to efficiency are traceable. In some fields, these approaches seem to converge faster than in others. Competition policy is an interesting example. This book argued that governance mechanisms play a role in the convergence of ideas over what the best policy is.

Securities law is a special example. The financial crisis that began in 2007/2008 revealed regulatory failures, and regulatory arbitrage is claimed to be among the causes.[65] The post-crisis reforms therefore aim to address these regulatory failures, and the single rule book aims to exclude regulatory divergence completely. Legal experimentation and mutual learning, however, are more promising forms of legal actors' interaction. The recent crisis may trigger a paradigm shift in economic, legal and political thinking (over the long term). Reserving a place for mutual learning in this process would be an idea to consider.

6.4 Private Regulation and Regulatory Competition in Europe

The narrowing of private regulators' competences was observed in both securities and company law (takeover regulation). The EU directive[66] covering takeover regulations in company law requires regulatory

---

[65] Indeed the extent of potential externalities imply that legal actors, as well as industry, left to compete without substantial safeguards will necessarily lead to welfare reduction.

[66] Directive 2004/25/EC of the European Parliament and of the Council of 21 April 2004 on takeover bids.

approval of private regulatory arrangements, such as that of the UK. In securities law it is proposed that so-called non-regulated markets that were regulated by private actors will come under the scope of EU regulation[67] and rating agencies have passed from self-regulation to public regulation.[68] Private regulation as such does not play any role in competition law but private ordering, in terms of choice of law, does. In the case of damages actions, forum and applicable law are influenced by the parties' contract or, where they are not in a contractual relationship, by the choice of the claimant(s). At present, the European legislator has not shown any intention of removing or narrowing the scope of private actors' choices in this field.[69]

The impact assessment methodology calls for an analysis of alternative legal designs, especially non-binding tools, so self-regulation is examined as an option in most impact assessments. But its analysis is still rather superficial or based on examples of past failures rather than presenting a forward-looking analysis of alternative regulatory mechanisms involving private legal actors.

6.5 Signalling and Branding Across Borders

It also appears from the analysis of the previous chapters that in the different legal fields where choice of law is available, regulatees do opt into stricter legal regimes in order to signal to the markets their quality. This can be observed not only in the case of trading rules of different markets in securities law, but also in the case of accounting standards, for example. In many cases, it appears that the choice between laxer or stricter standards depends on whether business partners or consumers are in a position to recognise or understand the different standards. In reality regulatees cannot always use signalling towards retail investors or clients, due to information problems. In the case of non-adjusting creditors, such as trading partners of firms, it is questionable whether they can assess the quality of different legal systems from among which a firm may choose its governing law and whether they are in a position to modify their contracts accordingly. In financial transactions, as behavioural research

---

[67] Proposal for a Directive of the European Parliament and of the Council on markets in financial instruments repealing Directive 2004/39/EC of the European Parliament and of the Council. 2011/0298 (COD).

[68] Regulation (EC) No 1060/2009 of the European Parliament and of the Council of 16 September 2009 on credit rating agencies OJ L 302.

[69] See, e.g. the Green Paper on Consumer Collective Redress COM(2008) 794.

has also shown, retail investors are only able to assess the quality of the financial products offered if the information is clear to them and comparable across products.

The policy choice to be made in these cases is between regulatory intervention aiming to restrict the choice of law, or an intervention aiming to improve the information asymmetries. Clearly, in several situations the beneficiaries of regulation are not one homogeneous group but can also be broken down to more and less sophisticated groups of clients. A free choice regime may lead to a race to the top *vis-à-vis* professional business partners, whereas, in the case of retail clients, information is not so easily managed. This could be abused by regulatees, leading overall to a race to the bottom.

In the case of securities law and financial services in general, the events leading up to the financial crisis even put in question the assumption that professional clients can process information efficiently. More recently, the discussion, given the recent development of more and more complex and more intermediated market structures, has been about whether information is either spread or processed well across layers of intermediaries, and, even if they have the ability, whether these layers of actors have the right incentives to process information perfectly. In other words, it is the entire chain of interactions that need to be analysed before concluding whether there is an opportunity for signalling. But in cases of negative outcomes with free choice, intervention can have different targets, and we can observe that in some cases (for example in the case of the key investor information document) the European legal actor harmonises the format of disclosure in order to facilitate consumers' information processing and comparison across products and across borders.

7. CONCLUSIONS

7.1 Drivers of Regulatory Competition

This book has looked at the driving forces of competition between legal actors. It has identified a number of issues worth examining in this context, and it has looked at three European policy fields to test how each of these drivers impact on regulatory competition. It has found that in order to examine the emergence and functioning of regulatory competition, one has to look at

- Market failures and efficiency theories
- Channels of competitive interaction
- Regulatees' incentives and the allocation of choice of law (if any)
- Competence allocation among legal actors
- The incentive structure of legal actors

Earlier literature on regulatory competition aims to identify the drivers of competitive law-making, viewed as pieces of a puzzle.[70] This book has explored some of these drivers through an analysis of three different legal fields.

7.1.1 Regulatees

With regard to regulatees, it is important to observe whether they have incentives for regulatory arbitrage. Incentives for arbitrage can be thought of as a cost benefit calculation between the choice of staying in the default (home) regime, or changing for another set of governing norms. These costs are composed of several elements, of which five important considerations are listed below.

1. First of all, regulatees may have different strategies when facing new legal rules, and they may or may not be interested in changing legal regimes. So, we should not think of regulatees as a homogeneous group of actors. (Legal actors may have different strategies, too, which ultimately may lead to perfect sorting of regulatees with different preferences into different jurisdictions.)
2. The default rule matters, because changing the default rule always requires action, which comes with transaction costs.
3. Whether regulatees have perfect information about the alternative legal rules will be another cost-driving factor. But it is important to remember that not only regulates but also their contracting parties need to have (close to perfect) information about foreign legal rules, in order for law shopping to pay off to regulatees and deliver welfare gains. If contracting third parties do not have information about non-default (that is, foreign) rules, they either will not enter into transactions with regulatees who opted out, or they will contract with them but can easily be the victims of law shopping, and financiers of regulatees' benefits derived from it.
4. Bundled legal products often cause the cost benefit calculus to change. Bundling is common, since connecting norms are often the

---

[70] After Radaelli; see Radaelli (2004).

same for the norms of several different legal fields. Regulatees will ideally look at the bundle of the most relevant legal norms before deciding about regulatory arbitrage.

5. Further cost drivers include the actual costs of administrative measures to change legal regimes, or the costs of moving physically from one regime to the other, if this is a prerequisite for changing governing law.

7.1.2 The different channels of competitive interaction

The above remarks are valid for regulatory competition with free choice of law or mobility. The present inquiry has analysed, however, further channels of competition (yardstick competition, trade competition, and production factor competition), and we should thus ask whether those work differently.

The situation with regard to competition through mobility of capital and labour is quite similar to the case described above, given that capital holders or employees can be thought of as regulatees, even if only in an indirect way.

- Capital investment can move into or out of a jurisdiction in order to search for more convenient legal rules, and the incentives for such arbitrage work similarly to the situation described above.[71]
- Trade competition and yardstick competition are different, however, in that regulatees do not necessarily need to have perfect information about the alternative governing legal norms. In the case of trade competition a perfect market with a perfect pricing mechanism will do the job of discovering which legal regime is more efficient. It is clear, though, that in such situations, without clear comparability of each field of law, different jurisdictions compete with their entire package of legal rules, as well as their specific endowments and trade advantages. This can make it difficult to

---

[71] An example of this is capital investment moving across jurisdictions in order to search for more suitable legal rules (resulting also in cheaper production). If capital holders do not have perfect information, this arbitrage will not necessarily trigger competition with positive welfare effects. If the contracting parties (e.g. firms' consumers) have full information about the differences in norms, they may reward or punish certain arbitrage strategies. Corporate social responsibility or fair trade are fit examples, where traceability of products may bring about product offering (with selected legal governing norms) that is demanded; but false or incomplete information can result in harmful arbitrage strategies.

identify whether a successful trade balance is due to the superior legal norms, or other factors.

- In the case of yardstick competition, this overview showed that regulatees do not need to have perfect information about different legal regimes, as long as legal actors are motivated to compete with each other through channels other than the threat of not being re-elected. Legal actors who are not directly elected will have other incentives. They may also strive to stay in office or be renewed in their appointment, and compete on their performance in order to achieve this. What motivates these legal agents, however their reappointment is determined, will vary along with the legal actor's independence, the person who holds the power to reappoint them, and potential performance indicators that may have been set in advance, and which may or may not reflect a better quality of norms produced.

7.1.3 Legal actors animating regulatory competition

With regard to the legal actors, it was argued here that their incentives to engage in competition with one another cannot be presumed. Regulatory arbitrage resulting in the exit of regulatees, or its threat, is not a sufficient condition if the legal actors are not motivated to retain regulatees. Their motivation may be monetary as well as reputational. This study did not resolve the debate over what exactly drives legal actors in their discretionary decision-making. Instead, several theories were put forward, acknowledging that more in-depth research would be necessary to identify motives. As an issue for further research, a more detailed inquiry into organisational set-up and motivational arrangements (financing power of nomination or removal from office, and so on) could perhaps reveal which competitive or cooperative legal outcome can be expected under what conditions.

This study proposed that certain legal actors may be more responsive to competitive pressures through certain competitive channels than others. For example, the legislator and government may be driven more by concerns of GDP and trade (which are general markers of their performance) than courts, private regulators or even independent regulatory agencies. The latter, once their performance is comparable with other, similar independent regulatory agencies from other jurisdictions, are likely to compete over performance related to a given economic theory or certain substantive indicators (even as simple as the number of actions taken in a year).

In theory, the different channels of competition are likely also to engage with each other through the interaction of different legal actors who are motivated through one channel or another. The legislator and the government, who are likely to be concerned with trade-related indicators, may transmit this interest to independent regulatory agencies (to the extent that the independence of the latter allows) through benchmarks set to measure performance. Private regulatory actors are following their individual or industry-wide market-related interests. These interests, in reality, often translate into retaining or attracting regulatees, and co-regulatory mechanisms should reflect this. Finally, independent and apolitical legal actors (such as the judiciary and some independent regulatory agencies) should be more responsive to yardstick competition than the other channels, provided that attracting regulatees is not a major motivation for institutional survival. In any legal field there will be a multitude of legal actors involved at national level.

Their interaction within any given jurisdiction has been referred to here as intra-jurisdictional competition. The result of such intra-jurisdictional competition is the starting point of inter-jurisdictional regulatory competition between different countries. Since each Member State may be free to choose its own institutional set-up, it can happen that one jurisdiction's legal outcome is dominated by the judiciary, while in others regulatory agencies shape the final norms. These differences may be one source of different regulatory strategies across Member States when it comes to legal fields where competition can occur.

7.1.4 Questions for further research

It appears that the pieces of the institutional and regulatory competition puzzle can and should be further researched. It emerged from the analysis that many of these drivers of competitive interactions can be linked up with other determinants of competition, which allows us to get further in understanding why, when, and how competition among legal actors can work within Europe. Legal, economic and political science research reveals ever more about this subject.

The most relevant directions for further research suggested by the present analysis relate to the following issues:

- How to identify the incidence of competition?
- A better definition of yardstick competition, distinguishing it from other forms of institutional competition.
- What drives legal decision-making? Current literature proposes several hypotheses, but none of them have proven unequivocally more powerful than others. An interesting path for further research would be to test different theories of actors' behaviour and motivations in a regulatory environment with competitive pressures

(including not only competition for regulatees but also trade and yardstick competition). Such research could also examine, for example, whether differences in any legal actor's institutional set-up influences the pattern of behaviour (distinguishing drivers of behaviour such as economic benefits, reputational advantages, entrenchment or budget maximisation, and so on), and see whether specific institutional arrangements result in decisions that fit one theory better than another.

7.2 Regulatory Competition in the Internal Market

7.2.1 An evolving legal framework

In the second part of this chapter, the relationship between regulatory competition and the EU Internal Market was explored. It was shown that the legal rules governing competence allocation have an evolving interpretation by the European Court of Justice. However, the criteria elaborated by the Court do not always result in a clear-cut rule in reality. Academic interpretations of the Court's case law range from legal through economic to interdisciplinary approaches. By the nature of its arguments, regulatory competition and its potential advantages are best reflected in economic (or interdisciplinary) interpretations. Some of these even propose a checklist for the European legal actors to assess the advantages and drawbacks of centralisation, accounting explicitly for the positive (or negative, as the case might be) effects of regulatory competition. In their current practice, legal actors at EU level do examine the economic rationale for intervention, and the issues of subsidiarity and proportionality are included in this analysis (reinforced by the Lisbon Treaty's protocol, which gives national parliaments a right of scrutiny). However, these practices are not yet at the level of a predefined in-depth analysis,[72] not least because the case law of the Court of Justice does not easily lend itself to practical application. Under the current arrangement, the European Commission, when carrying out a subsidiarity and proportionality analysis, could establish a checklist for examining the potential for regulatory competition. Alternatively, national parliaments could call for such analysis, or the Court of Justice could establish more precise guidance on these issues. It is to be seen whether such a regulatory competition test will ever be established. But, if it is, whichever of these

[72] No doubt there is a rigorous subsidiarity and proportionality analysis in every impact assessment accompanying legislative (and even many non-legislative) acts. But these do not systematically include an examination of issues related to the potential advantages of regulatory competition.

actors takes the first step in defining a more precise test for competitive designs is likely to have a first mover advantage and will be likely to shape this test to its taste (somewhat like competition among legal actors to define the applicable rule).

7.2.2 Cross-sectoral trends in regulatory competition within the internal market

Throughout the analysis of EU company, securities and competition law, three general trends emerged. One such trend was a move towards *more economic analysis*, not only in competition law, but also in securities law[73] and even in company law.[74] Adopting an economic approach to policy issues can be seen as a form of competition[75] to formulate the best rule. Other legal actors following an economic approach are really engaged in mere imitation or mutual learning (with these economic theories constantly evolving of themselves[76]).

A further trend in the European legal landscape is the use of *more complex governance mechanisms* to engineer the interaction of multiple legal actors within a policy field. Competition policy and securities law are good examples of this, whereas there is no such complex institutional set-up for company law, which has evolved through harmonisation and competition – either competition at the EU level in the form of a new 28th regime, or competition among member states following the market opening of the case law of the Court of Justice. In securities law there has been a recent wave of harmonisation, aiming for a single rule book, as a consequence of the financial crisis. In competition law, the centralisation element has been strong from the beginning, given that this is an

---

[73] See the example of behavioural economic studies in retail financial markets, e.g. Decision Technology Ltd et al. (2010), 'Consumer Decision-Making in Retail Investment Services: A Behavioural Economics Perspective', Study for the European Commission, November 2010. Available at: http://ec.europa.eu/consumers/strategy/docs/final_report_en.pdf (last accessed: 10 February 2012).

[74] See the impact assessment of the proposal on cross-border seat transfer: Commission staff working document, 'Impact assessment on the Directive on the cross-border transfer of registered office' SEC(2007) 1707.

[75] See McChesney, F.S. (2003), 'Talking 'bout my Antitrust Generation', *Emory Law Journal*, vol. 52, pp. 1401–1438.

[76] Budzinski, O. (2008), 'Monoculture versus Diversity in Competition Economics', *Cambridge Journal of Economics*, vol. 32, no. 2, pp. 295–324.

exclusive competence of the European legislator. In this field, decentralisation took place with the Regulation[77] that entered into force in 2004. In both fields the governance framework provides for transparency, cooperation on cross-border issues, and a central body to settle disputes and oversee consistency in the application of the rules, and so on. The institutional design in both fields (despite substantial differences) contributed to achieve cooperative, rather than competitive, outcomes.

An observation emerging from the previous chapters, which is generally applicable in the EU context, is that the *race to the bottom has a specific interpretation within the EU*. As Member States often have different legal and socio-economic systems, their interpretation of what is the optimal policy and policy outcome can differ substantially. These different systems are underpinned by often equally plausible but mutually exclusive economic efficiency theories about optimal regulatory intervention. In these cases one either adopts one single efficiency theory to judge what the welfare impacts of competitive interactions are, or accepts that from any country's point of view negative impacts may arise as soon as the efficiency theory adopted there is infringed. This poses some real difficulties in determining when a race to the top or race to the bottom occurs. In the EU decision-making process this overall EU welfare perspective is probably even less significant than any potential negative externality imposed on a number of Member States.

7.2.3 Observations for better policy design

Finally, three observations can be made, of a forward-looking and normative dimension, for policy design. These relate to the focus of intervention and the regulatory regime adopted.

First, an *ex-ante* analysis of *legal actors' incentives* would be advisable before any new competence allocation or governance design. This would serve the purpose of identifying which actors are best placed to create the rules. Such an analysis would, ideally, include the assessment of any advantages or risks of a centralised versus decentralised solution. In the context of multiple legal actors with competence, the policymaker should look at the incentives of each actor for competitive behaviour (under any channel of competition). A full analysis of potential drivers of competition would allow more predictability as to when regulatory competition can arise and where it is likely to lead.

---

[77] Council Regulation 1/2003 of 16 December 2002 on the implementation of the rules on competition laid down in Arts 81 and 82 of the Treaty OJ 2003 L/1.

Secondly, it appears from the above analysis that regulatory intervention should more often *target the information problems* between market participants, rather than correcting the symptoms that such problems can cause in different markets. These information asymmetries do not necessarily require heavy handed, expensive and compulsory disclosure mechanisms. Instead, the possibility of creating different information regimes and allowing transacting parties to avail themselves of branding should be explored. If a regime can establish itself as trustworthy and transparent enough, it may not need to be mandated.

The third observation concerning the regulatory regime adopted is that *private regulatory actors* are not always exploited fully. Analysis of new legal interventions at EU level does not explore in-depth the possibilities of involving private legal actors in the regulatory and governance design. There are cases where this happens but it could become part of a more systematic analysis for future legislation, along with the examination of the potential benefits of regulatory competition.

To conclude, a comparative approach revealed some interesting insights into what influences the emergence and functioning of competitive interactions among legal actors. In a European context, these findings can provide a starting point for institutional design that accounts for regulatory competition in achieving a desired legal and market outcome. The findings of this analysis may offer ideas for additional research that will hopefully take regulatory competition literature further in becoming useful to forward looking policy design.

Bibliography

Aggrawal, R. and Dahiya, S. (2006), 'Demutualization and Public Offerings of Financial Exchanges', *Journal of Applied Corporate Finance*, vol. 18, no. 3, pp. 96–106.

Ahmad, E. and Brosio, G. (2006), *Handbook of Fiscal Federalism* (Cheltenham, UK: Edward Elgar).

Allen, F. and Gale, D. (1999), *Comparing Financial Systems* (Cambridge, MA: MIT Press).

Alter, K.J. (2001), *Establishing the Supremacy of European Law. The Making of an International Rule of Law in Europe* (Oxford: Oxford University Press).

Anderson, R.C. and Reeb, D.M. (2003), 'Founding Family Ownership and Firm Performance: Evidence from the S&P 500', *Journal of Finance*, vol. 58, no. 3, p. 1301.

Armour, J. (2006), 'Legal Capital Requirements: An Outdated Concept?', *European Business Organization Law Review*, vol. 7, no. 1, p. 5.

Armour, J. and Skeel, D.A. Jr. (2007), 'Who Writes the Rules for Hostile Takeovers, and Why? The Peculiar Divergence of US and UK Takeover Regulation', *Georgetown Law Journal*, vol. 95, p. 1727.

Arrow, K. (1951), *Social Choice and Individual Values* (New York: Wiley).

Baddeley, M. et al. (2007), 'Herding and Social Pressure in Trading Tasks: A Behavioural Analysis', Cambridge Working Papers in Economics CWPE no. 0730.

Bainbridge, S. (1986), 'The Insider Trading Prohibition: A Legal and Economic Enigma', *University of Florida Law Review*, vol. 38.

Barbou des Places, S. (2003), 'Evolution of Asylum Legislation in the EU: Insights for Regulatory Competition Theory', IUE, Robert Schumann Center Working Paper, RSC No. 2003/16.

Barca, F. and Becht, M. (2002), *The Control of Corporate Europe* (Oxford: Oxford University Press). (For comparative data see pp. 21–25.)

Barontini, R. and Caprio, L. (2005), 'The Effect of Family Control on Firm Value and Performance. Evidence from Continental Europe', ECGI Finance Working Paper No. 80/2005.

Barros, P.P. and Cabral, L. (1994), 'Merger Policy in Open Economies', *European Economic Review*, pp. 1041–1055.

Basedow, J. (2007), 'Jurisdiction and Choice of Law in Private Enforcement of EC competition Law', in Basedow, J. (ed.) *Private Enforcement of EC Competition Law* (Alphen aan den Rijn: Kluwer).

Bebchuk, L.A. (2005), 'The Case for Increasing Shareholder Power', *Harvard Law Review*, vol. 118, no. 3, p. 833.

Bebchuk, L.A. and Ferrell, A. (1999), 'Federalism and Corporate Law: The Race to Protect Managers from Takeovers', *Columbia Law Review*, vol. 99, p. 1168.

Bebchuk, L.A. and Ferrell, A. (2001), 'New Approach to Takeover Law and Regulatory Competition', *Vanderbilt Law Review*, vol. 87, p. 111.

Bebchuk, L.A. and Hamdani, A. (2002), 'Vigorous Race or Leisurely Walk: Reconsidering the Competition over Corporate Charters', *Yale Law Journal*, vol. 112, pp. 553–615.

Bendor, J., Taylor, S. and Van Gaalen, R. (1987), 'Politicians, Bureaucrats and Asymmetric Information', *American Journal of Political Science*, vol. 31, no. 4, pp. 796–828.

Benston, G.J. (1973), 'Required Disclosure and the Stock Market: An Evaluation of the Securities Exchange Act of 1934', *American Economic Review*, vol. 63, p. 132.

Bergh, A. and Hoijer, R. (2008), *Institutional Competition* (Cheltenham, UK: Edward Elgar).

Berkowitz, D., Pistor, K. and Richard, J.F. (2003), 'The Transplant Effect', *The American Journal of Comparative Law*, vol. 51, no. 1, pp. 163–203.

Berle, A.A. and Means, G.C. (1967), *The Modern Corporation and Private Property*, 2nd edition (New York: Harcourt, Brace and World).

Bernard, K. and Deakin, S. (2001), 'Market Access and Regulatory Competition', Jean Monnet Working Paper 9/01, p. 4.

Besley, T. and Case, A. (1995), 'Incumbent Behaviour: Vote-Seeking, Tax-Setting, and Yardstick Competition', *American Economic Review*, vol. 85, no. 1, pp. 25–45.

BEUC (2010), 'Country Survey of Collective Redress Mechanisms: Where does Collective Redress for Individual Damages Exist?' (updated in July 2010) (The European Consumers' Organisation (BEUC)), available at: http://www.groupaction4consumers.eu/docs/Country%20survey_Traffic%20Lights.pdf (last accessed: 11 February 2012).

Bhide, A. (1993), 'The Hidden Costs of Stock Market Liquidity', *Journal of Financial Intermediation*, vol. 34, pp. 1–51.

Black, B. et al. (1999), 'Russian Privatisation and Corporate Governance: What Went Wrong?' *Stanford Law Review*, vol. 52, p. 1731.

Black, B.S. (2001) 'The Legal and Industrial Preconditions for Strong Securities Markets', *UCLA Law Review*, vol. 48, p. 781.

Black, J. (1997), *Rules and Regulators* (Oxford: Oxford University Press).

Black, J. (2003), 'Enrolling Actors in Regulatory Systems: Examples from UK Financial Services Regulation', *Public Law*, pp. 63–91.

Bloomfield, R. and O'Hara, M. (2000), 'Can Transparent Markets Survive?', *Journal of Financial Economics*, vol. 55, p. 425.

Boot, A.W. and Thakor, A.V. (1997), 'Financial System Architecture', *Review of Financial Studies*, vol. 10, pp. 693–733.

Bratton, W.W. and McCahery, J.A. (1999), 'Comparative Corporate Governance and the Theory of the Firm: The Case Against Global Cross Reference', *Columbia Journal of Transnational Law*, vol. 38, no. 2, pp. 213–297.

Bratton, W.W. and Watcher, M.L. (2008), 'Shareholder Primacy's Corporatist Origins: Adolf Berle and the Modern Corporation', *Journal of Corporate Law*, vol. 34, p. 99.

Bratton, W.W. et al. (eds) (1996), *International Regulatory Competition and Coordination* (Oxford: Clarendon Press).

Brennan, G. and Buchanan, J.M. (1980), *The Power to Tax. Analytical Foundations of a Fiscal Constitution* (Cambridge: Cambridge University Press).

Brown, J.G. (1996), 'Competitive Federalism and Legislative Incentives to Recognize Same-Sex Marriage', in Bratton, W.W. et al. (eds) *International Regulatory Competition and Coordination* (Oxford: Clarendon Press).

Budzinski, O. (2006), 'Economic Perspective on the Jurisdictional Reform of the European Merger Control System', *European Competition Journal*, vol. 2, p. 119.

Budzinski, O. (2008), 'Monoculture versus Diversity in Competition Economics', *Cambridge Journal of Economics*, vol. 32, pp. 295–324.

Buxbaum, R.M. (1987), 'The Threatened Constitutionalization of the Internal Affairs Doctrine in Corporation Law', *California Law Review*, vol. 75, p. 29.

Cafaggi, F. (2005), 'Self-regulatory Competition', presentation prepared for the first SIDE Conference, Siena, 25 November, available at: http://www.eui.eu/Documents/DepartmentsCentres/Law/Professors/Cafaggi/Nov05.pdf (last accessed: 17 October 2012)

Cafaggi, F. (2006a), 'Self-regulation in European Contract Law', EUI Working Paper Law 2006/43.

Cafaggi, F. (2006b), 'Rethinking Private Regulation in the European Regulatory Space', in Cafaggi, F. (ed.) *Re-framing Self-regulation in European Private Law* (The Hague: Kluwer Law Institute).

Carney, W.J. (1997), 'The Political Economy of Competition for Corporate Charters', *Journal of Legal Studies*, vol. 26, no. 1, p. 303.

Cary, W.L. (1974), 'Federalism and Corporate Law: Reflections Upon Delaware', *Yale Law Journal*, vol. 83, at p. 664, quoting Mr Justice Brandeis in an early case from 1933: *Ligett Co.* v *Lee* 288 U.S. 517, 562–563 (1933).

Choi, S.J. and Guzman, A.T. (1997), 'National Laws, International Money: Regulation in a Global Capital Market', *Fordham Law Review*, vol. 65, p. 1855.

Chordia, T. et al. (2008), 'Liquidity and Market Efficiency', *Journal of Financial Economics*, vol. 87, no. 2, pp. 249–268.

Christiansen, H.B. et al. (2008), 'Incentives or Standards: What Determines Accounting Quality Changes around IFRS Adoption?' *AAA 2008 Financial Accounting and Reporting Section (FARS) paper*, available at: ssrn.com/abstract=1013054.

Coffee, J.C. (2001), 'The Rise Of Dispersed Ownership: The Roles of Law and the State in the Separation of Ownership and Control', *Yale Law Journal*, vol. 111, p. 1.

Coffee, J.C. (2002), 'Competition Among Securities Markets: A Path Dependent Perspective', Columbia Law and Economics Working Paper No. 192.

Cooter, R. and Ulen, T. (2008), *Law and Economics*, 5th edition (Boston: Pearson Education).

CSES Report, 'Study on the Impact of the Prospectus Regime on EU Financial Markets', June 2008, available at: http://ec.europa.eu/internal_market/securities/prospectus/index_en.htm

Dammann, J. (2003), *The US Concept of Granting Corporations Free Choice among State Corporate Law Regimes as a Model for the European Community*, available at: http://ssrn.com/abstract=418660.

Davies, J. (consulting editor) (2007), 'Merger Control 2007, the International Regulation of Mergers and Joint Ventures in 61 Jurisdictions Worldwide', *Global Competition Review Special Report 2007* (London: Law Business Research Ltd).

Davies, J. et al. (2004), *Anatomy of Corporate Law: A Comparative and Functional Approach* (Oxford: Oxford University Press).

Deakin, S. (2006), 'Legal Diversity and Regulatory Competition: Which Model for Europe?', *European Law Journal*, vol. 12, no. 4, pp. 440–454.

Deakin, S. (2008), 'Regulatory Competition in Europe after Laval', University of Cambridge, Center for Business Research Working Paper no. 364.

Deakin, S. and Carvalho, F. (2010), 'System and Evolution in Corporate Governance', ECGI – Law Working Paper no. 150/2010.

Demarchi, M. and Foucault, Th. (2000), 'Equity Trading Systems in Europe: A Survey of Recent Changes', *Analyse d'Economie et de Statistique*, vol. 60, pp. 73–115.

Denozza, F. (2007), 'Fairness and Welfare', in Cafaggi, F. et al. (eds) *Law, Economics and Institutional Complexity* (New York: Routledge).

DeVisser, M.C.B.F. (2009), *Network-based Governance in EC Law: The Example of EC Competition and EC Communications Law* (Modern Studies in European Law, 19) (Oxford: Hart Publishing).

Devroe, W. (2001), 'Neglected Players? The Role of the National Judiciary and of Private Enterprise', in De Witte, B. et al. (eds) *The Many Faces of Differentiation in EU Law* (Antwerp: Intersentia).

Dimson, E. and Mussavian, M. (1998), 'A Brief History of Market Efficiency', *European Financial Management*, vol. 4, no. 1, p. 91.

Dorf, M.C. (2006), 'Whose Ox is Being Gored? When Attitudinalism Meets Federalism', Columbia Public Law Research Paper no. 06-102.

Dow, Sh. (2008), 'Mainstream Methodology, Financial Markets and Global Political Economy', *Contributions to Political Economy*, vol. 27, no. 1, pp. 13–29.

Dowling, M. and Lucey, B.M. (2005), 'The Role of Feelings in Investor Decision-Making', *Journal of Economic Surveys*, vol. 19, no. 2, pp. 211–237.

Downs, A. (1957), *An Economic Theory of Democracy* (New York: Harper and Brothers).

Dragomir, L. (2010), *European Prudential Banking Regulation and Supervision: The Legal Dimension* (New York: Routledge).

Drahos, M. (2001) *Convergence of Competition Laws and Policies in the European Community: Germany, Austria, and the Netherlands* (The Hague: Kluwer Law International).

Dworkin, R. (1980), 'Is Wealth a Value?', *Journal of Legal Studies*, vol. 9, p. 191.

Dyer, B.K. (1992), 'Economic Analysis, Insider Trading and Game Markets', *Utah Law Review*, vol. 1, pp. 1–66.

Easterbrook, F.H. and Fischel, D.R. (1984), 'Mandatory Disclosure and Protection of Investors', *Vanderbilt Law Review*, vol. 70, p. 669.

Easterbrook, F.H. and Fischel, D.R. (1991), *The Economic Structure of Corporate Law* (Cambridge, MA: Harvard University Press).

Edwards, V. (1999), *EC Company Law* (Oxford: Oxford University Press).

Enriques, L. (2002), 'Do Corporate Law Judges Matter? Some Evidence From Milan', *European Business Organization Law Review*, vol. 3, no. 4, pp. 756–821.

Enriques, L. (2003), 'Off the Books, but on the Record: Evidence from Italy on the Relevance of Judges to the Quality of Corporate Law', in

Milhaupt, C.J. (ed.) *Global Markets, Domestic Institutions: Corporate Law and Governance in a New Era of Cross-Border Deals* (New York: Columbia University Press).

Enriques, L. (2004), 'EC Company Law and the Fears of a European Delaware', *European Business Law Review*, vol. 15, no. 6, pp. 1259–1574.

Enriques, L. and Troger, T.H. (2008), 'Issuer Choice in Europe' *Cambridge Law Journal*, vol. 67, pp. 521–559.

Enriques, L. and Volpin, P. (2007), 'Corporate Governance Reforms in Continental Europe', *Journal of Economic Perspectives*, vol. 21, pp. 117–140.

Estella, A. (2002), *The EU Principle of Subsidiarity and its Critique* (Oxford: Oxford University Press).

Esty, D.C. and Geradin, D. (2001), *Regulatory Competition and Market Integration* (Oxford: Oxford University Press).

Ferran, E. (2004), *Building an EU Securities Market* (Cambridge: Cambridge University Press).

Ferrarini, G. (1999), 'The Regulation of Stock Exchanges: New Perspectives', *Common Market Law Review*, vol. 36, p. 569.

Ferrarini, G. (2002), 'Pan-European Securities Markets: Policy Issues and Regulatory Responses', *European Business Organization Law Review*, vol. 3, p. 249.

Fox, E.M. (2000), 'Antitrust and Regulatory Federalism: Races Up, Down and Sideways', *New York University Law Review*, vol. 75, pp. 1781–1807.

Fox, E.M. (2001), 'Antitrust Law on a Global Scale: Races Up, Down, and Sideways', in Esty, D.C. and Geradin, D. (eds), *Regulatory Competition and Economic Integration* (Oxford: Oxford University Press).

Fox, M.B. (1997), 'Securities Disclosure in a Globalizing Market: Who Should Regulate Whom?', *Michigan Law Review*, p. 2626.

Fox, M.B. (1999), 'Retaining Mandatory Securities Disclosure: Why Issuer Choice is not Investor Empowerment', *Virginia Law Review*, vol. 85, pp. 1335–1419.

Garon, P.S. et al. (2006), 'Challenging Delaware's Desirability as a Haven for Incorporation', *Wm. Mitchell Law Review*, vol. 32, p. 769.

Gennaioli, N. and Schleifer, A. (2006), 'Judicial Fact Discretion', National Bureau of Economic Research, NBER Working Papers no. w12679.

Geradin, D. and McCahery, J.A. (2004), 'Regulatory Competition and Coopetition', in Jordana, J. and Levi-Faur, D. (eds) *The Politics of Regulation: Institutions and Regulatory Reforms for the Age of Governance* (Cheltenham, UK: Edward Elgar).

Geradin, D. et al. (2005), *Regulation through Agencies in the EU: A New Paradigm of European Governance* (Cheltenham, UK: Edward Elgar).
Gerber, D.J. (1998), *Law and Competition in Twentieth Century Europe: Protecting Prometheus* (Oxford: Clarendon Press).
Gerber, D.J. (2007), 'The Objectives of Competition Policy: Protecting Consumers, Protecting the Competitive Process, Fostering Efficiency?', in Ehlerman, C-D. and Marquis, M. (eds) *European Competition Law Annual 2007* (Oxford: Hart Publishing).
Gilardi, F. (2005), 'The Formal Independence of Regulators: A Comparison of 17 Countries and 7 Sectors', *Swiss Political Science Review*, vol. 11, no. 4, pp. 139–167.
Gilardi, F. (2008), *Delegation in the Regulatory State: Independent Regulatory Agencies in Western Europe* (Cheltenham, UK: Edward Elgar).
Gilson, R.J. and Kraakman, R.H. (1984), 'The Mechanisms of Market Efficiency', *Virginia Law Review*, vol. 70, p. 549.
Goodhart, C. et al. (1998), *Financial Regulation: Why, How and Where Now?* (London: Routledge).
Goshen, Z. and Parchomovsky, G. (2001), 'On Insider Trading, Markets, and "Negative" Property Rights in Information', *Virginia Law Review*, vol. 87, p. 1229.
Govaere, I. and Demaret, P. (2001), 'The TRIPS Agreement: A Response to Global Regulatory Competition or an Exercise of Global Regulatory Coersion?' in Esty, D.C. and Geradin, D. (eds) *Regulatory Competition and Economic Integration* (Oxford: Oxford University Press).
Grunbishler, A. and Darlap, P. (2003), 'Integration of EU Financial Markets Supervision: Harmonisation or Unification?', consultation document of the FMA, Finanzmarktausicht, Austria.
Gunther, N. et al. (2009), 'Drivers of Earning Quality in a Bank-based Economy: Evidence from Voluntary vs. Mandatory IFRS adoption in Germany', available at: ssrn.com/abstract=1413145
Guzman, A. T. (1998), 'Is International Antitrust Possible?', *New York University Law Review*, vol. 73, pp. 1501–1548.
Handy, W. (1929), *The Yardstick of Public Utility Operations and Construction Costs* (Baltimore: Williams and Wilkins).
Hansmann, H. (1993), 'Worker Participation and Corporate Governance', *University of Toronto Law Journal*, vol. 43, no. 3, pp. 589–606.
Harrison, J.L. (1979), Yardstick Competition: A Prematurely Discarded Form of Regulatory Relief', *Tulane Law Review*, pp. 465–491.
Hawkins, K. (1992), *The Uses of Discretion* (Oxford: Clarendon Press).
Head, K. and Ries, J. (1997), 'International Mergers and Welfare under Decentralized Competition Policy', *Canadian Journal of Economics*, vol. 30, no. 4, pp. 1104–1123.

Heine, K. and Kerber, W. (2002), 'European Corporate Laws, Regulatory Competition and Path Dependence', *European Journal of Law and Economics*, vol. 13, pp. 47–71.

Helpman, E. and Krugman, P. (1985), *Market Structure and Foreign Trade: Increasing Returns, Imperfect Competition, and the International Economy* (Cambridge, MA: MIT Press).

Henderson, L. (1936), 'The Consumer and Competition', *Annals of the American Academy of Political and Social Science*, vol. 183, *Government Finance in the Modern Economy* (Jan. 1936), pp. 263–271.

Héritier, A. (2003), 'New Modes of Governance in Europe: Increasing Political Capacity and Policy Effectiveness?', in Börzel, T.A. and Cichowski, R.A. (eds) *The State of the European Union, vi: Law, Politics, Society* (Oxford: Oxford University Press).

Hertig, G. (2001), 'Regulatory Competition for EU Financial Services', in Esty, D.C. and Geradin, D. (eds) *Regulatory Competition and Market Integration* (Oxford: Oxford University Press).

Hervé, D. and Jeunemaître, A. (1996), 'The Convergence of Competition Policies in Europe: Internal Dynamics and External Imposition', in Berger, S. and Dore, R. (eds) *National Diversity and Global Capitalism* (Ithaca, NY: Cornell University Press), pp. 216–238.

Holmstrom, B. and Tirole, J. (1993), 'Market Liquidity and Performance Monitoring', *Journal of Political Economics*, vol. 101, pp. 678–709.

Holzinger, K. and Knill, Ch. (2003) 'Explaining Cross-national Policy Convergence' (typescript, Bonn: University of Jena, Max Planck Institute).

Holzinger, K. and Knill, Ch. (2005), 'Causes and Conditions of Cross-national Policy Convergence', *Journal of European Public Policy*, vol. 12, no. 5, pp. 775–796.

Hopt, K.J. et al. (2004), 'European Corporate Governance in Company Law and Codes', report prepared for the European Corporate Governance Conference on 18 October, The Hague, The Netherlands. Available at http://www.ecgi.org/presidency/presentations/2004_thehague_final_report.pdf (last accessed: 17 October 2012).

Inman, R.P. and Rubinfeld, D.L. (1997), 'The Political Economy of Federalism', in Muller, D.C. (ed.) *Perspectives on Public Choice: A Handbook* (Cambridge: Cambridge University Press).

Inman, R.P. and Rubinfeld, D.L. (1997), 'Making Sense of the Antitrust State-Action Doctrine: Balancing Political Participation and Economic Efficiency in Regulatory Federalism', *Texas Law Review*, vol. 75, no. 6, pp. 1203–1299.

Jackson, H.E. and Pan, E.J. (2001), 'Regulatory Competition in International Securities Markets', *Business Lawyer*, vol. 56, p. 653.

Jensen, M.C. and Murphy, K.J. (1990), 'Performance Pay and Top-management Incentives', *Journal of Political Economics*, vol. 98, pp. 225–264.

Kahan, M. and Kamar, E. (2002), 'The Myth of State Competition in Corporate Law', *Stanford Law Review*, vol. 55, p. 679.

Kaldor, N. (1939), 'Welfare Positions of Economics and Interpersonal Comparisons of Utility', *The Economic Journal*, vol. 49, no. 195.

Kaplan, M.C. and Reaugh, D.M. (1939), 'Accounting, Reports to Stockholders, and the SEC', *Yale Law Journal*, vol. 48, p. 935.

Kaplow, L. and Shavell, S. (2003), 'Fairness versus Welfare: Notes on the Pareto Principle, Preferences, and Distributive Justice', *Journal of Legal Studies*, vol. 32, no. 1, pp. 331–362.

Keininger, E.M. (2004), 'The Legal Framework for Regulatory Competition Based on Company Mobility: EU and US Compared', *German Law Journal*, vol. 6, no. 4, p. 747.

Kemp, M.C. (2001), *International Trade and National Welfare* (London: Routledge).

Kerber, W. and Budzinski, O. (2004), 'Competition of Competition Laws: Mission Impossible?', in Greve, M.S. and Epstein, R.A. (eds) *Competition Laws in Conflict: Antitrust Jurisdiction in the Global Economy* (Washington, DC: AEI Press).

Kerber, W. and Eckardt, M. (2007), 'Policy Learning in Europe: The Open Method of Coordination and Laboratory Federalism', *Journal of European Public Policy*, vol. 14, no. 2, pp. 227–247.

Kerber, W. and Van den Bergh, R. (2008), 'Mutual Recognition Revisited: Misunderstandings, Inconsistencies, and a Suggested Reinterpretation', *Kyklos*, vol. 61, no. 3, pp. 447–465.

Kerber, W. and Vanberg, V. (1994), 'Institutional Competition Among Jurisdictions: An Evolutionary Approach', *Constitutional Political Economy*, vol. 5, pp. 193–219.

Kieninger, E.M. (2004), 'The Legal Framework for Regulatory Competition Based on Company Mobility: EU and US Compared', *German Law Journal*, vol. 6, no. 4.

Kirchner, C. et al. (2004), 'Regulatory Competition in European Corporate Law after Inspire Art: Unbundling Delaware's Product for Europe', University of Illinois Law and Economics Working Paper no. LE04-001.

Krugman, P.R. and Obstfeld, M. (2009), *International Economics: Theory and Policy*, 8th edition (Boston: Pearson Education).

Kumm, M. (2006), 'Constitutionalising Subsidiarity in Integrated Markets: The Case of Tobacco Regulation in the European Union', *European Law Journal*, vol. 12, no. 4, pp. 503–533.

La Porta, R. et al. (1998), 'Law and Finance', *Journal of Political Economy*, vol. 106, pp. 1113–1155.

La Porta, R. et al (2000), 'Investor Protection and Corporate Governance', *Journal of Financial Economics*, vol. 58, no. 1–2, pp. 3–27.

Laffont, J.J. and Tirol, J. (1990), 'Politics of Government Decision Making: Regulatory Institutions', *Journal of Law, Economics and Organization*, vol. 6, no. 1, p. 1.

Langille, B.A. (1996), 'Competing Conceptions of Regulatory Competition in Debates on Trade Liberalisation and Labour Standards', in Bratton, W. et al. (eds) *International Regulatory Competition and Coordination* (Oxford: Clarendon Press).

Larouche, P. (2005), 'Coordination of European and Member State Regulatory Policy – Horizontal, Vertical and Transversal Aspects', in Geradin, D. and Petit, N. (eds), *Which Regulatory Authorities in Europe?* (Cheltenham, UK: Edward Elgar).

Lejano, R. (2006), *Frameworks for Policy Analysis: Merging Text and Context* (London: Routledge).

Lele, P.P and Siems, M.M. (2006), 'Shareholder Protection: A Leximetric Approach', ESRC, Center for Business Reseach Working Paper.

Levine, R. (2002), 'Bank Based or Market Based Financial System: Which is Better?', *Journal of Financial Intermediation*, vol. 11, no. 4, pp. 398–428.

Levine, R. and Zervos, S. (1998), 'Stock Markets, Banks, and Economic Growth', *American Economic Review*, vol. 88, pp. 537–558.

Lindseth, P.L. (2006), 'Agents without Principals? Delegation in an Age of Diffuse and Fragmented Governance', in Cafaggi, F. (ed.) *Re-framing Self-regulation in European Private Law* (The Hague: Kluwer Law International).

Linklaters (2011), 'Collective Actions Across the Globe – A Review', available at: http://www.linklaters.com/pdfs/mkt/london/A13187695%20v0.0%201103_Collective%20actions.pdf

Llewellyn, D. (1999), 'The Economic Rationale for Financial Regulation', FSA Occasional Paper Series, at p. 37.

Lombardo, S. (2002), *Regulatory Competition in Company Law in the European Community: Prerequisites and Limits* (Frankfurt: Peter Lang).

Majone, G. (1996), *Regulating Europe* (London and New York: Routledge).

Majone, G. (1997), 'The Agency Model: The Growth of Regulation and Regulatory Institutions in the European Union', *European Institute of Public Administration Working Paper.*

Majone, G. (2003), 'The Politics of Regulation and European Regulatory Institutions', in Hayward, J. and Majone, G. (1996) *Regulating Europe* (London: Routledge).

Mateus, A.M. (2007), 'Why should National Competition Authorities be Independent and how should they be Accountable?', paper presented at the 10th anniversary of the Romanian Competition Council. Available at: http://www.unctad.org/sections/wcmu/docs/c2clp_ige8p20aPortugal_pca_en.pdf

Mattei, U. and Cafaggi, F. (1998), 'Comparative Law and Economics', in Newman, P. (ed.), *The New Palgrave Dictionary of Economics and the Law*, vol.1, pp. 346–351.

McCahery, J.A. and Vermeulen, E.P.M. (2004), 'The Evolution of Closely Held Business Forms in Europe', in McCahery, J.A. et al. (eds) *The Governance of Close Corporations and Partnerships: US and European Perspectives* (Oxford: Oxford University Press).

McCahery, J.A. and Vermeulen, E.P.M. (2005), 'Does the European Company Prevent the Delaware Effect?', TILEC Discussion Paper.

McCheseny, F.S. (2003), 'Talking 'bout my Antitrust Generation', *Emory Law Journal*, vol. 52, no. 3, pp. 1401–1438.

McKinsey Global Institute (1998), *Driving Productivity and Growth in the UK Economy*, (London: McKinsey and Company), p. 10.

Meessen, K.M. (1989), 'Competition of Competition Laws', *Northwestern Journal of International Law and Business*, vol. 10, pp. 17–30.

Meessen, K.M. (ed.) (2009), *Economic Law as an Economic Good: Its Rule Function and Its Tool Function in the Competition of Systems* (Munich: Sellier).

Meidinger, E. (1985), 'Regulatory Culture: A Theoretical Outline', *Law and Policy*, vol. 9, no. 4, pp. 355–386.

Melis, A. (2004), 'Corporate Governance Failures. To What Extent is Parmalat a Particularly Italian Case?', available at: http://papers.ssrn.com/paper.taf?abstract_id=563223

Merton, R.C. and Bodie, Z. (1995), 'A Conceptual Framework for Analyzing the Financial Environment', Harvard Business School Working Paper no. 95-062.

Mitschke, A. (2008), *The Influence of National Competition Policy on the International Competitiveness of Nations* (Heidelberg: Physical Verlag).

Muir-Watt, H. (2003), 'Choice of Law in Integrated and Interconnected Markets: A Matter of Political Economy', *Columbia Journal of European Law*, vol. 9, pp. 383–409.

Mulligan, C. and Shleifer, A. (2005), 'The Extent of the Market and the Supply of Regulation', *Quarterly Journal of Economics*, vol. 120, no. 4, pp. 1445–1473.

Murno, A. (2009), *Bounded Rationality and Public Policy: A Perspective from Behavioural Economics* (Dordrecht: Springer).

Murphy, D.D. (2004), *The Structure of Regulatory Competition: Corporations and Public Policies in a Global Economy* (Oxford: Oxford University Press).

Nelson, P. (1970), 'Information and Consumer Behaviour', *Journal of Political Economy*, vol. 78, no. 2, pp. 311–329.

Nordhaus, R.R. (1998), 'Yardstick Competition in a Deregulated Electricity Industry', *Natural Resources and Environment*, vol. 12, pp. 256–260.

Oates, W.E. and Schwab, R.M. (1988), 'Economic Competition among Jurisdictions: Efficiency Enhancing, or Distortion Inducing?' *Journal of Public Economics*, vol. 35, pp. 333–354.

Ogus, A. (1999), 'Competition between National Legal Systems: A Contribution of Economic Analysis to Comparative Law', *The International Comparative Law Quarterly*, vol. 48, no. 2, pp. 405–418.

Olson, M. (1971), *The Logic of Collective Action: Public Goods and the Theory of Groups* (Cambridge, MA: Harvard University Press).

Paredes, T.A. (2004), 'A Systems Approach to Corporate Governance Reform: Why Importing US Corporate Law Isn't the Answer', Washington U. School of Law Working Paper no. 04-02-01.

Pareto, V. (1896), *Cours d'Economie Politique* (Lausanne: F. Rouge).

Parisi, F. et al. (2006), 'Two Dimensions of Regulatory Competition', *International Review of Law and Economics*, vol. 26, pp. 55–66.

Partnoy, F. (2002), 'ISDA, NASD, CFMA and SDNY: The Four Horsemen of Derivatives Regulation? Public Law and Legal Theory', Working Paper no. 39, University of San Diego School of Law. Available at: http://ssrn.com/abstract_id=293085

Pelkmans, J. (2006), *European Integration: Methods and Economic Analysis*, 3rd edition (Essex: Pearson Education Ltd).

Pistor, K. et al. (2000), 'Law and Finance in Transition Economies', *Economics of Transition*, vol. 8, p. 325.

Posner, R.A. (1983), 'Toward an Economic Theory of Federal Jurisdiction', *Harvard Journal of Law and Public Policy*, vol. 6, pp. 41–50.

Posner, R.A. (1985) *Antitrust Law* (Chicago: The University of Chicago Press).

Posner, R.A. (2008), *How Judges Think* (Cambridge, MA: Harvard University Press).

Quack, S. and Djelic, M.L. (2005), 'Adaptation, Recombination and Reinforcement: The Story of Antitrust and Competition in Germany and Europe', in Streeck, W. and Thelen, K. (eds) *Beyond Continuity: Institutional Change in Advanced Political Economies* (Oxford: Oxford University Press).

Radaelli, C. (2004), 'The Puzzle of Regulatory Competition', *Journal of Public Policy*, vol. 24, no. 2, pp. 1–23.

Ramakrishnan, R.T.S. and Thakor, A.V. (1984), 'Information Reliability and a Theory of Financial Intermediation', *Review of Financial Studies*, vol. 51, pp. 415–432.

Ramos, F. (2002), 'Judicial Cooperation in the European Courts: Testing Three Models of Judicial Behavior', *Global Jurist Frontiers*, vol. 2, no. 4.

Randall, M. et al. (2005), 'Corporate Governance, Economic Entrenchment and Growth', *Journal of Economic Literature*, vol. 43, no. 3, pp. 655–720.

Reidenbach, D. (2004), 'Executives' Liability for Incorrect Ad Hoc Announcements – A Comment on the Decision of the German Federal Court of Justice (BGH) in In re Infomatec AG, BGH II ZR 217/03, 218/03 and 402/02 of 19 July 2004', *German Law Journal*, vol. 5, no. 9.

Revesz, R.L. (1992), 'Rehabilitating Interstate Competition: Rethinking the "Race to the Bottom" Rationale for Federal Environmental Regulation', *New York University Law Review*, vol. 67, p. 1210.

Ribstien, L.E. (2004), 'Cross-listing and Regulatory Competition', *Review of Law and Economics*, vol. 1, no. 1.

Roe, M.J. (2003), *Political Determinants of Corporate Governance: Political Context, Corporate Impact* (Oxford: Oxford University Press).

Romano, R. (1985), 'Law as a Product: Some Pieces of the Incorporation Puzzle', *Journal of Law, Economics and Organization*, vol. 1, pp. 225–244.

Romano, R. (1993), *The Genius of American Corporate Law* (Washington: AEI Press).

Romano, R. (2001), 'The Need for Competition in International Securities Regulation', *Theoretical Inquiries in Law*, vol. 2, p. 387.

Romano, R. (2005), 'Is Regulatory Competition a Problem or Irrelevant for Corporate Governance?', ECGI Working Paper no. 26/2005, available at: http://ssrn.com/abstract=693484 (last accessed: 2 February 2012)

Roosenboom, P. and van Dijk, M. (2009), 'The Market Reaction to Cross-listings: Does the Destination Market Matter?' *Journal of Banking & Finance*, vol. 33, no. 10, pp. 1898–1908.

Salmon, P. (1987), 'Decentralisation as an Incentive Scheme', *Oxford Review of Economic Policy*, vol. 3, no. 2, pp. 24–43.

Schammo, P. (2011), *New Perspectives on Regulatory Competition in Securities Markets* (Cambridge: Cambridge University Press).

Schiller, R.J. (1981), 'Do Stock Prices Move Too Much to be Justified by Subsequent Changes in Dividends?', *American Economic Review*, vol. 71, p. 421.

Schumpeter, J. (1975), *Capitalism, Socialism and Democracy* (New York: Harper).

Schutze, Robert (2009), 'Subsidiarity after Lisbon: Reinforcing the Safeguards of Federalism?', *Cambridge Law Journal*, vol. 68, no. 3. pp. 525–536.

Schwartz, R.A. and Steil, B. (1996), 'Equity Trading: Institutional Investors' Trading Practices and Preferences', in Steil, B. (ed.) *The European Equity Markets* (London: Royal Institute of International Affairs).

Scott, C. (2005), 'Agencies for European Regulatory Governance: A Regimes Approach', in Geradin, D. et al. (eds), *Regulation through Agencies in the EU: A New Paradigm of European Governance* (Cheltenham, UK: Edward Elgar).

Sen, A. and Williams, B. (eds) (1982), *Utilitarianism and Beyond* (Cambridge: Cambridge University Press).

Shleifer, A. and Vishny, R.W. (1997), 'A Survey of Corporate Governance', *Journal of Finance*, vol. 52, no. 2, p. 737.

Sinn, H.W. (1997), 'The Selection Principle and Market Failure in Systems Competition', *Journal of Public Economics*, vol. 88, pp. 247–274.

Sinn, H.W. (2003), *The New Systems Competition* (Malden, MA: Blackwell Publishing).

Sinn, S. (1992), 'The Taming of Leviathan: Competition among Governments', *Constitutional Political Economy*, vol. 3, no. 2, pp. 177–196.

Sirri, E.R. and Tufano, P. (1995), 'The Economics of Pooling', in Crane, D.B. et al. (eds) *The Global Financial System: A Functional Approach* (Cambridge, MA: Harvard Business School Press), pp. 81–128.

Smets, H. and Van Cayseele, P. (1995), 'Competing Merger Policies in a Common Agency Framework', *International Review of Law and Economics*, vol. 15, no. 4.

Spindler, G. (2011), 'Behavioural Finance and Investor Protection Regulations', *Journal of Consumer Policy*, vol. 34, pp. 315–336.

Soskice, D. (1999), 'Divergent Production Regimes: Coordinated and Uncoordinated Market Economies in the 1980s and 1990s', in Kitschelt, H. et al. (eds) *Continuity and Change in Contemporary Capitalism* (Cambridge: Cambridge University Press).

Stead, W.H. (1942), 'Democracy and Social Controls in Industry', *American Sociological Review*, vol. 7, no. 2, pp. 176–184.

Stout, L.A. (1988), 'The Unimportance of Being Efficient: An Economic Analysis of Stock Market Pricing and Securities Regulation', *Michigan Law Review*, vol. 87, no. 3, pp. 613–709.

Stout, L.A. (2007), 'The Mythical Benefits of Shareholder Control', *Vanderbilt Law Review*, vol. 93, p. 789.

Streeck, W. and Thelen, K.A. (eds) (2005), *Beyond Continuity: Institutional Change in Advanced Political Economies* (Oxford: Oxford University Press).

Stuyck, J. et al. (2007), 'An Analysis and Evaluation of Alternative Means of Consumer Redress other than Redress through Ordinary Judicial Proceedings – Final Report'. Available at: http://ec.europa.eu/consumers/redress/reports_studies/comparative_report_en.pdf (last accessed: 19 October 2012).

Subramanian, G. (2002), 'The Influence of Antitakeover Statutes on Incorporation', *University of Pennsylvania Law Review*, vol. 150, no. 6, p. 1795.

Szyszczak, E. (2006), 'Experimental Governance: The Open Method of Coordination', *European Law Journal*, vol. 12, no. 4, pp. 486–502.

Thatcher, M. (2002), 'Delegation to Independent Regulatory Agencies: Pressure, Functions and Contextual Mediation', *West European Politics*, vol. 25, no. 1, pp. 125–147.

Tiebout, C. (1956), 'A Pure Theory of Local Expenditures', *Journal of Political Economics*, vol. 64, no. 5, p. 416.

Tirole, J. (1986), 'Hierarchies and Bureaucracies: On the Role of Collusion in Organizations', *Journal of Law Economics and Organization*, no. 2, p. 181.

Tirole, J. (1988), *The Theory of Industrial Organisation* (Cambridge, MA: MIT Press).

Trachtman, J.P. (2001), 'Regulatory Competition and Regulatory Jurisdiction in International Securities Regulation', in Esty, D.C. and Geradin, D. (eds), *Regulatory Competition and Economic Integration: Comparative Perspectives* (Oxford: Oxford University Press).

Tröger, T.H. (2005), 'Choice of Jurisdiction in European Corporate Law – Perspectives of European Corporate Governance', *European Business Organization Law Review*, vol. 6, pp. 3–64.

Tung, F. (2006), 'Before Competition: Origins of the Internal Affairs Doctrine', available at ssrn.com (last accessed: 28 May 2008).

Ullrich, H. (1998), *Comparative Competition Law: Approaching an International System of Antitrust Law* (Baden-Baden: Nomos).

Van den Bergh, R. (2000), 'Towards an Institutional Legal Framework for Regulatory Competition in Europe', *Kyklos*, vol. 53, no. 4, pp. 335–466.

Van den Bergh, R.J. (2004), 'Towards Efficient Self-regulation in Markets for Professional Services', in Ehlerman, C.D. and Atanasiu, I. (eds) *European Competition Law Annual 2004: The Relationship between Competition Law and Liberal Professions* (Oxford: Hart Publishing).

Ventoruzzo, M. (2006), 'Experiments in Comparative Corporate Law: The Recent Italian Reform and the Dubious Virtues of a Market for Rules in the Absence of Effective Regulatory Competition', Bocconi University Research Paper no. 06-02.

Vogel, David (1995), *Trading Up. Consumer and Environmental Regulation in a Global Economy* (Cambridge, MA: Harvard University Press).

Voigt, S. (2006), 'The Economic Effects of Competition Policy – Cross-Country Evidence Using Four New Indicators', ICER Working Paper No. 20/2006.

Waelbroeck, D. et al. (2004), 'Study on the Conditions of Claims for Damages in case of Infringement of EC Competition Rules', 'Ashurst Report', 31 August 2004, available at: http://ec.europa.eu/competition/antitrust/actionsdamages/study.html (last accessed: 18 January 2012).

Weatherill, S. (2011), 'The Limits of Legislative Harmonization Ten Years after *Tobacco Advertising*: How the Court's Case Law has become a "Drafting Guide"', *German Law Journal*, vol. 12, no. 3, pp. 827–864.

Weil, Gotshal and Manges LLP (2002), 'Comparative Study of Corporate Governance Codes Relevant to the European Union and its Member States', study on behalf of the European Commission, DG Internal Market. Available at: http://ec.europa.eu/internal_market/company/docs/corpgov/corp-gov-codes-rpt-part1_en.pdf (last accessed: 19 October 2012).

Wenger, E. and Kaserer, C. (1998), 'The German System of Corporate Governance: A Model which Should not be Imitated', in S.W. Black and M. Moersch (eds) *Competition and Convergence in Financial Markets: The German and Anglo-American Models* (New York: North-Holland Press), pp. 41–78.

Winter, R. (1977), 'State Law, Shareholder Protection and the Theory of the Corporation', *Journal of Legal Studies*, vol. 6, p. 251.

Woolley, P. (2011), 'Why are Financial Markets so Inefficient and Exploitative – and a suggested remedy', in *The Future of Finance and the Theory that Underpins It* (London: London School of Economics).

Wymeersch, E. (1999), 'Centros: A Landmark Decision in European Company Law', Financial Law Institute, Working Paper 1999-15.

Wymeersch, E. (2003), 'Corporate Law in a Turmoil and the Way to "Global Company Practice"', *Journal of Corporate Law Studies*, vol. 3, p. 283.

Zerbe, R.O. (2001), *Economic Efficiency in Law and Economics* (Cheltenham, UK: Edward Elgar).

Zumbansen, P. (2006), 'Spaces and Places: A Systems Theory Approach to Regulatory Competition in European Company Law', *European Law Journal*, vol. 12, no. 4, pp. 534–556.

Zweigert, K. and Kotz, H. (1998), *Introduction to Comparative Law*, 3rd edition (Oxford: Oxford University Press).

LIST OF EUROPEAN LEGISLATION, REGULATION AND OTHER OFFICIAL DOCUMENTS

Commission Decision 2001/527/EC.

Commission Decision establishing the European Corporate Governance Forum, 15 October 2004 (2004/706/EC), OJ L 321/53 22.10.2004.

Commission Impact Assessment (2008) Staff Working Document accompanying the White Paper on Damages actions for breach of the EC antitrust rules Brussels, 2.4.2008; SEC(2008) 405.

Commission Notice on the co-operation between the Commission and the courts of the EU Member States in the application of Articles 81 and 82 EC (2004/C 101/04) 27.4.2004

Commission Recommendation on the role of non-executive or supervisory directors of listed companies and on the committees of the (supervisory) board, 15 February 2005, (2005/162/EC) OJ L 52/51, 25.2.2005.

Commission Staff Working Document 'European Financial Integration Report' SEC(2007) 1696, available at: http://ec.europa.eu/internal_market/finances/docs/cross-sector/fin-integration/efir_report_2007_en.pdf (last accessed: 16 December 2011)

Commission Staff Working Document 'Impact assessment on the Directive on the cross-border transfer of registered office' SEC(2007) 1707

Commission Staff Working Paper accompanying the Report from the Commission on Competition Policy 2010 Commission Staff Working Paper (2010). Available at: http://ec.europa.eu/competition/publications/annual_report/2010/part2_en.pdf (last accessed: 6 February 2012).

Communication from the Commission 'Mutual recognition in the context of the follow-up of the action plan for the single market' COM(1999) 299.

Communication from the Commission 'Reinforcing sanctioning regimes in the financial sector' 8 December 2010, COM(2010) 716.

Communication from the Commission to the European Parliament, the Council, the European Economic and Social Committee and the Committee of the Regions 'Reinforcing sanctioning regimes in the financial services sector' Brussels, 8.12.2010 COM(2010) 716 final.

Council Decision 1999/468/EC, of 28 June 1999, replacing the original Comitology Decision of the Council of 1987.

Council Decision of 28 June 1999, (1999) OJ L 184, 23.

Council Directive 2001/23/EC of 12 March 2001.

Council Directive 2001/86/EC of 8 October 2001 supplementing the Statute for a European company with regard to the involvement of employees OJ L 294, 10.11.2001, pp. 22–32.

Council Directive 2005/19/EC of 17 February 2005 amending Directive 90/434/EEC on the common system of taxation applicable to mergers, divisions, transfers of assets and exchanges of shares concerning companies of different member states.

Council Regulation (EC) No 2157/2001 of 8 October 2001 on the Statute for a European company (SE) OJ L 294, 10/11/2001, 0001-21. Art. 8 paragraph 1.

Council Regulation 1/2003 of 16 December 2002 on the implementation of the rules on competition laid down in Articles 81 and 82 of the Treaty OJ 2003 L/1.

Council Regulation 44-2001 of 22 December 2000, on jurisdiction and the recognition and enforcement of judgments in civil and commercial matters, 2001, OJ (L 12), 1. 8.

Directive 19/94/EC on Deposit Guarantee Schemes.

Directive 2000/12/EC of the European Parliament and of the Council of 20 March 2000 relating to the taking up and pursuit of the business of credit institutions.

Directive 2002/14/EC of the European Parliament and of the Council of 11 March 2002.

Directive 2002/83/EC of the European Parliament and of the Council of 5 November 2002 concerning life assurance.

Directive 2002/87/EC of the European Parliament and of the Council, on the supervision of credit institutions, insurance undertakings, and investment firms in a financial conglomerate.

Directive 2003/6/EC on insider dealing and market manipulation, of 28 Jan 2003.

Directive 2003/71/EC of the European Parliament and the European Council of 4 Nov 2003, on the prospectus to be published when securities are offered to the public or admitted to trading and amending Directive 2001/34/EC.

Directive 2004/109/EC on the harmonisation of transparency requirements in relation to information on issuers whose securities are admitted to trading on a regulated market (amending directive 2001/34/EC).

Directive 2004/39/EC on markets in financial instruments (amending directives 85/611/EEC, 93/6/EEC, and 2000/12/EC and repealing Directive 93/22/EEC) of 21 April 2004.

Directive 2010/73/EU of the European Parliament and of the Council of 24 November 2010 amending Directives 2003/71/EC on the prospectus to be published when securities are offered to the public or admitted to trading and 2004/109/EC on the harmonisation of transparency requirements in relation to information about issuers whose securities are admitted to trading on a regulated market (2010) OJ L 327/1.

Directive 68/151 EEC, O.J. EC L 249/25 of 10/3/1969.

Directive 98/78 EC of the European Parliament and of the Council on the supplementary supervision of insurance undertakings in an insurance group.

Draft report on the proposal for a regulation of the European Parliament and of the Council on jurisdiction and the recognition and enforcement of judgments in civil and commercial matters (recast) (COM(2010)0748 – C7-0433/2010 – 2010/0383(COD))

European Commission White Paper on damages actions for breach of the EC antitrust rules COM(2008) 165.

Feedback statement on the public consultation 'Towards a Coherent European Approach to Collective Redress' Available at: http://ec.europa.eu/competition/antitrust/actionsdamages/index.html (last accessed: 12 February 2012)

Final Report of the Committee of Wise Men on the Regulation of European Securities Markets. Brussels, 15 February 2001.

Green Paper on Consumer Collective Redress COM(2008) 794.

Green Paper on Damages actions for breach of the EC antitrust rules COM(2005) 672, 19.12.2005

Proposal for a Council Directive amending Directive 90/434/EEC of 23 July 1990 on the common system of taxation applicable to mergers, divisions, transfers of assets and exchanges of shares concerning companies of different member states, COM 2003 (613) final.

Proposal for a Directive of the European Council and the Parliament Amending Directives 1998/26/EC, 2002/87/EC, 2003/6/EC, 2003/41/EC, 2003/71/EC, 2004/39/EC, 2004/109/EC, 2005/60/EC, 2006/48/EC, 2006/49/EC, and 2009/65/EC in respect of the powers of the European Banking Authority, the European Insurance and Occupational Pensions Authority and the European Securities and Markets Authority, Brussels, 26.10.2009 COM(2009) 576 final.

Proposal for a Directive of the European Parliament and of the Council on markets in financial instruments repealing Directive 2004/39/EC of the European Parliament and of the Council (Recast) SEC(2011) 1226 and SEC(2011) 1227.

Proposal for a Directive of the European Parliament and of the Council on markets in financial instruments repealing Directive 2004/39/EC of the European Parliament and of the Council. 2011/0298 (COD).

Proposal for a Directive of the European Parliament and of the Council on criminal sanctions for insider dealing and market manipulation, Brussels, 20.10.2011 COM(2011) 654 final.

Proposal for a Directive of the European Parliament and of the Council on cross-border mergers of companies with share capital, 18.11.2003. COM (2003) 703 final.

Proposal for a Regulation of the European Parliament and of the Council on jurisdiction and the recognition and enforcement of judgments in civil and commercial matters (Recast) Brussels, 14.12.2010 COM(2010) 748 final 2010/0383 (COD).

Regulation (EC) No 1060/2009 of the European Parliament and of the Council of 16 September 2009 on credit rating agencies OJ L 302.

Regulation No 182/2011 of the European Parliament and of the Council of 16 February 2011 laying down the rules and general principles concerning mechanisms for control by Member States of the Commission's exercise of implementing powers OJ L 55/13.

Single European Act, OJ L 169, 29.6.1987.

Treaty on European Union, (Maastricht Treaty), OJ C 191 of 29.7.1992.

Treaty on the Functioning of the European Union OJ C 115/47 9.5.2008.

LIST OF CASES

European Case Law

Case 120/78, Rewe/Bundesmonopolverwaltung für Branntwein, Judgment of 20 February 1979, ECR 79 p00649.

Case 81/87, The Queen v Treasury and Commissioners of Inland Revenue, ex parte Daily Mail and General Trust [1988] ECR 5483.

Case C-12/03, Commission v Tetra Laval [2005] ECR I-987.

Case C-167/01, Kamer van Koophandel v Inspire Art [2003] ECR I-0000.

Case C-2/97, Borsana, [1998] ECR I-8597.

Case C-208/00, Überseering BV v Nordic Construction Company Baumanagement GmbH (NCC). [2002] ECR I-09919.

Case C-210/03, Swedish Match AB and Swedish Match UK Ltd v Secretary of State for Health 2004 ECR I-11893.
Case C-212/97, Centros Ltd v Erhvervs-og Selskabsstyrelsen [1999] ECR I-1459.
Case C-35/96, Italian Customs Agents ECR 1998 I-03851.
Case C-376/98, Germany v Parliament and Council, 2000 E.C.R. I-8419.
Case C-453/99, Courage v Crehan, 2001 ECR I-6297.
Case C-491/01, The Queen v Secretary of State for Health, ex parte British American Tobacco (Investments) Ltd and Imperial Tobacco Ltd, 2002 ECR I-11453.
Case C-58/08, Vodafone, O2 et al v Secretary of State, 2010 ECR I-04999.
Case C-6/03, Deponiezweckverband Eiterköpfe v Land Rheinland Pfalz, Judgment of 14 April 2004.
Case C-68/93, Judgment of 7 March 1995, Shevill and others/Presse Alliance (C-68/93, ECR 1995 p. I-415).
Case T-251/00, Lagardère SCA and Canal+ v Commission [2002] ECR II-4825.
Case T-3310/01, Schneider Electric v Commission [2002] ECR II-4071.
Case T-342/99, Airtours v Commission [2002] ECR II-2585.
Case T-5/02, Tetra Laval v Commission [2002] ECR II-4381.
Joined Cases C-295/04 to C-298/04, Manfredi [2006] ECR I-6619.
Opinion of AG Poiares Maduro in Case C-446/03, Marks and Spencer Plc v. David Halsey (HM Inspector of Taxes), delivered on 7 April 2005.

Dutch Case Law

DES, Court of Appeal Amsterdam of 1 June 2006, *NJ* (2006), 461.
Dexia, Court of Appeal Amsterdam of 25 January 2007, *NJ* (2007), 427.

German Case Law

LG Dortmund, Az. 13 O 55/02 Kart., Vitaminkartell III, [2004].
Mainz District Court, decisions of January 15 2004, Cases 12 HK.O 52/02, 12 HK O 55/02 and 12 HK O 56/02, published in NJW-RR 2004, 478.
Oberster Gerichthof (OGH) decision of 7/15/1999 Österreichisches Recht der Wirtschaft (RdW) 719 (1999).

French Case Law

Tribunal de commerce de Nanterre, judgment 'Arkopharma / Roche' 11 May 2006.

UK Case Law

Provimi Ltd. v Aventis Animal Nutrition & Others [2003] EWHC 961 Comm.

Competition Appeal Tribunal

1077/5/7/07 Emerson Electric Co and others v Morgan Crucible Company plc.
1078/7/9/07 The Consumers Association v JJB Sports PLC.
1088/5/7/07 ME Burgess, JJ Burgess and SJ Burgess (trading as JJ Burgess & Sons) v W Austin & Sons (Stevenage) Limited and Harwood Park Crematorium Limited.
1105/5/7/08 (1) Freightliner Limited (2) Freightliner Heavy Haul Limited v English Welsh & Scottish Railway Limited.
1106/5/7/08 Enron Coal Services Limited (in liquidation) v English Welsh & Scottish Railway Limited.
1108/5/7/08 N J and D M Wilson v Lancing College Limited.
1078/7/9/07 The Consumers Association v JJB Sports PLC.
1060/5/7/06 Healthcare at Home v Genzyme Limited.

Index